CULTURAL
CAPITAL

CULTURAL CAPITAL

THE PROBLEM OF LITERARY CANON FORMATION

JOHN GUILLORY

THE UNIVERSITY OF CHICAGO PRESS
CHICAGO AND LONDON

The University of Chicago Press, Chicago 60637
The University of Chicago Press, Ltd., London
© 1993 by The University of Chicago
All rights reserved. Published 1993

Printed in the United States of America
02 01 00 99 98 97 96 95   2 3 4 5

ISBN: 0-226-31043-4 (cloth)
       0-226-31044-2 (paper)

Library of Congress Cataloging-in-Publication Data

Guillory, John.
    Cultural capital : the problem of literary canon formation / John
Guillory.
        p.   cm.
    Includes bibliographical references and index.
    1. English literature—History and criticism—Theory, etc.
    2. English literature—Study and teaching—Case studies.
    3. Capitalism and literature.   4. Literature and society.   5. Canon
(Literature)
    PR21.G85   1993
    820.9—dc20   92-34597

CONTENTS

Preface   vii

Acknowledgments   xv

Part One: Critique

1   Canonical and Noncanonical: The Current Debate   3

Part Two: Case Studies

2   Mute Inglorious Miltons: Gray, Wordsworth,
and the Vernacular Canon   85

3   Ideology and Canonical Form: The New
Critical Canon   134

4   Literature after Theory: The Lesson of
Paul de Man   176

Part Three: Aesthetics

5   The Discourse of Value: From Adam Smith
to Barbara Herrnstein Smith   269

Notes   341
Index   385

PREFACE

Symbolic struggles are always much more effective (and therefore realistic) than objectivist economists think, and much less so than pure
social marginalists think. The relationship between distributions
and representations is both the product and the stake of a permanent
struggle between those who, because of the position they occupy
within the distributions, have an interest in subverting them by mod-
ifying the classifications in which they are expressed and legitimated,
and those who have an interest in perpetuating misrecognition, an
alienated cognition that looks at the world through categories the
world imposes.

—BOURDIEU, *The Logic of Practice*

The largest thesis of this book is that the debate about the canon has been
misconceived from the start, and that its true significance is one of which
the contestants are not generally aware. The most interesting question
raised by the debate is not the familiar one of which texts or authors will be
included in the literary canon, but the question of why the debate represents a crisis in literary study. In order to understand the conditions which
gave rise to this crisis, however, it will be necessary first to call into question
the intuitive hypothesis of "exclusion" which currently governs historical
accounts of canon formation. In the chapters that follow I propose a thorough displacement of this explanatory hypothesis. Where the debate
speaks of the literary canon, its inclusions and exclusions, I will speak of
the school, and the institutional forms of syllabus and curriculum. I will
argue that evaluative judgments are the necessary but not sufficient condition for the process of canon formation, and that it is only by understanding the social function and institutional protocols of the school that we will
understand how works are preserved, reproduced, and disseminated over
successive generations and centuries. Similarly, where the debate speaks
about the canon as representing or failing to represent particular social
groups, I will speak of the school's historical function of distributing, or
regulating access to, the forms of cultural capital. By insisting on the interrelation between representation and distribution, I hope to move beyond a
certain confusion which both founds and vitiates the liberal pluralist cri-

tique of the canon, a confusion between representation in the political sense—the relation of a representative to a constituency—and representation in the rather different sense of the relation between an image and what the image represents. The collapse of the latter sense into the former has had the unfortunate effect of allowing the participants in the "symbolic struggle" over representation in the canon to overestimate the political effects of this struggle, at the same time that the participants have remained relatively blind to the social and institutional conditions of symbolic struggles. I will argue that the concept of cultural capital can provide the basis for a new historical account of both the process of canon formation and the immediate social conditions giving rise to the debate about the canon. For while the debate seems to its participants to be about the contents of the literary canon, its significance goes well beyond the effects of any new consensus about a truly "representative" canon. The canon debate signifies nothing less than a crisis in the form of cultural capital we call "literature."

The concept of "cultural capital" is derived from the work of Pierre Bourdieu, where it facilitates a revisionary sociology of great depth and complexity. The purpose of importing the term into the debate about the canon is not to endorse Bourdieu's project in its totality (I have dissented on occasion from particular conclusions of Bourdieu's) but to introduce an entirely different theoretical perspective into the present debate. The theory of cultural capital implies that the proper social context for analyzing the school and its literary curriculum is *class*. Yet the argument of this book is not simply, on that account, "Marxist." For Bourdieu the concept of class is preeminently a sociological concept, and one which is, as Marxists know, undertheorized in Marx himself. If there exists a form of capital which is specifically symbolic or *cultural*, the production, exchange, distribution, and consumption of this capital presupposes the division of society into groups that can be called classes. Bourdieu's sociology assumes such a division, but it does not assume that an economic account of classes is sufficient in itself.[1] Such an account would omit precisely what in Bourdieu's theory is "cultural." The theory of cultural capital belongs to the general field of what in France goes by the name of "post-Marxist" thought; but this is an affiliation which is much harder to claim in our own country, where there is no indigenous Marxist tradition to overthrow or move beyond. Without aspiring either to a consistent Marxism or post-Marxism, I have sought rather to make visible the relative absence of class as a working category of analysis in the canon debate. This may seem surprising to participants in the debate, who have always argued that exclusions from the canon are determined by the race, gender, or class identities of authors. But the argument of this book is that one cannot infer a process of exclusion from the canon by setting out from the category of class, a fact which explains why examples of excluded authors always happen to be those whose identities are marked by race or gender. The fact of class determines whether and how individuals gain access to the means of literary production, and the system regulating such access is a much more efficient mechanism of social exclusion than acts of judgment. By foregrounding the question of the relation between social groups and the means of literary production, I have thus attempted to resist the easy assumption that whatever one says about race and gender goes without saying for class too.

What *should* go without saying is that the emphasis on class in the following argument does not imply the theoretical privileging of class over race and gender. Without venturing here into what is now a quasi-theological controversy, I would insist only that a given social problem should be understood in relation to the context which yields the best explanation for that problem. In the case of the literary curriculum, I propose that the problem of what is called canon formation is best understood as a problem in the constitution and distribution of cultural capital, or more specifically, a problem of access to the means of literary production and consumption. The "means" in question are provided by the school, which regulates and thus distributes cultural capital *unequally*. The largest context for analyzing the school as an institution is therefore the *reproduction* of the social order, with all of its various inequities. The particular authors who happen to be canonical have a minor role in this system of reproduction, but the far larger role belongs to the school itself, which regulates access to literary production by regulating access to literacy, to the practices of reading and writing. The literary syllabus is the institutional form by means of which this knowledge is disseminated, and it constitutes capital in two senses: First, it is *linguistic* capital, the means by which one attains to a socially credentialed and therefore valued speech, otherwise known as "Standard English." And second, it is *symbolic* capital, a kind of knowledge-capital whose possession can be displayed upon request and which thereby entitles its possessor to the cultural and material rewards of the well-educated person. For reasons to be argued more fully within the chapters of this book, I regard these two kinds of capital as ultimately more socially significant in their effects than the "ideological" content of literary works, a content which the critics of the canon see as reinforcing the exclusion of minority authors from the canon by expressing the same values which determine exclusionary judgments. Literary works must be seen rather as the vector of ideological notions which do not inhere in the works themselves but in the context of their institutional presentation, or more simply, in the way in which they are taught.

For the purposes of a sociologically informed history of canon formation, it is the category of "literature" which invites the closest scrutiny.
That category organizes the literary curriculum in such a way as to create
the illusion of a fixed and exclusive "canon," an illusion which is belied by
the real history of literary curricula in the schools. For that very reason,
calling the canon into question has failed to inaugurate a historico-critical
inquiry into the category of literature, even while it has registered a crisis in
the cultural capital so denominated. The overarching project of the present
study is an inquiry into just this crisis, one which attempts to explain why
the category of literature has come to seem institutionally dysfunctional, a
circumstance which I will relate to the emergence of a technically trained
"New Class," or "professional-managerial class."[2] To put this thesis in its
briefest form, the category of "literature" names the cultural capital of the
old bourgeoisie, a form of capital increasingly marginal to the social function of the present educational system. From this perspective the issue of
"canonicity" will seem less important than the historical crisis of literature, since it is this crisis—the long-term decline in the cultural capital of
literature—which gives rise to the canon debate. The category of literature
remains the *impensé* of the debate, in spite of what passes on the left as a
critique of that category's transcendent value, and on the right as a mythological "death of literature."

After offering an analysis of the current debate in Chapter 1, along the
lines suggested above, I proceed in the second part of this book to examine
the historical category of "literature" as the organizing principle of canonical selection at three moments in the history of the English vernacular
canon. These case studies are keyed to the level of the school system and are
intended to demonstrate the articulation of the school's institutional
agendas with social struggles in the society at large. The context of the first
case study is the institution of a vernacular literary curriculum in the primary schools of the eighteenth century. Taking as the occasion of my analysis the peculiar canonical significance of Gray's *Elegy Written in a
Country Churchyard*, a poem which appears to thematize canon formation in its topos of the "mute, inglorious Milton," I attempt to show that
the poem's notorious popularity is an effect of its very successful "translation" of classical literacy into an anthology of quotable vernacular phrases.
This translation could then be appropriated in an eighteenth-century polemic on behalf of instituting a vernacular curriculum, a curriculum which
preserved a place of honor for Gray's *Elegy* at its very threshold. The emergence of a vernacular curriculum tended ultimately to fix criteria of selection for canonicity which no longer privileged the standards derived
from the Greek and Roman classics, and thus no longer privileged figures

such as Waller and Denham, who were thought to embody such standards. If the "middling sort," especially those trained in the Dissenting Academies, embraced English literature as a politically empowering educational program, because it facilitated entrance into the relatively homogenized linguistic arena of the "public sphere," this revaluation of the cultural capital of vernacular literary works was responsible for the emergence of the category of literature itself, as well as for the first crisis in the status of the vernacular canon, the problem of assimilating new vernacular genres such as the novel. Wordsworth and Coleridge responded to this crisis with a programmatic attempt to reaffirm the High Cultural status of traditional canonical works in English against, on the one hand, popular novels and narrative poetry, and, on the other, the quasi-Latinate "poetic diction" supposed to have characterized especially the work of Gray. The effect of that program, which was of course shared by a literary culture much larger than the circle of Wordsworth and Coleridge, was to reserve the term "literature" for High Canonical works, and in this way to maintain the cultural capital of those works.

It will be useful to emphasize here what this book is not: It is not an institutional history of literary study. I have not, for example, undertaken an account of the emergence of literary study such as that provided by Gerald Graff in his invaluable *Professing English*. The current interest of university professors in the origins of their profession is entirely legitimate, but it may also have tended to obscure the significance of the earlier institution of the vernacular syllabus in the lower levels of the school system. My intention throughout has been to stress the interconnectedness of the educational system, and hence I have constructed the second case study around a moment in which the vernacular curriculum in the university became strongly distinguished from the curriculum in the primary and secondary levels. This was the moment of the great canonical reformation of the New Critics. In Chapter 3 I give an account of the New Critical revision of the English canon, which canonized the moderns and revalued the metaphysical poets, by setting this reformation in the context of a project for redefining the cultural capital produced by literary study in the university. In the circumstance in which the linguistic capital defined by "Standard English" was being more or less successfully disseminated at the lower levels of the school system, the literary curriculum at the university level acquired a new kind of distinction when the New Critics attributed to literary works a conceptual and linguistic difficulty that could only be approached by the technique of "close reading." This distinction of literary language, for which the metaphysical and the modern poets provided the canonical exemplars, in turn became the vector of a certain "ideology" of literary culture. I argue, however, that the ideology of the New Critical canonical form is not reducible to the explicitly political ideas of the New Critics, but rather produces its effects when the cultural capital of literature is set against a "mass culture" which at once reveres and neglects the monuments of High Culture.

Chapter 4 turns to the highest level of the educational system, the graduate school, where in the last twenty-five years the literary syllabus has been supplemented by a list of texts which effectively circulate as a "canon of theory." This new syllabus, consisting largely of philosophical works, was thought to inaugurate a definitive challenge to the authority of an exclusively literary syllabus, although the syllabus of theory was also always indissolubly bound to that syllabus, as the means for producing new readings of literary works. In order to understand in retrospect how the texts of theory came to be canonically organized in programs of graduate study, I offer a reading of Paul de Man's crucial intervention into the dissemination of theory. I propose specifically a "symptomatic reading" of the oeuvre of de Man, one which attempts to demonstrate (1) that the dissemination of the theory-canon was dependent on the emergence of charismatic "master thinkers"; (2) that theory in its preeminent "deconstructive" form resurrected the discipline of rhetoric as a means of redefining literature, and as a way of extending the properties of literariness to nonliterary (primarily philosophical) texts; and (3) that the social context for the emergence of the theory-canon can be located in new institutional conditions of intellectual work. These conditions, the transformation of the professional literary critic's intellectual labor by the technobureaucratic restructuring of the university, ultimately account for the dual form of the syllabus in the graduate schools, the two canons of literature and theory. The syllabus of theory has the oblique purpose of signifying a rapprochement with the technobureaucratic constraints upon intellectual labor, symptomatically registered as a fetishization of "rigor." The moment of theory is determined, then, by a certain defunctioning of the literary curriculum, a crisis in the market value of its cultural capital occasioned by the emergence of a professional-managerial class which no longer requires the (primarily literary) cultural capital of the old bourgeoisie. This crisis calls forth a redefinition of literature itself, a redefinition which incorporates as a new aspect of literary study the "technical" quality of the knowledge valued by the professional-managerial class. Needless to say, the emergence of theory is the symptom of a problem which theory itself could not solve. The fact that today we so easily recognize the names of the master theorists confirms the emergence of these names as a "canon" supplementing the canon of literature in the graduate schools, and testifies to the perceived inadequacy of the literary syllabus to constitute a program of study complete in itself. I intend to demonstrate finally that the failure of theory to construct a new rationale for the literary curriculum was a necessary condition for the development of a new critique of the curriculum, the "canon debate" of the last decade.

The three case studies described above do not constitute a history of literary canon formation, but attempt to redirect the focus of the debate away from the question of who is in or out of the canon to the question of the canonical *form* in its social and institutional contexts. The form we call "literature" organizes the syllabus and determines criteria of selection much more directly than the particular social biases of judgment which have been invoked to explain the canonical or noncanonical status of particular authors. Yet the argument that such social bias is the determinant of canon formation has been so generally accepted in critical discourse that it is now capable of being elaborated into a general critique of aesthetic judgment. In its most extreme form this critique seeks to discredit the concept of the aesthetic altogether, as intrinsically repressive. In the final chapter of this book I argue that the extrapolation of a critique of aesthetics from the critique of the canon is mistaken in its fundamental premise. This premise takes the form of a refusal of "aesthetic value," on the grounds that aesthetic values cannot be distinguished from any other values in the social realm, not even economic value. This argument has received its most sophisticated treatment in Barbara Herrnstein Smith's *Contingencies of Value*, which disables the category of the aesthetic by reversing the cardinal principle of Kantian aesthetics—the "uselessness" of the work of art—and discovering in every work of art the manifest expression of economic "use value." The persuasiveness of this argument is belied, however, by its failure to historicize the concept of value itself. So far from being the transhistorical equivalent of judgment, the concept of value has a very specific origin in the eighteenth-century discourse of political economy. The value-concept has a history of which the canon debate remains unaware, and which needs to be recovered before one sets out to critique the concept of a specifically "aesthetic" value. I proceed in Chapter 5 to reconstruct the historical relation between aesthetics and political economy in order to demonstrate the origin of the value-concept in the struggle to distinguish the work of art from the commodity. The reduction of aesthetic value to economic use value forgets precisely the fact that the problem of the work of art was crucial for political economy's founding distinction between use value and *exchange value*. The conflation of these two terms in current anti-aesthetic arguments betrays how much the present critique of judgment has actually forgotten about the intimate historical relations between aesthetic and economic discourses. The cost of that amnesia is a kind of false enlightenment, the restatement in altogether more reductive terms of a relation between the aesthetic and the economic much more interestingly and problematically engaged in eighteenth-century moral philosophy than in our recent neorelativist critiques.

Turning finally to Bourdieu's sociology of art, I argue that the simple reduction of aesthetics to the quasi-economic concept of "use value" loses sight of what Bourdieu describes as the emergence of aesthetic production as a "relatively autonomous" field of cultural activity in the eighteenth century. That is to say, the production and distribution of cultural works as cultural capital cannot be explained by making *no distinction* between cultural and material capital. The consequences of this argument for our understanding of what we call canon formation are profound. For the specificity of aesthetic judgment is not on this view simply an illusion to be exploded, but rather a privileged site for reimagining the relation between the cultural and the economic in social life.

The strangest consequence of the canon debate has surely been the discrediting of judgment, as though human beings could ever refrain from judging the things they make. But if this notion has been bad sociology, it has proven to be even worse politics. The argument that one should suspend judgment on behalf of the politically urgent objective of making the canon more "representative" of diverse social groups invited the reactionary objection to the abandonment of "standards." The most politically strategic argument for revising the canon remains the argument that the works so revalued are important and valuable cultural works. If literary critics are not yet in a position to recognize the inevitability of the social practice of judgment, that is a measure of how far the critique of the canon still is from developing a sociology of judgment. The theory of cultural capital elaborated in this book is an attempt to construct just such a sociology.

ACKNOWLEDGMENTS

Parts of Chapter 1 appeared in *ELH* and *Transition*. An earlier version of Chapter 3, now thoroughly revised, appeared in *Critical Inquiry*. I thank these journals for permission to reprint work here.

This book has been a long time in writing, and much to my surprise the canon debate has outlasted my response to it. I am very grateful to many friends and colleagues whose patience and encouragement saw me through to conclusion. I thank especially Jeff Nunokawa for the extraordinary gift of his intellectual friendship; Margaret Ferguson for the unfailing generosity of her support; Mary Poovey for consistently responsive readings and encouragement; and Jonathan Goldberg for the benefit of his conversation on matters both canonical and noncanonical. At various times I have had crucially helpful exchanges (my interlocutors did not always know they were crucial) with Christopher Miller, Neil Hertz, Henry Abelove, Toril Moi, David Simpson, Anthony Appiah, Henry Finder, Jerome Christensen, and David Rodowick. I would also thank Susan Staves and Ronald Paulson for helpful comments on Chapter 2. Various chapters of the book were delivered as lectures, or discussed in seminars, at several institutions, including Columbia, Yale, the University of Colorado at Boulder, Wesleyan, the Mellon Fellows conference at Bryn Mawr, the Clark Library, and the Women's Studies Seminar at Johns Hopkins. I owe more than I can begin to acknowledge to my respondents on these occasions. I thank in addition Alan Thomas and the editorial staff at the University of Chicago Press for their patience and their enthusiasm for this project.

The thoughts expressed in this book represent my part in an ongoing conversation with Jennifer Wicke. For that conversation, and so much else, I will always be grateful. This book is for her.

Part One
Critique

Chapter One

Canonical and Noncanonical: The Current Debate

The Imaginary Politics of Representation

> Not only in their answers but in their very questions there was a mystification.
>
> —MARX, *The German Ideology*

Social Identity

In recent years the debate about the literary canon has entered a new phase, with the emergence in the university and in the popular media of a strong conservative backlash against revisions of the curriculum.[1] Given the renewal and even intensification of the debate after what had seemed a successful transition to an expanded syllabus of literary study, the moment may now have arrived for a reassessment of the debate, and particularly of the theoretical assumptions upon which the practice of canonical revision has been based. These assumptions derive without question from the political discourse—liberal pluralism—to which we owe the most successful progressive agendas of the last three decades. It will not be my intention to question social objectives whose realization is both necessary and urgent, but to demonstrate that a certain impasse in the debate about the canon follows from the fundamental assumptions of liberal pluralism itself. This impasse is visible, for example, when the distinction between "canonical" and "noncanonical" works is institutionalized in two very different and even contradictory ways: as the canonization of formerly noncanonical works, and as the development of distinct and separate noncanonical programs of study. I shall argue in this chapter that the vulnerability of curricular revision to attack from the right is one consequence of the contradiction between integrationist and separatist conceptions of curricular revision, a contradiction that can be traced to theoretical problems with pluralism itself, and that threatens to disable an effective response to the conservative backlash.

While the explicitly political ends of canonical revision are obvious, it has not been sufficiently acknowledged how much the language of revision owes to a political culture which is specifically American. It will be my contention that however easy it has been for both progressive academics and their reactionary critics to conflate the critique of the canon with the forms of leftist and even Marxist thought, the terms and methods of canonical revision must be situated squarely within the prevailing conventions of American pluralism. These conventions have been usefully summarized by Gregor McLennan, in his *Marxism, Pluralism, and Beyond,* as follows:

—a sociology of competing interest groups;
—a conception of the state as a political mechanism responsive to the balance of societal demands;
—an account of the democratic civic culture which sets a realistic minimum measure for the values of political participation and trust;
—an empiricist and multi-factorial methodology of social science.[2]

Within traditional liberal pluralist thought, individuals are conceived in their relation to the state as members of groups whose interests are assumed to conflict. Hence the object of representing these groups within the legislative institutions of the state is to negotiate among the interests of particular social groups or constituencies. "Representation" in political institutions now describes an important objective for many social groups, defined by a variety of forms of association: women, trade union members, the elderly, consumers, the sick, the disabled, veterans, and most recently members of minority ethnic or racial groups, the communities which constitute our pluralist society. In the context of the long-term development of democratic culture, the pluralist version of liberalism emergent in post–World War II American society registers a certain deepening crisis in the institutions of political representation, the sense (not necessarily conscious) of having reached an apparent limit in the capacity of these institutions to represent diverse social groups.[3] This crisis has reached a new stage with the decline of postwar liberalism in American political culture and the resurgence of a strongly reactionary politics which now designs to purge liberalism from political culture in the same way that it formerly (and successfully) purged socialism. In response to an increasingly hostile climate of opinion, it would seem that the political culture of liberalism has established a last redoubt in the university, where the very extremity of its situation has deformed its discourse by rigidifying certain defensive postures.[4] The deterioration of what was in the United States always a very limited program of economic socialization, along with a general decline in the credibility of democratic political institutions, constitute the immediate conditions for the development of a political critique of "representation" in contexts other than those formerly conceived as political. In retrospect it was only in the wake of liberalism's apparent defeat in American political culture that such agendas as "representation in the canon" could come to occupy so central a place within the liberal academy.[5] The new curricular critique made it possible for the university to become a new venue of representation, one in which new social identities might be represented more adequately, if also differently, than in existing political institutions of American society.

If the politics of canon formation has been understood as a politics of representation—the representation or lack of representation of certain social groups in the canon—this circumstance may well be a consequence of the fact that, as McLennan points out, the "whole relationship between subjects, individuals and their identity as members of certain social categories is one which has been dramatically unsettled in recent social theory."[6] Because the concept of "social identity" has undergone a kind of mutation, with which democratic institutions have not yet caught up, the venue of representation can be displaced to new arenas of contestation. But that displacement, while it reconceives a process such as canon formation as "political," leaves unclarified the question of the precise relation between a politics of representation in the canon and a democratic representational politics. In order to answer the question of what "representation in the canon" means within the larger context of American political culture, we must acknowledge at the outset that our concept of "social identity" is a product of that culture, and that only within that culture can the category of an author's racial, ethnic, or gender identity found a politics of curricular revision. Any reconsideration, then, of canon critique in its political context must begin with the notion of "social identity."

I propose to offer here a critique of the assumptions underlying the current understanding of the canon, a critique which derives its premises from a set of terms and arguments closer to Marxism than to liberal pluralism. But the point of such a reorientation is not to argue for the mutual exclusivity of Marxism and pluralism. I take it for granted that Marxism itself has theoretical limitations, which recent "post-Marxist" confrontations with pluralist methodology (for example, that of Laclau and Mouffe) have had to confront, with important theoretical results.[7] The major terms of my analysis are drawn from the arguably post-Marxist theory of "cultural capital" elaborated in the works of Pierre Bourdieu.[8] Insofar as the concept of cultural capital presupposes the concept of capital, and inasmuch as it foregrounds the category of class, Bourdieu's theory must be located within the Marxist rather than the pluralist critical tradition. The object at the present moment of advancing a Marxist critique (however qualified) of liberal pluralist revisions of the canon would be to indicate the inherent limitations in pluralist analysis in order to bring to light certain questions occluded by the current problematic of "representation." These questions concern the *distribution* of cultural capital, of which canonical works constitute one form. I will assume, following Bourdieu, that the distribution of cultural capital in such an institution as the school reproduces the structure of social relations, a structure of complex and ramifying inequality. However, it will not be possible to explore the relation between the canon and access to the forms of cultural capital, until we have first demonstrated the inherent limitations in the problematic of representation, in the very questions it asks.

For the purposes of that critique, we can extract from the current debate about the canon two pervasive theoretical assumptions: The first of these assumptions is implicit in the word "canon" itself, not until recently a common term in critical discourse.[9] The word "canon" displaces the expressly honorific term "classic" precisely in order to isolate the "classics" as the object of critique. The concept of the canon names the traditional curriculum of literary texts by analogy to that body of writing historically characterized by an inherent logic of *closure*—the scriptural canon. The scriptural analogy is continuously present, if usually tacit, whenever canonical revision is expressed as "opening the canon." We may begin to interrogate this first assumption by raising the question of whether the process by which a selection of texts functions to define a religious practice and doctrine is really similar *historically* to the process by which literary texts come to be preserved, reproduced, and taught in the schools. This question concerns the historicity of a particular kind of written text, the "literary." Since the hypothesis of closure is a historical conjecture, it is subject to historical proof or disproof, a task I shall undertake in this and subsequent chapters.

The first assumption of canonical revision operates in concert with a second, which posits a homology between the process of *exclusion,* by which socially defined minorities are excluded from the exercise of power or from political representation, and the process of *selection,* by which certain works are designated canonical, others noncanonical. The second assumption clearly requires the first—literature as quasi-scripture—in order to make the claim that the process of canonical selection is always also a process of social exclusion, specifically the exclusion of female, black, ethnic, or working-class authors from the literary canon. The unrepresentative content of the canon is described in the rhetoric of canonical critique as a kind of scandal, after two millennia a scandal which has gone on long enough. If the forces of exclusion have been so powerful as to prevail without challenge until recent years, the strategy for their defeat has been surprisingly obvious, even simple. It has only been necessary to "open" the canon by adding works of minority authors to the syllabus of literary study. In this way the socially progressive agenda of liberal pluralism could be effected in a particular institution—the university—by transforming the literary syllabus into an inclusive or "representative" set of texts.

Again, it will not be necessary to dissent from the larger aims of the progressive social agenda (far from it) in order to raise a question at the level of theoretical assumptions about the relation between the literary curriculum and "representation." The movement to open the canon to noncanonical authors submits the syllabus to a kind of demographic oversight. Canonical and noncanonical authors are supposed to *stand for* particular social groups, dominant or subordinate. One can easily concede that there must be *some* relation between the representation of minorities in positions of power and the representation of minorities in the canon, but what is that relation? The difficulty of describing this relation is in part a consequence of the fact that a particular social institution—the university—intervenes between these two sites of representation. Given the only partially successful social agenda of educational democratization in the last three decades, we may conclude that it is much easier to make the canon representative than the university. More to the point, those members of social minorities who enter the university do not "represent" the social groups to which they belong in the same way in which minority legislators can be said to represent their constituencies. The sense in which a social group is "represented" by an author or text is more tenuous still. The latter sense of representation conceives the literary canon as a hypothetical *image* of social diversity, a kind of mirror in which social groups either see themselves, or do not see themselves, reflected. In the words of Henry Louis Gates, Jr., the "teaching of literature" has always meant "the teaching of an aesthetic and political order, in which no women and people of color were ever able to discover the reflection or representation of their images, or hear the resonances of their cultural voices."[10] I shall argue that the sense of representation as *reflection* or image inhabits what may be called the field of "imaginary" politics. But by the latter term I do not mean what is opposed to the real but a politics which is manifestly a politics *of the image*. Such a politics

7

belongs to the same political domain as the ongoing critique of minority images in the national media, to the project of correcting these images for stereotyping, or for a failure to represent minorities at all. Such a politics has real work to do, as complex and interesting as images themselves, but it is also inherently limited by its reduction of the political to the instance of representation, and of representation to the image. It is only the first step toward a political critique of the literary curriculum to say that it is a *medium* of cultural images. This mode of canonical critique reduces the curriculum to such a medium, and thus, as we shall see, to a mass cultural form. In this sense the critique of the canon betrays its determination by certain postmodern conditions, by those conditions in which media images have the central ideological function of organizing our responses to virtually all aspects of our lives.[11] If there is any difference worth considering between the politics of image-critique and the politics of canonical revision, this difference must inhere in the latter's institutional location. The literary curriculum is precisely not the site of mass cultural production and consumption, but the critique of the canon has proceeded as though it were, as though canon formation were like the Academy Awards. Clearly a "representative" canon does not redress the effects of social exclusion, or lack of representation, either within or without the university; nor would the project of canonical revision need to make this claim in order to justify the necessity of curricular revision. But in construing the process of canon formation as an exclusionary process essentially the same as the exclusion of socially defined minorities from power, the strategy of opening the canon aims to reconstruct it as a true image (a true representation) of social diversity. In so specifying "representation" as the political effect of the canon, the liberal pluralist critique fails to consider what other effects, even political effects, the canon may have at its institutional site.

Whatever effects the canon as an image of equal or unequal representation may actually produce within the university, we must nevertheless insist that the politics of canonical revision is in its present form an imaginary politics, a politics of the image. That is just the reason why the social effects of a representative canon are so difficult to determine.[12] What the project of canon-critique still lacks is an analysis of how the institutional site of canonical revision mediates its political effects in the social domain. There is no question that the literary curriculum is the site of a political practice; but one must attempt to understand the politics of this practice according to the specificity of its social location. The specificity of the political here cannot mean simply a replication of the problem of "representation" in the sphere of democratic politics, and therefore it cannot mean simply importing into the school the same strategies of progressive politics which sometimes work at the legislative level.[13] Should we not rather rethink the whole question of what the "political" means in the context of the school as an institution? The institutional question bears directly, I shall argue, on the current impasse at which the pluralist agenda is lodged, its vacillation between integrationist and separatist institutional strategies, between the incorporation of noncanonical works into the curriculum on the grounds that such works ought to be canonical, and the establishment of separate or alternative curricula of works which continue to be presented as "noncanonical" in relation to the traditional curriculum.

With respect to the latter alternative, it is relatively easy to see why it has seemed necessary to many progressive critics to present certain texts by minority authors as *intrinsically* noncanonical, as unassimilable to the traditional canon. The separatist strategy follows from the same basic assumption of pluralist canonical critique as the integrationist, that the process of the inclusion or exclusion of texts is identical to the representation or nonrepresentation of social groups. In the context of curricular revision, the category of the noncanonical loses its empty significance as merely the sum total of what is not included in the canon, and takes on a content specified by the contemporary critique: the noncanonical must be conceived as the *actively* excluded, the object of a historical repression. But paradoxically, the most surprising aspect of the current legitimation crisis is the fact that the "noncanonical" is not what fails to appear in the classroom, but what, in the context of liberal pedagogy, *signifies exclusion*. The noncanonical is a newly constituted category of text production and reception, permitting certain authors and texts to be *taught* as noncanonical, to have the status of noncanonical works in the classroom. This effect is quite different from the effect of total absence, of nonrepresentation *tout court*. What it means is that the social referents of inclusion and exclusion—the dominant or subordinate groups defined by race, gender, class, or national status—are now represented in the discourse of canon formation by two groups of authors and texts: the canonical and the noncanonical. It is only *as* canonical works that certain texts can be said to represent hegemonic social groups. Conversely, it is only *as* noncanonical works that certain other texts can truly represent socially subordinated groups. This fact must be grasped in order to understand why the critique of the canon has proceeded in recent years to reinstate at the level of institutional practice, of curriculum, the same opposition—between the canonical and the noncanonical—that its early agenda of "opening the canon" called into question.

If the objective of representation in the syllabus is the expression of an imaginary politics, this objective does not exhaust the agenda of the liberal pluralist critique. The sense in which a canonical author represents a dominant social group, or a noncanonical author a socially defined minority, is continuous with the sense in which the work is perceived to be immediately expressive of the author's *experience* as a representative member of some social group. The primacy of the social identity of the author in the pluralist critique of the canon means that the revaluation of works on this basis will inevitably seek its ground in the author's experience, conceived as the experience of a marginalized race, class, or gender identity. The author returns in the critque of the canon, not as the genius, but as the representative of a social identity. We scarcely need to be reminded of the fact that just as the first wave of theory called into question such categories as that of the author (along with notions of genius, tradition, etc.), much other contemporary theory calls the valorization of experience itself into question, in order to critique the very concept of representation. Laclau and Mouffe, for example, set out from the recognition that the coherent identity demanded by a practice assuming the perfect fit of identity and experience is in fact unavailable to anyone:

> there is no social identity fully protected from a discursive exterior that deforms it and prevents it becoming fully sutured. Both the identities and their relations lose their necessary character. As a systematic structural ensemble the relations are unable to absorb the identities; but as the identities are purely relational, this is but another way of saying that there is no identity which can be fully constituted.[14]

Such theoretical arguments (which evoke the vexed question of "essentialism") have surprisingly coexisted in the present debate with an otherwise incompatible rhetoric of canonical revision in which it is precisely the fit between the author's social identity and his or her experience that is seen to determine canonical or noncanonical status. The typical valorization of the noncanonical author's experience as a marginalized social identity necessarily reasserts the transparency of the text to the experience it represents.[15] If the practice of canonical revision cannot pause to indulge theoretical scruples about such assertions, its urgency betrays an apparently unavoidable discrepancy between theory and practice, an incapacity as yet to translate theory into political practice *at the site of institutional practices.* Hence the critique of the canon remains quite vulnerable to certain elementary theoretical objections, but this fact is itself symptomatic of a political dilemma generated by the very logic of liberal pluralism. It suggests that the category of social identity is too important politically to yield any ground to theoretical arguments which might complicate the status of representation in literary texts, for the simple reason that the latter mode of representation is *standing in for* representation in the political sphere. We must speak here (and perhaps generally in postmodern culture) of a certain displacement of the political which is the condition for the new politics of representation. Hence the *theory* of representation, and the *politics* of representation, have begun to move in quite different directions.

While we may readily acknowledge that the relation of theory to practice is never easy to specify, we may also wonder whether practice is really condemned to invoke theoretical assumptions so manifestly deficient as those which govern liberal pluralist practice, in its present incarnation as "identity politics." Consider, for example, the invocation of "race, class, and gender" as the categories which are supposed to explain the historical process of canon formation. It would be difficult to deny that the canon critique's assumption of the text's transparency to the race, gender, or class experience of the author has been instrumental in the short term, in that this assumption has served as the immediate basis for canonical revision; but the ubiquitous invocation of these categories of social identity continually defers their theoretical discrimination from each other on behalf of whatever political work is being done by pronouncing their names in the same breath as practice. But what work is that? What political work requires the deferral of theory, despite the fact that one must always gesture to some future, as yet unelaborated, analysis of the *relations* between race, class, or gender? It is not so much that such analyses are presently unavailable—in fact, they are[16]—but that in the context of canonical critique and revision they have no obvious application. In that context the equation of all minority writers as "noncanonical" brings their social identities into ontological correspondence, and equates their works as the expression of analogous experiences of marginalization. For the present, it would appear that there is much greater pressure to equate the social identities of minority authors than to distinguish them in a systemic analysis of the modes of domination specific to different social groups.

The telegraphic invocation of race/class/gender is the symptom of just the failure to develop a systemic analysis that would integrate the distinctions and nuances of social theory into the practice of canonical revision. We can indicate briefly here what is at stake in the difference between a Marxist/post-Marxist and a liberal critique of the canon by insisting upon the theoretical and practical incommensurability of the terms race, class, and gender: the modes of domination and exploitation specific to each of these socially defined minorities thus cannot be redressed by the *same* strategy of representation. It is by no means evident that the representation of blacks in the literary canon, for example, has quite the same social effects as the representation of women, precisely because the representation of blacks *in the university* is not commensurable with the representation of women. It remains difficult, if not impossible, within a pluralist critique to express the practical political implications of the fact that race and gender do not merely signify analogous experiences of marginalization but incommensurable modes of social identification.[17] Even within the category of race, socially constructed racial identities are as different as the modes of racism specific to the oppression of different races (and these modes are obviously very different). A politics presuming the ontological indifference of all minority social identities as defining oppressed or dominated groups, a politics in which differences are sublimated in the constitution of a minority identity (the identity politics which is increasingly being questioned within feminism itself)[18] can recover the differences between social identities only on the basis of common and therefore commensurable experiences of marginalization, which experiences in turn yield a political practice that consists largely of *affirming* the identities specific to those experiences. For this reason the differences or antagonisms that exist within and between dominated social groups tend to become the basis for the constitution of new social identities or subgroups, rather than the occasion for an analysis of the systemic nature of social antagonisms. This point has been made with particular persuasiveness by Peter Osborne, whose discussion of Laclau and Mouffe's version of identity politics is worth quoting at some length:

> Claiming an "identity" on the basis of the experience of a specific oppression is seen here as the ground for a wholly new kind of politics, for which the affirmation and validation of experiences of "difference" are at least as important as the analysis of the basis of oppression and its location within the perspective of a wider oppositional movement—if not more so. On this model, oppressed social identities are transformed *directly* into oppositional political identities through a celebration of difference which inverts the prevailing structure of value but leaves the structure of differences untouched.
>
> . . . . the problem with [this] position is that it tends to reduce radical politics to the expression of oppressed subjectivities, and thereby to lead to the construction of moralistic, and often simply additive, "hierarchies of oppression," whereby the political significance atttributed to the views of particular individuals is proportional to the sum of their oppressions. Such a tendency both positively encourages a fragmentation of political agency and harbours the danger of

exacerbating conflicts between oppressed groups. It also makes
group demands readily recuperable by the competitive interest-
group politics of a liberal pluralism.[19]

Granted the theoretical perspicacity of Laclau and Mouffe's analysis of the
category of social identity, that analysis, in Osborne's view, fails to produce
anything like a practical politics; hence the gesture toward the coalition
politics of "hegemony" provides no indication of any expressly *political*
means for the formation of such coalitions and falls back upon the same
practice of affirming discrete and autonomous social identities their own
theory subjects to a definitive critique. In Osborne's formulation, such a
politics "ends up *reducing* political to social identities."[20] This reservation
is worth emphasizing, not because it vitiates every aspect of Laclau and
Mouffe's theoretical argument, but because it calls attention to the symptomatic discrepancy between the theory of social identity and the practice
of identity politics. If liberal pluralism has discovered that the cultural is
always also the political (which it is), it has seldom escaped the trap of reducing the political to the cultural.[21] There is surely no more exemplary
instance of this trajectory of pluralist critique than the canon debate, which
remains preeminently an expression of identity politics.

The above argument may explain why a culturalist politics, though it
glances worriedly at the phenomenon of class, has in practice never devised
a politics that would arise from a class "identity." For while it is easy
enough to conceive of a self-affirmative racial or sexual identity, it makes
very little sense to posit an affirmative lower-class identity, as such an identity would have to be grounded in the experience of deprivation per se. Acknowledging the existence of admirable and even heroic elements of
working-class culture, the *affirmation* of lower-class identity is hardly compatible with a program for the abolition of want. The incommensurability
of the category of class with that of race or gender (class cannot be constructed as a social identity in the *same way* as race or gender because it is
not, in the current affirmative sense, a "social identity" at all) does not, on
the other hand, disenable a description of the relation between these social
modalities. This was after all the problem sociology once addressed by
means of the distinction between class and *status*. The current equation of
gender, race, and class as commensurable minority identities effaces just
this structural distinction.

The underlying theoretical problem here, one might speculate, is the result of an as yet unacknowledged theoretical slippage between the concepts
of "subject" and "identity." While it is typical enough for current practice
to use these terms interchangeably, it is worth recalling that the problematic of the subject derives from theoretical projects which were at the time

of their inception (in the 1960s) explicitly Marxist or psychoanalytic. As these projects were assimilated into American liberal pluralist discourse, the problematic of the subject was more or less displaced by that of identity, or simply confused with that concept. This confusion is evident in the argument sometimes expressed within feminist thought, that theory's overthrow of the autonomous subject somehow conflicts with a feminist political practice. That overthrow might on the contrary have been the *basis* for such a practice. Without reprising at this point the various debates within the critique of the subject, we can say that the problematic of the subject always emphasized the complex formation of subject positions by unconscious processes or by impersonal forms of social structuration. The politics implied by such a theoretical problematic was always addressed to the exposure of these unconscious or structural modes of subject formation. The problematic of identity, on the other hand, insofar as it has developed a voluntarist politics of self-affirmation, has little use for the subject of Marxist or psychoanalytic theory. This is not to say that the latter theories do not continue to circulate alongside a liberal pluralist practice, but that their actual incompatibility with that practice tends to go unrecognized. The fact that identity politics is brought up short before the concept of class suggests the limit, in one direction, of the concept of identity, but it also argues for the urgency of theorizing the relation between subject and identity, since "identification" (whether affirmative, negative, or in Laclau and Mouffe's view, constitutively incomplete) belongs to the process of subject formation as one of its moments.[22]

Meanwhile, we may say that the incommensurability of different subject formations (and, likewise, the "experiences" of these subjects) is the condition for an accurate description of the systemic relations between race, class, and gender. In the context of the present critique of the canon, the actual incommensurability of these categories as *author*-identities remains to be acknowledged. The fact of incommensurability explains why the revisionist critique of the canon has in practice been incapable of identifying "noncanonical" works by lower-class writers who are not already identified by race or gender. For how would such "identities" be registered as self-affirmative? The name of "D. H. Lawrence," for example, may signify in the discourse of canonical critique a white author or a European author, but it does not usually signify a writer whose origins are working-class. Within the discourse of liberal pluralism, with its voluntarist politics of self-affirmation, the category of class in the invocation of race/class/gender is likely to remain merely empty. But this fact only confirms that the critique of the canon does indeed belong to a liberal pluralist discourse, within which, as Gregor McLennan has pointed out, the category of class has been systematically repressed.[23]

Canon Revision or Research Program?

We are in a position now to make the even stronger claim that the category of "social identity" is entirely inadequate to explain how particular works become canonical in the first place, in a particular set of historical conditions. Let us approach this question first from its end point, from the canonical history currently being made in the classroom: What does it mean in the real conditions of institutional practice to open the syllabus of canonical works to works regarded as "noncanonical," that is, to works by authors belonging to socially defined minorities? I would suggest that the objective of canonical revision entails in practice shifting the weight of the syllabus from older works to *modern* works, since what is in question for us are *new* social identities and new writers. In fact, the history of the literary curriculum has always been characterized by a tendency to modernize the syllabus at the expense of older works. The "opening" of the classical curriculum to vernacular writing in the eighteenth-century primary-school system, in response to certain cultural demands of the nascent bourgeoisie, is one momentous example, ultimately responsible for displacing many Greek and Roman works from the curriculum altogether. Closer at hand, and slightly less momentous, are the generic modernizations of the canon, the inclusion of the novel in syllabi of the later nineteenth century, or film since the 1960s. By defining canonicity as determined by the social identity of the author, the current critique of the canon both discovers, and misrepresents, the obvious fact that the older the literature, the less likely it will be that texts by socially defined minorities exist in sufficient numbers to produce a "representative" canon. Yet the historical reasons for this fact are insufficiently acknowledged for their theoretical and practical implications. The reason more women authors, for example, are not represented in older literatures is not primarily that their works were routinely excluded by invidious or prejudicial standards of evaluation, "excluded" as a consequence of their social identitity as women. The historical reason is that, with few exceptions before the eighteenth century, women were routinely excluded from *access to literacy,* or were proscribed from composition or publication in the genres considered to be serious rather than ephemeral. If current research has recovered a number of otherwise forgotten women writers from the period before the eighteenth century, this fact is not directly related to canon formation as a process of selection or exclusion on the basis of social identity, but to the present institutional context of a valid and interesting *research program* whose subject is the history of women writers and writing. No other defense is required for studying these writers than the aims of the research program (and these could well be *political* aims). It is not necessary to claim canonical status for noncanonical works in order to justify their study, as the archive has always been the resource of historical scholarship. If the feminist research program has recovered from the archives the works of a number of women writers now all but forgotten, such as Lady Mary Wroth or Katherine Philips, it must also be borne in mind that the archives preserve (and bury) hundreds and thousands of writers, of various social origins and identities. The question for us, in reconsidering the rhetoric of canon revision, is why any particular noncanonical author discovered by a research program has to be presented as *excluded* from the canon. The hypothesis of exclusion has more to do with a misrecognition of the political work accomplished by the research program than with any actual historical circumstances of judgment.[24] But this misrecognition itself has certain political consequences, since it effaces the historical significance of literacy in the history of writers and writing.

The social conditions governing access to literacy before the emergence of the middle-class educational system determined that the greater number of writers, *canonical or noncanonical,* were men. The number of canonical texts represents in turn only the minutest percentage of these works, and the body of canonical authors could never in that case have reflected the actual social diversity of their times or places—not even, it might be added, in the case of women writers of the early modern period, who were literate by and large as a consequence of being aristocratic.[25] The retroconstruction of early modern women writers as expressing the marginalized experience of women in general, as though the difference between an aristocratic woman and a peasant were indifferent, is thus only the obverse of the error identifying the writings of these women as excluded from the canon merely as a consequence of the fact that they were written by women. If much feminist theory now problematizes the category of "woman" itself, what theoretical inhibition disallows the problematization of the "woman writer" in the canon debate?[26]

One might nevertheless want to object here that even if the most socially consequential process of exclusion occurs primarily at the level of access to literacy, it might still be the case that canon formation functions to exclude works by minority writers who do manage to acquire the means of literary production. For reasons I shall now indicate, even this qualified hypothesis is in crucial ways inaccurate. It is without question true that some past writers have suffered an undeserved oblivion; indeed the history of canon formation offers many examples of writers rediscovered after periods of obscurity. What seems dubious in historical context is that such cases can be *generally* explained by invoking the categories of race, class, or gender as the immediate criteria of inclusion or exclusion. These categories might well explain at the present time why some writers have been recovered from the archive, but not necessarily why they ceased to be read. Nor does the circumstance of their being read now mean that they have become canonical—only that they are read now.

Let us consider once again the category of gender as a hypothetical criterion for exclusion from the canon: The existence of canonical women authors, even before the revisionary movement of the last decade, invalidates in strictly logical terms the category of gender as a *general* criterion of exclusion; which is to say that in the case of an excluded woman author, it will not be sufficient merely to invoke the category of gender in order to explain the lack of canonical status. The principle that explains the exclusion of Harriet Beecher Stowe from the canon on the basis of gender cannot really account for the complexity of the historical circumstances governing the reception of Stowe's work, for the same reason that it cannot account for the counterexample of Jane Austen's canonical status. This is not to say that the category of gender is not a *factor* in the subsequent reputation of Stowe, or of any woman author. We can expect that many factors will enter into the situation of the reception of a given author's work, and that these factors will advance and recede at different moments in the history of the work's reception. This point can be briefly underscored by citing the famous opening sentence of F. R. Leavis's *The Great Tradition,* whose canonical intentions are entirely explicit: "The great English novelists are Jane Austen, George Eliot, Henry James and Joseph Conrad—to stop for the moment at that comparatively safe point in history."[27] Leavis seems not to be thinking of gender at all in pronouncing his canonical judgments. His project rather has to do, as readers of Leavis know, with defining a High Cultural novelistic canon in opposition to the depredations of what he sees as the emergence concurrently of modern mass culture and the novel (his canonical list excludes Dickens on the grounds of his mass cultural affiliations, despite his "great genius"). We can hardly attribute the apparently equal representation of men and women authors in Leavis's novelistic canon to the absence of bias, much less to any feminist sympathies. The point of the example is that the historical process of canon formation, even or especially at the moment of institutional judgment, is too complex to be reduced to determination by the single factor of the social identity of the author.

If the social identity of the author appears to us now as the condition of canonicity or noncanonicity, this is as much as to say that the categories of race and gender are contemporary conditions of canon formation; they are historically specific. These categories will not bind future critics either to the canonical choices of the present or to the categories of liberal pluralist critique. Social identities are themselves historically constructed; they mean different things at different historical moments, and thus the relation of different social groups to such cultural entitlements as literacy will be differently constructed at different times. Acknowledging the conditional force of literacy in the history of canon formation would thus disallow us from ever assuming that the field of writing is a kind of *plenum*, a textual repetition of social diversity, where everyone has access to the means of literary production and works ask only to be judged fairly. The fact that the field of writing is not such a *plenum* is a social fact but also an *institutional* fact. Linda Nochlin arrives at much the same conclusion in rejecting the premise of the question, "Why are there no great women artists?" The answer to this question lies not in the supposition that there must exist many unjustly forgotten great women artists but in reckoning the social consequences for women of "our institutions and our education."[28] An "institutional" fact such as literacy has everything to do with the relation of "exclusion" to social identity; but exclusion should be defined not as exclusion from representation but from access to the *means of cultural production*. I will define literacy accordingly throughout this book not simply as the capacity to read but as the *systematic regulation of reading and writing,* a complex social phenomenon corresponding to the following set of questions: Who reads? What do they read? How do they read? In what social and institutional circumstances? Who writes? In what social and institutional contexts? For whom?[29]

The question of literacy foregrounds what is at stake in the difference between a pluralist and a Marxist/post-Marxist conception of canon formation: for literacy is a question of the distribution of cultural goods rather than of the representation of cultural images.[30] From the point of view of such a materialist critique, it would seem that pluralism can only apprehend the history of canon formation as a history of consumption, the history of the judgment of cultural products. But if the socially unrepresentative content of the canon really has to do in the first place with how access to the means of literary production is socially regulated, a different history of canon formation will be necessary, one in which social identities are historical categories determined as much by the system of production as by consumption. The present tendency to restrict canonical critique to the reception of images attests to the absence of any theoretical understanding of the relation between a real historical silence—exclusion from the means of literary production—and the sphere of reception, in this case, the university. What becomes visible there is an immense collection of works, among which only a few can be "canonical," selected for inclusion within the curriculum of literary study. A critique which is confined to the level of consumption must necessarily misrepresent the historicity of literary production, the systemic effects of the *educational system* in the determination of who writes and who reads, as well as what gets read, and in what contexts. The educational institution performs the social function of systematically regulating the practices of reading and writing by governing access to the means of literary production as well as to the means of consumption (the knowledge required to read historical works). Nothing confirms the failure to ground the critique of the canon in a systemic analysis of the educational system more than the failure to reflect upon the most salient fact of the canon debate, its locus in the university. No one speaks there of the relation between canonical revision and the primary levels of the educational system, where for a much larger part of the population the content of the university curriculum is simply irrelevant. If literacy is a problem of the distribution of cultural resources, this problem is very much larger than the problem addressed by a politics of "representation in the canon."

Canonical and Noncanonical Values

In recent years the distinction between canonical and noncanonical works has been invoked to organize the curriculum in a new way, by institutionalizing that distinction in distinct syllabi. It would be difficult to overestimate the significance of this second phase of canonical critique, since it discovered a new project of representation for the curriculum. While the category of social identity continued to be employed to account for the historical lack of representation in the canon, it was no longer necessary to rectify that circumstance solely by the strategy of inclusion. In the second phase of canonical critique, the curriculum became representative in another sense, by reflecting the *actual* division of the social order into dominant and dominated social groups, each now represented by its own syllabus of works. In this context of representation, the "values" according to which works were canonized could themselves be called into question or declared to be simply incommensurable with the "values" embodied in subordinate cultures. This phase of canonical critique was raised to the level of theory in Barbara Herrnstein Smith's *Contingencies of Value*, which argues that works cannot become canonical unless they are seen to endorse the hegemonic or ideological values of dominant social groups:

> since those with cultural power tend to be members of socially, economically, and politically established classes . . . the texts that survive will tend to be those that appear to reflect and reinforce establishment ideologies. . . . they would not be found to please long and well if they were seen *radically* to undercut es-

tablishment interests, or *effectively* to subvert the ideologies that support them.[31]

Conversely, noncanonical works can be seen to express values which are transgressive, subversive, antihegemonic. While it would be easy enough to demonstrate that most historically noncanonical works are not characterized by any such political effectivity, we need to remember that the critique of the canon was never concerned with most noncanonical works, only with those works already marked by the socially defined minority identity of their authors. If one can successfully extend the critique of the canon from the category of social identity to the category of *cultural value,* then it would indeed follow that the inclusion of noncanonical works in the canon misrepresents the social significance of the canon by failing to recognize it as the inevitable embodiment of hegemonic cultural values. On this account canonical and noncanonical works are by definition mutually exclusive; they confront each other in an internally divided curriculum in the same way that hegemonic culture confronts nonhegemonic subcultures in the larger social order.

The canon debate has given rise in recent years to a general critique of values, particularly "aesthetic" value, on grounds both philosophical and sociopolitical, a critique well exemplified by Herrnstein Smith's neorelativist position; but I should like to postpone until a later chapter a full consideration of that theoretical by-product of the debate, since what is at issue in the reassertion of cultural "relativism" is the very possibility of a specifically aesthetic value. It will not be necessary here either to dismiss or to defend that possibility in order to register a large reservation about the mapping of the distinction between canonical and noncanonical texts onto specific cultures and their values. It will suffice to open the terrain of this reservation to note a certain peculiar convergence in the characterization of the canon in the rhetoric of both progressive critique and reactionary defense. Here, for example, is the egregious William Bennett, whose polemics in the 1980s as director of the NEH, and later as secretary of education, popularized the revanchist reaction to curricular revision:

> For some 15 to 20 years now there had been a serious degree of embarrassment, of distancing, even of repudiation of that culture on the part of many of the people whose responsibility, one would think, is to transmit it. Many people in our colleges and universities aren't comfortable with the ideals of Western civilization.
>
> Bennett stands up and says, "You know, I really think people should be familiar with Homer and Shakespeare and George

Eliot and Jane Austen," and they say, "We don't do that any-more. Why should we have to do that?" All right, if the purpose of the institution is not to transmit that culture, then what is the institution's purpose?[32]

Such remarks, presented more formally in the NEH publication "To Re-claim a Legacy," have been widely provoking, but not because Bennett's conception of what constitutes cultural value has itself been contested. On the contrary, pluralist critics of the canon would agree that canonical works do represent the "ideals of Western civilization," and that these ide-als or values constitute a "culture." Whether Homer, Shakespeare, Eliot, and Austen actually express in some homogeneous way a culture of "West-ern civilization" is not in question on either side of the debate.

In this circumstance it has become surprisingly difficult to define a pro-gressive political rationale for the teaching of canonical texts. Leaving aside the option of not teaching them at all (an entirely logical alternative, if the teaching of canonical texts actually disseminates hegemonic values), pro-gressively inclined teachers of these texts must reground the politics of their pedagogy on assumptions that are themselves theoretically weak. Hence it might seem necessary to assume that a politically progressive reading will consist of *exposing* the hegemonic values of canonical works. Whenever liberal pluralist critique slides into such a characterization of its object, we can say that it has found its way back to what was once considered to be a "vulgar" Marxism; but the more important point is that such a rediscovery of "reflection theory" is determined by the internal logic of pluralism itself, by its theory of representation as reflection, as image.

Just as weak theoretically is the liberal position that claims for canonical texts an intrinsic subversiveness, that discovers in the intrinsically "liberat-ing" effect of these texts the reason of their canonicity.[33] The deficiency of this compromise with the rhetoric of canonical critique is apparent as soon as its genealogical relation to the liberalism of the old bourgeoisie is re-vealed. For that apparently egalitarian ideology was always implicitly "elit-ist," in the sense that it divided the population into those who were capable of being so liberated and those who were not. Thus the defense of the canon on these grounds will inevitably resurrect the charge of elitism, as the bad conscience of its own bad theory, as in the following statement: "If we are alert to these elements of freedom in the canon of great literature, the charge of elitism will be less destructive of cultural values, and we will not have to stand mute before claims that inarticulateness, ignorance, occult mumbling, and loutishness are just as good as fine literature."[34] The latter author fears becoming what he has been made to behold: the condition of muteness is nothing other than exclusion from literary *production*. But why should the coming-into-writing of those formerly excluded from the means of literary production be experienced as the degeneration of cultural values? Or, on the other hand, why must the writing of minority authors be considered *intrinsically* subversive, as the overturning of supposedly hegemonic values represented by Homer or Shakespeare? These alternatives are only enjoined upon us by the supposition that canonical works can be characterized politically in some universal way, as either progressive or regressive in their social effects.

The virtual agreement of the progressive and the reactionary participants in the canon debate about the relation between culture and value suggests that the positions of these antagonists are more complexly interrelated than a narrative of hegemony and resistance would imply. We will have to say rather that the two positions are mutually constitutive, and even more that they both fall well within the normative assumptions of American political culture, even within the normative principles of liberal pluralism. (It is important to remember in this context that even the reactionary defenders of the canon are scrupulous to "include" token minority works in their conception of "Western civilization").[35] Here I would like to consider briefly three propositions about cultural value to which both progressive and reactionary critics would presumably assent, in order to demonstrate that these propositions are questionable, on whatever side of the debate they happen to be argued.

1. *Canonical texts are the repositories of cultural values.* The equation of the values expressed in a work with the value *of* the work is assumed by both the revanchists and the revisionists when they conceive literary texts as the means of transmitting specific values in the classroom. It is certainly the case that at the primary levels of the educational system "values" are simply decanted from carefully chosen texts which are not always the same texts taught at higher levels. In the stratosphere of pluralist pedagogy, the same reified values are often exposed and ritually qualified, subverted, or rejected, as though the work were simply the container of such values. What fails to be noted about this institutional arrangement is that the pedagogic relation between value and the literary work is very much keyed to the level of the educational system. At the level of the graduate school and the professional conference, the educational capital specific to that level can be signalled by a certain refusal of the rhetoric of "great works" characteristic of the lower levels of the system. Hence Michael Ryan, commenting on the surprising number of sessions at the 1984 MLA convention critical of the canonical epic tradition, can present the thesis that the epic is "a renowned bastion of male self-aggrandizement" as merely the con-

sensus of these sessions.[36] Yet, as I hope to demonstrate more fully at a later point in this argument, the meaning of patriarchal or misogynist values, in contradistinction to "Homeric" values, is enormously attenuated when spread over thousands of years and dozens of social formations. "Homeric values" are not transmitted to students any more than Homer expresses immediately the "ideals of Western civilization." The latter ideals are specific to individual social formations, to successive ideologies of tradition, and they are expressed in determinate social conditions of reading. These conditions are of course pedagogic, but it is a measure of the theoretical deficiency of the canon critique that "values" transmitted in the classroom can simply be conflated with the contents of historical works.[37]

2. *The selection of texts is the selection of values.* Within the world of reified and ahistorical values, aesthetic value confronts the reader, the consumer of values, as just another value, not in any conceivable way more important than the value of justice or social equality. Thus Lillian Robinson writes of the feminist critique of the canon: "At its angriest, none of this reintrepretation offers a fundamental challenge to the canon *as canon;* although it posits new values, it never suggests that, in the light of those values, we ought to reconsider whether the great monuments are really so great, after all."[38] The desirability of such a reconsideration is hinted by Nina Baym, on behalf of a version of feminist criticism operating vigorously in the last two decades in the field of canon revision: "it is time perhaps . . . to reexamine the grounds upon which certain hallowed American classics have been called great."[39] The distinction between masculine and feminine values has been relatively easy to superimpose upon the field of writing, especially as women writers in the modern European languages emerged earlier than writers of other minority groups. There is accordingly a larger body of writing by women to organize in alternative canonical form, and in such a way as to confirm the alignment of canonical and noncanonical texts with hegemonic and antihegemonic values.

The entrance of women into literary culture, however, is not a simple transition to an unambiguous literacy, as though writing were the neutral medium for the conveyance of gendered values. To acknowledge only the most conspicuous complication of the transition, for example, one might invoke, as does Myra Jehlen in her critique of Nina Baym, the historical relation between writing by women and the division of public writing into "serious" and "popular" genres; for Jehlen this is a question of women's "relationship to writing as such."[40] The distinction between serious and popular writing is a condition of canonicity; it belongs to the history of literacy, of the systematic regulation of reading and writing, as the adaptation of that system's regulatory procedures to social conditions in which the practice of writing is no longer confined to a scribal class. The explosion of popular writing in the eighteenth century was an effect of the fact that writing itself was becoming "popular." Thus the generic category of the popular continues to bear the stigma of nonwriting, of mere orality, within writing itself, since popular works are consumed, from the point of view of High Culture, as the textual simulacra of ephemeral speech. This is not to say anything of the actual importance of popular writing, of its multiple social effects, or of why one may wish to read it or study it. It should also be stressed that the distinction between serious and popular is a far less stable mechanism for enforcing social stratification than the sexual hierarchy itself, and it thus permits (because it cannot always prevent) the production of "serious" works by strategically placed members of groups to whom it means to assign devalorized textual practices—a contradiction marking the history of writing by women as the relation between their writing and the novel, itself a noncanonical genre until the end of the nineteenth century. The canonization of novels written by women was thus conditional upon the legitimation of the novel form, the canonization of a popular genre.

Considerably more would need to be said here in order to give even a brief creditable account of hierarchizing procedures within the field of writing and their complex relation to social stratification; but the above remarks should indicate at the least how unhistorical it is to claim, as Jane Tompkins does in *Sensational Designs: The Cultural Work of American Fiction,* that popular fiction "has been rigorously excluded from the ranks of 'serious' literary works,"[41] as though the two categories did not define *each other* in a system of literary production. Or to claim that the evaluation of popular writing by women can be subjected to a canonical reversal simply by revaluing the values expressed in these works: "My own embrace of the conventional led me to value everything that criticism taught me to despise" (xvi). Tompkins's project of "reconstituting the notion of value in literary works" dissolves the aesthetic, in a gesture now foundational in the critique of canon formation, by substituting for it a pseudo-historicism disguising the fact that the values being "revalued" are very simply *contemporary* values: "Instead of asking whether a work is unified or discontinuous, subtle, complex, or profound, one wants to know, first, whether it was successful in achieving its aims; and second, whether its aims were good or bad" (xvii). Hence the assertion that Susan Warner and Harriet Beecher Stowe offer "in certain cases a critique of American society far more devastating than any delivered by better-known critics such as Hawthorne and Melville" is defended not on the basis of a symptomatic reading of their texts in historical context, but on explicitly moral grounds, namely the affirmation of such values as the "sanctity of motherhood and the family" or "the saving power of Christian love" (145). If one demurs at endorsing these values, one need not look beneath this ground of value for a mythical elephant or tortoise, a fact perhaps not interesting with respect to the values in question but immediately indicative that values in this context always mean *moral* values.

The reversion to moralism is determined by the equation of text-selection with value-selection. For this reason much of what passes for political analysis of historically canonical works is nothing more than the passing of moral judgment on them. The critique of the canon moves quickly to reassert absolute notions of good and evil; the overturning of Kant's autonomous aesthetic is brought up short before Nietzsche's critique of morality. One need only compare Tompkins's theory of canon formation with Hans Robert Jauss's equally revisionary concept of "horizonal change" to see that a fall into moralism will occur regardless of what values are set against the category of the aesthetic. Tompkins argues that the "text succeeds or fails on the basis of the 'fit' with features of its immediate context, on the degree to which it provokes the desired response, and not in relation to unchanging formal, psychological, or philosophical standards of complexity, or truth, or correctness" (xviii). Her statement yields a spectacular but in the end illusory contrast to Jauss's historicization of literary tradition:

> The distance betweeen the horizon of expectations and the work, between the familiarity of previous aesthetic experience and the "horizonal change" demanded by reception of the new work, determines the artistic character of a literary work, according to an aesthetics of reception: to the degree that this distance decreases, and no turn toward the horizon of yet-unknown experience is demanded of this receiving consciousness, the closer the work comes to the sphere of "culinary" or entertainment art.[42]

The difference between Jauss and Tompkins disappears entirely when Jauss comes to define how it is that a work can frustrate the expectations of its initial readers. The formal innovation Jauss admires rather more than Tompkins (his example is Flaubert's *style indirect libre,* valued over the conventionality of Feydeau) is finally only the vehicle for the introduction of new moral values, which may be "immoral" from the standpoint of the old: "If one looks at the moments in history when literary works toppled the taboos of the ruling morals or offered readers new solutions for the moral casuistry of his lived praxis, which thereafter could be sanctioned by the consensus of all readers in the society, then a still little-studied area of research opens itself up to the literary historian" (454). Whatever pleasure is produced by *style indirect libre,* or style as such, is thoroughly chastened in this Whiggish history of "the competitive relationship between literature and canonized morals." If Jauss's theory can then be used to *devalue* the same popular works Tompkins desires to revalue as the embodiment of excluded, counterhegemonic values, this paradox has less to do with any absolute difference between these two critics than with the inadequacy of reductively moralistic theories to account for the process of canon formation.

3. *Value must be either intrinsic or extrinsic to the work.* As we have just noted, the Kantian aesthetic is distantly engaged in the critique of canon formation by the argument that value is not intrinsic but rather relative, contingent, subjective, contextual, or, in other words, extrinsic. The distinction between intrinsic and extrinsic value accords well at the level of pluralist theory with a historical narrative of inclusion or exclusion. According to that narrative, the canonical judgments of dominant groups have been typically justified by an appeal to transcendent norms of judgment, as though history itself were the judge of works, or as though individuals could really transcend the conditions of their specific judgments. Yet the exploding of such fictions of intrinsic, universal, or transcendent value, which was a necessary means of recovering a sense of the historicity of judgment, does not necessarily clarify the actual circumstances in which judgments are made and have effect. Further, the strategy of exposing intrinsic value as simply extrinsic has the curious effect of disabling at the outset any project of revaluation, where the object revalued is the work, and not (as in Tompkins) other extrinsic (moral) values. In the case of devalued or forgotten works, revaluation typically appeals to the "real" value or quality of the work; nothing other than a strong assertion of such value is likely to succeed in the actual institutional circumstances of canonical revision. Recently it has been possible to argue that the process of valuation is grounded in the consensus of a particular community where, for the members of such a community, such values function as though they were absolute. On this account values are indeed extrinsic to the work but they are at the same time intrinsic or internal to what Stanley Fish calls, in the most prominent version of this argument, an "interpretive community."[43] Hence it is only in the *absence* of consensus that a distinction between intrinsic and extrinsic value need arise at all with reference to particular works. Elizabeth Meeese discovers the answer to the vexing question of "the failure of so many feminist commentaries aimed at demonstrating the stature of neglected works by women" in Fish's unapologetic observation

that "the act of recognizing literature . . . proceeds from a collective decision as to what will count as literature, a decision that will be in force only
so long as a community of readers and believers continues to abide by it."[44]
Such an argument implies that a different community of readers—women
readers, for example—will very likely express different values by valuing
different works, that is, by positing a different canon of "literature." Having faced the fact that judgments cannot be reconciled under a universal norm of value, or by a surreptitious appeal to a transcendent court of
judgment, advocates of this theory need no longer be troubled by the distinction between intrinsic and extrinsic value: judgment can always be
grounded in some community or other.[45]

One can see in retrospect that the formulation of such notions as that
of the "interpretive community" provided an early theoretical justification for the separatist phase of canon critique, since it is only necessary to
claim that the university is host to more than one "interpretive community" in order to justify the institutionalization of different canons—
canons of the noncanonical. Once consensus is achieved by any "community of readers," however, that community enters into what looks like a
state of mass delusion, in which valuation can proceed without reference to
any constraints imposed by the social function of the school itself or by the
difficulty of constituting a community sufficiently homogeneous in its interests or identity to operate by consensus. Hence those who dissent from a
given consensus are compelled either to fall back upon assertions of the
innate value of the cultural products they value or to constitute themselves
as another distinct "community of readers"—a sequence of action and reaction repeatedly characterizing the canon debate. Shall we not say in this
circumstance that "consensus" has the same relation to value within a particular "interpretive community" as the notion of transcendent value once
had for a "community of readers" which imagined itself to be the only such
community? But one only has to consider the fact that value judgments can
and do come into conflict *within* an interpretive community in order to call
into question the notion of consensus as the name for how judgments
achieve canonizing force. Literary culture in general, and the university in
particular, are by no means structurally organized to express the consensus
of a community; these social and institutional sites are complex hierarchies
in which the position and privilege of judgment are objects of competitive
struggles.

The problem of value is scarcely resolved by recourse to the notion of the
community as its hypothetical ground. On the contrary, consensus is the
pleasant ideological shift by which social determinations are mystified as
"collective decisions" that are finally only the sum of individual decisions.

In this polity texts confront readers in an artificial social vacuum like the space of the voting booth, behind the curtain of private judgment. Disagreements about value within such a pseudodemocracy are comfortably absorbed in a continuous plebiscite within which even the coming to power of the loyal opposition changes nothing structurally, since there is no theoretical limit to the number of "interpretive communities," and since each one believes itself to function in exactly the same way, by consensus. The democratic metaphor is quite potent here, since the conflation of judgment with a kind of election betrays the fact that the terms of the canon debate are entirely determined by the basic assumptions of liberal pluralism.[46] This is why the critique of the canon has always constructed the history of canon formation as a conspiracy of judgment, a secret and exclusive ballot by which literary works are chosen for canonization because their authors belong to the same social group as the judges themselves, or because these works express the values of the dominant group.[47] The poverty of this historical reconstruction determines the limits of the response to it—the notion that dominated groups must choose their own canonical works by a kind of pseudoelection or "consensus." If the process of judgment is more complicated than the electoral analogy suggests, this model of canon formation will have to be discarded. While the selection of texts for preservation certainly does presuppose acts of judgment, which are indeed complex psychic and social events subject to many kinds of determination, these acts are necessary rather than sufficient to constitute a process of canon formation. An individual's judgment that a work is great does nothing in itself to preserve that work, unless that judgment is made in a certain institutional context, a setting in which it is possible to insure the *reproduction* of the work, its continual reintroduction to generations of readers. The work of preservation has other, more complex social contexts than the immediate responses of readers, even communities of readers, to texts; as we shall see, these institutional contexts shape and constrain judgment according to *institutional* agendas, and in such a way that the selection of texts never represents merely the consensus of a community of readers, either dominant or subordinate. The scene in which a group of readers, defined by a common social identity and common values, confronts a group of texts with the intention of making a judgment as to canonicity, is an *imaginary* scene. That imaginary scene must now be set against what happens in a real place, the school.

The Pedagogic Imaginary

The socioinstitutional constraints upon the process of canon formation are well exemplified by such welcome and necessary projects as the *Norton*

Anthology of Literature by Women, or the forthcoming *Norton Anthology of Afro-American Literature.* The constituency for these anthologies will continue to consist largely of university students, who will use them as *textbooks,* or as instruments of research. This fact is a condition for the production of both anthologies, but it is a condition whose force is easily forgotten when the critique of the canon assumes that the selection of texts for canonicity represents the consensus of some community, either dominant or subordinate, and therefore that the anthologies represent "alternative canons." For many compelling social reasons neither the *Norton Anthology of Literature by Women* nor the *Norton Anthology of Afro-American Literature* can represent the consensus of hypothetical *communities* of women or Afro-Americans. The responsibility of selecting texts for the purpose of defining a tradition of literature by women, or by Afro-American writers, resides much more narrowly in the editors of the anthologies, whose relation to female or Afro-American culture is considerably more complex than might be indicated by the term "representation." This circumstance is neither scandalous nor extraordinary; it means nothing more than that judgments with canonical force are institutionally located.[48]

It is nevertheless an interesting consequence of the canon debate that it has called every act of judgment into question, not simply because judgment is always historical, local, or institutional, but more profoundly because it is exercised at all. The latter position is expressed unequivocally by a participant in the debate over the Stanford "Western Culture" course:

> The *notion* of a core list is inherently flawed, regardless of what kinds of works it includes or excludes. It is flawed because such a list undermines the critical stance that we wish students to take toward the materials they read. . . . A course with such readings creates two sets of books, those privileged by being on the list and those not worthy of inclusion. Regardless of the good intentions of those who create such lists, the students have not viewed and will not view these separate categories as equal.[49]

It is difficult to see how the logic of such an argument would allow *any* works to be taught, since every syllabus of study selects some works rather than others. The curious logic of this argument conflates the syllabus, a selection of texts for study in a particular institutional context, with the canon itself—the sum total of works supposed to be "great." A syllabus will necessarily be limited by the constraints of a particular class and its rubric, even by the irreducibly material constraint that only so much can be read or studied in a given class. In no classroom is the "canon" itself the object of study. Where does it appear, then? It would be better to say that the canon is an *imaginary* totality of works. No one has access to the canon as a totality. This fact is true in the trivial sense that no one ever reads every canonical work; no one can, because the works invoked as canonical change continually according to many different occasions of judgment or contestation. What this means is that the canon is never other than an imaginary list; it never appears as a complete and uncontested list in any particular time and place, not even in the form of the omnibus anthology, which remains a selection from a larger list which does not itself appear anywhere in the anthology's table of contents. In this context, the distinction between the canonical and the noncanonical can be seen not as the form in which judgments are actually made about individual works, but as an effect of the syllabus as an institutional instrument, the fact that works not included on a given syllabus appear to have no status at all.[50] The historical condition of literature is that of a complex continuum of major works, minor works, works read primarily in research contexts, works as yet simply shelved in the archive. Anyone who studies historical literatures knows that the archive contains an indefinite number of works of manifest cultural interest and accomplishment. While these works might be regarded as "noncanonical" in some pedagogic contexts—for example, the context of the "great works" survey—their noncanonical status is not necessarily equivalent in anyone's judgment to a zero-degree of interest or value. The fact that we conventionally recognize as "the canon" only those works included in such survey courses or anthologies as the Norton or the Oxford suggests to what extent the debate about the canon has been driven by institutional agendas, for which the discourse of the "masterpiece" provides such a loud accompaniment. The merest familiarity with historical context brings the continuum of cultural works back into focus and demonstrates that the field of writing does not contain only two kinds of works, either great or of no interest at all. For this reason the category of the "noncanonical" is entirely inadequate to describe the status of works which do not appear in a given syllabus of study.

What does have a concrete location as a list, then, is not the canon but the syllabus, the list of works one reads in a given class, or the curriculum, the list of works one reads in a program of study. When teachers believe they have in some way challenged or overthrown the canon and its evaluative principles, what they have always really done is devise or revise a particular syllabus, as it is only through the syllabus that they have any access to the imaginary list which is the canon. While this point is in some respects quite obvious, it nevertheless usefully exposes the fallacy of using a revision of the syllabus against the *principle* of the canon. So far from being the case that the canon determines the syllabus in the simple sense that the syllabus is constrained to select only from canonical works, it is much more historically accurate to say that the syllabus posits the existence of the canon as its imaginary totality. The imaginary list is projected out of the multiple individual syllabi functioning within individual pedagogic institutions over a relatively extended period of time. Changing the syllabus cannot mean in any historical context overthrowing the canon, because every construction of a syllabus *institutes* once again the process of canon formation.

To illustrate the latter point let us consider at somewhat greater length the much controverted "Western Culture" course offered at Stanford University, since revised so as to include works by various minorities, as well as works by non-Western writers:

Ancient World

Required:
Hebrew Bible, Genesis
Plato, *Republic,* major portions of books 1–7
Homer, major selections from *Iliad, Odyssey,* or both
At least one Greek tragedy
New Testament, selections, including a gospel

Strongly recommended:
Thucydides
Aristotle, *Nicomachean Ethics, Politics*
Cicero
Virgil, *Aeneid*
Tacitus

Medieval and Renaissance

Required:
Augustine, *Confessions,* 1–9
Dante, *Inferno*
More, *Utopia*
Machiavelli, *The Prince*
Luther, *Christian Liberty*
Galileo, *The Starry Messenger, The Assayer*

Strongly recommended:
Boethius, *Consolation of Philosophy*
Aquinas, selections
A Shakespearean tragedy
Cervantes, *Don Quixote*
Descartes, *Discourse on Method, Meditations*
Hobbes, *Leviathan*
Locke, *Second Treatise of Civil Government*

Modern

Required:
Voltaire, *Candide*

Strongly recommended:
Rousseau, *Social Contract, Confessions, Emile*

Marx and Engels, *Commu-nist Manifesto*	Hume, *Enquiries, Dialogues on Natural Religion*
Freud, *Outline of Psycho-analysis, Civilization and Its Discontents*	Goethe, *Faust, Sorrows of Young Werther*
Darwin, selections	Nineteenth-century novel
	Mill, *Essay on Liberty, The Subjection of Women*
	Nietzsche, *Genealogy of Morals, Beyond Good and Evil*

If one glances over the list of works on this syllabus, one sees that no wo-men writers are required (the nineteenth-century novel category makes one slot for a woman available). There are no nonwhite authors (depending upon how one defines the race of St. Augustine—and this question is not an uninteresting complication of our notions of social identity); and the far-ther back one goes in the list, the more likely that the author comes from a privileged class, priestly or noble. Obviously in order to "open" this canon, one would have to *modernize* it, to displace the preponderance of works from earlier to later. And there are of course many good reasons to do so. The pressure to modernize the curriculum has succeeded again and again despite the inertial conservatism of the educational institution, and it is this pressure which is largely responsible for many historically signifi-cant *exclusions:* The fact that we read Plato but not Xenephon, Virgil but not Statius, has nothing to do with the social identities of Xenephon or Statius, something more to do with later evaluations of their relative inter-est; but the necessity of choosing between them has everything to do with the modernization of the curriculum, with the imperative of *making room* for such later writers as Locke or Rousseau. The totality of the canon as an imaginary list is always in conflict with the finite materiality of the syllabus, the fact that it is constrained by the limits imposed by its institutional time and space.

Nevertheless this fact has been hard to acknowledge, perhaps because none of us will ever be familiar with more than a fraction of what has been written that might be considered to be worth reading or studying. Every-thing that counts as "knowledge" is a selection from a continually expand-ing aggregate. What sense would it make, then, to argue that the Stanford curriculum "excludes" Herodotus, Ovid, two of the three major Greek tra-gedians, medieval romances, Rabelais, Calvin, Montaigne, Bacon, Kant, Hegel, the Romantic poets, Proust, Joyce, Mann, not to mention Virginia Woolf, Simone Weil, Richard Wright, or Zora Neale Hurston? If one replaced some entries in the Stanford syllabus with the names just cited, would the Stanford course have been more (or less) representative of something called "Western Culture"? I would suggest that it would be better to begin a critique of this course with the notion of Western culture, the umbrella term under which all these different texts take shelter from the labor of critique, the labor of reading. (It is perhaps worth noting here that the concept of Western culture is itself of relatively recent origin—perhaps no earlier than the eighteenth century—and that it is constructed by suppressing the elements of African and Asian culture it has assimilated, as well as the difficult suturing of the Judaic and the Hellenic; but of this I shall have more to say in the next section.) The homogenizing concept of Western culture hints that all these texts are in accord about certain fundamental issues, or that they all share something that might go by the same name. However much they may all be worth reading, one would have to say that they do not necessarily share anything in the way of fundamental notions.[51] It would be absurd to conclude from a critique of the canon that one should not read any particular work; one should of course read as much as one can. But the construction of a syllabus begins with selection; it does not begin with a "process of elimination." What is excluded from the syllabus is not excluded in the *same way* that an individual is excluded or marginalized as the member of a social minority, socially disenfranchised. What is wrong with the Stanford curriculum has less to do with its inclusions or exclusions than with the fact that it is not and *cannot* be a course on Western culture.[52] It is because the construction of the syllabus works backward from this notion that it takes the form that it does. Hence, as soon as any of these works begin to be taught as expressive of a homogeneous and overarching culture extending from the fifth century B.C. to the present, they begin to be *misread*.

What one would like to comprehend with a finer set of terms is the relation between the material constraints of the syllabus, as an instrument of pedagogy, and the various imaginary totalities projected out of historical curricula. The syllabus has the form of a list, but the items on the list are given a specious unity by reference to a whole from which they are supposed to be a representative selection. This specious unity indeed characterizes not only the canon but the syllabi we call English literature, Romantic literature, women's literature, Afro-American literature. The canon achieves its imaginary totality, then, not by embodying itself in a really existing list, but by retroactively constructing its individual texts as a *tradition*, to which works may be added or subtracted without altering the impression of totality or cultural homogeneity. A tradition is "real," of course, but only in the sense in which the imaginary is real.[53] A tradition always retroactively unifies disparate cultural productions (and this is no less true for the tradition of women writers or the tradition of Afro-American writers); while such historical fictions are perhaps impossible to dispense with, one should always bear in mind that the concept of a given tradition is much more revealing about the immediate context in which that tradition is defined than it is about the works retroactively so organized. Also, and perhaps more interestingly, the larger and more disparate the body of works to be retroactively unified, the more urgent and totalizing the concept of tradition is likely to be. If a principle of specious unity is implicit in the construction of any syllabus, this means that the form of the syllabus sets up the conditions within which it is possible to forget that the syllabus is just a list, that there is no concrete cultural totality of which it is the expression. The confusion of the syllabus with the canon thus inaugurates a pedagogy of misreading, wherein a given text's historical specificity is effaced as it is absorbed into the unity of the syllabus/canon.

Here it will be possible to raise a larger question about the social context of the present canonical reformation, since the construction of alternative canons (that is, alternative syllabi) is very much concerned to reassert the cultural *unity* of subcultures or countercultures. The syllabus functions in a pedagogical context to embody that unity by projecting an alternative or oppositional "canon" out of the synecdochic list which is the syllabus. I would suggest that the present very anxious fixation on the canon (and on the syllabus as its avatar) by both its defenders and its critics, can be read as symptomatic of a certain anxiety associated with the perceived disunity of contemporary society. The critique of the canon responds to the disunity of the culture as a whole, as a *fragmented* whole, by constituting new cultural unities at the level of gender, race, or more recently ethnic subcultures, or gay and lesbian subcultures. The real question before us is not whether these subcultural formations produce a demonstrable regularity of behavior in certain social groups (they obviously do), but whether the concept of "community" accurately names the site and mode of operation of these cultural regularities. The absence of any other concept in the present debate for describing the site of culture represents a serious defect in the sociological vocabulary of liberal pluralist discourse, a poverty that is especially evident if we were to invoke the distinction between *Gemeinschaft* and *Gesellschaft* introduced long ago by Ferdinand Tönnies in his 1887 study of that name. It is immediately apparent that while liberal pluralism continually employs an implicitly sociological concept of *Gemeinschaft* (community), it has no concept of *Gesellschaft* (association) at its disposal at all. Hence it is unable to describe the political effect of any form of association which does not entail the assumption of cultural unity, or "community." Tönnies's distinction was intended to address the fact that modern societies are in fact characterized by the predominance of *Gesellschaft* over *Gemeinschaft*. Whether or not we can speak of a politicization of *Gemeinschaft*—and there may indeed be many reasons why we should wish to do so, reasons which have to do with the "postmodern" condition—such a politics is not likely to prove effective if it forgets the conditions which actually complicate the existence of communities, if it forgets modernity itself. Our postmodern tribalism does not make these conditions disappear. To return this argument to the context of the canon debate, a forgetting of modernity can be seen to correspond to a forgetting of the institutional being of the university, its being as "association." The desire to reduce the question of the canon to a relation between a set of texts and a given community forgets the fact that the university is not a community, despite its misrecognition as such in the pedagogic imaginary.

The discursive form which mediates between the pedagogic scene of debate about the canon and the social scene of perceived social fragmentation or *Gesellschaft* is the *list itself*. I would like to suggest that an obsession with the form of the list defines a version of what Cornelius Castoriadis and Claude Lefort have called the "social imaginary," the entire realm of imaginary significations organizing social life as something beyond the satisfaction of material needs or functions, and positing the unity of "society" in the face of social division.[54] What I will call the "pedagogic imaginary" similarly organizes the discursive and institutional life of teachers in excess of the simple function of disseminating knowledge by projecting a unity of the "profession" in the ideality of its self-representation, the discourse of its own being as a kind of community.

In order to make the pedagogic imaginary visible as a fetishizing of the syllabus/list, let us consider the example of the list which is appended to E. D. Hirsch's *Cultural Literacy,* and which has the simple function of communicating what Hirsch believes to be a quantity of knowledge prerequisite to functional literacy. We need not linger here over the peculiarity of an argument which offers as information prerequisite to reading the same information one ordinarily acquires as a *consequence* of reading. If Americans are "culturally illiterate," this fact is evidence of the educational system's failure to install a motive for reading in a nominally literate population. For the purposes of the example, however, I am less interested in disputing Hirsch's argument (it has been well and throughly contested by others)[55] than in explaining why the knowledge defining cultural literacy must take the form of a *list;* and in fact I would argue that it is really the form of the list which has allowed Hirsch's book to produce effects of fascination in both the social and the pedagogic imaginary. The list which defines a common culture of the "culturally literate" (that is, the culturally advantaged) is itself an exemplary artifact of *mass* culture, with its lists of ten-best-everything. As such, the form of the list is a significant instance of the social imaginary at work; but within that imaginary what does it signify? One would have to invoke Lukács or Adorno to undertake a critique of the nostalgia for community that pervades this aspect of mass culture, in the midst of its carnival of cultural diversity, its infinite dispersal and fragmentation of knowledge. The fetishized list is one symptom of what Lyotard has described (and also celebrated) as the "postmodern condition of knowledge."[56] Indeed nothing can be more alienating (in the full range of Marxian senses) than to read through Hirsch's list, from which I excerpt the following sequence for comment: Agamemnon, aggression, Agnew (Spiro), agnosticism, agreement (grammar), agribusiness, air pollution, air quality index, Akron, Ohio.[57] From Agamemnon to Akron, Ohio is, to be sure, quite a stretch; it is Western culture on the rack. Nothing *makes sense* of the sequence, least of all its origin in the house of Atreus. Nevertheless the relations among these terms are not so difficult to recover at another level of analysis, at the level of a critique which takes as its object not the content but the *form* of the list, the form which unifies these terms as constitutive of that cultural capital called "cultural literacy." The latter form of capital has everything to do, as we shall see, with the kind of knowledge that *grammar* is, the kind of knowledge conveyed by a literary education; but it does not of itself reveal the relation between agribusiness and air pollution, or between Spiro Agnew and aggression. Its specious unity is a repression of the *systemic* relations between the very terms which might signify (with surprising accuracy) the world of late capitalism, where the detritus of "Western" culture is merely juxtaposed to the name of Akron, Ohio, the center, as Hirsch's subsequent *Dictionary of Cultural Literacy* tells us, of rubber production in the United States. The form of the list forecloses any systemic analysis of its own terms on behalf of a nostalgia in which Agamemnon and Akron might truly belong to a "common culture." The nonexistence of this culture, or its actual existence as mass culture, is just the fact which Hirsch's list both manifests and denies.

I would suggest further that the fetishized mass cultural form of the list, as an instance of the social imaginary, determines the form of the critique of the canon in the university, the fixation on the syllabus as an exclusive list. A nostalgia for community pervades the debate about the canon on both the right and the left sides of the debate—on the one side as the unity of Western culture, and on the other as the unity of its individual countercultures, represented by canons of "noncanonical" works. Both unities contend with the actual dominance of mass culture by projecting an imaginary totality out of mass culture's image of cultural diversity—the form of the list. There is no question that cultural unities, especially unities in opposition, have political effects, that the concept and experience of "solidarity" is essential to any struggle. But the pedagogic imaginary within which the critique of the canon has been advanced is at once in excess of that solidarity, because it constructs out of its alternative canon/syllabus/list a culture (of women writers, or Afro-American writers, etc.) more homogeneous than it actually is, and in defect of that solidarity, because the image of cultural homogeneity it disseminates is only an image for those who consume it in the university, where it is consumed *as* an image. The "open" canon can lay claim to representational validity in the experience not of "women" or "blacks" but of women or blacks in the university—which is not itself a *representative* place. The university is nevertheless a locus of real power (for the distribution of cultural capital), and therefore a good place for a political praxis to define its object. Such an object should not be the imaginary alone, the canon as image, even if such a praxis must sometimes act upon the image, or mobilize the potent force of the imaginary. The imaginary has real and sometimes beneficial social effects, but these effects are always mediated by the institutional form within which they are expressed.[58]

The difference between the canon and the syllabus, then, is the difference between the pedagogic imaginary, with its images of cultural or countercultural totality, and the form of the list, as the instance of mass culture's social imaginary, with its simultaneous denial and manifestation of cultural heterogeneity. As teachers we should of course never let the syllabus determine pedagogy, even or especially when we "change the syllabus." The fact that we have conceived of the latter project as changing or even overthrowing the canon itself means that the form of the syllabus fails to be recognized as a mediating structure in its institutional place. To decline the theoretical and practical labor of analyzing pedagogic structures in their institutional sites is to cede everything to the imaginary, to play the game of culture without understanding it. It is only in the pedagogic imaginary that changing the syllabus means in any *immediate* sense changing the world; what is required now is an analysis of the institutional location and mediation of such imaginary structures as the canon in order first to assess the real effects of the imaginary, and then to bring the imaginary itself under more strategic political control.

It is a fact, to be sure, that many more women authors are taught in literature classes than used to be, just as it is a fact that there are now many more women authors, and just as it is a fact that there are now many more women in professional and managerial fields. It is also a fact that the burden of poverty in the last decade has been shifted more and more onto the shoulders of women. What is the relation between these facts? The critique of the canon can at present offer no analysis of the relation between the forms of cultural and material capital, nor will it ever if it merely confirms the imaginary ego ideal of a newly constituted professional-managerial class, no longer exclusively white or male. Those who have never been taught, or have been very inadequately taught, the *practice* of reading have little occasion to rejoice at being "represented" in the canon. Such representation does not address or compensate for the socioeconomic conditions of their existence so long as the school continues to distribute cultural capital unequally. Let us recognize, then, that the university belongs to an educational *system,* inclusive of every level and every kind of school, higher and lower, public and private. If we have undertaken a necessary modernization of the curriculum in the last decade, we should reflect upon the fact that what has been revised is a curriculum in the *university,* in response to social pressures registered much more ambiguously at the lower levels of the educational system, where the democratization of the school has been simultaneously subverted by the withdrawal of public funding, the "deskilling" of teachers, and the virtual removal of texts, literary or otherwise, from the classroom.[59] What would it mean to redefine the object of our critique as the institution of the school, of which the syllabus is only an instrumentality? It would mean acknowledging that the canonical reformation has somewhat less social effect as an agency of change than it claims, by which I mean, precisely, "less." To have drawn up a new syllabus is not yet to have begun teaching, nor is it yet to have begun reflection upon the institutional form of the school.

Multicultural Interlude: The Question of a Core Curriculum

Every relationship of "hegemony" is an educational relationship.
　　　　　　　　　—GRAMSCI, *Prison Notebooks*

While the debate over the canon concerns what texts should be taught in the schools, what remains invisible within this debate—too large to be seen at all—is the school itself. The absence of reflection on the school as an institution is the condition for the most deluded assumption of the debate, that the school is the vehicle of transmission for something like a national culture. What is transmitted by the school is, to be sure, a kind of culture; but it is the *culture of the school.* School culture does not unify the nation culturally so much as it projects out of a curriculum of artifact-based knowledge an imaginary cultural unity never actually coincident with the culture of the nation-state. In this way the left hand of the educational system—the dissemination of a supposedly national culture—remains ignorant of what the right hand is doing—the differential tracking of students according to class or the possession of cultural capital. If the structure of the system, its multiple levels and its division between public and private institutions, divides the population in this way, the culture the *university* produces (as opposed to other kinds or levels of school), can only be "national" for that plurality which acquires this level of education. What this group may learn to think of as a national culture is always a specific *relation* to the knowledge defined by the university curriculum.[60]

The extraordinary effects of confusing school culture with national culture are most conspicuous when the national culture is made to swallow whole the even larger fish called "Western culture," and in such a way as to produce an image of the American nation as the telos of Western cultural evolution. Here we may adduce William Bennett's complacent version of this narrative in "To Reclaim a Legacy":

> We are a part and a product of Western civilization. That our society was founded upon such principles as justice, liberty, government with the consent of the governed, and equality under the law is the result of ideas descended directly from great epochs of Western civilization—Enlightenment England and France, Renaissance Florence, and Periclean Athens. These ideas, so revolutionary in their times yet so taken for granted now, are the glue that binds together our pluralistic nation. The fact that we as Americans—whether black or white, Asian or Hispanic, rich or poor—share these beliefs aligns us with other cultures of the Western tradition.[61]

The interesting point about this argument is not the typically American chauvinism Bennett immediately denies ("It is not ethnocentric or chauvinistic to acknowledge this"), or the dubious assimilation of Western thinkers to democratic political principles many or even most of them would not in fact have endorsed. What remains interesting and consequential in Bennett's statement is a confusion which, as we shall see, characterizes both Bennett and his opponents in the canon debate: the slippage between *culture* and *civilization*. The semantic burden of the latter term obliquely recognizes what the concept of the national culture denies—the necessity of defining that culture largely by reference to the High Cultural artifacts to which access is provided in the schools. Bennett admits as much, without drawing any adverse conclusion from this point: "No student of our civilization should be denied access to the best that tradition has to offer." Is "our civilization," then, the same as "our culture"? One may reasonably question what necessary *cultural* relation a university-trained suburban manager or technocrat has to Plato or Homer by virtue of his or her American citizenship—no more, in fact, than an educationally disadvantaged dweller in the most impoverished urban ghetto. The suburban technocrat and the ghetto dweller on the other hand have very much more in common culturally with each other than either of them ever need have with the great writers of Western civilization. If "Western" civilization—defined by a collection of cultural artifacts—can imaginarily displace the real cultural continuities that obtain at the national level, such an exemplary expression of the social imaginary is the effect of a crucial ambiguity in the concept of culture itself, an ambiguity familiar enough in the history of the concept as the distinction between culture in the sense of refinement—in this case, familiarity with the great works of "civilization"—and in the ethnographic sense of common beliefs, behaviors, attitudes—what a "national culture" would really have to mean.[62] The attempt to make the first sense of culture *stand for* the second names a certain project for the university, but one which it seems less well suited to undertake than ever (for reasons I will consider presently). The apparent failure of the university's cultural project of constituting a national culture elicits from the New Right the clamorous demand for a return to what was after all the *bourgeois* school, the institution enabling the old bourgeoisie to identify itself culturally by acquiring the cultural capital formerly restricted to the aristocratic or clerical estates. This capital consisted of nothing other than the "great works" of Western civilization.

If the national cultural project of the school is no longer a real possibility (it was always a class project anyway), the canon debate has nevertheless decisively problematized the notion of culture in its controversial language. The absence, however, of any concept of a specific *school* culture in the debate has meant that the perceived monolith of Western culture has had to be contested by the assertion of an antithetical "multiculturalism" as the basis of a politically progressive curriculum. Multiculturalism defines Western culture as its political antagonist, and vice versa. Yet the rather too neat polarization of these terms elides the question of what school culture really is, that is, what *relation to culture* is produced by the formal study of cultural artifacts. Whatever other effects the introduction of multicultural curricula may have, the *theory* of multiculturalism perpetuates the confusion of culture as the study of preserved artifacts with the sense of culture as common beliefs, behaviors, attitudes. It is by no means the case that the study of cultural works simply operates as the agency of cultural transmission in the second sense—although school culture, as Bourdieu has shown, does its part to install a *class* habitus in the subjects of its pedagogy. This habitus is defined not by the content of cultural works (Plato is not really part of "our culture"), but by the relation to culture inculcated by the school, the relation named precisely by Bennett's "legacy"—a relation of *ownership*. It is not the ideas expressed in the great works that account for their status in arguments such as Bennett's, but the fact that these works are appropriated as the cultural capital of a dominant fraction. That appropriation is in turn justified by representing the ideational content of the great works as an expression of the same ideas which are realized in the current social order, with its current distribution of cultural goods.

In order to accomplish the cultural task of appropriation, however, the school must traverse the heavily mined terrain of a certain alienation produced by the formal study of cultural works. We should not forget that the effects of this alienation are sometimes permanent, and that it is precisely "one's own" culture which sometimes fails to survive the culture of the school (that is to say, the school sometimes produces, despite its acculturative function, dissident intellectuals). Similarly the formal study of cultural works produced within minority cultures is not a means of reproducing minority culture (in the ethnographic sense). If the formal study of Latin-American novels in the university does not really transmit or reproduce Latino culture, it follows that the relation of even Latino students to these artifacts will not be entirely unlike the relation of "American" students to the works of "Western" (American or European) culture. The question is what this relation is, or what it should be.

One conclusion to be drawn immediately from this argument is that there is no ground of commensuration between Western cultural artifacts on the one hand, if examples of these are the *Odyssey* or the Parthenon; and Latino culture on the other, if the latter means the totality of a living culture, and not just its artifacts. Insofar as it is only the *works* of Western or Latino culture to which one has direct access in the school, these works will ultimately be constructed and legitimated as objects of study *in the same way*, by a process of deracination from the actual cultural circumstances of their production and consumption.[63] If works by Afro-American, Latin-American, or postcolonial writers are read now in formal programs of university study, this fact may be the immediate result of a political project of inclusion, or the affirmation of cultural diversity. But the survival of these works in future school curricula will be seen otherwise, as a consequence of their status as interesting and important cultural works that no intellectually responsible program of study can ignore. The current project of affirming *cultures themselves* through the legitimation of cultural works in university curricula is enabled by the very conflation between the senses of culture to which I have drawn attention. The very intensity of our "symbolic struggle" reduces cultural conditions of extreme complexity to an allegorical conflict between a Western cultural Goliath and its Davidic multicultural antagonists. Hence it is never really Greek culture, or French culture, or Roman culture, that is compared with Latino culture or Afro-American culture, but always "Western" culture. Multiculturalism finds itself in the position of having to credit both the reality and the homogeneity of that fictional cultural entity, which achieves its spurious self-identity only by consisting of *nothing but* cultural artifacts.[64]

If the fiction of the cultural homogeneity of the West is nevertheless a very powerful one (because it is ideological), perhaps the better strategy for resisting its domination-effect may be to expose the relation between the "culture" it pretends to embody and the institution which is its support in reality. It is just by suppressing culture in the ethnographic sense—or reserving that sense of culture for non-"Western" artifacts—that the traditional curriculum can appropriate the "great works" of Western civilization for the purpose of constituting an imaginary cultural unity such as Bennett or Hirsch envisions. The deracination of the text tradition thus forces us to define the intertextual relation, say, between Aquinas and Aristotle as evidence of the continuity of Western culture, but it allows us to set aside the fact that Aristotle and Aquinas have almost nothing in common *culturally.* It should be remarked here also that the construction of Western culture depends more upon a body of philosophical than literary texts. If the canon debate originated in university literature departments, the defenders of the canon extended the debate to the question of the humanities curriculum as a whole—the "core" curriculum—by resurrecting the philosophical text tradition as the basis for that core curriculum. This text tradition can be invoked more easily than national vernacular literatures to maintain the fiction of a profound evolution or destiny of Western thought extending from the pre-Socratics to the present.[65] Yet the fact remains that this continuity was always the historical support for *nationalist* agendas. The schools in the early modern nation-states provided an instrument by means of which the state could dissolve the residually feudal bonds of local sovereignty and reattach personal loyalty to itself. Nationalism is, as we have seen, entirely on the surface in Bennett's document. In the early modern period, the great vernacular literary works of the nation-states were taught in such a way as to constitute retroactively a pre-national "West" (usually classical rather than medieval), a continuity intended to cover over the traumatic break of early modern societies with traditional feudal cultures. The "West" was always the creation of nationalism, and that is why one observes that the assertion of the continuity of Western tradition exactly corresponds in its intensity to the assertion of nationalism itself.[66]

The homogenizing textual effects of deracination are even more obvious when we consider the fact that, for us, Plato and Aristotle, Virgil and Dante, are great works of literature *in English*. The translation of the "classics" into one's own vernacular is a powerful institutional buttress of imaginary cultural continuities; it confirms the nationalist agenda by permitting the easy appropriation of texts in foreign languages. Yet the device of translation should not be regarded as extraordinary or atypical of school culture, for translation is only a more explicit version of the same technique of deracination by which all cultural works are constructed as objects of study. This point may clarify the otherwise confusing status of "oral literature," which has become a favored site for the contestation of Western culture's hegemony. It is not a mere contingency that oral works must become "written" in order to be brought into the arena of curricular conflict as "noncanonical" works, excluded or devalued by the Western text tradition. In fact, oral works *cannot* otherwise enter the institutional field, since orality as a cultural condition can only be studied at all ethnographically, as the "writing of culture." When the condition of oral production is on the other hand ignored in the context of interpreting or evaluating these works (by treating oral works as though they were other written works), the real difference between school culture and the culture which gives rise to works disappears from view. By suppressing the context of a cultural work's production and consumption, the school produces the illusion that "our" culture (or the culture of the "other") is transmitted simply by contact with the works themselves. But a text tradition is not sufficient in itself either to constitute or to transmit a culture, and thus school culture can never be more than a part of a total process of acculturation which, for societies with schools, is always complex and has many other institutional sites.

The function imposed upon schools of acculturating students in "our" culture often thus requires that texts be read "out of context," as signs of cultural continuity, or cultural unity. We need not deny that the text tradition can sustain intertextual dialogue over centuries and millennia, however, in order to insist that what is revealed by the historical context of this dialogue is cultural discontinuity and heterogeneity.[67] A rather different pedagogy, one that emphasizes historical contextualization, would at the very least inhibit the assimilation of cultural works to the agenda of constituting a national culture, or the Western culture which is its ideological support.[68] For the very same reason, only the simplest countercultural pedagogy can make the works of the multicultural curriculum stand in a "subversive" relation to Western culture. The historicization of these works too will have to confront the mutual influence and interrelation between dominant Western and dominated non-Western cultures (in the case of post-colonial works, for example, the fact that "Western culture" appears as a cultural unity *only* through the lens of the colonial educational system, and that postcolonial literatures are in constant dialogue with the works taught in that system). While there exists a multiplicity of sites of cultural production, then, this multiplicity can never really be equated with the multiplicity of cultures, as though every cultural work were only the organic expression of a discrete and autonomous culture.[69] The fact that we now expect the curriculum to reflect as a principle of its organization the very distinctness of cultures, Western or non-Western, canonical or non-canonical, points to a certain insistent error of culturalist politics, its elision of the difference the school itself makes in the supposed transmission of culture.

From the perspective of long-term developments in the educational system, the canon debate itself may seem oddly beside the point. Bennett and his associates already acknowledged in their 1984 document that the "crisis of the humanities" refers to the fact that fewer undergraduates choose to major in traditional humanities than in the past. One has the impression in surveying the musings of the right-wing pundits that this fact is the result of nothing less than abdication by the professors of their duty to teach the traditional texts.[70] Nothing could be further from the truth—these texts still constitute the vastly greater part of the humanities curriculum—and in that sense the complaint of the New Right is simply fraudulent. A welcome reality check is provided by Patrick Brantlinger in his analysis of the "crisis":

> Tradition gives the humanities an importance that current funding and research priorities belie. At giant public "multiversities" like the Big Ten schools, humanities courses are taken by many students only as requirements—a sort of force-feeding in writing skills, history, great books, and appropriate "values" before they select the chutes labeled "pre-professional"—pre-med, pre-law, and so forth. . . . Clearly, one doesn't need to blame the radical sixties for the current marginalization and sense of irrelevance that pervades the humanities today.[71]

The crisis of the humanities is the result not of university professors' unwillingness to teach great works (the idea is an insult especially to those teachers and graduate students who could not find employment in the recessions of the 70s and 80s) but of the decisions students themselves make in the face of economic realities. Granted the fact that the crisis is not the result of curricular decisions by humanities teachers, why is the content of the curriculum the site of such controversy? The canon debate will not go away, and it is likely to intensify as the positions of the right and of the multiculturalists are further polarized. The very strength of the reactionary backlash, its success in acquiring access to the national media and funding for its agitprop, suggests that the symptomatic importance of the debate is related in some as yet obscurely discerned way to the failure of the contestants to give an account of the general decline in the significance of the humanities in the educational system. It has proven to be much easier to quarrel about the content of the curriculum than to confront the implications of a fully emergent professional-managerial class which no longer requires the cultural capital of the old bourgeoisie. The decline of the humanities was never the result of newer noncanonical courses or texts, but of a large-scale "capital flight" in the domain of culture. The debate over what amounts to the supplementation (or modernization) of the traditional curriculum is thus a misplaced response to that capital flight, and as such the debate has been conducted largely in the realm of the pedagogic imaginary. I would propose, then, that the division now characterizing the humanities syllabus—between Western and multicultural, canonical and noncanonical, hegemonic and nonhegemonic works—is the symptom of a more historically significant split between two kinds of cultural capital, one of which is "traditional," the other organic to the constitution of the professional-managerial class.

In this larger socioeconomic context, the polarization of the debate into a conflict between Western culture and multiculturalism has proven to be a political misstep for the left. For both the reactionary scapegoating of the noncanonical syllabus as the cause of the crisis of the humanities, and multiculturalism's reduction of canonical works to the ideology of a monolithic Western culture fail to recognize the real relations between the humanities curriculum and the social forces which operate on it. If the debate is ever to acknowledge the presence of these forces, it will have to move beyond the curricular distinction between the canonical and the noncanonical; it will have to raise the much larger question of what is at stake in the relation between the kinds of cultural capital. Since both canonical and noncanonical works constitute at base, despite their apparent conflict, the same *kind* of cultural capital, the social forces displacing this kind of capital will sooner or later strand the participants in the canon debate on an ever shrinking island within the university itself.

What needs urgently to be recognized now is that the polarization of the curriculum into canonical and noncanonical works is very much more in the interest of the right than of the left. The investment of the right in the great works of Western civilization—a "core" curriculum—is in extreme bad faith. For Bennett has already decided that what Bloom calls the "big questions" have been given definitive answers in the American social and political system, which rests on the unshakeable foundation of the *free market.* Yet it is the market itself which produces the effect of cultural capital flight. The professional-managerial class has made the correct assessment that, so far as its future profit is concerned, the reading of great works is not worth the investment of very much time or money. The perceived devaluation of the humanities curriculum is in reality a decline in its *market* value. If the liberal arts curriculum still survives as the preferred course of study in some elite institutions, this fact has everything to do with the class constituency of these institutions. With few exceptions, it is only those students who belong to the financially secure upper classes who do not feel compelled to acquire professional or technical knowledge as undergraduates. The professional-managerial class, on the other hand, many of whose members have only recently attained to middle and upper middle-class status, depends entirely on the acquisition of technical knowledge in order to maintain its status, or to become upwardly mobile. The challenge posed to a class analysis of culture by the professional-managerial class has been well described by Gouldner in his *The Future of Intellectuals and the Rise of the New Class:* "What is needed for the systematic analysis of the old and new class is a *general theory of capital* in which moneyed capital is seen as part of the whole, as a special case of capital. Conversely, what is required for the understanding of culture as capital is nothing less than a political economy of culture."[72] Whether such a political economy of culture has been successfully elaborated in the work of Gouldner or Bourdieu, it is entirely indicative of the conceptual limits of the curriculum debate that it could be carried on for over a decade virtually without reference to either figure.

In this context the right-wing design of purging noncanonical works from the curriculum has as one of its evident objectives the revaluation of the cultural capital of canonical works by associating them with currently popular nationalist and xenophobic sentiments. Mary Louise Pratt is surely correct in identifying the aim of this polemic as the creation of "a narrowly specific cultural capital that will be the normative *referent* for everyone, but will remain the *property* of a small and powerful caste that is linguistically and ethnically unified."[73] The crucial question, however, is not how "narrowly specific" this cultural capital is to be, but how it is to produce the effect of unifying a "caste." Because this unity is not preexistent in American society—capital itself is dispersed now among a number of ethnicities, genders, and even linguistic groups—it must be constituted in the university *after the fact,* as a new project for that institution. This circumstance explains why the right's agenda for the university always makes room for *some* members of minority groups, because the right believes these self-made individuals can be assimilated to the "caste" of all those with an interest in preserving the rights and privileges of their acquired capital. Such assimilation will leave (and has left) the grossly inequitable social structure more or less unchallenged. It is not quite the case, then, that the New Right wishes to purge the university of all linguistic or ethnic others, but that it sets the university the project of unifying the new possessors of cultural capital by cultural means, by means of a "common" curriculum which will identify them as (justly) privileged. In this way Bennett's "legacy" can be reclaimed for its proper inheritors, those who leave the university possessed of capital, of whatever kind. The cultural legacy so probated will present an image to a somewhat more ethnically heterogeneous propertied class of its unified cultural identity as the inheritors of cultural capital.

If this analysis is correct it does not seem the most effective strategy for the left to cede to the right the *definition* of cultural capital; but this is exactly what multiculturalism does when it yields canonical works to the right, when it accepts the right's characterization of the canonical syllabus as constitutive of a unified and monolithic Western culture. Basing its agenda upon such assumptions, a left politics of representation seems to have no other choice than to institutionalize alternative syllabi as representative images of non-Western or "counter"-cultures. This is finally why the project of legitimizing noncanonical works in the university produces an irresolvable contradiction between the presentation of these works as equal in cultural value to canonical works, and at the same time as the embodiment of countercultural values which by their very definition are intended to delegitimize the cultural values embodied in canonical works. The polarization of the debate into Western culturalism versus multiculturalism must then be seen not as a simple conflict between regressive and progressive pedagogies but as the symptom of the transformation of cultural capital in response to social conditions not yet recognized as the real and ultimately determining context of the canon debate. Both the right-wing attempt to shore up the cultural capital of the "great works" by advocating a return to a core curriculum, and the pluralist advocacy of multiculturalism respond to the same demographic circumstances, the heterogeneous constituency of the university. But neither version of culturalist politics responds to the heterogeneous constitution of cultural capital, and hence both movements are condemned to register this condition symptomatically, as a false perception of the mutual (cultural) exclusivity of canonical and noncanonical works.

It is chastening to recall that a leftist analysis of the heterogeneity of cultural capital was available long before Bourdieu or Gouldner, in the work of Antonio Gramsci. In his prescient notes on the subject of education, Gramsci recognized that the displacement of the classical curriculum by professional and technical knowledge would have the effect of precipitating the "humanist" curriculum into what seems to be a permanent state of crisis:

> The basic division of schools into classical (i.e. grammar) and trade schools was a rational scheme: trade schools for the instrumental classes, classical schools for the ruling classes and intellectuals. The development of the industrial base in both town and country led to a growing need for a new type of urban intellectual: alongside the classical school there developed the technical school (professional but not manual), and this brought into question the very principle of the concrete orientation of general culture based on the Greco-Roman tradition. This orientation, once brought into question was in fact doomed, since its formative capacity was largely based on the general and traditionally indisputable prestige of a particular form of civilization.[74]

Gramsci expresses in his notes what may seem to the present liberal academy a surprising conservatism on curricular issues. Without arguing for the retention of the classical curriculum—Gramsci allows that it had to be replaced—he was concerned to point out the paradoxical social effects of the "new type of school" which, while it "appears and is advocated as being democratic" is actually "destined not merely to perpetuate social differences but to crystallize them in Chinese complexities."[75] The apparently conservative tenor of his remarks should not be confused, then, with the usual complaint about "specialization," which expresses nostalgia for the even less democratic educational system of the past (Gramsci insists that the older system was always "intended for the new generation of the ruling class"). The question is not whether technical or professional knowledges will or should be taught, but whether there exists a body of knowledge to which *everyone* should have access in the schools. Gramsci's solution to the emergence of a "crisis of the humanities" was to propose the formation of a "single, humanistic, formative, primary school of general culture which will correctly balance the development of ability for manual (technical, industrial) work with the development of ability for intellectual work."[76] Gramsci's proposal may seem, at this date, uncritical of the content of such a curriculum, since he did not have to consider his own society as in our sense "pluralist"; but we should remember that his sense of a politically strategic educational practice is supported by what is perhaps the most powerful theory of intellectual labor in the Marxist tradition, as well as by the very concept of hegemony that is invoked in virtually all forms of current cultural criticism. For these reasons a serious consideration of Gramsci's analysis may be in order.

What Gramsci called the "unitary school" was supposed to "break [the] pattern" of the traditional educational system, in which "each group has its own type of school, intended to perpetuate a specific traditional function, ruling or subordinate."[77] The new technical and professional schools reinstated the division of society "into juridically fixed and crystallized estates rather than moving towards the transcendence of class divisions." The issue here is not only class division but the conditions of possibility for democratic self-government, since Gramsci rightly sees the schools as providing the means for participating in government: "But democracy, by definition, cannot mean merely that an unskilled worker can become skilled. It must mean that every 'citizen' can 'govern' and that society places him, even if only abstractly, in a general condition to achieve this" (318). This is of course an old theme, but the simultaneous and not unrelated decline of both public education and participatory democracy in the United States should confirm its continued pertinence. For reasons too obvious to belabor, Gramsci's "unitary school" was never a goal in this country; but since our concern is with the American educational system, we can at least note that the very limited "democratization" of that system has been accompanied by the gradual displacement upwards to the university level of the curriculum Gramsci conceived as the basis of a "unitary school." This arrangement accomplishes the effect of class fractioning by tracking most students into the work force at the end of their primary or secondary schooling (an effect reinforced also by the distinction between public and private schools). Given the social pressure to enforce vocational tracking at the lower levels of the educational system, and to dispense more highly valued professional and technical knowledge at the university level, the slot into which the humanities curriculum is confined is very small—as we know, the first two years of college study. In the absence of a "unitary school" at the primary or secondary levels, the possibility of installing a core curriculum of philosophical or literary works exists only during this brief period. Many colleges, of course, have always had some form of a core curriculum, but the important point is that the formal study of a set list of "great works" is condemned to have something of a remedial status for those students who have not read literary or philosophical works, either historical or contemporary, at the lower levels of the system, and who will not continue to study them after their sophomore year. It is only by first recognizing the remedial status of the first two years of college study that we can then pose the question of what Gramsci's analysis may have to offer the present debate.

It will first be necessary to exit the social imaginary by acknowledging that there is no question of producing a *national* culture by means of a *university* curriculum. Or conversely of producing a national multiculturalist ethos by the same means. The question is rather what social effects are produced by the knowledges disseminated in the university, and by the manner of their dissemination. It should not be the business of the university to produce a "common culture," even if the educational system inevitably produces a school culture, a specific relation to knowledge among its subjects. The objective of political integration is not to be confused with the altogether questionable objective of cultural assimilation. Gramsci's analysis suggests that a necessary social condition of democracy is the general exercise of a certain kind of intellectual labor, and that a specific body of knowledge (by which is meant neither *information* in Hirsch's sense, nor *culture* in Bennett's) is the necessary medium in the schools for the exercise of this intellectual labor. The point of the unitary school is that it is a school for everyone; by definition it is not the university. A necessary objective of a Gramscian reconsideration of the curriculum debate would thus be the rearticulation of that debate in the context of the educational system *as* a system. In this context, we can recognize that the constraints upon the university curriculum at its present moment and in its present form account for the fact that the project of a core curriculum is so easily annexed to a socially regressive agenda. Time is one such constraint, since it intensifies the effect of deracination to the point of reducing the study of "great works" to a shallow rehearsal of contextless ideas; such "ideas" turn out unsurprisingly to be nothing more than the clichés of right-wing ideology.[78] It has been all too easy as a consequence for the left/liberal professoriate to identify the only respectable adversarial stance with opposition to a core curriculum. The institutionalization of the distinction between canonical and noncanonical works thus emerges as the necessary response to any attempt to reinstitute an exclusively traditional curriculum. As an expression of the same culturalist politics which confuses school culture with culture in general, this adversarial position unfortunately also deprives the teaching of canonical works of an adequate progressive rationale.

It is perhaps time for progressive teachers to take back the humanities curriculum—all of it—as an integrated program of study. Such a program will be severely limited by the narrow stratum of the educational system which it is forced to inhabit, but until we can begin to think and speak about education as a system of interrelated levels, these limits will continue to function subliminally, beyond analysis or intervention. In the meantime, we can imagine that an integrated curriculum would supersede the distinction between canonical and noncanonical works in the recognition that a syllabus of study always enacts a negotiation between *historical* works and *modern* works. There is no question now, nor has there ever been, of the inevitability of curricular change: the latter-day curriculum is the archaeological evidence of its own sedimented history. When we read Plato or Homer or Virgil in a humanities course, then, we are reading what *remains* of the classical curriculum after the vernacular revolutions of the early modern period. The fact that we no longer read these works in Greek or Latin, or that we read far fewer classical Greek or Latin works than students of premodern school systems, represents a real loss; but this loss must be reckoned as the price of the *integration* of these works into a modern curriculum. The inevitable loss of older works in any humanities curriculum, even one hypothetically much larger than current programs tend to be, is the result, as we have observed, of the *absolute* accumulation of cultural works. The reactionary defense of the traditional "canon" thus betrays itself as ignorant of the cultural history sedimented in the very syllabus it desires to fix. On the other hand it should no longer be necessary to present certain other works, "noncanonical" works, as intrinsically opposed to a hegemonic principle of canonicity, as this is likewise to forget the history sedimented in any syllabus of study.

An alternative theoretical formulation of the curriculum problem will thus have to repudiate the practice of fetishizing the curriculum, of locating the politics of pedagogy in the anxious drawing up of a list of representative names. The *particular* names matter even less at the university level, since the number of historical and modern works worth studying is vastly greater than any (remedial) course of study could begin to consider. The syllabus should rather be conceived as the means of providing *access* to cultural works, both historical and modern (the contrary assumption—that works not on the syllabus will never be read—is an entirely disreputable assumption for teachers to make). Since noncanonical works are in every case either historical works (the objects of research or revaluation) or modern works (the objects of legitimation for the first time as cultural capital), they are in fact what all canonical works once were. To contend otherwise is to commit oneself to the notion that some works are intrinsically canonical, simply expressive of the dominant ideology, and other works intrinsically noncanonical, utterly unassimilable to hegemonic culture. If that were true, what would the struggle to legitimize new works as objects of study be *for*? Hegemony, in Gramsci's sense, is to be fought for; it is something that is continually won and lost by struggles which take place at the specific sites of social practice.

What difference would such a reformulation of terms make? First, that current research programs such as women's studies, or Afro-American studies be recognized as such, as research programs and not as the institution of separate curricula for separate constituencies. But even more important, the humanities curriculum should be presented as an integrated program of study in which the written works studied constitute a certain kind of cultural capital, and in which works therefore cannot be allegorized as intrinsically canonical or intrinsically noncanonical, intrinsically hegemonic or intrinsically antihegemonic. No cultural work of any interest at all is simple enough to be credibly allegorized in this way, because any cultural work will *objectify* in its very form and content the same social conflicts that the canon debate allegorizes by means of a divided curriculum. Further, a conception of an integrated curriculum would make it impossible to forget that what one internalizes in the school is not one's own culture but the culture of the school (which has in turn a certain relation, but not a relation of identity, to culture in the ethnographic sense). The school produces a culture, then, neither unambiguously good or bad, but it does not simply reproduce a given culture, hegemonic or antihegemonic, through the *content* of the curriculum. If it is a defensible objective of the school to disseminate knowledge about the "multicultural" diversity of the nation (defensible because the nation *is* so diverse), it follows from this very objective that it is just as important for majority students to study the cultural products of minority cultures as it is for minority students to be able to study the cultural works of their own cultures. Hence when works by minority writers are legitimized as cultural capital by becoming objects of study in the university, it will follow that everyone will have a right of access to them.

Especially in the wake of a reactionary backlash which indicts the liberal critique of the canon for the abandonment of all standards of judgment, it is no longer politically strategic to argue for the necessity of teaching certain "noncanonical" works solely on the grounds that these works represent social minorities. It is on the contrary much more strategic to argue that the school has the social obligation of providing access to these works, *because they are important and significant cultural works.* In this way we will disabuse ourselves and our students of the idea that canonical or noncanonical syllabi have natural constituencies, the members of dominant or subordinate cultures respectively. The latter notion operates tacitly in the canon debate as the illegitmate displacement of liberal concepts of representation to a site—the school—where democratic objectives are better served by the modestly coercive structure of (in Gramsci's terms) a "unitary" curriculum. Extrapolating from Gramsci's analysis of the relation between the school and democracy, we can predict that different curricula for different constituencies will produce the same effects of social stratification as different schools for different classes. There is not, and should not be, one national culture, but there is, and there should be, one educational system.

But here we return to the fundamental point: pluralism has been able to affirm different cultures but not the fact that cultures are inescapably interdependent both at the moment of a cultural work's production and at that of its consumption. The question is whether or not the school is to acknowledge this "postmodern" condition. It is certainly acknowledged in the domain of mass culture, where cultural products are very often produced for particular constituencies, but where their circulation "interculturally" is virtually assured by the restless promiscuity of commodity exchange. These conditions need not be denied in the university but rather made the occasion of what Christopher Miller, in responding to Hirsch's notion of a national culture, has called "intercultural literacy": "Intercultural literacy would consist of a mode of inquiry that respects the accumulation of shared symbols (thus the term *literacy*) but also invites research into the processes by which cultures are formed and particularly encourages analysis of how cultures constitute themselves *by reference to each other*."[79]

An integrated curriculum would imply a second, pragmatic assumption: It is just as important for both minority and nonminority students to study historical works as it is for both groups to study modern works. The study of historical works need not be justified as an apotropaic exercise—because these works are supposed to embody hegemonic values—but because they *are* historical works. The cultures which give rise to them are as other to all of us as minority cultures are to some of us. Here we can take leave of another fetish of the canon debate, namely, the exclusive emphasis on cultural artifacts as representative of cultures, in the absence of real knowledge about the history of these cultures. The relative lack of reference to history in the curriculum debate is symptomatic of how the concept of culture is deformed in the mirror of the pedagogic imaginary, all the more so since this deformation fails to account for the immanent historicity of even the most recent works. No program of multiculturalism will succeed in producing more than a kind of favorable media-image of minority cultures if it is not supported at every point by an understanding of the historical relations between cultures. At the same time one must insist that it is no longer intellectually defensible to equate historical knowledge with "Western history." It has always been the case (if not always acknowledged) that Western history is the history of the *global* relations of Western states, societies, and cultures; and even more that it is only as a consequence of its global relations that the "West" could conceive or write its own history. If the curriculum is to produce intercultural literacy, in recognition of the imbricated sites of cultural production, we must assume that the context of cultural production is nothing *less* than global.

Were the left/liberal academy to reappropriate the "humanities," that is, to take back the authority to define the cultural capital embodied in its curriculum of study, it would have to devise a rationale for an integrated curriculum of textual/historical study exceeding the laudable objective of affirming cultural diversity. A left rationale for an integrated curriculum would have to present all of the cultural works in that curriculum, whatever their provenance, as a species of cultural capital constitutively different from the capital embodied in technical and professional knowledge. This difference can be defined by the proposition that *everyone* has a right of access to cultural works, to the means of both their production and their consumption. The dissemination of these means produces at every level of the educational system a form of "literacy," or what we would otherwise recognize as the practices of *reading* and *writing*. It would make an immense social difference if the knowledge designated by the latter terms were the property of everyone; but we are speaking here of what may be called "socialized" education, that is, of something that does not exist in this country. If the current educational institution does indeed (like every other social institution) reproduce social inequities, it achieves this effect by the unequal distribution of cultural capital, or by presenting cultural works in the classroom as the organic expression of the dominant classes' entitlement to those works. This effect cannot be undone by changing the university curriculum alone, because it is an effect of the educational *system,* of which the university is only a part. Does this mean that curricular reform is pointless, or that it has no social consequences? On the contrary, the university curriculum is at this moment a privileged site for raising questions about the educational system as a whole, just because it is the site at which a "crisis" of cultural capital (or the "humanities") has occurred. The claim of the present argument is that an analysis of this crisis in terms of the distribution of cultural capital will produce a more strategic theory of curricular reform than will a pluralist critique.

If progressive teachers have a considerable stake in disseminating the kind of knowledge (the study of cultural works as a practice of reading and writing) that is the vehicle for critical thinking, this knowledge is nevertheless only the vehicle for critical thought, not its realization. As cultural capital it is always also the object of appropriation by the dominant classes. The pluralist strategy of institutionalizing the category of the noncanonical is incapable of grasping this essential ambiguity of the school as an institution. For the same reason that a syllabus of canonical works cannot reproduce a culture of the dominant outside a certain total structuration of the educational system, no syllabus of noncanonical works can function ipso facto as the embodiment of that system's critique. To demand that critical thinking be institutionalized entails an obvious contradiction, but the desire for the institutionalization of a pluralist critique is what drives the current form of curricular revision. We can at most, however, institutionalize the *conditions* of critical thought, in this case a curriculum that makes possible the maximum dissemination of the practices of reading and writing. Inasmuch as the study of cultural works in historical context constitutes a good condition for these practices, no curricular intervention which does not *reaffirm* the cultural capital of these works can ensure the viability of that condition. In the present regime of capital distribution, the school will remain both the agency for the reproduction of unequal social relations and a necessary site for the critique of that system.

Literature as Cultural Capital: An Alternative Analysis

> What need for purists when the demotic is built to last,
> To outlast us, and no dialect hears us?
> —JOHN ASHBERY, "PURISTS WILL OBJECT"

The School and the Reproduction of Social Relations

The defense of the noncanonical may justly take as its epigraph Walter Benjamin's remark that "there is no document of civilization which is not at the same time a document of barbarism."[80] Benjamin offers no unequivocal response to the fact of barbarism, rather a certain "cautious detachment"; but what is the barbarism congealed in the work such that one can remove oneself to a distance from it? This question is further complicated by the continuation of Benjamin's thought: "And just as it [the document of civilization] is itself not free of barbarism, neither is the process of transmission [*Überlieferung*] by which it descends from one to another." The latter statement suggests how one might begin to conceptualize the social effects of the canonical form. Canonicity is not a property of the work itself but of its transmission, its relation to other works in a collocation of works—the syllabus in its institutional locus, the school. Is the barbarism of transmission, then, the same barbarism we find in the "document of civilization"? Ultimately no doubt, but not immediately. Whatever the relation of the work to its initial audience, it must certainly have other relations as a canonical work. The failure to make this distinction is the premise of every ideology of "tradition," if tradition implies the supposed reproduction of cultural values by the monuments of culture themselves. Yet if canonical works do not all by themselves reproduce cultural values, it is significant— even integral—to the real social process of reproduction that they are thought to do so. The real social process is the reproduction not of values but of *social relations*. These relations consist of much more than a relation of text to reader.

The form of the canon belongs to the process of the reproduction of social relations, but it does not enter this process immediately. The canon does not accrete over time like a pyramid built by invisible hands, nor does it act directly and irresistibly on social relations, like a chemical reagent; in its concrete form as a syllabus or curriculum, the canon is a discursive instrument of "transmission" situated historically within a specific institution of reproduction: the school. We may define the latter institution as a more or less formal arrangement for undertaking intensively educational functions also distributed extensively across the institutional breadth of any social formation. The system of educational institutions reproduces social relations by distributing, and where necessary redistributing, knowledges. The canon is thus not grounded in an "institution of criticism," as is sometimes said. Criticism is not an institution but a disciplinary discourse inhabiting a historically specific educational institution.

The instrumentality of the canon within this system is a function of its status as an objectification of the reproduction process, Benjamin's "cultural treasure," or Bennett's "legacy," which is inexhaustible because it appears to reproduce itself—it is wealth never consumed by consumption. The educational apparatus regulates, because it makes possible, access to this inheritable treasure. Individual works are taken up into this system (preserved, disseminated, taught) and confront their receptors first as canonical, as cultural capital. There is no other access to works: they must be confronted as the cultural capital of educational institutions, a circumstance proven rather than disproven by the exceptional case of the autodidact. The question of access, however, is far from simple. The school does not exist merely to lift a veil of ignorance, or to set one at the threshold of the temple. The school functions as a system of credentialization by which it produces a specific *relation* to culture. That relation is different for different people, which is to say that it reproduces social relations.

To give an account of the exact constitution of these relations is to index the "barbarism" of which Benjamin writes: the social relations of domination and exploitation. But to foreground the particular barbarities of the historical record, as though mere exposure to canonical works were the same as exposure to these barbarities, is to misrecognize certain recurrent structural features of the institutions which constitute the mechanism of social reproduction. The implications of this fact are immensely significant if the duration of educational institutions can be shown to be (in part) an effect of formal objectifications of reproduction, such as canons of texts. The institution elicits out of its very structure a demand for the subordination of the historical specificity of individual works to the ideology of the canonical form (tradition), and this subordination is recognizable in pedagogic practice as a homogenizing of dogmatic content, the positing of universal truths discovered and rediscovered in the great works. Against this inert narrative one can respond with Benjamin's determination to "brush history against the grain"; but this is never a simple act, for reasons Bourdieu persuasively argues. Institutions of reproduction succeed by taking as their first object not the reproduction of social relations but the reproduction of the institution itself.[81] No institution is in that sense reducible to its social function. Only by reason of its relative autonomy does an institution succeed in the remote function of reproducing social relations. Autonomy in no way transcends social formations but rather takes the form of a structural atavism existing in complex relation to the motors of social change. Hence major reorganizations of social relations alter only very slowly the larger structural features that allow the school historically "to occupy homologous positions in the system of relations which link it to the dominant classes" (129). Elsewhere Bourdieu draws a stark conclusions from such facts: "it is no doubt in the area of education and culture that the members of the dominated classes have least chance of discovering their objective interest and of producing and imposing the problematic most consistent with their interests."[82] This conclusion might be qualified, but not until the full measure of its force is acknowledged.

Bourdieu's argument will seem most surprising to those critics who would like to represent education as a means of directly effecting social change. Schools have seldom conceived of themselves in this way, and in fact it is only at certain privileged moments of crisis that consistently adversarial pedagogic practices have been cultivated. From the perspective of the present analysis, we can say that strategies such as the "opening of the canon," or the institution of noncanonical syllabi, repress the fact of reproduction through institutional forms in the belief that social relations are directly acted upon in the classroom. To insist again on what may now seem an obvious point, the apparatus of stratification by which knowledge is socially distributed—the educational system itself, with its multiple levels of access and procedures of credentialization—remains largely untouched by such programs; and it is unfortunately also a fact that adversarial pedagogies are largely restricted to elite institutions. More important, only a very impoverished notion of reproduction represents it as incompatible with social change. In the present socioeconomic order the reproduction of the system as a whole demands rapid transformations in social relations in response to rapid changes in the relations of production and consumption. In this context, the very success, for example, of feminist revisions of the literary canon must be read not simply as the victory of an oppositional culture but as a systemic feature of the reproduction of the sexual division of labor, the most recent form of which is manifested by the entrance (not without struggle) of middle-class women into expanded professional and managerial fields. Educational institutions facilitate the production of new relations (in necessary conflict with other institutions of reproduction, such as the family) and thus facilitate the reproduction of the system as a whole. This is to say nothing, of course, about the desirability of these new relations, or about the possibility of their use as a staging ground for more systemic strategies of resistance. Progressive teachers must first intervene, however, at the site of reproduction, *and even as one of its agents,* in order to put into circulation any critique of the system as the whole.

To repress the fact of the school's institutional structure, as though the classroom had no walls, does not mean that the social effectivity of such strategies as curricular revision is merely illusory, but rather that it will never be quite what is intended, that pedagogy is never wholly within the control of pedagogues. But it is better to be aware of this fact than not, particularly in the case of the canonical/noncanonical distinction, which, as we have seen, has effects which exceed the immediate intention of affirming the cultural products of minority cultures. The crucial point in extending and qualifying Bourdieu's account of an apparently homeostatic system of reproduction is the question of institutional atavism, Bourdieu's insistence that "by ignoring all demands other than that of its own reproduction, the school most effectively contributes to the reproduction of the social order."[83] Such a condition certainly obtains in the short run (even countercultural movements, once institutionalized, direct a good deal of their energy to ensuring the reproduction of their institutional forms); but Bourdieu's analysis seems to beg the question of very large systemic transformations.[84] Any given social formation constructs itself out of much older apparatuses of reproduction that must be adapted to new social relations. These older apparatuses coexist with and complicate the social space of recent, perhaps more organic institutions (the capitalist corporation, for example). In the face of inevitable struggles within and at the juncture of institutional ensembles, the most atavistic features of older institutional structures serve to legitimate and stabilize what is always illegitimate and unstable—the momentary conjunctural order.[85] But let us name this situation exactly: it is contradiction. John B. Thompson draws a similar conclusion to the one implied here in his critique of Bourdieu, when he argues that social reproduction is not so much "a concert performed without a conductor" (Bourdieu's phrase) as it is a "cacaphony of divergent and discordant notes." Reproduction succeeds in late capitalist society as the effect of the proliferation of difference itself, the extreme divergence of interests resulting in "a lack of consensus at the very point where oppositional attitudes could be translated into political action."[86] This observation stops short of theorizing a mechanism of systemic transformation, displacing it to the effects of extremely dispersed struggles upon the social totality. But no such theorization is necessary to advance the present argument, only a recognition of the exponentially increasing complexity of reproduction in the context of a historical *durée* in which many institutions survive long after the conditions of their emergence have disappeared.

Canons of texts belong to the *durée* of the school as both an objectification of "tradition" and as a list of texts (syllabus, curriculum) continuously changing in response to the frictional relations between institutional and social reproduction. Yet the significance of this tension between the two sites of reproduction is concealed from revisionists of the canon, who see a direct relation between the canon and social struggle but misrecognize the institution mediating this relation as a mythical "interpretive community," or as an autonomous "profession." The profession is not an institution any more than criticism is: it is the self-representation in the "pedagogic imaginary" through which teachers misrecognize their relation both to their discursive practices and to the institution of the school. The objective history of canon formation, if the latter is an effect of syllabus construction and revision, exhibits enormous variation, but this history can be recovered only in the context of the history of the school, whose invariant social function is the distribution of knowledge by means of techniques of dissemination and rituals of credentialization. The invariant function of credentialization, however, does not determine what constitutes credentials in a given social order, the certifiable possession of skill, knowledge, judgment, taste, genius, or whatever. The forms of cultural capital are rather determined within the whole social order as arenas of both certification and contestation, because the social totality is structured by the multiple and relatively incommensurable distinctions of class, sex, race, national status (to name only the crudest of many), distinctions produced and reproduced in a system that never closes upon its objective of homeostasis.

If the critique of the canon posited a direct relation of "representation" between social identity and the canonicity of certain texts, the effect of that correlation was to dehistoricize the forms of cultural capital, as well as the forms of social identity. This fact can be demonstrated by raising the specific question of what historical forms of cultural capital are embodied in *literary* texts. The answer to this question will of course entail recognizing the historicity of the category of literature itself, the recognition that its history cannot be dissociated from the history of the school. Let us begin with an example drawn from R. R. Bolgar's authoritative study, *The Classical Heritage and Its Beneficiaries,* an encyclopedic account of the transmission of classical literature from late antiquity through the end of the Renaissance. The example concerns the teaching of Graeco-Roman literature in the provinces of imperial Rome, and it is chosen both because it is an extreme case, and because its extremity disturbs Bolgar's narrative of transmission in instructive ways:

> As the protective might of the legions weakened, so the imperial government came to rely to an ever greater extent on its intangible assets; and the excellence of Graeco-Roman culture was turned into useful bait for retaining the loyalty of uncertain provincials. Steel was in short supply. So the provinces were to be grappled to the soul of Rome by hoops of a different make. Literature was taught with great zeal as an introduction to the Roman way of life; but what it introduced men to was in the last analysis the old life of the city-states.[87]

When Bolgar reaches this point in his account, his prose is excited into an unusual state of figurative radiation by the spectacle of what Bourdieu calls "symbolic violence," "the imposition of a cultural arbitrary (*arbitraire*) by an arbitrary power."[88] The legions withdraw and are replaced by schools. But for Bolgar this fact in no way compromises the excellence of Graeco-Roman literature. On the contrary, the reproduction of the Roman system in the provinces comes to rely in part upon the very quality of its literature, which for Bolgar remains uncontaminated by the business of imperial administration. It would seem that the original context of a work's production becomes simply irrelevant when individual works are appropriated by the empire's ideological machinery, which flattens local cultures in its path. Bolgar is struck by this discrepancy and cannot refrain from noting and even belaboring the bewildering circumstance that the literature read in the provincial curriculum seemed to reflect favorably the "old life of the city-states" rather than the contemporary norms of the imperium.

There is indeed a real and irresolvable discrepancy in the relation between the historical specificity of works and the factitious universality of the canonical form, which aspires to transhistorical validity by masking the pedagogic function of disseminating this year's orthodoxy. But the puzzle of why this discrepancy does not seem obvious to everyone is not nearly so inexplicable in the context of Bourdieu's point that social reproduction is not effected directly through the contents of the curriculum. At the moment when the spectacle of symbolic violence begins to play on the stage of empire, it becomes easy to forget what is elsewhere for Bolgar merely given, that the first objective of the educational system in the provinces was to teach future colonial subalterns the Latin language. As students of Roman education, these administrators had a different relation to Latin than native speakers, as well as a different relation to their own languages. If the primary objective of education in the provinces was to produce this linguistic differentiation of the subject populace as a technical means of administration—government by symbolic rather than by physical violence—then the signifying effects of Latin literature, its ideological "contents," were necessarily mediated, diffused, or even contained by the effects of this superimposed social stratification. The primary fact about the teaching of Latin literature was thus not that it conveyed Roman cultural values but that it was the vehicle for the teaching of the Latin language. This goal was important enough to overwhelm any objection that might have been raised to particular Latin works whose contents may not have been wholly compatible with the norms of the imperium. As carriers first and foremost of *linguistic capital* these works could then become the vector of ideological motifs not necessarily expressed within the works themselves.

The example of imperial education is not exceptional. The situation of provincial adminstrators was not markedly different from that of the educated citizenry of Rome itself, where the Roman way of life also had to be reproduced. This fact is quite apparent in Bolgar's discussion of the "well organized educational system of the Empire," which had for its main aim not so much to teach the Roman way of life as to teach the two literary languages of Latin and Greek. These were not, of course, the languages learned by Roman infants; they were languages "remote from ordinary speech" (22), second languages learned in the formal context of an institutional relation between teacher and student, and by means of that abstract alienation of language known in the classical world as "grammar." At this point the question of literacy may be taken up again, in recognition of the fact that the systematic regulation of reading and writing belongs to the project of social reproduction. What one learns to read is always another language, and because that language is unequally distributed, it is a form of capital. The internal differentiation of language produced by the classical educational system as the distinction between a credentialed and a non-credentialed speech reproduces social stratification on the model of the distinction between the tribe or nation and its sociolinguistic other, the "barbarian." Incorrect speech is marked from the first appearance of Alexandrian grammars as "barbarism," a characterization persisting into the present as a strategy for mobilizing xenophobia in the service of an internal linguistic stratification constructed upon and reproducing internal social distinctions. The barbarism about which Benjamin writes is nothing other than the ironic inversion of that ideological representation of the dominated lower classes as the barbarians *within the walls*.

It has long been known that the appearance of literature as a collection of canonical texts was from the first a scholarly pedagogic device of the classical grammarians. Thus E. R. Curtius, in his *European Literature and the Latin Middle Ages:* "In antiquity, the concept of the model author was oriented upon a grammatical criterion, the criterion of correct speech."[89] Quintilian writes of the classical world's primary educators, the *grammatici,* that they were concerned to teach "the art of speaking correctly" and "the interepretation of the poets," the one by means of the other.[90] They developed procedures for the selection of texts that sometimes constituted the sole means of their preservation (for example, the anthological handbooks within which many classical authors survive as exemplary fragments). Nor is the formation of textual canons merely accidentally allied to the emergence of grammatical speech as socially marked. The constitutive link in classical education between the selection of texts and the distribution of cultural capital in linguistic form is remarked by Curtius in connection with Aulus Gellius's extension of the term *classicus,* one of Rome's five propertied classes, to the best of the poets, "a first class and taxpaying author, not a proletarian"—about which Curtius comments, "What a tidbit for a Marxist sociology of literature" (250). But this genealogy of the classics has remained merely an etymological joke (and Curtius himself is seldom cited in the canon debate) because selections of texts historically have the appearance of having selected themselves. This is certainly the case in any very complex social conditions of literary production, where the literary tradition is generalized as the heritage of a homogeneous literary culture, whose text tradition is curiously independent of the institutions transmitting that tradition. It is by no means necessary to reduce the former to the latter in order to see what lies plainly before us: a process of unnatural selection, a social history. The literary canon has always functioned in the schools as a pedagogic device for producing an effect of linguistic distinction, of "literacy." The production of this effect does not depend upon the biasing of judgment—the educational system works better with better works—nor is it a question of insuring the ideological orthodoxy of texts by extraordinary procedures of exclusion and censorship (these measures have for the most part been imposed from above, by church or state). Literary curricula, historically the substance of most educational programs, are capable of assimilating the otherwise dangerous heterodoxies expressed in some works by means of homogenizing methods of textual appropriation exercised within institutional structures of symbolic violence. The ideological effect rides on the back of the effect of sociolinguistic differentiation produced by access to the literary language, which is therefore its vector. Only in this way can one explain the use of the *same* canonical works to inculcate in different generations of students many different and even incompatible ideologies.

Authors themselves do not produce the effect of linguistic differentiation, any more than their works can produce for later generations of readers the same effects of persuasion they may have intended for readers of their own time, and which, when we set out to critique these effects, we call "ideological." Authors cannot be said to write *for* the educational system but in a determinate relation to it, *as the subjects it produces.* The history of canon formation belongs to the history of literary production, therefore, as a condition of production; in the same way, literary production is a condition of reproduction, of the history of canon formation. Hence the production of literary texts cannot be reduced to a specific and unique social function, not even the ideological one. Authors confront a monumentalized textual tradition already immersed as speakers and writers in the social condition of linguistic stratification that betrays at every level the struggle among social groups over the resources of language, over cultural capital in its linguistic form. When these authors are joined to the frieze upon which they formerly gazed, the record of struggle seems to pass into oblivion as the unwritten. Yet that record is immediately available in works themselves as the *language of literature,* out of which literature is made, and in the process of canon formation as the institutional intervention by which the literary curriculum becomes the pedagogic vehicle for producing the distinction between credentialed and uncredentialed speech.

Literary Language as Linguistic Capital

If the pedagogic form of the canon always assumes (as well as activates) an ideology of tradition, that ideology collapses the history of canon formation into an autonomous history of literature, which is always a history of writers and not of *writing.* The critique of the canon fails to overcome this ideology, and thus it has consistently fallen back on notions of tradition, in the form of various countertraditions of noncanonical writers. A history of writing would by contrast have to pose first the question of what genres of writing count as "literature" in a given historical context, a question that logically precedes the question of what criteria of value may affirm or deny the canonicity of particular writers.

In this context, it is well worth reconsidering the first theoretical movement in the twentieth century explicitly to reject the concept of tradition, namely, Russian Formalism. The Formalists attempted to move beyond the history of writers by displacing the agency of change within literature from the psychology of authors (genius, originality) to the "literary system," conceived as a specific and irreducible linguistic system with its own immanent laws of evolution. Here I would like to follow the Formalist argument, very summarily, to its theoretical conclusion, the dead end that cleared the way for the advances of the Bakhtin school. In retracing this history, I propose to make several points preliminary to constructing a historico-theoretical sketch of canon formation. The first of these points is that twentieth-century literary theory has usually attempted to define literature by reference to linguistics, because this adjacent, apparently more scientific discipline seems to offer some assurance against lapsing into psychologistic notions of genius or originality. The Formalists, much in advance of what came to be called "theory" in the 1960s, worked through certain hypotheses about the autonomy of the "linguistic system," and discovered at the end of this project that they were forced to affirm the inseparability of the linguistic from other aspects of the social. Second, since the problem of canon formation has emerged at the margins of theory (and sometimes, as we have seen, in direct opposition to it), it has tended merely to regard the question of the relation between literature and language as having nothing to do with the process by which certain *authors* have been excluded from the canon. Yet histories of canon formation, when they consist primarily of a narrative of *reputations,* of the names which pass in and out of literary anthologies, explain nothing. Such narrative histories fail to recognize generic or linguistic shifts which underlie the fortunes of individual authors by establishing what counts as literature at a given historical moment. In this context the Bakhtinian response to Formalism makes available a strategic method that might now be used to address at the level of theory the neglected philological evidence presented in the preceding section. I refer to the Bakhtin circle's reformulation of the question of literary language as the question not of an *essentially* different kind of language (literariness) but of linguistic differentiation as a social fact.

While the critique of the canon is now being advanced in critical debate in conjunction with a thorough skepticism about the narrow discursive category of literature, any simple dismissal of this category would fail to recognize its historical force. The ontological groundlessness of literature in no way diminishes its social effects as a means of marking the status of certain texts and genres. To their credit, the Russian Formalists recognized the historical variability of literature without dismissing it as a mere fiction. For that reason the question of generic transformation in history was first and last on their theoretical agenda: they were interested to understand what counts as literature in a given organization of social life. From a very early point, with the publications of the *Opayaz* movement, the solution to this problem was founded upon a distinction between "poetic" and "ordinary" language. This distinction cut across the historical forms of literature, which were deduced from the more fundamental concept of "literariness," in Eichenbaum's words, "an element of such specificity that its study can be productive only in immanent evolutionary terms."[91] The question of literariness, as opposed to literature, is the opening move of theory, even today, at the most sophisticated levels of rhetorical reading, and long after Medvedev's definitive critique of that concept in his 1928 volume, *The Formal Method in Literary Scholarship*. With regard to Shklovskii's typical discussion of poetic language, Medvedev objects, for example, "to the continual naive confusion of the linguistic definition of language (Sumerian, Latin) with its poetic significance ('heightened language'), confusion of dialectological characteristics (Church Slavonicisms, popular dialects) with the poetic functions of language."[92] Yet the polarization of linguistic practices into the poetic or literary, and the ordinary or practical, generated an attractively simple and elegant model of historical transformation conceived as an oscillation between the processes of familiarization and defamiliarization (*ostranenie*). This model (in Medvedev's terms, a pseudo-dialectic) seemed finally to bypass the agency of individual psychology; literary evolution produces its effects in the fashion of waves moving through authors as through a medium. In fact, as Medvedev argues, the model of evolution by defamiliarization is wholly grounded in individual psychology, in the form of an invoked psychic law of perception, an oscillation between the stimulus of the new and the fatigue of long-standing perceptions.[93] In this sense, the supposedly immanent-evolutionary model turns out to be not immanent to the literary system at all, but rather an effect of an unchanging law of human psychology. Now this theoretical deficiency, a dead end acknowledged implicitly by Tynjanov in his later writing (in particular, "On Literary Evolution"), as well as by Marxist critics of Formalism, is well worth pondering: beneath the thin ice of linguistics lies the ocean of the psyche. It will be necessary to return from this depth, where grammar itself is supposed to have been found, in order to recognize literariness as *literary* language, as writing.

This practice is institutionalized first in the teaching of grammar, which, so far from being a structure to be recovered from a depth, is a linguistic practice upon the two-dimensional plane of the text.[94]

Hence it can be said that what the Bakhtin school salvaged from the wreck of Formalism was precisely linguistics. In the absence of a concept of literary language, no explanatory model could be brought to bear upon the variable historical forms of literary production, much less upon the formation of textual canons. One had only to place the concept of literary language in its proper category—not aesthetics but sociolinguistics, what Medvedev called "sociological poetics." In Bakhtin's writing, the axis upon which literature appears as a particular kind of valorized language is rotated away from the essentialist scale of automatization/defamiliarization and repositioned along a hierarchy of socially marked forms of speech. Bakhtin stages this axial rotation to the vertical as a defense of that language which erupts into the literary from beneath, as its antagonist or object of colonization. The literary language and its other, what Bakhtin calls *heteroglossia*, are defined relationally and contextually at the moment of their contact. Here it is necessary to quote a key passage from "Discourse in the Novel":

> In different national languages and different epochs, the general and, as it were, extra-generic category of the "literary language" is filled with a variety of concrete content; it has different degrees of importance in the history of literature as well as in the history of literary language. But everywhere and always "literary language" has as its area of activity the conversational language of a literarily educated circle (in the example cited above, the language of "respectable society"), the written language of its everyday and semiliterary genres (letters, diaries, etc.), the language of socio-ideological genres (speeches of any kind, pronouncements, descriptions, printed articles, etc.) and ultimately of the artistic prose genres, in particular the novel. In other words, this category attempts to regulate the area of literary and everyday (in the sense of dialectological) language not already regulated by the strict previously coalesced genres, with the specific and well-differentiated demands they make on their own languages; the category of a "general literariness" does not of course apply at all in the areas of the lyric, the epic, and the tragedy. The concept of "general literariness" regulates the area of spoken and written heteroglossia that swirls in from all sides on the fixed and strict poetic genres—genres whose demands spring neither from conversational nor from everyday

written language. "General literariness" attempts to introduce
order into this heteroglossia, to make a single, particular style
canonical for it.[95]

"Literary language" does indeed ride the crest of a historical wave, but not
as the defamiliarized or the new. On the contrary, it forms at the interface
between the language of preserved literary texts and the context-bound
speech that continually escapes total regulation and hence *changes*. It is
different from both. Within this complex one glimpses the operation of certain institutional forms hinted by Bakhtin. If the "older poetic genres,"
preserved as nothing other than canonical texts, exert a kind of drag on the
velocity of linguistic change, the product of which interaction is "literary
language" (or Bakhtin's "general literariness"), the place at which this
braking action is applied is a specific social locus—primarily, if not exclusively, the school. Bakhtin has a highly metaphoric spatial sense of what
this means, expressed in his image of colliding centrifugal and centripetal
linguistic forces. With the exception of such "concrete forces" as genre
(other such forces would be "an academic grammar, a school, salons") he
prefers to emphasize more abstract terms of analysis, although he is by no
means reluctant to identify the function of literary language as the preservation of "the sealed-off quality of a privileged community" (382). Nevertheless a certain referential vagueness at this point in his argument suits
the purpose of revaluing and universalizing heteroglossia, analytically abstracted from its social base as that which lies just outside the reach of linguistics, marking the boundary of that discipline.

The theoretical difficulties thrown off by this program have scarcely begun to be resolved, but they need to be acknowledged if it is desirable to
retain the concept of heteroglossia as the necessary complement to the sociolinguistic concept of literary language. These difficulties are most acute
in Bakhtin's description of the novel as a genre, specifically the "noncanonical genre," by which he means that it never develops generic rules
(canons) even as it accumulates a repertoire of works. The novel as noncanonical genre is privileged for Bakhtin as the genre which welcomes the heteroglossic: "The novel senses itself on the border between the completed,
dominant literary language and the extraliterary languages that know
heteroglossia" (7). This border is permeable in either direction, making
heteroglossia accessible to hegemonic cultural forms and vice versa. Hence
the boundaries of the genre itself cannot be fixed, nor can its appearance as
a modality in other High Cultural genres (what Bakhtin calls "novelization") be easily contained. What is important for Bakhtin in the valorization of the novel as genre is the recovery of a determinable mechanism of
change in literary history from the vertiginous domain of social relations.

In this Bakhtin's project is still very much in accord with such Formalist themes as Shklovskii's "canonization of the junior branch."[96] This objective accounts for certain peculiarities in the theory, for example, the argument Todorov has reasonably questioned, that the novel flourishes during periods in which the central power (centripetal force) weakens.[97] If genre is indeed the important concept in constructing a history of literary production, that history need not seek to explain the appearance of new works.[98] It already follows from Bakhtin's discussion of literary language that this language and heteroglossia cannot be opposed as old and new—they are exactly contemporary. Literary language (as the product of the educational system) will always mediate between canonical texts (the syllabus of study) and the production of new literary works; but literary language is neither necessarily inhibiting nor enabling in relation to new works. The relation will rather be differently constituted at different times according to the total complex of institutional forms and social/linguistic stratification. Hence, while it is simply (but not trivially) correct to say that literature must be written in the literary language, with its linguistic and generic constraints, it does not necessarily follow that the heteroglossic is the wellspring of the new, but rather that it acts through texts upon the literary language and its genres. Literary language also changes, if at a slower pace than extraliterary language, or heteroglossia, and this is the crucial point. Canonical texts, institutionally preserved and disseminated, constitute the paradigmatic basis of literary language, the guarantor at the lower educational levels of simple grammatical speech, the exemplar, at higher levels, of more expansive as well as more elite standards of linguistic use (stylistic or rhetorical rather than simply grammatical norms), even the licensed abuses that are now virtually identified with the language of high canonical literature. Hence canonical texts cannot be reduced wholly to exemplars of the literary language or the grammatical speech abstracted from them, and that difference is as consequential as the perpetual difference of the heteroglossic. This point seems to me congruent with Bakhtin's argument in preserving his picture of colliding sociolinguistic forces, but with the focus of analysis shifted from a perennial genre—the novel as the heteroglossic mechanism of literary transformation—to a perennial social-institutional situation. This displacement is necessary in order to isolate the concept of literary language as a linguistic fact with the same duration as the school.

Literary language therefore cannot be characterized monolithically as the recurrent foregrounding of a particular linguistic feature (not even rhetoricity), nor need it be equated with a unique kind of speech act (such as fiction). In very useful discussions of the allied term "literature," Raymond Williams has emphasized the historical distinction between the sense of literature as everything that is written, and the more modern sense, dating from the later eighteenth century, of literature as particular kinds of writing (poetry, plays, etc).[99] If the term "literature" can be retained to indicate a transhistorical phenomenon at all, it would have to be defined as the canonical genres of writing, whatever these genres happen to be in any particular time or place, and whatever name may have been given to them collectively. We are speaking, then, of certain genres of *writing* which become paradigmatic for a socially differentiated *speech*.

Sociolinguists have referred to the recurrent historical relation between a body of writing (literature), and a socially marked "literary language" as *diglossia*, defined in a seminal essay by the sociolinguist Charles Ferguson as

> a relatively stable language situation in which, in addition to the primary dialects of the language (which may include a standard or regional standards), there is a very divergent, highly codified (often grammatically more complex) superimposed variety the vehicle of a large and respected body of written literature, whether of an earlier period or in another speech community, which is learned largely by formal education and is used for most written and formal spoken purposes but is not used by any sector of the community for ordinary conversation.[100]

Aside from providing an interestingly different perspective on precisely what we call "canon formation," Ferguson's study demonstrates (we shall have occasion to reflect upon this fact) how faithfully sociolinguistics follows in the path of that defunct literary discipline, "philology." Ferguson derives the concept of diglossia, defining high and low language varieties in a given speech community from such classical precedents as the distinction in ancient Greek between *katharévusa* and *demotic*. It now seems apparent that Ferguson's strict distinction between dialects and diglossic language varieties is too narrow, since in many cases diglossic hierarchy is unquestionably superimposed upon preexistent spoken dialects. Nor is it necessary to deny that bilingual cultures can erect diglossia on the basis of fully distinct languages, especially if one is to understand the operation of imperial languages within colonized territories. In an important revision of Ferguson's argument, Joshua Fishman has suggested that diglossia is most usefully conceived as "the social allocation of functions to different languages or varieties," whether or not this functional distinction appears within a single language or upon a base of dialectal or multilingual diversity.[101]

Diglossia defined as a differentiation of social/linguistic function does not permit a simple identification of hierarchized languages with the hierarchy of classes. The distinction between high and low is a distinction of function only, and access to function can be regulated in various ways, many of which are far more subtle that the mechanism of inclusion/ exclusion. For example, it was not especially important for the medieval nobility to be literate in the high language, Latin, a language mainly reserved for the clergy. The control of the medieval clergy over the functions allocated to the high variety served to reproduce with relative stability and efficiency the ideological discourses of feudalism, with its specifically religious mode of symbolic domination. From the perspective of sociolinguistics, it does not matter what combination of generic options constitutes the high variety of writing (literature in the transhistorical sense), a fact that can be verified by comparing the medieval curriculum, founded upon specialized discourses of knowledge (the trivium and quadrivium), with the curriculum of the early modern humanist schools, founded upon a canon of classical literary works, and from which is derived a repertoire ("copia") of literary styles. But this transition, which relegated to obscurity a great number of medieval works, has unfortunately appeared to literary historians primarily as a revaluation of particular authors and texts. Here the inadequacy of empirical literary history to theorize canonical reformations as anything other than the rise and fall of individual reputations is matched by the inadequacy of sociolinguistics to theorize changes in the literary language as anything other than a process of linguistic erosion, the devolution of the distinction between an original *katharévusa* and an original *demotic*. The linguistic model isolates literary language as a social fact, but it also overemphasizes features of stability and duration whose social function is masked in the normative prescriptions of grammar. Bakhtin's concept of heteroglossia disrupts both static models by reminding us that if the difference between the written and the spoken is at stake in the continuous transformation of the literary language, this difference can be made to take the charge of many other differences constitutive of social struggles. Hence it is no tragedy that linguistic analysis must always arrive too late upon the scene of heteroglossia, that heteroglossia can never be isolated before it comes into contact with what Bakhtin calls "official language." The silence that follows this lapsed conversation is always legible as the written itself—literature, of whatever genre. The oppositional terminologies Bakhtin mobilizes in order to hear these conversations—the distinction between the dialogical and the monological, carnival and official culture—need less to be applied in a quasi-Bakhtinian reading than invoked as a possible (but not the only) means of theorizing the history of the *social relations of writing.* The facts of this history are already very well known. The following sketch is intended not only to recollect these facts, as they have been recounted by Auerbach, Curtius, and others, but to enact a return, with theoretical hindsight and with a different political agenda, to this "philological" narrative.

The Historical Forms of the Literary Canon

Grammar and poetry. The category of "literary language" is of course foundational for philology; it was given consummate treatment by Auerbach in his *Literary Language and Its Public in Late Latin Antiquity and in the Middle Ages,* first published in 1958. Auerbach's identification of literary language, what he calls *Hochsprache,* by the signal features of "selectivity, homogeneity, and conservatism," agrees precisely with Ferguson's description of diglossia.[102] Neither Auerbach nor Ferguson, however, recognizes the generally recurrent structure of the phenomenon they observe: a technical arrangement for the distribution of cultural capital in linguistic form. The history of literature, the history of textual canons, the history of languages—these histories yield nothing but facts if they do not bring into view this structural arrangement. Within the history of canon formation we will always be able to discern the arrangement and rearrangement of (1) an institutional practice, or pedagogy; (2) a body of preserved and disseminated writings, or canon; and (3) a produced linguistic knowledge, or *Hochsprache.*

Auerbach insists that the literary language must be regarded as "not only the written language but also the spoken, everyday language of the educated classes" (249). This point characterizes more accurately than does Ferguson's account the diglossic situation of classical Latin, which Latin writers themselves acknowledged in the distinction between *sermo rusticus* and *sermo urbanus.* Setting aside the obviously interesting geographical basis for this distinction (as well as the bilingualism of the Greek-reading literati), it is worth emphasizing that the literary language is always also a speech, a *sermo.* The Roman educational system was designed to train the upper social classes for oral performance, a task delegated to the highest level of the system, the schools of rhetoric. "Literacy," the knowledge of how to read and write, was a prerequisite to that higher training. The degree of correspondence between the written language as it was abstracted and formalized from a body of writing, and the actual speech of the "educated classes" is not known, but it can be conjectured that the formalized written language had to some degree diverged from the speech of educated Romans by the end of the first century B.C., when Ennius, who survives now only in fragmentary form, was replaced in the school curriculum by Virgil, a more up-to-date model of grammaticality and style. This is not to say that the pedagogic need for grammatical models is an exclusive determinant of preservation or canonicity (though it was, in fact, for many Greek authors). Grammaticality, correct speech, becomes an increasingly complex social practice precisely because the literary language changes without discarding older literary works. One consequence of this fact is that bodies of canonical texts are internally organized in later phases of accumulation to reflect distinctions such as "archaic," "classical," or "modern," which are indifferently both "literary-historical" and "linguistic" categories.

The scriptorium. The distinction between *sermo urbanus* and *sermo rusticus* does not, as one might expect, disappear over the following centuries. On the contrary, as Auerbach notes, the "High Latin" of the senatorial aristocracy had become virtually unintelligible to the common man by the fifth century A.D., while vulgar Latin, in continuous creolizing contact with the "barbaric" languages, evolved into the dialectal variety of the early Romance tongues (252). This primeval forest of philology concerns us only insofar as it conditions a new arrangement of institution-canon-*Hochsprache,* with very different social effects. Nothwithstanding the *sermo humilis* of the early church fathers, the Latin *Hochsprache* ceased to have a broad social base until classical educational institutions had been fully appropriated by the literate clergy. And this development waited upon an accumulation of Christian writing in Latin (including a Latin Bible) sufficient to undergo canonical organization, and to which other classical writing might be subordinated in various ways. The fusion of early Christian scriptural form, with its severe canonical and doxological anxieties, with the surviving texts of classical pedagogy, produced an extremely complex canonical arrangement within which the category of literature in the narrow sense (poetry, plays, etc.) may be said to have been completely irrelevant. The medieval *scriptorium* had no need for such a category, and it does not emerge until much later. The medieval pedagogic canon was selected according to the criterion of *truth.* It is a question of how a work like Virgil's *Aeneid* will be read: the criterion of truth enjoins a practice of interpretation so different from our own that it would indeed be inaccurate to say that Virgil was read at this time as "literature." Even the late medieval parodic texts celebrated by Bakhtin interrupt this regime of truth not as fictions but as the linguistic complement of the truth, namely, the lie.[103]

Access to the *scriptorium,* to what counts as literacy in the Middle Ages, was successfully regulated without installing the Latin *Hochsprache* as a (ruling) class language. Rather, the linguistic differentiation of literate clergy and illiterate nobility marked the relative cultural autonomy of the "estates," as well as their historical complicity (since the ranks of the higher clergy were generally drawn from the nobility). The collapse of this pure allocation of functions (in Auerbach's words, the clerical "monopoly on writing") dates from the eleventh and twelfth centuries, with the simultaneous revival of classical Latin and the emergence of vernacular writing. Auerbach is uncomfortable with the problem of explaining this origin (now of course the subject of intense research and controversy), and while glancing briefly at such economic factors as the expansion of trade and the growth of towns (both of which imply secular uses of literacy), he is finally determined to credit the "spontaneous force" that "gives rise to individual talents" (276). A different sense of how certain social struggles give rise to new kinds of literary production is conveyed by Natalie Zemon Davis, in her discussion of the changing relation between the medieval nobility and the clergy: "from the twelfth through the fourteenth centuries in France, knights and noble landowners were trying to set themselves off from the clergy and forge an independent cultural identity."[104] This project, which no doubt responded to many pressures including the paradoxical one of a relative relaxation (or delegation) of military functions among the warrior class, involved the appropriation of literacy as a form of cultural capital, but not the *Hochsprache* or pedagogic canon of the scribal class.[105] The appropriation of literacy was accomplished in conjunction with another appropriation—of that popular, folk culture from which the nobility had never distinguished itself. Hence the elaboration of narrative material of folk culture into vernacular forms of writing came to be consumed at the court in a different way than such material had formerly been consumed by the folk. The emergence of a vernacular High Culture not only weakened the major clerical form of domination—its monopoly of literacy—it laid the groundwork for the cultural alienation of the nobility from the lower classes by instituting a linguistic differentiation within the vernacular where none had existed before.[106] This linguistic alienation, an analogical extension of the norms of Latin grammaticality into vernacular speech, forms one basis of that aristocratic culture about which Norbert Elias writes in his major study, *The Civilizing Process*. This process concealed its origins in the violent forms of feudal domination behind the finery of acquired taste, culture, civility.[107]

Neoclassicism. The measure of this double appropriation has only begun to be taken; it remains difficult to assess because its effects are not necessarily produced by an extraordinary increase in the absolute magnitude of literacy. It was sufficient to alter the entire structure of linguistic stratification that the educational apparatus no longer function as a clerical monoply. The acquisition of literacy by noble (and eventually also, bourgeois) culture is the condition for the appearance of diglossia within the vernaculars, as opposed to the bilingualism of medieval "international" culture. Dante glimpses this development when he distinguishes in *De Vulgari Eloquentia* between a primary speech "which we learn without any rules in imitating our nurse," and "another speech which is dependent on this one called by the Romans 'grammar'."[108] Dante's "eloquence" will eventually require the institutional mediation of that same grammar. The production of vernacular grammatical speech is as complex as the incipient nationalism of the early modern period, and thus difficult to describe. Dante's survey of Italian dialects in quest of a literary language, for example, dreams of a national language, however far removed a national polity may be from realization. The problem here, as Gramsci argues in his very helpful discussion of this subject, is not just the erection of one dialect over others as the language of writing (Bakhtin's "generalized literariness"), but the persistence of bilingualism among the intellectuals, not all of whom now are clergy.[109] That is to say, these intellectuals are laymen, but not *laicus*, "ignorant of Latin." Hence the paradigms of Latin grammar continue to dominate and deform vernacular grammaticality (as ever since), producing an ever more severe diglossic distinction of high and low, and at the level of literary production, an intensifying classicism. Gramsci argues that "for the Humanists the vernacular was like a dialect," and that they were "therefore continuators of the universalism of the Middle Ages" (233). This construction of the humanist cultural project is entirely compatible with the now firmly established picture of the early modern absolute monarchy as, in Perry Anderson's words, "a redeployed and recharged apparatus of feudal domination."[110] Such a state required, according to Gramsci, a new *noblesse de robe* of "administrators, scholars, and scientists, theorists, non-ecclesiastical philosophers etc.," but their authority, especially pedagogic authority, was defined in contradistinction to the authority of the clergy and its *Hochsprache*, as the prestige of classical Latin or Greek, purged of medievalism.[111]

At the point of the Latin language's maximum pressure upon vernacular diglossia, it becomes possible for the accumulation of vernacular writing to be submitted to its first canonical organization, according to criteria of judgment manifestly classical. An example here would be Sidney's *Defence of Poetry*, with its survey of English poets under the rubric of classical genres, as well as its strictures against the "mixing" of genres, an inhibition which already evinces humanism's inability to assimilate medieval genres to the new order of neoclassicism. Those literary productions most in conformity with classical paradigms are momentarily advantaged vis-à-vis canonicity, but (as we shall see) only momentarily. It is also the case that vernacular writing continually falls away from classicist paradigms, even actively resists them with the same gesture of cheerful resignation with which Shakespeare entrusted his book to the flood. The very severity of the distinction between high and low culture now partially inhibits the late medieval appropriation of popular, folk culture by the new High Cultural vernacular writers and occasions instead what Graham Pechey has rightly called "that irruption into 'high' culture of an unofficial (but potent and ubiquitous) sub-cultural formation—that entry of popular 'carnival' forms into the classical form of writing which is traditionally called the Renaissance."[112] Canon formation within the early vernaculars thus appears as a conservative discourse of classicism among the intellectuals, who occupy an unstable position between the traditional pedagogic institutions of the clergy, the political structures of absolutism, and a continually re-nascent popular culture. Within this conjuncture it is a vernacular *Hochsprache* that finally emerges as most politically useful to the nobility of the sword, even if the nobility of the robe stakes its claim to autonomy and status upon its bilingualism, its knowledge of classical languages.[113]

The vernacular canon. The instability of the conjunctural position of literary culture in England is manifest as early as Sidney but reaches its first point of crisis in the judicial rhetoric of Dryden's critical essays, where the imperative to judge literary merit according to linguistic or even "grammatical" criteria vexes the question of the relative merits of Jonson and Shakespeare.[114] It would be misleading to dismiss this problem of judgment as a *lusus culturae,* as it persists in many versions through Samuel Johnson and beyond (for example, as the problem of the sublime, the question of the value of flawed works of genius versus "correct" works). The place of Shakespeare within the English canon is perhaps the result of the working through of this problem. Its definitive resolution, however, waits upon the entrance of vernacular writing into the school curriculum (earlier for the lower levels, later for the higher). In the meanwhile, vernacular literature occupies the place of a more or less unofficial culture in relation to existent pedagogic institutions still dominated by the clergy (and therefore by the Latin *Hochsprache*), but not to the new, transitional configuration of classes that come to be known as *la cour et la ville.* In his discussion of this hybrid culture ("polite society") Auerbach writes of its distinctive valuation of *le bon usage,* in retrospect a remarkable fetishization of grammar.[115] The rigorous simplification of grammaticality from the more latitudinarian norms of Renaissance humanism facilitates a cultural homogenization of aristocracy and bourgeoisie at a very high social level, where the aristocracy was finally "stripped of its feudal character" and the "weathy bourgeoisie had begun to turn away from gainful occupations toward *otium cum dignitate.*[116] At this moment too, ephemeral institutions such as the salons produce and reproduce vernacular literary language as the prototype of a national standard language. Auerbach points out that the "public," that is, the polite reading public, "came . . . to be dominated by *la ville,* the bourgeoisie" (333). This development is somewhat easier to trace in England, where an early version of what we now call Standard English is being developed not only in the salons but more significantly in such institutions as the coffeehouse. These official/unofficial institutions are thrown across the gap between the still structurally medieval schools and the appropriation of the pedagogic apparatus by a hegemonic bourgeoisie whose administrative and ideological needs require a standardization of the vernacular language.[117] It is in this climate of cultural transformation that a polemic is generated by such writers as Thomas Sheridan on behalf of a vernacular curriculum which, in Sheridan's view, would confirm for everyone that the works of English literature are fully the equal of the Greek and Latin "classics."[118]

The eventual retooling of the school as it turns out the new product of Standard English by means of a new curriculum of English writing does not transform the school beyond recognition; the vernacular curriculum required more than a century to rise from elementary schools to the university level, and the classics continued in the meanwhile to function as the rarest and most expensive form of cultural capital. But in another sense it is only vernacular writing that has the power to bring into existence the category of "literature" in the specific sense of poetry, novels, plays, and so on. The brackets that close around a particular set of genres at this time increasingly distinguish it on the one side from philosophical and scientific writing, and on the other from scripture—but this is not to say that "literature" does not claim for itself a "truth" which communicates and competes in some fashion with both these kinds of writing. The very fact that the body of literary works can be analogized to the scriptural "canon" betrays the fact that vernacular writing must borrow the slowly fading aura of scripture as a means of enhancing and solidifying its new prestige.[119] Indeed the retroactive annexing of the Bible itself to the history of literature in our own time has effects that are quite distinguishable from the humanist *imitatio* of the Greek and Latin classics. The vernacular canon belongs to a nationalist agenda, quite distinct from the multilingual cultural internationalism of the Renaissance humanists. To mistake the emergence of the vernacular "canon" for a process like the formation of scripture, then, is to confuse the institutions of the church and the school. Even more, it is to misunderstand the functional atavism that allows the bourgeois school to be staffed by an unreconstructed clergy.

While the vernacular canon as pseudo-scripture takes its place in the emergence of national "traditions," the ends of nationalism were served not simply by the establishment of vernacular classics but even more crucially by the use of these texts in the schools as a means of standardizing the vernacular language. We can recognize that the vernacular curriculum is a vector of nationalist ideology (in addition to whatever other cultural pieties may be transmitted in the classroom), but that recognition does not in itself explain the relation between these ideological motifs and the linguistic project of standardization. That relation is extraordinarily complex, since it is the standardization of the vernacular that enables some social groups to achieve upward mobility and other groups to be more effectively administered, kept in their places. This is to emphasize once again a cardinal principle of the present analysis, that literacy is not a simple matter of knowing how to read or write, but refers to the entire system by which reading and writing are regulated as social practices in a given society.

The ambiguous effects of that system are well exemplified by the phenomenon literary history denominates as the "rise of the novel," since the novel was an arena of literary production which challenged the restrictive generic definition of literature almost as soon as that definition was put into practice. The question raised by the novel was whether poetry or prose ought to provide the paradigms for a national standard language. In Bakhtin's terms the novel represented a "centrifugal" force, opening the domain of writing to a much larger populace, consisting of readers and writers whose class or gender would formerly have excluded them from literate culture. The existence of the novel at the interface between literate and illiterate culture produced a crisis in poetic production itself, symptomatically registered by the Romantic break with the "poetic diction" of eighteenth-century poetry, and its turn to a prose paradigm of "generalized literariness." Thus Wordsworth writes in the Preface to *Lyrical Ballads* that "there neither is, nor can be, any essential difference between the language of prose and metrical composition."[120] Without inquiring any further into the ambivalence of Wordsworth himself about the new prose paradigm of generalized literariness, we can at least affirm that by the beginning of the nineteenth century, such a paradigm was firmly established.

Literary language. Once installed as the triumph of a class-based sociolect over regional dialects, the standard becomes the condition of literary production, just as the literary curriculum becomes the institutional means for the reproduction of the standard. This linguistic/institutional fugue has been analyzed by Renée Balibar and Dominique Laporte in studies of the French language which have as yet no exact parallel in English criticism.[121] In addition to their admirable rigor in insisting upon the mutual relation between the school and the discursive category of literature, these studies have the advantage of making visible the reappearance of diglossia in the different ways in which literature is taught at different levels of the school system. In their theoretical summary of Balibar and Laporte's work, Pierre Macherey and Etienne Balibar describe this difference as "different practices of the same language."[122] Hence the distinction between the practices they designate as "basic language" and "literary language" is not simply a repetition of the distinction between *katherévusa* and *demotic,* nor between the standard and the dialect, although one may say that all forms of diglossia are homologous with respect to the function of social stratification. This point is rather more significant than might at first appear. Macherey and Balibar describe literature as "the *agent* for the *reproduction* of ideology in its ensemble," an agency it is able to enact by displacing the contradictions of class struggle onto the linguistic plane of a common language (56). While in my view this formulation does not always escape from an essentialism that attributes the same ideological function and content to all literary works, it is unquestionably the case that the "literary" language of which Renée Balibar and Dominique Laporte speak is a fission of the bourgeois sociolect resulting from the very success of its dissemination. Thus, while the standard or "common" language seems to efface social stratification by making language itself the vehicle of a common national identity, the "literary" language reinstates at another level a linguistic difference by which the upper classes can continue to mark their cultural distinction.

The difference of which Macherey and Balibar speak is not easy to define; yet it is immediately recognizable as the difference between *spoken* and *written* language. That is to say, "standard" spoken English becomes something different when its norms begin to imitate the norms of written English. Let us acknowledge here the truth of the still popular Strunk and White and say that this difference is produced by the "element of style," that is, by the practice of writing. But the two-handed engine which the new grammarians have wielded to harrow the ranks of the ungrammatical does not know its own doubleness, and Strunk and White are thus able to say, in a telling conflation, that style, by which they mean *written* style, is "a matter of ear, of reading the books that sharpen the ear."[123] Style may seem natural and individual, but it is the effect of a "good" education, that is, of contact with the *right* books. Even more tellingly, "Only a writer whose ear is reliable is in a position to use bad grammar deliberately." Style is nothing other than a certain relation to grammar, a relation most visible at the vanishing point of grammar's abrogation.

The effect of style, as we now know it, is ultimately a product of that

system within which the texts canonically organized for the purpose of instituting grammatical speech are not the same texts used to produce the
element of style. Hence the emergence, beginning in the nineteenth century,
of a canon of texts specific to the primary levels of the educational system, a
canon consisting of writers and texts who are relatively "minor" in relation
to the High canonical writing.[124] To these writers is entrusted the task of
producing in the general populace a standard language, whose somewhat
rigid norms are then relaxed, though in an altogether regulated way, with
the introduction of more properly "literary" texts at the higher levels of the
school system.[125]

Literature and composition. The difference between standard and literary language roughly corresponds to the levels of the school system, but it
also characterizes the university curriculum itself in the form of the cognate
programs of composition and literature, yet another way in which "different practices of the same language" are inculcated in the school. The present urgent expansion of composition in the university undoubtedly
exposes a failure to install the standard vernacular at lower levels of the
educational system, or the return of what appears to be a condition of dialectal multiplicity (actually, a multiplicity of class, racial, and ethnic sociolects). The disintegration of the standard also throws into relief the
institutional interdependence of composition and literature, widely misrecognized as a disrelation. Macherey and Balibar's analysis would lead us
to conclude that "composition" is simply the belated attempt to install
grammatical norms in college students by means of the linguistic form in
which grammaticality is embodied, namely, "good" writing. But the program of composition has never been so limited as to identify grammaticality as its sole end; it has on the contrary posited grammaticality as
the means to emancipatory political ends which are not finally different
from the posited political ends of literary education.[126] Like the law, grammar is the same for everyone, except of course that it is not. The inflation of
vernacular grammaticality into a universal speech, the language of participatory democracy, now goes by the ancient name of "rhetoric." In this way
the classical sequencing of credentialization, first in grammar (literature)
and last in rhetoric (oral performance), is reversed, but in order to produce
a new kind of "oral performance" on the basis of the new kind of writing
practice inculcated in the compositional syllabus. We will have no difficulty
in recognizing what this speech sounds like: it is the speech of the
professional-managerial classes, the administrators and bureaucrats; and
it is employed *in its place,* the "office." It is not "everyday" language. The
point of greatest historical interest about this speech is that its production
bypasses the older literary syllabus altogether. Students need no longer im-

merse themselves in that body of writing called "literature" in order to acquire "literary" language. In taking over the social function of producing a distinction between a basic and a more elite language, composition takes on as well the ideological identity of that sociolect, its pretension to universality, its status as the medium of political discourse.

The fact that the universal speech is entirely based on the practice of writing marks the contradiction between its universality and the fact that it is not for everyone, a contradiction that subtends both the most ideologically mystified position on the relation of composition to the vernacular standard (E. D. Hirsch: "The normative character of a national written language lies in its very isolation from class and region"), and the avowedly progressive "writing across the curriculum" (James Kinneavy: "[Students] must be taught the common language of humanity in its full rhetorical scales").[127] Mistaking the class-based sociolect for the language of "humanity" is an Enlightenment dream from which the political subject is not meant to awaken. Hence we may read the ideology of composition, the curricular distinction by which composition names a practice of writing and literature a practice of reading, as obfuscating the real social relations between writing, reading, and speech, as concealing a conflict between the literary syllabus and the composition syllabus over what kind of writing will furnish the paradigms for the New Class sociolect. For this reason the boundary between the two syllabi has been subject to considerable surveillance, brusquely registered in composition theorist Edward Corbett's warning that "literary texts will more often than not serve as a distraction from, rather than a promoter of, the objectives of a writing course."[128]

Sociolects. As the vernacular standard reaches the borders of internal colonization, manifest destiny turns over into defeat: it is no longer possible for these national borders to be ruled from a linguistic center, from within literature. In fact we know that fewer students are now routed through the curriculum of literature, although this is not a matter of numbers only—the center of the system of social reproduction has moved elsewhere, into the domain of mass culture. Hence the current state of the literary language, in which stylistic norms derived from literature have the anachronistic aura of "old money," no longer yields to an analysis identifying the literary text as "the privileged agent of ideological subjection."[129] The crisis of the literary syllabus is that it is indeed no longer such a privileged agent, because it is no longer the basis of the vernacular standard. Its very claim to universality meant that it took upon itself the universalization of every specific system of domination, and that it therefore opened itself to every specific force of resistance. This is one reason why the literary syllabus should seem to us now so vulnerable to the charge of a failure to "represent" various social groups, while the syllabus of composition proceeds quietly with the work of producing a language that is at once manifestly privileged, and which aspires at the same time to "universality," the same claim that was once asserted virtually without dissent for the literary curriculum. The students who regard composition as a necessary prerequisite for entry into professional life know this, without knowing what it is that they know. In this context, the movement to open or expand the canon might be regarded, among other things, as a belated attempt to save the bourgeois sociolect by expanding its base of textual representation, but to save that sociolect *for literature.* So long as this movement fails to recognize the social relation between writing and speech, or the institutional relation between literature and composition, it will not be capable of understanding the historical forces which compel the literary canon to manifest itself as *linguistic capital.* The relative decline of literary study in the schools is proof that the status of literary works as cultural capital depends to a significant degree upon their status as linguistic capital.

The disintegration of the vernacular standard as grammatical speech—the old bourgeois sociolect—is currently being registered in the universities as a critique of the discursive category of literature itself. This critique implies neither the "death of literature" nor the degradation of reading—it may even make possible a more historical understanding of the fortunes of literature, the sort of understanding Raymond Williams has been concerned to promote. Nevertheless we have to recognize that Standard English has dwindled to an impoverished scribal formulaic that takes refuge in the fortress of composition, where it defends itself against the continual invasion of barbarian tongues. This invasion, not of dialects but of sociolects, proceeds from "below" as the failure of Standard English (a process of creolization, the political consequences of which are perhaps not yet visible), but also from above, as the fracturing of the standard into technical jargons and styles of speech. "Writing across the curriculum," for example, already acknowledges that there no longer exists a single paradigm for the New Class sociolect, even if composition theorists still continue to speak of a "common" language. In their very multiplicity, the new sociolects may appear to parody the vernacular standard, vacillating between the hyper-grammatical and the ungrammatical, between eloquence and awkwardness. Moreover, these sociolects are as much laterally competitive as they are vertically hierarchizing: they enact strategies of mutual derogation, of stylistic differentiation, responsive to social conditions which militate against the formation of a new standard. In the situation of apparent mutual incomprehension between different disciplines or professional fields, we recognize one form of what Lyotard calls the delegitimation of the "emancipation narrative," or the refusal of one speech for all, because the language of emancipation has always also been the language of the *ones* who speak for all:

> In the context of delegitimation, universities and the institutions of higher learning are called upon to create skills, and no longer ideals—so many doctors, so many teachers in a given discipline, so many engineers, so many administrators, etc. The transmission of knowledge is no longer designed to train an elite capable of guiding the nation toward its emancipation, but to supply the system with players capable of acceptably fulfilling their roles at the pragmatic posts required by its institutions.[130]

Lyotard goes as far as it may be possible to go in celebrating the carnival of sociolects, and he raises for us the crucial question of whether a systemic critique (such as that proposed here) must be articulated within and through such archaically hegemonic forms as a "common language," installed in the populace by means of a privileged (literary) curriculum. No doubt Lyotard is rather too eager to conclude that the "emancipation narrative" is disqualified by virtue of the fact that it has always been written in a "universal" language, but it would be a mistake to suppose that critique is identical to such a language; we should say rather that critique undertakes to criticize everything, including its own language.[131] The poverty of Lyotard's merely celebrating the rise of sociolects is the same poverty that finds a solution to the problem of "representation" in the practice of cultural separatism. I shall continue to insist that the project of political integration is distinct from the project of cultural assimilation, and is in fact the basis for the latter's critique. Critique insists upon analyzing the systemic relations that exist between all the sites of cultural production and consumption. A politically effective critique of literary education would be better served now by discarding the problematic of representation for a problematic whose object is the systematic constitution and distribution of cultural capital. For if social groups now imagine that they are too different to speak the same language, or to be represented by the same cultural works in the schools, they are nevertheless always exchanging the same currency, even in the symbolic form of cultural capital. In the case of literature the problematic of cultural capital will always return us to the question of the relation between the means of literary production and the institutions of social reproduction within which speakers succeed or fail to speak for themselves.

Part Two
Case Studies

Chapter Two

Mute Inglorious Miltons: Gray, Wordsworth, and the Vernacular Canon

Putting Gray in His Place

Mr. Coleridge (in his Literary Life) says, that his friend Mr. Wordsworth had undertaken to show that the language of the Elegy is
unintelligible: it has, however, been understood!
— HAZLITT, *Lectures on the English Poets*

The preceding chapter argues that there can be no *general* theory of canon
formation that would predict or account for the canonization of any particular work, without specifying first the unique historical conditions of that
work's production and reception. Neither the social identity of the author
nor the work's proclaimed or tacit ideological messages definitively explain
canonical status. If this were not true, ideologically heterodox works
would never achieve canonicity, nor would writing produced by any member of a socially defined minority. If the literary canon has historically been
capable of assimilating enormously heterogeneous productions, that is because the ideological integration of these works has always been the task of
the school, not of works themselves. Yet the project of replacing the current
critique of the canon with something like a sociology of writing and reading raises an interesting question about the actual relation between the
ideological contents of particular literary works and the immediate historical circumstances of their canonization. I should like to begin answering
this question by considering at some length a canonical work, Gray's *Elegy
Written in a Country Churchyard,* whose ideological resonance has always
been perceived as related in an especially intimate way to its canonicity.

The example of Gray's *Elegy* is offered here with the additional purpose
of magnifying a cross section from the historical sketch concluding Chap-

ter 1, the moment at which the vernacular English canon enters the school system as a literary curriculum in competition with the classical curriculum. While Gray's *Elegy* is indisputably a monument, in Empson's well-known reading of the poem, of "bourgeois ideology," that ideology does not in itself account for the poem's canonicity, its utility in a syllabus of English literature. As soon as we understand canonicity as a form of cultural capital, we recognize that whatever agreeable messages may have been derived from the poem by its initial readers (and these messages were by no means unambiguous), it also circulated as capital in at least two senses: First as *property*, in both the literal sense of its commodity status (it made considerable money for its publisher), and in the extended sense of its accessibility only to those who already possessed a certain quantum of cultural capital (specifically, vernacular literacy). And second, as *linguistic* capital, as the means by which that literacy was produced in the schools. There is much evidence to suggest that Gray's *Elegy* accrued enormous capital of the latter sort, since it rapidly established itself in the school system as a perfect poem for introducing schoolchildren to the study of English literature. Of what does this perfection consist? Not, I will argue, primarily or only its perceived ideology, for this ideology does not operate independently of other more "formal" aspects of the poem. It is rather in the relation between what the poem means and what it formally embodies that we may understand its canonical position.

We may twist and turn the poem as we wish, then, examining each facet of its ideology, and we will not grasp its canonical essence. Yet surely the most curious aspect of the poem's canonical status is that the *Elegy* sets out what looks very like a problematic of canon formation in its reflection on the "mute, inglorious Milton," or the undiscovered "gem of purest ray serene"—both phrases which raise the issue of *literacy*. I will return periodically to the example of Gray's gem in order to look more closely at that scenario in which one imagines the literary productions of the unlettered as having the status of the gem in its underwater cavern, precisely what in our discourse is called the "noncanonical." Such works are supposed to exist in a realm in which they do not circulate but nevertheless have value, a kind of *unvalued* value. In the case of the gem itself, its value in a real-world economy is constituted as a relation between its social production as a gem—the fact that it is not found but *sought*—and its material properties. These relations are complex enough for the gem, but even more so for a literary text, whose material properties are nothing other than properties of pure signification. Here we can begin to speak about the relation of a particular work to the actual desire of its author for canonical status: This relation includes not only the poem's intertextual relations with other canonical poems, its situatedness in an always retroactively constructed tradition, but its relation to the entire linguistic/institutional field within which the form of the canon appears as both the space of the work and its time, past and future. For Gray's *Elegy* that context is, I will show, the space and time of vernacular literacy as that form of literacy is produced by the institutionalization of the vernacular canon in the primary schools of the eighteenth century. Wordsworth's meditation on certain issues raised by Gray's position in the vernacular canon will provide a retrospect on the moment of that canon's institutionalization and, more broadly, on the emergence of "literature" as the discursive category devised to accommodate vernacular works in the schools.

In order to locate the poem in the precise social/institutional context of its production and reception, we will first have to describe as exhaustively as possible the relation between the poem's formal characteristics and the institutional conditions which both enable its composition and select it as the perfect text for reproduction in teaching anthologies. These conditions are as follows.

A compositional matrix. The most striking formal feature of Gray's poem has always been acknowledged as the density of its intertexuality; its phrases sound familiar even in the absence of identified pretexts, as though it were the anonymous distillation of literary *sententiae*. It may no longer be possible now to distinguish this effect from the effect of the poem's recitation or memorization in the classroom, since the *Elegy* has been adopted as such a school text for nearly two centuries. Leslie Stephen could remark casually in his 1909 study, "Gray and his School": "Everyone knows his [Gray's] poetry by heart. The *Elegy* has so worked itself into the popular imagination that it includes more familiar phrases than any poem of equal length in the language."[1] That this impression of familiarity even upon first reading is by no means simple is confirmed by the slightly reserved praise of nineteenth-century critics for the insinuated inevitability of the poem; thus Edmund Gosse in 1882: "The *Elegy* may almost be looked upon as the typical piece of English verse, our poem of poems, not that it is the most brilliant or original or profound lyric in our language, but because it combines in more balanced perfection than any other all the qualities that go into the production of a poetical effect."[2] The total impression of an immediate but sophisticated accessibility locates the poem within a literary culture which may very well now be based upon an anthology of literary clichés available to every minimally educated reader (a trivial "cultural literacy"),[3] but which in Gray's own time was equally likely to consist in the use of an actual text known as the "commonplace book," a text uniquely both public and private. It is this text which functions as the matrix of composition, as the base over which the locodescriptive or topographical lyric, the pastoral, the elegiac, are laid in successive veneers. By looking closely at this matrix of compositional practice, we can begin to characterize the conditions of production specific to Gray's poem.

Gray compiled three folio commonplace books in his lifetime, within which he transcribed and translated quotations, as well as drafts of his own poetry, including the *Elegy.*[4] Wordsworth's complaint that "Gray wrote English verses as his brother Eton schoolboys wrote Latin, filching a phrase now from one author and now from another"[5] is an accurate characterization of a compositional process mediated by a text whose dual status as a means of both producing and consuming texts is now all but forgotten. The practice of keeping a commonplace book translated into a *writing* practice the classical rhetor's mnemonic technique of finding (*inventio*) the "topic" or "line of argument" (*locus communis*) appropriate to a given performative occasion. These performances of classical rhetoric were both oral and public. In the early modern period, the motive of public persuasion that accompanied rhetorical practice began to recede (very slowly at first) with the successful dissemination in the sixteenth century of works such as Erasmus's *De Copia,* which adapted the stylistic norms of rhetoric to written production. Hence Erasmus's specific pedagogic injunction that schoolchildren "have paper books ready" within which to record selected passages from their reading.[6] These transcriptions insured the memorability of chosen passages, in whatever context of recollection, and hence the transformation of "topics" into the modern conception of indexical categories of any sort. In 1706, Locke published "A New Method of a Common-Place Book" organized around just this indexical, or nonrhetorical, principle; evidently Gray followed Locke's plan in organizing his own folio volumes. Nevertheless it would be incorrect to detect in this historical sequence the disappearance of the persuasive motive, which lingers in the very conception of "commonplace," that is, truths generally believed. If Gray's *Elegy* is indeed composed in much the same manner as a commonplace book, its "sententiousness" takes the strictly Aristotelian form of the enthymeme, or rhetorical syllogism, an abbreviated logic negotiating a move from the general proposition to the particular, specifically from the assertion of a universal mortality to a deduction of the individual's (the speaker's). The doubling back of the rhetorical motive upon what might be called a purely anthological principle marks the point at which the "commonplace" itself becomes synonymous with banality, or mere truism. One might speculate also that the commonplace book had to be discarded as a matrix of composition in order for the Romantic locodescriptive lyric to set itself against the rhetorical commonplace, or to resist the compositional methods of eighteenth-century poetry.

But the confusion of the rhetorical and the anthological motives is in fact even more complex and interesting, as it is without question the loco-descriptive poem—the generic matrix of so much Romantic lyric—that engages the semantic ambiguity of the topos, which was perhaps even in Aristotle an unstable sliding between a "place" in the visual memory and in a text. The locodescriptive poem literalizes the metaphor of place as an organizational principle of composition. From its very inception it exhibited a tendency toward digressive, generalized reflection which exceeded the didacticism of the georgic, upon which it was probably founded, and thus required a new generic designation. Johnson calls this new form "local poetry" in his *Life of Denham:*

> *Cooper's Hill* is the work that confers upon him the rank and dignity of an original author. He seems to have been, at least among us, the author of a species of composition that may be denominated *local poetry,* of which the fundamental subject is some particular landscape to be poetically described, with the addition of such embellishments as may be supplied by historical retrospection or incidental meditation.[7]

The possibility of dullness or banality inherent in this generic project is only the complement of the pleasure arising from expatiation upon the commonplace. We may discern, then, in the evidence of the *Elegy's* composition the conditions of its production in the refunctioning of the commonplace book, which is at base an instrumentality of the early modern school.

A generic matrix. The nexus of textual/institutional relations privileging the sententious within locodescriptive poetry must then be set within a larger historical conjuncture which sees the emergence of "landscape" as a value in the cultural-aesthetic domain. The career of such landscape gardeners or estate planners as Capability Brown depends upon the same social valuation of "landscape" one finds in the painting and locodescriptive poetry of the period (the ubiquitous recourse to views, prospects, and the like), but equally fundamentally upon the transformation of the traditional "common" into private property as a result of a long process of what was described at the time as agricultural "improvement."[8] The invisible grid of property makes possible the reconstruction of the land as "landscape." The social significance of this concept has been superbly analyzed by John Barrell in connection with Thomson's *Seasons,* where the key landscape descriptions drive toward the representation of the national social order as a harmonious totality. In Barrell's analysis, it is crucial that this totalizing impulse can be indulged only by depopulating the "landscape," by reducing the laboring many, as in this passage from Thomson's "Spring," to a metonymic sign, the "smoke" of the villages on the horizon (the same sign reappears in the depopulated landscape of Wordworth's "Tintern Abbey"):

> Meantime you gain the height, from whose fair brow
> The bursting prospect spreads immense around;
> And, snatched o'er hill and dale, and wood and lawn,
> And verdant field, and darkening heath between,
> And villages embosomed soft in trees,
> And spiry towns by surging columns marked
> Of household smoke, your eye excursive roams—
> Wide-stretching from the Hall whose kind haunt
> The hospitable Genius lingers still,
> To where the broken landscape, by degrees
> Ascending, roughens into rigid hills. . . .
>
> "Spring," 950–60[9]

Barrell comments: "It is of course particularly easy to see a vast prospect as a harmonious composition, if in its foreground is a landscaped park designed to organize the world beyond it into a pictorial unity from a carefully chosen station."[10] Lord Lyttleton, the gentleman addressed in Thomson's lines, views the national order from Hagley Park: everything beyond the park is shrunk by means of perspective to the margin of his property. This effect might be described briefly, if not redundantly, as the landscape topos, a totalizing pictorial representation that permits the return of the rhetorical commonplace, with its agenda of persuasion, by appeal to common truth or common sense. The landscape topos is just where Gray begins, with a landscape that modulates or "fades" into a reflection on the entire social order: "Now fades the glimmering landscape on the sight." And in Gray, as in Thomson, the very expatiatory possibilities of this generic matrix allow reflection on the nation's literature, indeed provide the occasion for a reflection on that literature as *national*.[11]

A linguistic matrix: When Johnson comes to praise the *Elegy,* he locates its power precisely in the evocation of the "common," and the language of his panegyric thus functions as symptomatic discourse, as a commentary on the text-milieu itself:

> In the character of his *Elegy* I rejoice to concur with the common reader; for by the common sense of readers uncorrupted with literary prejudices, after all the refinements of subtilty and the dogmatism of learning must finally be decided all claim to poetical honours. The *Church-yard* abounds with images which find a mirrour in every mind, and with sentiments to which every bosom returns an echo. The four stanzas beginning

"Yet e'en these bones" are to me original: I have never seen the
notions in any other place; yet he that reads them here per-
suades himself that he has always felt them. Had Gray written
often thus it had been vain to blame, and useless to praise him.
(II, 441)

The poem Johnson describes seems to be uttered by the *Zeitgeist,* as though
it were the consummate expression of a social consensus. This is not to say,
however, that the social totality merely speaks its own truth through Gray
(or Johnson). The *Elegy* does not abound with images which find a mirror
in *every* mind. Johnson has already eliminated from his consensus everyone
who will not read the poem because he or she cannot read. What is the
relation then between "every mind" and the "common reader"? The claim
to a "common sense" embraces everyone in the same way that everyone is
embraced by a mortal fate. The instancing of a universal fate is the ground
of a claim to a universal truth that does not even allow of an "original"
thought unless that thought can be experienced at the same time as "always
felt." This paradox has been subjected to the sharpest critique by Empson
in his now unavoidable sentences on the "massive calm" and "complacence" of the poem: "The truism of the reflections in the church-yard, the
universality and impersonality this gives to the style, claim as if by comparison that we ought to accept the injustice of society as we do the inevitability of death."[12] But if both Empson and Johnson describe *avant la
lettre* what Althusserian ideology-critique calls "interpellation," the hailing of the subject,[13] this process has only very little to do with the truth of
the commonplaces themselves—which are indeed nothing but banalities—
and everything to do with the "style," with the peculiar force of banalities
expressed in a specific linguistic form.

The tradition of Romantic criticism has been suspicious enough of the
commonplaces to wonder at the source of their power, and even to trouble
itself about the value of a truth which anyone might possess (Gray himself
was contemptuous of the *Elegy's* popularity, for reasons to be considered
later). I. A. Richards, whose theoretical apparatus was mobilized to a high
degree of readiness against banality of all sorts, exempts Gray's *Elegy* from
this charge on the ground of its successful "tone," which he defines as "a
perfect recognition of the writer's relation to the reader." Gray's flawless
staging of this conspiracy compels Richards to repeat the very terms of
Johnson's praise, doubly symptomatic now for the defensiveness of the
rhetoric:

Gray's *Elegy,* indeed, might stand as a supreme instance to
show how powerful an exquisitely adjusted tone may be. It
would be difficult to maintain that the thought in this poem is

striking or original, or that its feeling is exceptional. It embodies a sequence of reflections and attitudes that under similar
conditions arise readily in any contemplative mind. Their character as commonplaces, needless to say, does not make them
any less important, and the *Elegy* may usefully remind us that
boldness and originality are not necessities for great poetry.[14]

A footnote adds to this statement a small quibble with Johnson, denying
the originality of the lines beginning "yet e'en these bones." In fact it is important for Richards to deny any originality at all to the poem in order to
make the strongest possible argument for its overcoming of banality by ex-
quisiteness of tone. But it is hard to see how this argument has not been
anticipated by Johnson's gesture of merely joining a unanimous and harmonious chorus, to which indeed he already belonged. This chorus cannot
be reduced to the company of "any contemplative mind"; nor can it be
expanded to include everyone who would agree that "the paths of glory
lead but to the grave" (presumably everyone). On the contrary, Johnson has
already identified the social locus of "common sense" in the "common
reader." If the question of tone concerns the relation of writer to reader,
that relation is defined not solely by the exchange of commonplaces but, in
Empson's words, as an effect of "complacence," that is, a species of pleasure. It is against this pleasure that Empson reacts with "irritation," the
precisely antithetical affect ("Many people have been irritated . . . by the
complacence . . . ").

The affect of complacence is produced, as Empson rightly argues, by the
relation of the commonplace as such—the continuous quotation from the
rhetorical/anthological commonplace book of eighteenth-century literary
culture—to the "universality and impersonality" of the style. I would like
to propose that this style is produced by the *systematic linguistic normalization of quotation,* a compositional method of translation, decontextualiz-
ation, and grammatical revision. By this means both classical literary
works and older works of English literature are absorbed into the poem in
a linguistically homogeneous form, the proto-"Standard English" of mid-
eighteenth-century England. Linguistic normalization is not invented by
Gray but "supremely instanced" by his poem. The cento of quotable quotations which *is* the poem thus generates a reception-scenario characterized by the reader's pleased recognition that "this is my truth," while at
the same time concealing the fact that this pleasure is founded upon the
subliminal recognition that "this is my language." Johnson's images of
"mirror" and "echo" accurately track the sequence of these recognitions.
The pleasure elicited by them is undoubtedly narcissistic, but it is not the

pleasure of an individual's recognition of his or her individuality; rather it takes the form of identification with a social body expressed or embodied in the common possession of writer and reader, a common language.

Carrière ouverte aux talents

> The *Elegy* is not concerned with protest against or acquiescence in contemporary social conditions. Gray simply sets down the social facts, which are subsumed under the more important question of individual fulfillment.
> —FRANK BRADY, "Gray's Elegy: Structure and Meaning"[15]

The foregrounding of the question of language does not at all relieve one of having to read the poem, of determining the relation of linguistic normalization to what the poem "says." Such a foregrounding is only the premise of a correct reading of this relation, as well as a correct reading of the many interpretations of the poem that manage to bracket its apparent social critique. For example, the "complacence" of the above quotation may be taken merely to reproduce the poem's supposed ideology, but it also usefully exemplifies the work of pedagogy by which the historical specificity of the poem is canceled and rewritten as the *universal* problem of the *individual*. Such a reading is interesting just because it raises a question it cannot answer: What is "individual fulfillment" apart from certain social conditions? How would it be experienced or recognized? The question of what the poem actually says about the social inequality of the class structure is on the other hand not at all easy to answer. I would like to argue that this is really a question of what the class structure signifies in the poem and not what signifies class structure in the poem. The poem actively reflects upon this structure and does not merely reflect it.

The latter point is what Empson brings out in reading the famous "gem" stanza; the distinction between the rich and the poor does not signify immediately a historically specific class structure—the rich and the poor have always been with us—but rather a problem of *social mobility*, which is in turn specific to a certain historical class structure. It is only in the context of problematizing the possibility of movement between classes that Gray's characteristic strategies of ironizing wealth or power under the shadow of death, or granting to poverty a noble pathos, become intelligible; and it is in this context that we must read Empson's remarks:

> Gray's *Elegy* is an odd case of poetry with latent political ideas: [quotes "Full many a gem . . ."] What this means, as the context makes clear, is that eighteenth-century England had no scholarship system or *carrière ouverte aux talents*. This is

stated as pathetic, but the reader is put into a mood in which one would not try to alter it. (It is true that Gray's society, unlike a possible machine society, was necessarily based on manual labour, but it might have used a man of special ability wherever he was born.) By comparing the social arrangement to Nature he makes it seem inevitable, which it was not, and gives it a dignity which was undeserved. Furthermore, a gem does not mind being in a cave and a flower prefers not to be picked; we feel that the man is like the flower, as short-lived, natural, and valuable, and this tricks us into feeling that he is better off without opportunities. The sexual suggestion of *blush* brings in the Christian idea that virginity is good in itself, and so that any renunciation is good; this may trick us into feeling it is lucky for the poor man that society keeps him unspotted from the World. The tone of melancholy claims that the poet understands the considerations opposed to aristocracy, though he judges against them; the truism of the reflections in the church yard, the universality and impersonality this gives to the style, claim as if by comparison that we ought to accept the injustice of society as we do the inevitability of death.

Many people, without being communists, have been irritated by the complacence in the massive calm of the poem, and this seems partly because they feel there is a cheat in the implied politics; the "bourgeois" themselves do not like literature to have too much "bourgeois ideology." (4–5)

These sentences still stand in my view against all the refutations of them because they set against Gray's pathos an equally powerful performance of Enlightenment reason. The elements of the pathos seem not to survive this analysis. And yet the wasting of human potential, in Empson's own words, "cannot but be felt deeply," and indeed this pathos is the motive of Empson's critique of Gray. Empson claims both that there is too much "bourgeois ideology" in Gray's poem, and that "all the great poetic statements [of the wastage of human powers] are in a way 'bourgeois'," a contradiction that sets up his striking translation of the "gem" stanza into an explicit statement about the absence of any institutional structure facilitating social mobility. What this stanza means is "that eighteenth-century England had no scholarship system or *carrière ouverte aux talents.*" But in fact, as historians have amply demonstrated, there was a much greater degree of social mobility in mid-eighteenth-century England than in the caste or "estate" system of feudalism, or in the transitional early modern period.[16] The fact of increased upward mobility is at once the premise of "bourgeois ideology"—that anyone can succeed—and its prime source of social anxiety. Hence the continuous appropriation by the bourgeoisie of aristocratic caste traits, precisely in order to reinforce and stabilize a class structure founded upon a necessary degree of instability or fluidity. Needless to say, this functional instability of social hierarchy requires complex practical and discursive strategies in order to maintain the structure as a whole; there must be neither too little nor too much social mobility. In the same way, mobility must be valued neither too little nor too much. The narrative scenario in which Gray imagines what the illiterate peasant might have been (the unfound gem) valorizes the process of social mobility as *circulation* per se: What cannot move (up) is waste, and waste is at the same time the necessary *cost* of circulation: every success is at the expense of another's failure.[17]

In this context the fact that Empson implicitly identifies a particular institution—the school—as the site at which social mobility is choked off is a perversely brilliant intuition. Contemporary eighteenth-century guardians of class structure were worried about just those mobilizing and possibly destabilizing effects of education, and as a consequence they were likely to argue that the availability of knowledge had to be actively restricted. In the previous century Locke had suggested that the children of the poor should not be taught to read at all, and this opinion was more or less the consensus of educated social commentators.[18] In 1757 Soam Jenyns remarks typically that ignorance is a "cordial, administered by the gracious hand of providence, of which [the poor] ought never to be deprived by an ill-judged and improper education."[19] Not until the later eighteenth and early nineteenth century were the poor provided in any numbers with the means to acquire literacy, and then primarily as an adjunct to the disciplining of their everyday life (the program, for example, of the Society for the Promotion of Christian Knowledge, or of the new "monitorial" systems of basic education).[20] If knowledge is a real form of property or wealth, it is difficult to see how this property can come to be possessed by the endemically impoverished, how indeed a "mute, inglorious Milton" can ever come to write, for better or worse. Clearly the question of social mobility, as it is raised by access to knowledge, does not refer to the poor at all, except as they represent *in extremis* a condition of deprivation that is in fact *relative* for certain other social groups. Only those in possession of some capital are in a position to acquire the knowledge that in turn signifies the at once attractive and dangerous possibility of upward mobility, even if this mobility is essentially enacted in the realm of the imaginary, as the imitation of upper-class behavior or educated manners, that is, as social *emulation*.

Here we may return to Bourdieu's concept of "cultural capital" in order to identify the motive force behind a variety of developments that traverse the market, the class structure, and literary discourses. These are: the wider availability of vernacular printed matter, particularly subscription series such as the *Spectator;* the establishment of quasi-educational bodies such as the literary clubs, the coffeehouses, and the lending libraries; and the rise of for-profit grammar schools and vocational academies designed specifically for the commercial classes.[21] In these latter schools, not only professional knowledges such as accounting and surveying are disseminated. Traditional knowledges—of classical languages and literatures—are also disseminated as the sign of acquired rather than inherited capital, and as a means of exhibiting status. Such social emulation expresses itself not as antagonism between classes but as the bourgeois embrace of aristocratic culture, the complement of that commercialization of the nobility by which their revenues came to be invested more and more in capitalist agriculture or trade. As soon as we look at the educational sites of social emulation, we note that the curricular form of this emulation is marked by the clear distinction of "polite letters," of linguistic knowledges, from the nascent discourses of natural philosophy, pure or applied. This distinction, which would have been meaningless in the medieval university, emerges clearly in the seventeenth century with Locke's well-known critique of the Latin curriculum, which recognizes emulation as nothing more than pretension: "Can there be anything more ridiculous, than that a Father should waste his own Money, and his Son's time, in setting him to learn the Roman Language; when at the same time he designs for him a Trade, wherein he having no use of Latin, fails not to forget that little which he brought from School."[22] But Locke goes on to concede that a knowledge of Latin is of course the endowment of every gentleman. The vocational academies of the eighteenth century follow Locke's utilitarian principle in offering new courses in skills needful for various forms of commerce, and their rise is paralleled by a decline in the quality of the grammar schools, which had been vital institutions for disseminating classical literacy in the preceding two centuries, along with a certain ossification of university curricula accessible for the most part to the bored progeny of noble families.[23]

Two consequences follow from these curricular developments: First, the position of the classical languages, as the knowledge provided by the traditional curriculum, changes; but this knowledge does not suffer in the end a simple derogation in status. On the contrary, since the children of gentlemen continue to be educated in the traditional classical languages, their "useless" knowledge comes to stand by the later eighteenth century as a pure sign of their noble status.[24] Second, there is installed in the "middling" and commercial classes, as the upwardly mobile classes, a linguistic ambivalence which takes the form of suspicion toward the classical languages as useless knowledge, and envy of the social distinction they represent.[25] This ambivalence, as we shall see, is ultimately resolved with the entry of vernacular literature into the new, middle-class schools. The study of vernacular literature is thus at first a substitute for the study of Greek and Latin, but with the same object of producing a linguistic sign of social distinction, a distinctive language.

If it is not yet possible to say that in the later seventeenth or early eighteenth century this language is a bourgeois language—what we now call Standard English—that is because it has as yet only a limited dissemination. In the last chapter we observed it thrust itself above the sea of dialects first as the vernacular *Hochsprache* of the court nobility, who use it both as an administrative and as a literary language. But Standard English is a national language *derived* from its literary precursors, a complex derivation that requires the active intervention of institutional agencies. Once it has appeared, the literary language must be consciously and systematically *transformed* in order to regularize its distinctive differences from regional dialects; hence the production in the later seventeenth century of vernacular grammars, dictionaries, and rhetoric handbooks which are disseminated in the wider literary culture even more than in the schools. If England did not establish, as did France, an "academy" to lay down the linguistic law, it did develop an array of quasi-academic institutions within which the continuous correction of speech was undertaken—the coffeehouses, literary clubs, and salons.

The thematization of vernacular "polite" language so conspicuous in the writing of Swift, Addison, Johnson, and many others, is premised, as I argued in Chapter 1, on a fetishization of grammar, that is, a reduction of the stylistic norms of the courtly *Hochsprache* to an iterable system of rules. This fetishizing is duly if also anxiously expressed in literary culture as the project of correcting Renaissance English.[26] In his survey of neoclassical attempts at linguistic regularization, John Barrell usefully reminds us that the revolutionary effects of this agenda were dissimulated by the fact that "proper" or correct English was still conceptualized from the perspective of the gentleman: "The gentleman . . . was believed to be the only member of society who spoke a language universally intelligible; his usage was 'common,' in the sense of being neither a local dialect nor infected by the terms of any particular art."[27] Nonetheless the impetus behind the standardization of speech does not come from the landed nobility but from a much wider and more heterogeneous group, which is beginning to recognize itself not as other than aristocratic but as part of a society of "gentlemen," defined according to norms of behavior and education rather than blood: "For well before the 1730s it is clear that, though the gentleman may survive as the ideal of a comprehensive observer, he is no longer easily identifiable with any very considerable body of men within the society of England."[28] At a later point Barrell argues that this redefinition of the gentleman tends to erase the difference between the gentleman and the author who arrogates to himself both the power to define gentility and the power to legislate the norms of polite speech. Even if proper English is referred to the idea of the gentleman, then, Barrell's analysis confirms Auerbach's parallel argument that the site of linguistic regularization moves decisively from the court to the city (hence "polite" speech). One may wonder why the bourgeoisie does not recognize itself as the agency of transformation, but Auerbach's concept of cultural homogenization suggests why such a recognition is not possible: The acquisition of polite speech evidently cannot be the medium of class consciousness so long as this speech is defined by reference to the "gentleman." True class consciousness does not come to the bourgeoisie through polite speech until that speech is fully representable as a national language, that is, as a language actually spoken throughout the nation-state. Clearly this is not the case in the earlier eighteenth century, nor is this project capable of realization until the educational system is readapted to disseminate this speech. The interconnection of linguistic and nationalistic agendas has been interestingly examined in Benedict Anderson's study of nationalism, *Imagined Communities,* the following passage of which will stand as a summary overview of the largest historical context of the present argument:

> The relatively small size of traditional aristocracies, their fixed political bases, and the personalization of political relations implied by sexual intercourse and inheritance, meant that their cohesions as classes were as much concrete as imagined. An illiterate nobility could still act as a nobility. But the bourgeoisie? Here was a class which, figuratively speaking, came into being as a class only in so many replications. Factory-owner in Lille was connected to factory-owner in Lyon only by reverberation. They had no necessary reason to know of one another's existence; they did not typically marry each other's daughters or inherit each other's property. But they did come to visualize in a general way the existence of thousands and thousands like themselves through print-language. For an illiterate bour-

geoisie is scarcely imaginable. Thus in world-historical terms, bourgeoisies were the first class to achieve solidarities on an essentially imagined basis.[29]

Anderson goes on to suggest that such an imagined community necessarily had a natural limit in the extent of the vernacular language, and if this is so, the bourgeoisie comes to know itself not as an international class but as the nation itself, as the speakers of a national language. Until that imagined community comes to be, the "polite language" of earlier eighteenth-century literary culture continues to embody a *confusion* of aristocratic and bourgeois cultural norms, and an *ambivalence* in the relation of vernacular to classical literacy.

The trajectory sketched here is intended to make sense of one moment in that history of literary canon formation to which Gray's *Elegy* belongs, and which is nothing other than the field of institutional/linguistic forces conditioning both the production and the reception of his poem. This moment is virtually the last moment at which literary culture can sustain a discourse of polite letters in the vernacular without establishing this discourse in the schools. And it is virtually the last moment at which polite speech can easily be assimilated to the concept of the gentleman as aristocrat, and therefore to a class structure simply divided into aristocracy and commons. It is this class structure which appears in Gray's *Elegy*, not as a representation of the social order but as a generic anachronism—the pastoral; hence we are enjoined to ask what this structure signifies *as* an anachronism. William Temple characterized Gray himself in a letter to Boswell as just such a living anachronism: "he could not bear to be considered himself merely as a man of letters; and though without birth, or fortune, or station, his desire was to be looked upon as a private independent gentleman, who read for his amusement."[30] This biographical datum is a very relevant consideration, because Gray inserts himself into the *Elegy* as a figure just like the idle aristocrat in pastoral disguise, a surprisingly belated performance of what Empson calls the "trick" of Renaissance pastoral. Of course the gentleman who is quite out of place indulging his pastoral melancholy in the company of peasants happens to be, like Milton, the son of a scrivener. There is perhaps no better example of Barrell's point that the boundary between gentleman and author is effaced when "men of letters" arrogate to themselves the discourse of gentility. To this point I shall return. At present, I would like to place under greater magnification the event (in the 1740s and 1750s) which transforms English literary culture: the passage of English vernacular texts into the schools. Gray's *Elegy* bears a necessary if also an oblique relation to this event.

There was, to be sure, a discourse of canon formation within English literary culture prior to the 1750s. The important fact about this discourse is that it circulates outside the curriculum of the Latin schools but in a *mirror relation* to that curriculum. This point has not been sufficiently appreciated; it is why such poets as Denham and Waller could for so long enjoy reputations they could not sustain after English literature began to be taught in the schools. The teaching of vernacular literature meant the beginning of the end of this neoclassical hegemony, the end of a strict conformity of the English canonical form to the norms of Latin classicism. This development is the long-term consequence of an ultimate enabling cause: the 1662 Act of Uniformity, which excluded non-Anglicans from teaching in the grammar schools and universities. The Dissenting Academies which emerged as a result of that act initially merely reproduced for their constituencies the curriculum of the traditional schools, but this imitation clearly did not provide the cultural capital most desired by the "middling" sort— the commercial and professional classes who were most likely to be Dissenters in the first place. The decades-long campaign to replace Latin with vernacular texts had doubtless many determinants, but we might describe the particular moment under scrutiny as the temporary victory of linguistic ambivalence over social emulation. Just as the late medieval nobility acquired literacy but did not care to master the scholastic canon of the clergy, the middling sort wished to acquire polite speech but not necessarily a knowledge of Latin or Greek. In this way a *difference* from the aristocracy was preserved within the gradual process of cultural homogenization; and this difference expressed both a resentment against exclusions based upon class and religious belief, and a canny recognition that the dissemination of polite speech provided a cultural basis for the *dispersion* of political power. Hence the program to vernacularize the curriculum became urgent by midcentury, the subject of intense controversy. By the time that Thomas Sheridan wrote his important polemic, *British Education: Or the Source of the Disorders of Great Britain* (1756), the connection between vernacular linguistic refinement and a progressive political agenda was firmly entrenched, and took the pedagogic form in the dissenting academies of a revival of "political oratory," or rhetoric. It was in the context of a rhetorical program whose ends are also easily recognizable as nationalistic that Sheridan, like many others, urged a syllabus of English literature:

> . . . as models of style, Milton in the poetic, and Shakespeare in the dramatic, Swift, Addison, Dryden, and Sir William Temple (in some of his works) in prose, may be considered as truly classical, as the Virgil, Caesar, Tully, and Sallust of the Romans; nor is there any reason that they should not be handed down as such equally to the end of time. . . . And shall we not endeavor to

secure to future generations, entire and unchanged, their birth-
right in Milton, in Addison, and Swift? Or shall we put in the
power of one giddy and profuse age to dissipate, or render of no
value, the heaps of treasure now collected in the many excellent
books written by English authors?[31]

The anxiety expressed by Sheridan is that, in the absence of an institutional
form of dissemination, literary culture cannot be entrusted to preserve English works of the past; vernacular works must be revalued as equal in value
to classical works and therefore worthy to be taught in the schools. This is
the crucial point: the judgment of vernacular works throughout the sixteenth and seventeenth centuries already elevates some works over others,
but only the institutionalization of these works as a *curriculum* can revalue
their cultural capital as the equal of the classics.

The introduction of these works into school curricula exceeds the objective of instituting grammatical speech as a credential of gentility and discovers in this canonical form the paradigm of another linguistic practice,
the rhetorical or the "elocutionary," which, as we shall see, functions as a
claim to political entitlement on the part of those who are not gentle by
birth.[32] An account of the elocutionary use of vernacular literature in the
classroom of a dissenting academy is recorded in *The Monthly Repository*,
volume 8, which describes the technique of Dr. John Aiken of Warrington
Academy, perhaps the leading academy of the age (Joseph Priestly taught
there):

> After the exercises [practical sermons] were examined he would
> generally turn to some of the finest passages of the English po-
> ets, Milton, Pope, Thomson, Young, and Akenside, and having
> first himself read a considerable portion . . . he heard each of
> the students read, pointed out their defects and the proper
> mode of remedying them. This lecture was often the most satis-
> factory and improving of any in the whole course.[33]

Early vernacular anthologies such as William Enfield's frequently reprinted
The Speaker (1774), the Adamic ancestor of the Norton anthologies, were
thus organized for use in the classroom as texts for elocution practice.[34]
The Speaker, which was used in Warrington Academy, opens with an essay
on elocution and goes on to reproduce a recognizably modern selection of
English literary texts, notably different from the Norton Anthology perhaps only for a greater selection of minor mid-century writers and the relative absence of those Restoration poets whose language was paradigmatic
for the polite speech of the earlier eighteenth century. There appeared
then, within and in some sense also against, the *sermo urbanus* of the

"gentleman" a different linguistic practice, different but also the same. The difference roughly corresponds to the major political divisions of the century—between Tory and Whig—but these are divisions between parties whose common basis of power was always property. Even if the middle-class academies disseminated a form of cultural capital from which certain strata of this class had been excluded by the traditional schools, that dissemination ceased at the border of property. In cultural terms, this border marked the division between the literate and the illiterate.

Here it is possible to begin reading Gray's poem in its proper place, the place it occupies in the field of institutional/linguistic forces. At present this reading attempts nothing more than a general description: the generic form of pastoral simplifies the social structure by reducing it to the Renaissance status-hierarchy of aristocracy and peasantry. The poem's representation of such a structure facilitates an act of social emulation by which Gray inserts himself into his poem as a pseudo-aristocrat. But this elitism is also contradicted by Gray's own avowedly Whig sentiments, which are expressed in his fragment, "The Alliance of Education and Government." There he speculates seriously on what we would call the distribution of cultural capital, and he argues, much as Sheridan does, for a wider dissemination of knowledge on behalf of the nation's political health. Gray cannot say, however, what should be the content of such knowledge, and that is just the historical crux. The poem cannot really move beyond its metaphors to a domain of reference:

> As sickly Plants betray a niggard Earth,
> Whose barren Bosom starves her gen'rous Birth
> Nor genial Warmth, nor genial Juice retains
> Their Roots to feed, and fill the Verdant Veigns:
> And as in Climes, where Winter holds his Reign,
> The Soil, tho' fertile, will not teem in vein,
> Forbids her Gems to swell, her Shades to rise,
> Nor trusts her Blossoms to the churlish Skies. . . .
>
> (1–8)

I invoke this ghostly parallel of the more famous stanzas from the *Elegy* not only to underline the historical relation between polite letters and political economy (the "alliance" of education and government), but in order to make intelligible the contradiction between the *Elegy's* pathetic depiction of deprivation and the aloofness of the solitary, whom we cannot imagine condescending to teach the peasantry to read. The absurdity of such a hypothetical departure from the meditative narrative measures the peculiar force of a complex effect by which it is possible for readers to identify with either the state of privilege or the state of deprivation, to indulge in the pathos of sympathy or the ethos of resentment. I mean to describe by this effect not the reason for the poem's "canonization," but the fact that it cannot be other than it is, that its conditions of production are such that it must occupy this place and no other in the history of literary production and reception.

The necessity of conceiving the conditions of production and reception as an indivisible complex can be demonstrated by glancing briefly at the position of the *Elegy* in Enfield's *Speaker*. Gray's poem is reprinted under the section heading "Descriptive Pieces," and it is preceded by several other poems of his, as well as by poems of Goldsmith, Green, and Dyer. It is followed by a poem entitled "Warrington Academy," by one "Mrs. Barbauld," a writer no one would regard today as canonical. The adjacency of so titled a poem to Gray's calls attention either to itself or to Gray, or to both. Enfield also quotes several lines from Mrs. Barbauld's poem at the end of his opening dedication to John Lees, then president of Warrington Academy. The dedication boasts, as does the passage from Barbauld, of the successful careers pursued by graduates of the school:

> In this Seminary, which was at first established, and has been uniformly conducted, on the extensive plan of providing a proper course of Instruction for young men in the most useful branches of Science and Literature, you have seen many respectable characters formed, who are now filling up their stations in society with reputation to themselves and advantage to the Public. And, while the same great object continues to be pursued, by faithful endeavours to cultivate the understandings of youth, and by a steady attention to discipline, it is hoped, that you will have the satisfaction to observe the same effects produced, and that the scene will be realized, which OUR PO-ETESS has so beautifully described:
>> When this, this little group their country calls
>> From academic shades and learned halls,
>> To fix her laws, her spirit to sustain,
>> And light up glory thro' her wide domain
>> Their various tastes indifferent arts display'd
>> Like temper'd harmony of light and shade,
>> With friendly union in one mass shall blend,
>> And this adorn the state, and that defend.[35]

"Our Poetess," Anna Laetitia Barbauld, is the daughter of the tutor Dr. Aiken, whose classroom practice is described above. Barbauld was a tal-

ented poet, well known in her own day, and extremely possessed of that
mobility by which one travels in literary circles. In her later life she was a
friend of both Wordsworth and Coleridge. She produced an edition of English novelists in fifty volumes (including many women novelists) and later
a companion volume to Enfield's for women readers, entitled *The Female
Speaker*. Barbauld was very much in the vanguard, then, of that an-
thologizing movement by which English literature was given a canonical
form.[36] In this context the pendant position of "Warrington Academy" in
relation to Gray's poem is, as we may now demonstrate, not at all accidental: Barbauld's poem reads Gray's *Elegy* and so enacts its reception. But
what it reads is precisely a poem about the conditions of literary production. Here are the first lines of the poem:

> Mark where its simple form yon mansion rears,
> The nursery of men for future years!
> Here callow chiefs and embryo statesmen lie,
> And unfledged poets short excursions try:
> While Mersey's gentle current, which too long
> By fame neglected, and unknown to song
> Between his rushy banks (no poet's theme)
> Had crept inglorious, like a vulgar stream,
> Reflects th' ascending feats with conscious pride,
> And dares to emulate a classic tide.
>
> (1–10)

"Warrington Academy" belongs to the generic tradition of the topographical poem, of which Denham's "Cooper's Hill" provides, as Johnson remarks, the "original." The Mersey winds its way emblematically through
the landscape as does the Thames in Denham's poem. In so locating her
poem generically, Barbauld declines to pastoralize her subject, and this
strategy has the effect of lifting the pastoral scrim from Gray's pretty set.
Behind the generic veil certain social facts come sharply into focus: the
struggle of individuals and social groups to rise. Gray's peasants of course
do not struggle. Barbauld's word for the social fact she firmly grasps is
"emulation," which here has all of the senses to which I have assigned it,
preeminently "to compete by imitation." The important point here is that
the opening lines express the fact of struggle through a rhetoric of literary
culture; that culture is where the struggle takes place. So the Mersey emu-
lates a "classic" tide, perhaps the following neoclassic *locus classicus:*

> O could I flo like thee, and make thy stream
> My great example, as it is my theme!

> Though deep, yet clear, though gentle, yet not dull
> Strong without rage, without oreflowing full.

Denham reinscribes the ancient Ciceronian topos, the *universum flumen* of rhetorical topics, as the political topography of the Thames itself.[37] The effortless embodiment of the very fluidity they long for, these lines distill for Restoration culture everything that is left of the Renaissance nobility's *sprezzatura* into a single linguistic performance. And what unquestionably excited so many imitations of these lines was just the way in which its language becomes its referent. To imitate them is to celebrate the Restoration linguistic *politesse* as it stands for the Restoration polity. Barbauld opposes to Denham's Thames (picking up the rhyme on theme and stream) a naturally "gentle current" which is like a "vulgar stream" only in having had no poet to sing of it, or perhaps only a "mute, inglorious Milton" to languish on its "inglorious" banks. Gray's problem of wasted talent is regrounded in the language of the locodescriptive ur-text in order to set beside the stream of language itself the very institution within which that language is produced as a signifier of fluidity, of social mobility.

The distinction between "gentle" and "vulgar" thus activates the latent class referents of Denham's rhetoric while making a rather careful if also profound allusion to Gray's *Elegy:*

> Here nature opens all her secret springs,
> And heav'n born science plumes her eagle-wings:
> Too long had bigot rage, with malice swelled,
> Crush'd her strong pinions, and her flight withheld.
>
> (17–20)
>
> Ye generous youth who love this studious shade,
> How rich a field is to your hopes display'd!
> Knowledge to you unlocks the classic page;
> And virtue blossoms for a better age.
>
> (31–34)

Barbauld refers explicitly in the first set of lines to the laws by which Dissenters were excluded from access to institutions of learning. Her tropes supply a precise antecedent to the pronominal subjects of the universalized and abstracted condition of deprivation in the lines of the *Elegy* to which Barbauld alludes:

> But knowledge to their eyes her ample page
> Rich with the spoils of time did ne'er unroll;
> Chill Penury repressed their noble rage,
> And froze the genial current of their soul.
>
> (49–52)

Of these lines one must observe the *absence* of a specific referent; one must notice the fact of abstraction as it apparently generalizes particular deprivations. Empson replicates Barbauld's response to the level of generalization in Gray's poem similarly by supplying a referent: "Eighteenth-century England had no scholarship system or *carrière ouverte aux talents*. This is stated as pathetic, but the reader is put in a mood in which one would not try to alter it." Indeed the pathos of sympathy might well end just there, in a "mood." The ethos of resentment is quite another matter, an active response: it accounts for the fact that Barbauld can locate Warrington Academy in a different generic and social space than Gray's pastoral landscape; it accounts for her fierce praise of successful "emulation." But this resentment is itself not wholly absent from Gray's poem; on the contrary, it is there as the object of repression, as the "noble rage" abstractly repressed by the abstraction "Chill Penury." Gray's landscape contains no historical social institutions, no historical aristocrats or peasants, and that is just the point of it. It is a landscape of abstract repression: "Penury" represses "rage."

In this context it matters very much how we read the "noble rage" standing as the object of this subjectless repression. Gray's most recent editor, Roger Lonsdale, hastens to note that Gray means by "rage" not "anger" but "rapture, ardour, inspiration (equivalent to the favourable sense of furor)."[38] Of course Gray does mean this, but it seems prematurely defensive to rule out as simply irrelevant any other sense of rage, as though it were ridiculous to imagine that the perennially impoverished would be anything but content with the frustration of their native talents. Does this editorial gesture not itself repress the other sense of rage? This question can hardly be decided by appealing confidently to what Gray means. Let us grant that he too may be strenuously repressing the "unfavorable" sense of rage. Gray takes his chances, though, by lyricizing, latinizing, or "ennobling" this rage. The hands performing the pastoral trick are momentarily too fast to follow, and while the topos of innate nobility is a convention of the genre, the temporary ennobling of the peasants liberates an uncontrollable irony. The repression of a truly noble rage, freezing the very current of gentility, ought to provoke nothing less than outrage. In the absence of such a response, the irony lapses into the pathos of generalization: the common, because merely figurative, nobility of gentle and commoner. That the irony does not so lapse for Barbauld or Empson does not attest to inaccurate reading—they merely stand perplexed before the absence of anger. If Barbauld can then transpose Gray's "noble rage" into the "bigot rage" of the Anglican hegemony against the Dissenters, this projection reveals very tellingly how much repressed violence makes up the institutional agenda of "emulation." Imitation is the insincerest form of flattery. Barbauld reads into Gray's poem, then, the immediate circumstances of her own literary production, the very conditions that bring Warrington Academy into existence. Her reading discovers at the same time what is really there in the *Elegy*—an absence of reference, a structure of abstract repression, which Empson makes concrete once again by specifying that absence as the absence of a "scholarship system," the *carrière ouverte aux talents*.

Literacy and Literature in the *Elegy*

> Nor you, ye poor, of lettered scorn complain
> To you the smoothest song is smooth in vain.
> —CRABBE, "The Village"

The maudlin irony of Crabbe's lines, and indeed of "The Village" as a whole, may be said to mark the furthest and perhaps unintentionally the funniest actualization of that potential irony in Gray's elegy for unrealized potential. As such Crabbe's lines are an interesting reading of their pretext; they describe a repression so successful that its victims have not even the means to detect its operation. Hence the imperative verb "Nor . . . complain" turns out to be, after all, merely declarative: the poor can hardly complain about the contents of works they cannot read. Gray's more genteel syntactical choice is the Latinate subjunctive:

> Let not Ambition mock their useful toil,
> Their homely joys and destiny obscure;
> Nor grandeur hear, with a disdainful smile,
> The short and simple annals of the poor.

The slight drift of the last two lines in the direction of a Crabbe-like irony is arrested in the next stanza by the much greater irony of the figure of death, who, if he does not laugh last, smiles last. Beside the ironist who fatally embraces both the rich and the poor, the social repression that produces material inequality dwindles to insignificance. This irony has been a great comfort to many of Gray's critics, who have hailed the figure of death as the properly universal theme of the poem; indeed it would be difficult to argue that the poem is *not* about death. Yet critics have often been able to assert that the poem is about death only by asserting that it is not about something else: "The central subject of the *Elegy* is not the contrast between the poor and the great, but the nature and meaning of epitaphs."[39] The mise-en-scène speaks clearly to this point: the peasants whom the narrator evokes are all dead, and he is moved to speculate about what they might possibly have done in their lives. This meditative affect is so totally enveloping as to lull the idiot questioner in the critic, but a less sensitive reader might raise a point of simple logic: surely Gray is not saying the hypothetical accomplishments of the peasants were prevented by *death*? Surely they were prevented by the very conditions of peasant existence, by poverty? The slippage between these terms is nonetheless very functional; the concept of "death" is the slipperiest of signifiers, the most likely to take on the metaphoric task of signifying any blockage, failure, inhibition. The question of relevance to Gray's poem is what regions of signifying are traversed by the signifier "death." And here it is possible to propose a specific hypothesis: The invocation of death is the rhetorical mechanism by which the social structure of repression is *abstracted*, rendered subjectless and objectless.

The mechanism of abstraction is not instanced, then, simply by the metaphorizing of deprivation as death-like, the "chill" hands of Penury. The moment of death structures every micro-narrative of the nameless peasants' hypothetical other lives by allowing us to forget that their actual lives are foreshortened by poverty and not by death:

> Perhaps in this neglected spot is laid
> Some heart once pregnant with celestial fire;
> Hands that the rod of empire might have swayed,
> Or waked to ecstasy the living lyre. . . .

> (45–48)

The conditions preventing such accomplishment must obtain equally for the living peasants whom the narrator has just observed trudging wearily to their homes, and it will not do therefore to say that these conditions are by implication compared figurally to death. The "celestial fire" that might have eventuated in great deeds is only observed at all when it is irrecoverably buried, when the possibility of its expression is absolutely foreclosed. The micronarratives are founded, then, upon a logical contradiction, which is yet necessary in order to produce the pathos of these narratives. This contradiction consists, as I have hinted earlier, in the imaginary scenario of envisioning the invisible object of a perfect repression. Empson's irritable insistence that "a gem does not mind being in a cave, and a flower prefers not to be picked" strains against the illogic of the poem's imaginary scenario not by questioning the typically ideological motif of "naturalizing" social determinations, but by turning the tables of Gray's metaphor—giving flowers and gems a will which was not given to the peasants in the first place. They neither resist nor acquiesce in their repression, which is to say either that they are dead or that they do indeed suffer from a perfect and therefore asymptomatic repression.

If it is barely possible to speak in this context of repression without also invoking the domain of psychoanalysis, that temptation is quite instructive and should make it possible to look again at these most familiar lines of English poetry, which translate the process of canon formation into the occasion of an intense pathos by inviting us to imagine the great unwritten works of an unlettered populace. The (psycho)analytic gaze, however, might detect in the illogic of Gray's scenario of pathos the obvious betrayal of the supposedly perfect repression: "Full many a flower is born to *blush* unseen." Of course this blush has been caught unaware, since the flower may be said not to know that it is the object of anyone's gaze. Who blushes when alone? The blush is the failure and thus the only evidence of repression. This repression takes as its object another sort of passion than the "noble rage" of the preceding stanza. Empson rightly seizes upon this bizarre touch to expose yet another "trick" of Gray's pastoral: "The sexual suggestion of blush brings in the Christian idea that virginity is good in itself, and so that any renunciation is good; this may trick us into feeling it is lucky for the poor man that society keeps him unspotted from the World." That the blush conveys a "sexual suggestion" is unmistakable, but that the agency of this repression can be simply assimilated to "society" is worth considering more carefully. The psychosomatic blush implies a form of self-censorship, even if this censorship can then be referred to social constraints of various sorts. The attempt to keep down or repress a sexual passion takes over from "Chill Penury" the job of repression, and so converts a social into a psychic repression.

The model of repression that emerges from these lines structures the next four stanzas, which gradually substitute a more complex and ambiguous rage for the "noble rage" of the thirteenth stanza, a rage that first took the form of great "virtue" but finally comes to signify the sheer negativity of individual lusts and ambitions:

> Some village-Hampden, that with dauntless breast
> The little Tyrant of his fields withstood;
> Some mute inglorious Milton here may rest,
> Some Cromwell guiltless of his country's blood.

> Th' applause of list'ning senates to command,
> The threats of pain and ruin to despise,
> To scatter plenty o'er a smiling land,
> And read their his'try in a nation's eyes

> Their lot forbade: nor circumscrib'd alone
> Their growing virtues, but their crimes confin'd;

Forbade to wade through slaughter to a throne,
And shut the gates of mercy on mankind,

The struggling pangs of conscious truth to hide,
To quench the blushes of ingenuous shame,
Or heap the shrine of Luxury and Pride
With incense kindled at the Muse's flame.

Far from the madding crowd's ignoble strife,
Their sober wishes never learn'd to stray;
Along the cool sequester'd vale of life
They kept the noiseless tenour of their way.

(57–76)

The reappearance of "blushes" in the later stanza (line 69) only confirms its secret determination of the repressive process; nor would it be merely fanciful to say that the stanzas quoted stage a grand scene of blushing, as the only too modest speaker recoils against every excess of ambition. In the same peculiar way that a blush arouses desire by betraying a sexual feeling at the same time that it signifies modesty, these lines betray ambition *repressed*. Gray is quite caught up in this moment of betrayal by the blood, of failed repression. By the end of the last stanza quoted we are quite beyond the celebration of the peasantry's "noble rage." Their "sober wishes" are in perfect accord with the very repressive process that forbids them to wish for any object not defined as "sober." It is this process of "forbidding" which governs the strangely convoluted syntax of the wishes which are expressed only to be immediately canceled out:

Forbade: The struggling pangs of conscious truth to hide . . .
Forbade: To quench the blushes of ingenuous shame . . .

That is, the peasants are incapable of lying in the way that the ambitious lie when they successfully suppress the telltale blush at the magnitude of their crimes. These great ones are like pathological liars who can fool the polygraph machine, who can sin without blushing. The poor may desire what the wealthy and ambitious desire, but they blush with shame at the recognition of those desires, and as a consequence they can be approved for pursuing "the noiseless tenour of their way." When we relate this telltale blush to its predecessor in the line "Full many a flower is born to blush unseen," the homology of poverty and obscurity produces, as we may now demonstrate, a curious equation between social and *literary* ambition. It is in this sense that the poem meditates on the process of what we call canon formation, by projecting onto the figure of the peasant a certain pleasure in the very nonexistence of poems by the "mute, inglorious Milton." The very conditions enabling literary production can thus be reexperienced as morally inferior to the conditions which *constrain* production.

The reading proposed here does not yet address that contradiction by which the violence evoked in the stanzas quoted can signify either the violence imposed from above on inferiors in the social order or a more disturbing because *revolutionary* violence (signified by the allusion to Hampden, Milton, and Cromwell). All evocations of violence in the poem are tendentially assimilated to the motive of ambition, but by way of an allusion to the civil war, an allusion which imposes upon that conflict a certain reductive interpretation suggested by the phrase "ignoble strife." If there is no such thing as "noble strife" within the terms of the poem, the attempt to equate strife itself with the essentially ignoble is belied by the phrase "ingenuous shame," which activates the Latinate sense of *ingenuus,* meaning "of noble birth." The secondary but now standard sense— "frank, open, guileless"—attributes to the noble-born a quality of innate expressivity, an inability to conceal noble birth. "Ingenuous shame," on the other hand (the Latin hand), hints at a kind of class-shame, the noble's betrayal of his own blood at the moment at which the blushes are "quenched," when that blood fails to appear. "Ignoble strife" might very well be an appropriate term to bring into association with the nobility, inasmuch as it characterizes in a general way the political order Gray's contemporaries called "Old Corruption."[40] We might think in this context of the satiric productions of Grub Street, of its scandalous narratives of Ambition, Luxury, and Pride among real lords and ladies. Gray's desire to idealize aristocratic culture appears to contradict his simultaneous idealization of peasant culture, just because his social topography does not locate Ambition, Luxury, or Pride definitively in one social group. These terms can define what is in a generally metaphoric sense "ignoble," and conversely the absence of these same motives can define in a generally metaphoric sense what is "noble." The problem raised by the pastoral topos of the aristocrat-as-peasant, however, is that the metaphorical nobility of the peasants is supposed to characterize what is *really,* essentially, the class character of the nobility. It is in this context that we need to ask what Gray means when he substitutes Hampden, Milton, and Cromwell for Cato, Tully, and Caesar in the published version of lines 57–60. For that "translation" into the vernacular finally locates "Ambition" in *literary culture,* where the shrine of "Luxury and Pride" is heaped with "incense kindled at the Muse's flame." We may now conjecture that the appearance of Milton's name in connection with Hampden and Cromwell marks an attempt to reground literary production in an ethos entirely incompatible with that signified by "Ambition, Luxury, and Pride." This ethos, I would suggest, is aristocratic, but precisely in the sense governed by the pastoral topos of the aristocrat-as-peasant.

The nature of this ethos can be recovered by tracing the allusion in Gray's "quench the blushes" to its source in Act IV, scene iv, of *The Winter's Tale,* the very scene in which the innate nobility of the noble-born is proven in the figure of Perdita:

> Come, quench your blushes, and present yourself
> That which you are, mistress o' the feast.
>
> (IV, iv, 67–68)

In these lines the Old Shepherd chides Perdita for her "retirement," for behaving as though she were the "feasted one" and not simply the country hostess. But she is, after all, a real princess whose "noble rage" is repressed in her identity as peasant girl. Even in such a lowly setting, the innate expressiveness of the noble cannot be entirely repressed and betrays itself through the blood, as Perdita's "blush." What I will call Perdita's *expressive reserve* is an example of what Bourdieu, following Mauss, calls a habitus: "a system of durable, transposable dispositions" where disposition is defined as "a way of being, a habitual state (especially of the body.)"[41] The system of these dispositions and their interrelations, as determined in Bourdieu's account by class position, have the function of regulating the practices of social life. These dispositions need not be consciously articulated as motives, either class or individual, nor need they take the discursive form of ethical norms. Rather they are the result of an internalization of regulatory procedures capable of being objectified in the body itself as ways of speaking or moving. Perdita expresses the disposition of aristocratic grace in the perfect (and therefore imaginary) form of pure, expressive motion, which Florizel figures metaphorically as "a wave o' the sea," and which he desires to contemplate only and forever in this abstracted form: "move still, still so, and own no other function." That function is refined to an expression or objectification of noble blood so pure that individual actions lose any other function than the signifying of status: As Florizel says to Perdita, "all your acts are queens."

We are now prepared to take the full measure of Gray's investment in this pastoral topos. The hypothetical achievements of the peasantry can be represented in the poem as at once tragically repressed; but on the other hand, no achievements are named in the poem which are not deplored as instances of Ambition, Luxury, and Pride: hence Milton is flanked by Hampden and Cromwell. These figures of ambition are firmly displaced in the following stanzas by an ethos of serene resignation defining the ideal aristocratic habitus of expressive reserve, but a habitus which is *reflected* in the peasantry. The absence of social emulation that imaginarily defines the Perdita-like aristocrat—because she need never claim to be any more than *what she is*—is translated into pastoral terms as the proposition that the noble makes a better peasant than the peasant. No one is more modest than Perdita, farther from the madding crowd, and this is the sense in which, generically speaking, the peasant stands for the nobleman. Gray's appropriation of this topos is not merely belated, however. Gray is not after all recommending an ethos of noble reserve to the *peasant,* despite the unambiguous praise for the "noiseless tenour" of peasant life. The poem does not really address the peasantry. While the noble habitus can be represented by the imperturbable and natural nobility of literary peasants, these peasants cannot at the same time be represented as miserably impoverished.[42] The peasants, in other words, cannot be both *literary* and real peasants. This fact is quite obvious in the rejected manuscript conclusion to the poem, where Gray attributes the noble rage buried in pastoral obscurity not to the peasantry but to himself:

> The thoughtless World to Majesty may bow
> Exalt the brave, & idolize Success
> But more to Innocence their Safety owe
> Than Power and Genius e'er conspired to bless
>
> And thou, who mindful of the unhonour'd Dead
> Dost in these Notes their artless Tale relate
> By Night & lonely Contemplation led
> To linger in the gloomy Walks of Fate
>
> Hark how the sacred Calm, that broods around
> Bids ev'ry fierce tumultous Passion cease
> In still small Accents whisp'ring from the Ground
> A grateful Earnest of eternal Peace
>
> No more with Reason & thyself at strife;
> Give anxious Cares & endless Wishes room
> But thro' the cool sequester'd Vale of Life
> Pursue the silent Tenour of thy Doom.

The manuscript attributes the "silent Tenour" to Gray himself, but the published line reads: "Dost in these Notes *their* artless Tale relate" (emphasis mine). It is as though Gray had momentarily forgotten that he is not himself a peasant. But what is at stake after all in an identification with the peasantry? Here again we must insist that the referent of these negotiations is *literary culture*. This point is much clearer in the context of Gray's revision of the conclusion, where resignation becomes resignation not to poverty but to *obscurity*. The revision corrects the illogic of deriving from the deprivations of peasant existence a program of resignation to the speaker's rather different "doom"; and so "anxious Cares and endless Wishes" are given a specific content relating to the desire for *literary* fame.

The rejected manuscript conclusion brings out somewhat more explicitly than the published version the consistent analogy in the *Elegy* between political and literary ambition, between Cromwell and Milton, and conversely between the obscurity of the peasantry and the lack of literary fame. For this reason we can be relatively certain that the prospect of a "mute, inglorious Milton" focuses the largest and most intense anxiety in the poem. At this point we find ourselves disembarked upon the terrain of some traditional interpretations of the poem, which take as the premise of their readings the subjectivity of the poetic persona, whose "melancholy" suggests at once the inevitability of death and the tragedy of literary obscurity. This literary subjectivity is really the final product of the poem's composition (in its successive versions) and not at all the basis of that composition. The poem discovers this melancholy subject as the solution to its intractable problems, and hence the specular eye of the first stanza is refashioned in the final version into the pastoral poet who so oddly languishes in the countryside merely to die and be remembered as of that world and yet not of it. Here it might be easy to provide the motive of the melancholy, the reason for its convergence upon mourning, by invoking the convenient narrative of Gray's frustrated poetic ambitions (in the phrase Matthew Arnold liked so much, "he never spoke out").[43] But this argument reads a retrospective judgment upon Gray's production into the literary melancholy of the poem, as though Gray never wrote again, or as though he were not famous in his own time. I propose to read the surprising emergence of the melancholy poetic subjectivity at the end of the poem rather differently. The purpose of such a reading is not to reject the relevance of "poetic ambition," frustrated or otherwise, as a motive but to place that motive in relation to the "Ambition" already extensively thematized in the poem. What one is able to explain within this frame of argument is not Gray's attempt to write his personal frustrations, whatever they may be, into figurative or narrative terms, but the very ambivalence about social emulation that works itself out through and with reference to the conditions of literary production. For what characterizes the melancholy poet of the later stanzas is not simply acquiescence in, or resentment against, the frustration of ambition, but the contradiction between emulation (or ambition) and its *systematic self-repression*.

The published version of the poem thus effects a reconstellation of the

Elegy's generic terms, submitting the looseness of the locodescriptive lyric to the order of a pastoral narrative. Further, the construction of the melancholy poet as both subject and object of writing reorients the process of repression to bring to the fore the relation between literary fame and obscurity, while allowing the relation of wealth and poverty to recede into the background. The imagined death of the poet functions obviously enough as the repressive agency producing resignation to obscurity as a metonymic corrollary of resignation to death ("No farther seek his merits to disclose"). Yet one wants to observe how peculiar this scenario really is. Gray derives his concluding narrative without doubt from the poem he most frequently echoes in the *Elegy,* Milton's *Lycidas,* a poem whose argument is premised upon the causal relation, in Milton's anxious view, between the death of Edward King "ere his prime" and the foreclosure of fame, the very anxiety which constructs Edward King as the prototype of the "mute, inglorious Milton." Gray's melancholy poet is for this reason, and for no other, a "youth." Milton's grief is provoked by a strong identification with the dead Lycidas, an identification that sidetracks the poem almost immediately into the fantasized scenario of Milton's own death and funeral. Gray ends his poem here, where Milton begins:

> So may some gentle Muse
> With lucky words favor my destined Urn
> And as he passes turn
> And bid fair peace be to my sable Shroud.

Milton's solution to the problem of premature death is to place Lycidas at the threshold between life and death as the "genius of the shore," thus reassuring himself that he will not cross this threshold before he has accomplished the work that will gain him an "immortality of fame." The "uncouth swain" who shuffles off the coil of mortal thoughts is recreated by Gray as the "hoary-headed swain" who recounts the death of the alterego rustic poet. In that sense Gray may be said to identify more completely than Milton with the figure of Edward King. Gray's extension of the Miltonic scenario is surprisingly more complex than *Lycidas* itself; it requires a multiplication of Lycidean figures ("Thee," "swain," and "kindred spirit") as a means of shuttling between its imaginary temporal moments:

> For thee, who mindful of th' unhonour'd Dead
> Dost in these lines their artless tale relate
> If chance, by lonely contemplation led,
> Some kindred Spirit shall inquire thy fate,
>
> Haply some hoary-headed Swain may say . . .
>
> (93–97)

If the immediately following lines are caught in the abyssal trap of having to quote the swain on the death of the poet who is himself writing the lines the swain speaks, this instability of reference follows predictably from the problematic contradictions of the earlier stanzas.[44] The dead poet addressed as the projection of Gray's own self is imagined to speak from the grave just as the buried gem is imagined to shine in its unfathomed cave. It should be evident that Gray does not, as does Milton, express directly a fear of death. On the contrary, death is the signifier of an attractive self-repression (self-burial), an almost successful repression of a subject who yet leaves behind the trace of his repression in the form of a somewhat lengthy epitaph. As the sole remainder and reminder of the rustic poet's life and work, the graven epitaph is the means by which Gray's very belated deployment of pastoral is fused with the complex structure of Milton's elegy. The narrative that results brings the conditions of literary production into relation with the orders of social distinction by foregrounding in an egregious parenthesis the fact of literacy as a requisite to the reception of that text: "Approach and read (for thou canst read) the lay." Now this parenthetical admission has in a certain sense been implicit all along in Gray's choice of exemplary figures of ambition from the realms of politics and poetry, in retrospect an overdetermined linkage. While it may be no more than banally true that the conditions of peasant existence must prevent the rise of any one of them to power or wealth, the same conditions do not obtain with regard to literary production. *Only death* can silence Milton in the imaginary narrative future of *Lycidas,* but the "mute, inglorious Milton" of the *Elegy* is silenced by what constitutes *muteness*—not an inability to speak but an inability to read or write. Hence Gray dissociates himself from his "hoary-headed swain" by reclaiming his higher social station, by reasserting his position within (at the least) a literate culture. If it can nevertheless be said that Gray also casts himself as the "mute, inglorious Milton" of the *Elegy* by burying his poetic alter ego "ere his prime" in the country churchyard, this figure continues to resemble the Perdita-like character of the aristocrat-as-peasant in knowing somehow, as if congenitally, how to read and write. On this complex and subtly disingenuous mystification, we can do no better than to quote another of Shakespeare's country folk, Constable Dogberry: "To be a well-favoured man is a gift of fortune, but to read and write comes by nature." Such natural literacy betrays the rustic poet's class origins just as much as Perdita's ingenuous blush; it is the fact of literacy—writing as a mnemonic technology—that prevents the poet from being entirely lost in pastoral obscurity.

The absence of a class or institutional place of origin for Gray's solitary thus allows that figure to stand as an aristocrat in relation to the peasantry, and as a peasant in relation to the ruling class:

Here rests his head upon the lap of earth
A youth to fortune and to fame unknown.
Fair Science frowned not on his humble birth,
And Melancholy marked him for her own.

(117–20)

Where, after all, does this youth come from, if he ends up in the country churchyard? The very social dislocation of the figure is surely what determines his subject position as at once humble and *privileged:* "Fair Science frowned not on his humble birth." Gray's melancholy poet cannot be reduced to a projection of his writing anxieties, however large they may be; and the figure of the solitary is in fact already a convention of mid-century poetry. John Sitter names this convention "literary loneliness," and takes it to signify a recoil from public life and the large historical concerns so conspicuously foregrounded in post-Restoration literature.[45] While it may suffice to Sitter's argument to present this circumstance as merely a reaction to the perceived tumult of what Habermas calls the "bourgeois public sphere," this explanation is slightly misleading if it suggests that mid-century poets have themselves withdrawn from that sphere by disdaining certain "public" genres or themes.[46] The figure of the solitary expresses ambivalence about the emergence of the public sphere, but that expression itself belongs to the public sphere by virtue of being literary, by virtue of being *published*. This is the very paradox that Gray's poem inscribes by fetishizing the igorance of the peasant as a kind of covert nobility, by having it both ways. "Where ignorance is bliss, 'tis folly to be wise!"

What we shall now be able to demonstrate is the fact that such a strategy scarcely makes sense for either the aristocratic or the peasant writer (and we shall be introduced to one of the latter presently). Gray's solitary belongs neither to the aristocracy nor to the peasantry. If it now seems that by process of elimination the homeless solitary is in some sense "bourgeois," this identification is not at all simple. English society of the mid-eighteenth century is characterized structurally by a gradient of middle classes who identity themselves in a variety of conflicting and mutually exclusive ways (by economic, professional, political, religious affiliation) but not yet as a bourgeoisie. Even within the "middling sort" the difference between, for example, the merchant and the scholar is crucial with respect to self-identification. We can also expect that strategies of self-identification are intrinsically unstable wherever a claim is made to upward mobility of any sort, real or imagined; and that therefore the only identification of the bourgeoisie as yet available to the bourgeois in general is precisely a lack of stable self-identification. In the absence of a fully articulated "political economy" which might describe the relation between wealth and power in terms of the social consanguinity of all property, the self-identification of classes is itself an arena of social struggle. Rather than broaden the scope of these generalizations any farther, I propose only to characterize the social order (along the lines suggested by Benedict Anderson) in such a way as to underline the immense social significance of polite letters as a transformative cultural force, an arena at once of upward mobility and of the cultural unification of the ruling classes.

The emergence of a "common reader," a literary "public," was by no means universally welcomed; it could be actively resisted as a process of cultural *degeneration*. The "quarrel between the ancients and the moderns," for example, registers the level of anxiety produced by increased vernacular literary production in the public sphere. It was quite possible to regard the tendency toward a cultural homogenization of the middle and upper classes as the degeneration of culture itself. Here we can begin to understand how Gray's substitution of "Hampden, Milton, and Cromwell" for the manuscript version's "Cato, Tully, and Caesar" might be said to stigmatize the transition from classical to vernacular literacy as a kind of revolutionary violence, indeed as the "bourgeois revolution" itself. While the allusion to the civil war may express Gray's "personal" contempt for the public, his desire to be considered a "gentleman," these terms are less idiosyncratic than they may at first seem. The very extremity of Gray's reaction argues that the redistribution of cultural capital is in a very real sense a revolutionary process. If the cultural capital represented by vernacular literacy signifies to some social groups the possibility of upward mobility, it can also signify the devaluation of the cultural capital possessed by other individuals or groups. In Gray's famous ambivalence about publication, one sees how it is possible for polite letters to react *against itself*. Such moments in Gray, and in mid-century literary culture, represent a backward-flowing eddy in the stream of literary culture, as that stream broadens into the bourgeois public sphere. The cultural capital which in its "public" place becomes the means of upward mobility thus reappears within Gray's literary landscape as the occasion for a kind of vertiginous homelessness, for the dislocation of the melancholy poet who imaginarily identifies with the displaced aristocrat of Renaissance pastoral.

In a sense we have only taken rather literally the fact that the subject of withdrawal in Gray's poem is a poet. If the authorial subject has determinate relations to the institutions of cultural capital, one must say that the "Eton" Gray elsewhere apostrophized as a "distant prospect" is only just over the horizon of the *Elegy's* landscape. At this point my reading of the internal argument of the *Elegy* necessarily rejoins my reading of the poem's reception in stressing the essential rightness of Barbauld's revision of

Gray's poem in order to foreground the institution absent from the scene of the poem. She writes after the moment at which the solitary's cultural significance has peaked, and from a class position embracing unequivocally the effects of vernacular literacy. The difference between Eton and Warrington Academy, or between classical and vernacular literacy, marks two different and incompatible strategies of social emulation. For Barbauld there is no repression of ambition and equally no simple identification with the ethos of the gentleman. The withdrawal of Gray's solitary, by contrast, acts out the contradiction between social emulation and the idealized aris-tocratic habitus of expressive reserve by embodying that contradiction in the pastoral topos of aristocrat-as-peasant.

The imitation by would-be gentlemen such as Gray of what Norbert Elias calls the "drive-economy" of the nobility—all those norms of civility which function historically to sublimate competitive violence within the nobility—is thus demonstrably bourgeois.[47] The textual enactment of an imitative ethos belongs to a continuum of imitative social behaviors expressed most conspicuously, of course, by Gray's disdain for publication, as though he still belonged to a manuscript culture of courtly poets, but also by his disinclination to accept money for his poems, even though Dodsley, his publisher, made large sums printing them.[48] To dismiss these facts to the category of the anecdotal is to misjudge the real political force of polite letters. Gray's ambivalent relation to the public sphere is the exact inversion of Barbauld's resentment of the privilege of social superiors, but it unquestionably also participates in that resentment as a reaction formation. In the early modern period, contempt for the culture of the vulgar was expressed by the development of a new "humanist" High Culture, and took the linguistic form of a renewed valuation of classical literary production. This valuation was so universally assumed that Waller could write as late as the mid-seventeenth century, "poets that lasting marble seek,/Must carve in Latin, or in Greek."[49] The vernacular *Hochsprache,* because it both embodied and eventually overcame this inferiority complex, finally undermined the conditions for continued production in the classical languages, and by the middle of the eighteenth century there ceased to be a readership for such writing. At the same time the classical languages continued to define the most elite educational capital as against the actual social importance of the languages disseminated in the coffeehouses and the vocational academies.

The moment we are examining under high magnification here can be described in the terms formulated by Raymond Williams as a complex overlapping of "residual" and "emergent" cultural formations. The technique of linguistic normalization employed by Gray in the *Elegy* clearly negotiates a certain emergence, but its "residual" pastoralism also resists (as it happens, unsuccessfully) the very linguistic properties which made the poem uniquely *popular*. In most of his poetry, Gray was concerned to develop a rather different linguistic practice, a "poetic diction," which replicated *within the vernacular* a distinction like the distinction between classical and vernacular literacy. This distinction could be articulated as an essential difference between poetry and prose, which Gray describes and celebrates in his famous letter to Richard West:

> As to the matter of stile, I have this to say: the language of the age is never the language of poetry; except among the French, whose verse, where the thought or image does not support it, differs in nothing from prose. Our poetry, on the contrary has a language peculiar to itself: to which almost everyone, that has written, has added something by enriching it with foreign idioms and derivatives: Nay sometimes words of their own composition or invention. Shakespeare and Milton have been great creators in this way; and no one more licentious than Pope or Dryden, who perpetually borrow expressions from the former.[50]

But the difference celebrated in this letter was resisted by some of his readers, among them of course Johnson, who condemned it as the "refinements of subtlety and the dogmatism of learning." Only the *Elegy* was exempt from the reservation Johnson expressed about much the rest of Gray's poetry: "Gray thought his language more poetical as it was more remote from common use." Perhaps the most important fact for us to recognize now about the historical situation of the *Elegy* is that it is a linguistically anomalous production for Gray. The poet acknowledged this fact himself in disdaining his poem's popularity, its very commonness. In 1765 he remarked "with some acrimony" to his friend Dr. Gregory, "that the *Elegy* owed its popularity entirely to its subject, and that the public would have received it as well if it had been written in prose."[51] But to say that the poem was misread as though it were prose is to admit the degree to which the language of the poem is already the language of vernacular prose; it is to recognize the degree to which the poem normalizes its classical and Renaissance sources. The transparency of the *Elegy's* language to its commonplaces, the immediacy of its intelligibility, is not a measure, then, of public misperception so much as it is of the very pressure of the common language on the language of the poem. The place of the *Elegy* in the world of cultural production is just at the intersection of two opposing forces: the homogenizing forces expressed by the commonplaces and the common language;

and the differentiating forces expressed by the nostalgic evocation of the pastoral genre and the valorized withdrawal from the public sphere. The fact that the *Elegy's* language failed to be perceived, in Gray's own terms, as "the language of poetry" situates it where these forces have canceled themselves out, where poetic diction *fails to appear.* This unique place of rest, the place which is the poem, renders no reader illiterate by "refinements of subtlety and the dogmatism of learning." To every common reader is given the pleasure of the commonplace and the common language, and at the same time, the pleasure of withdrawal from the (urban) place—the scene of Ambition, Luxury, and Pride—where this language is formed as the product of a specific kind of struggle, the agon of social mobility. The *Elegy* is thus at once peculiarly accessible to a wide reading public at the same time that its narrative reinscribes this access as innate rather than acquired. The very attractiveness of its pastoralizing narrative effaces the struggle for cultural capital and propels the reader into that imaginary identification which, as Bourdieu has pointed out, continually misrecognizes bourgeois culture as a kind of "aristocracy of culture." The cultural entitlement that for Gray is defined by classical literacy, by his immense learning, is thus acquired by his readers at a *discount,* at the cost only of acquiring the vernacular literacy requisite to reading the poem.

If the difference between poetic diction and prose diction reproduces the effect of the distinction between classical and vernacular literacy, this difference has enormous significance for the process of canon formation, since the very possibility of canonical English prose depends upon the outcome of the negotiation between these two kinds of linguistic capital. The elision by which, in the two previous centuries, all literature was poetry and only poetry was literature, is no longer possible if the bourgeois sociolect is increasingly grounded in paradigms derived from prose, especially novelistic prose.[52] Gray understood that the distinction between poetry and prose was at stake in the popularity of the *Elegy,* but that distinction was at stake only because it had the force of a social distinction. This does not mean that the distinction between poetry and prose had never before corresponded to a distinction between high and low culture (as it does certainly in Shakespeare's plays), but that this difference was not a difference between the *language* of poetry and the *language* of prose. Renaissance prose remained as open to neologism, archaism, complex figuration, and foreign borrowing as Renaissance poetry. The same cannot be said for eighteenth-century prose, which defined itself against these very strategies, as a normalized national language. The social function served by the institution of a vernacular literary curriculum in the schools exerted considerable pressure on the process of canonical selection, since paradigms of grammatical speech could just as easily, if not more easily, be derived from prose narrative as from poetry. If certain genres of prose (the novel, for example) were ever to become canonical, the full implementation of such a judgment would have to wait for the development of a category of writing that would include both poetry and fictional prose. This category was of course to be "literature," but the important point is that "literature" in mid-century England did not yet refer to fictive or imaginative writing, as Raymond Williams is careful to remind us in his invaluable consideration of this category:

> Literature was still primarily reading ability and reading experience, and this included philosophy, history, and essays as well as poems. Were the new eighteenth-century novels "literature"? That question was first approached, not by definition of their mode or content, but by reference to the standards of "polite" or "humane" learning. Was drama literature? This question was to exercise successive generations, not because of any substantial difficulty but because of the practical limits of the category.[53]

Literature so defined corresponded in the bourgeois public sphere to the kind of literary producer known as the "man of letters." We can do no better here than to quote that most exemplary man of letters, David Hume, for a sense of what "literature" meant in mid-century England. The text is a letter to Gilbert Elliot of 1757, and the subject is the distinction of Scottish writers:

> Is is not strange that , at a time when we have lost our princes, our parliaments, our independent government,—even the presence of our chief nobility; are unhappy, in our accent and pronunciation; speak a very corrupt dialect of the tongue we make use of,—is it not strange, I say, that, in these circumstances we should really be the people most distinguished for literature in Europe?[54]

Hume's remark grasps with his usual precision the ambiguity of "literature," at once the vehicle in the schools for inculcating a practice of standardized *speech,* but also the medium by which the social limitations of an incorrect dialect, or a low class accent, might be circumvented. Hume's claim in this letter is interestingly framed by a portrait of his fellow countryman and "peasant poet," William Wilkie, one of the mid-century's many peasant poets.[55] Wilkie was the author of a pseudo-classical "Epigoniad," as noncanonical a poem as one might ever hope to rediscover. With considerable delight, Hume recounts the story of how his friend

Jemmy Russel brought an Englishman, a Dr. Roebuck, to visit Wilkie. Roebuck found the peasant poet in his fields, much besmirched with the grime of his labor, but happy to discourse with his visitor upon the Greek poets:

> Dr. Roebuck, who had scarce understood his rustic English, or rather his broad Scotch, immediately comprehended him, for his Greek was admirable; and on leaving him, he could not forbear expressing the highest admiration to Russel, that a clown, a rustic, a mere hind, such as he saw this fellow was, should be possessed of so much erudition.

Of course the point of this anecdote is chauvinistic, justly so; but we may derive from it another moral, with reference to the situation of Gray's mute, inglorious Miltons, who write no Epigoniads. Hume's peasant poet knows very well that what really counts as cultural capital is knowledge of Greek and Latin. Vernacular literacy appears not at all in this story; and yet it is writing in *English* which supports Hume's larger claim for his countrymen's distinction in "literature." It is the emergence of vernacular literacy which brings the category of "literature" to the forefront of the public sphere, and names the "man of letters" as its producer.

Jerome Christensen has recently argued for a reading of Hume's literary career that would allow us to recognize the appearance in the eighteenth century of an order of literature which temporarily canonized figures who have since been displaced from that order by the emergence of a much narrower category of literature: the "imaginative" genres—poetry, novels, and plays. Christensen points out that Hume very consciously "sought to create a canon that would have the classical, particularly Ciceronian virtues of comprehensiveness and independence."[56] The fact that Cicero still belongs to the canon of "classical literature," while Hume no longer belongs to the canon of English literature is a peculiarity of the history of canon formation which the present critique of the canon remains unable to see at all. But its consequences are immense, and testify to the larger point of this book, that canonical *forms,* the categories of textual appropriation and reproduction in their institutional sites, operate as mechanisms of selection before individuals exercise judgments, of whatever kind.

To summarize, then: between the sixteenth and the nineteenth centuries three such canonical forms appear: (1) *poetry,* which privileges the texts of classical literacy; (2) *literature* (in the general sense) or "polite letters," which privileges writing in the vernacular; and (3) *literature* (in the restricted sense) or "imaginative" writing, which privileges poetry, novels, and plays. In retrospect, it seems evident that Gray's resistance to being

identified as a "man of letters" situates his own literary production between the order of "poetry" and the order of "literature" in the general
sense. His valuation of "poetic diction" looks back to the Renaissance canonical form of poetry. Nevertheless one must immediately qualify that
statement by insisting that poetic diction is not simply archaic: it represents
a *reaction* against polite letters as the emergent discourse of the bourgeois
public sphere. In another sense such a reaction is not reactionary at all. It
presages the effort of literature at a later moment to distinguish itself from
the very kinds of writing which defined polite letters. The problem of poetic
diction is, after all, the problem of the cultural *distinction* of poetry, and in
that sense the argument for poetic diction argues for the greater cultural
capital of poetic forms within the forms of writing. If the very capaciousness of eighteenth-century "literature" implicitly privileged the language
of prose, Gray responded to that development by reworking the vernacular
precisely in order to *estrange it from itself,* to invent a kind of vernacular
Latin. But this is also a question of whether and how literature comes to be
estranged from the vernacular reading public, whose passion for novels
calls into question the traditional hierarchy of literary forms and genres.
This is a question which I should like to approach now by considering
Wordsworth's critique of Gray's poetic diction, and Coleridge's response to
that critique.

Lingua Communis and the Vernacular Canon

> Gray was at the head of those who, by their reasonings, have at-
> tempted to widen the space of separation betwixt Prose and Metrical
> composition, and was more than any other man curiously elaborate
> in the structure of his own poetic diction.
>
> —WORDSWORTH, Preface to *Lyrical Ballads* (1802)

In their respective engagements with Gray's *Elegy,* both Barbauld and
Empson gain entry to the poem at the level of the mise-en-scène, by reference to an absence—the school. The absence of the school from the poem
has perhaps been more than compensated by the importance of the poem
to the school, by its "canonization." The absence of poetic diction from the
Elegy is harder to see; it is visible as the unexpected transparency of the
poem's language at the historical moment of its composition, the moment
of a reactive "poetic diction." The fact that the hoary-headed swain and the
melancholy poet speak exactly the same language, devoid of provincialism
or obscurity, attests to the power of the new bourgeois sociolect to overcome resistance even within the generic stronghold of that resistance—the
pastoral. Donald Davie and others have argued that eighteenth-century

poetry was for the most part very close to prose in its diction, and that the practice of diction was largely confined to the "descriptive" genres, including among them the increasingly archaic genre of pastoral.[57] By the time Johnson delivers his very negative judgment of pastoral in his *Rambler* essay, the genre appears to elicit a question about the proper language of poetry which would scarcely have been conceivable in the Renaissance:

> Other writers, having the mean and despicable condition of a shepherd always before them, conceive it necessary to degrade the language of pastoral, by obsolete terms and rustic words, which they very learnedly call Dorick, without reflecting, that they thus becomes authors of a mingled dialect, which no human being ever could have spoken, that they may as well refine the speech as the sentiments of their personages, and that none of the inconsistencies which they endeavor to avoid, is greater than that of joining elegance of thought with coarseness of diction.[58]

What Johnson considered "coarseness of diction"—the archaism that degrades Spenser's *Shepheardes Calendar* as well as the contemporary productions that follow the Spenserian model—is the equally "learned" complement of that artificial elevation of diction which in Johnson's own time was likely to characterize descriptive/topographical genres, and which descends stylistically from the idiosyncratic English of Milton rather than from the standardized prose of eighteenth-century letter-writing. Hence Johnson's condemnation of Milton's *Lycidas* looks like a condemnation of poetic diction before it can be said that pastoral (or any poetry) is peculiarly marked by such diction. Johnson's censure extends to any diction which deviates from what Davie calls "the tone of the center, a sort of urbanity," that is, the standard London-based vernacular which authorizes a single diction for both poetry and prose.

Davie makes the further point that "the tie between the writing of poetry and the writing of letters makes it possible, and necessary, to speak of Johnson's diction as bourgeois."[59] The descriptive/topographical genres stage the conflict between homogenizing and differentiating sociolinguistic forces by removing the site of linguistic practice to the country, while claiming at the same time a privileged overview of the social order, a universalizing perspective. This perspective always has a tendency to drift nostalgically toward the vantage of the landed aristocracy, who still hold sway from their country estates. But when the topographical genres incorporate the topoi of the pastoral genre, with its simple transposing of the noble/peasant distinction upon a far more complex social geography, a surprising redirection of this nostalgia occurs: the return of pastoral in the later eighteenth century makes it possible to reground normative linguistic practice in what is thought to be the *actual* language of the peasantry. This is indeed what happens in the "antipastoral" of these later decades, and it is why the topographical genres never cease to be, in Empson's phrase, "covert pastoral." The reaction against the bourgeois sociolect that gives rise to poetic diction is therefore subject to another reaction that takes the form of a literalized pastoral diction; such a diction is described in John Aiken's 1772 essay on pastoral poetry as the folk source of the recognizably popular form of the ballad: "The rude original pastoral poetry of our country furnishes the first class of the popular pieces called ballads. Their language is the language of nature, simple and unadorned."[60] The imitation of rustic speech no longer attempts to reproduce the characteristics of dialect, then, but posits an aboriginal simplicity of rural language which has no real historical basis, and which can only be produced by imposing a new "simplicity" upon the now standardized language of polite letters. The literalization of pastoral speech is thus an unacknowledged idealization of the bourgeois sociolect; only in this context does Wordsworth's turn to such a simplified speech in the Preface to *Lyrical Ballads* appear to be something other than a mysterious and total rupture with eighteenth-century practice:

> The principal object, then, which I proposed to myself in these Poems was to choose incidents and situations from common life, and to relate and describe them, as far as was possible, in a selection of language really used by men. . . . Low and rustic life was generally chosen, because in that condition, the essential passions of the heart find a better soil in which they can attain their maturity, are less under restraint, and speak a plainer, more emphatic language.[61]

A. D. Harvey has reminded us in his *English Literature in a Changing Society,* that despite the claims of his theory, Wordsworth's poetic practice was scarcely anomalous in its literary milieu. Wordsworth himself, in the Advertisement to the 1798 *Lyrical Ballads,* invokes the models of Burns and Cowper. Harvey argues that "the point Wordsworth was making was not that he was the first to have written inartificial poetry, but that he was the first deliberately and systematically to avoid poetic diction."[62] In contrast to the Preface, the Advertisement describes his linguistic experiment as an attempt to "ascertain how far the language of conversation in the middle and lower classes of society is adapted to the purposes of poetic pleasure." The substitution of rustic language in the Preface for that of the middle and lower classes gives us another version of pastoral, which functions as the means to produce a linguistic differentiation apparently the inverse of poetic diction's complication of polite speech. The fact that Wordsworth simplifies rather than complicates the common language nonetheless does not move his project generically beyond its precursors, however initially alienating his more rigorous linguistic experiments happen to be. Like Gray, he wishes to produce a different language—but by simplification rather than by complication. Not surprisingly, when Coleridge comes to examine Wordsworth's linguistic practice in *Lyrical Ballads,* he cannot detect its difference from the language of an ordinary, educated, middle-class person:

> To this I reply: that a rustic's language, purified from all provincialism and grossness and so far reconstructed as to be made consistent with the rules of grammar . . . will not differ from the language of any other man of common-sense, however learned or refined he may be, except insofar as the notions which the rustic has to convey are fewer and more indiscriminate.[63]

Coleridge identifies the logical crux of Wordsworth's argument as the principle of "selection" or "purification," which is supposed of itself to "form a distinction far greater than would at first be imagined, and will entirely separate the composition from the vulgarity and meanness of ordinary life." Wordsworth gives no example of the principle of selection at work, and only the vaguest sense of what is actually subtracted from the language really spoken by men ("purified indeed from what appears to be its real defects, from all lasting and rational causes of dislike or disgust"). Coleridge fairly questions whether this process can be undertaken upon any other basis than the real social difference produced by a literary education: "For the very power of making the selection implies the previous possession of the language selected. Or where can the poet have lived?" This poet is as mysteriously homeless as Gray's elegist. If Wordsworth really means by "selection" only the process of subtracting provincialisms, dialect expressions, or grammatical errors from the language of peasants, then one merely arrives again at the vernacular standard, the language of educated Londoners. Coleridge goes on to correct Wordsworth's slip by arguing that "For real we must substitute *ordinary,* or *lingua communis.*" But this correction does not explain why Wordsworth substituted "rustic" for "common" language in the first place.

If the new language of poetry turns out to be nothing other than the language of the educated middle-class, a distinction without a difference, this sort of distinction complicates another important article in Wordsworth's manifesto: "There neither is, nor can be, any essential difference between the language of prose and the language of metrical composition." The distinction between poetry and prose depends in only a minor way on the fact of meter, which Wordsworth recommends for its superaddition of pleasure to the matter of poetry, and secondarily for its capacity to moderate the effects of strong emotions. These virtues do not in themselves seem sufficient to claim for poetry a higher status than prose, but Wordsworth does implicitly make such a claim by transferring the hierarchical burden of the distinction onto the character of the poet, whose refined sensibility reproduces the aristocrat's, but in the register of sensibility alone. These claims are very well known and I will not rehearse them here. I propose instead to set them in a generic context by reading the poet of the Preface as the protagonist of a submerged pastoral narrative. This poet is "distinguished from other men" but not linguistically; he moves among them as though he were one of them, speaking their language, and he only signals his difference by the choice of meter, the signal or signature of the poetic sensibility. Such a narrative not only reinscribes the major topos of Renaissance pastoral—the poet as peasant—it engages as well the specific problematic of Gray's *Elegy:* the socially distinct character of the poet threatened with effacement or obscurity in the very identification of his language with the language of the rustics. Thus Wordsworth fears that his readers "will look round for poetry, and will be induced to inquire by what species of courtesy these attempts can be permitted to assume that title." The threat of *indifference* is necessarily expressed as the failure of a social distinction, but this fact only brings to the surface the same fear that underlies the topos of the "mute, inglorious Milton." For Wordsworth to fail in producing what his readers will recognize as "poetry" would indeed condemn him to the state of being mute and inglorious. The narrative motifs of the *Elegy* are close enough to Wordsworth's own at this point to undermine Wordsworth's stigmatizing of Gray as the representative of an overthrown poetic practice. If the Preface secretly reproduces the *Elegy's* narrative structure, Wordsworth can only acknowledge this fact obliquely by singling out Gray's sonnet on the death of Richard West as his chief example of obsolete poetic diction. The Preface's epitaph for poetic diction stands in for that other epitaphic poem, the *Elegy* itself, as its *misplaced* gravestone.

Coleridge is again the best critic of Wordsworth's Preface, because his quite logical objections to the Preface have the effect of exposing the structure of Wordsworth's argument as a narrative logic, specifically the logic of covert pastoral. Further, by pointing up the arbitrariness of Wordsworth's assignment of some lines of Gray's sonnet to poetic diction (1–5; 9–12), some to the language of prose (6–8; 13–14), he is able to argue for the desirability of a poetic diction purged of the hackneyed "schoolboy im-age[s]" such as are supposed to blemish Gray's sonnet: "I write in meter because I am about to use a language different from that of prose." This language is intrinsically and justifiably elevated even in such particulars as the choice, for the sake of meter, between the voiced and unvoiced "e" in "beloved." The concrete linguistic object is reinstated as the bearer of dif-ference, and the character of the poet is reduced to logical irrelevance; it was after all only the displacement of a difference which has no other mode of being than the written text. I would hasten to add, however, that while the mythology of the poetic character has an obvious social force, it is only the force lent it by the preexistent social distinction between aristocrat and commoner. All social differentiation, even the most narcissistic of small dif-ferences, continues to be modeled on this distinction, and in this way the back door is left open for pastoral. It has been worth briefly recapitulating the dialogue between Wordsworth and Coleridge in order to make just this point: In the absence of a poetic diction, the distinction between poetry and prose must be maintained elsewhere, as an assertion of the difference em-bodied in the poetic sensibility. But that the distinction requires such a speculative theory to defend against the threat of indifference implies that the generic differences between poetry and prose have already been seri-ously eroded; and indeed, as A. D. Harvey has shown, poetic production at the dawn of the century is increasingly modified generically by the copre-sence of prose genres, prime among them the Gothic novel. Wordsworth's earlier poetry is in retrospect generically homogeneous with the poems of Cowper or Campbell, and the real generic break occurs with the Goth-icized poetic narratives of Scott and Byron. In Bakhtin's terms, Romantic poetry then becomes subject to the pressure of novelization, a pressure against which Wordsworth reacts by a programmatic co-optation of the language of prose rather than by an intensified poetic diction.

It should be possible to demonstrate now that the distinction between poetic diction and the *lingua communis* is really determined by a generic distinction—between poetic genres and prose genres. The fact that this dis-tinction was conceived by Wordsworth in exclusively linguistic terms is the index of a crisis, specifically a crisis in the history of vernacular canon for-mation. For the first time poetic genres and prose genres are comparable as *literary* genres; this point is immediately evident when we consider how difficult it is in the eighteenth century to conceptualize prose genres at all. One recalls in this context Johnson's attempt to conceive the fictions we now call "novels" under the category of "comic romance," a generic desig-nation that would derive them from the vernacular entertainments of the late medieval courts; these entertainments were subjected to High Culture norms (that is poetic norms) in the early modern period. Hence Johnson can argue that such fictions are "to be conducted by the rules of comic po-etry."[64] The difficulty of conceptualizing prose genres is intelligible in light of the fact that genres had always historically been categories of poetics: the earliest classical genres were simply distinctions between kinds of meter. New generic categories of prose are conceived in the later eighteenth century only because a sufficient amount of pressure exists to produce such categories after the fact, after they have already become paradigmatic for the *sermo urbanus* of both the bourgeoisie and the aristocracy.

We are now in a position to look at a simple fact about Wordsworth's Preface, with some understanding of why this fact is difficult to place in its proper context: The "real language of men" and the "language of prose" are *equivalent terms* in Wordsworth's argument, but they are by no means obviously or necessarily the same thing. "Prose" is a practice of writing, and it is only the bourgeois gentleman's learned error to think that conversation is prose. Wordsworth's embrace of prose as the language really spoken by men represents a compromise between his distaste for a clichéd poetic diction and his disdain for the taste of the public that neglects canonical works in favor of ephemeral novels, plays, and novel-like narrative poems:

> For a multitude of causes, unknown to former times, are now acting with a combined force to blunt the discriminating powers of the mind, and unfitting it for all voluntary exertion to reduce it to a state of almost savage torpor. The most effective of these causes are the great national events which are daily taking place, and the increasing accumulation of men in cities, where the uniformity of their occupations produces a craving for extraordinary incident, which the rapid communication of intelligence hourly gratifies. To this tendency of life and manners the literature and theatrical exhibitions of the country have conformed themselves. The invaluable works of our elder writers, I had almost said of Shakespeare and Milton, are driven into neglect by frantic novels, sickly and stupid German Tragedies, and deluges of idle and extravagant stories in verse.

The terms of Wordsworth's sociological analysis are in some respects superior to the terms of his poetics. The relation between the canonical form of literature (in the narrow sense) and the social constitution of the literate public appears to Wordsworth as a crisis, as the threatened disappearance of an audience for High Culture productions; a Milton unread is a mute, inglorious Milton. But the hypothesis of a vanishing audience for canonical poetry is better understood as a misrecognition of a division within the reading public—between an elite readership for High Culture works (for whom poetic works still have the greatest cultural status) and a larger general reading public for whom the novel becomes the primary object of literary consumption. The point, however, is that the *language* of the novel and the *language* of poetry are at this moment still virtually indistinct. It is this indistinction of language which Wordsworth unwittingly confirms in defending the language of prose, at the same time that he condemns the new reading public for neglecting poetry. When this new reading public appears, it becomes necessary to say that henceforth the domain of literary production is effectively cleft in two, and that some contemporary works will be *read differently* because they descend generically from High Canonical works. If we are rehearsing here the distinction between "serious" and "popular" literature, it should be emphasized that this distinction does not merely replicate the long-standing distinction between High Culture and Low Culture forms of writing; such a distinction was always available in the difference between the major poetic genres and, say, ballads, broadsides etc. What is new here is the distinction between serious and popular *literature*—a distinction between two bodies of writing which are alike in respect of being equally "fictional" or "imaginative," equally distinguishable from philosophy or history, but *unlike in value*. For the moment, this value distinction can be registered as the distinction between poetry and prose, a hierarchy of literary genres that concedes to poetry an unquestioned generic superiority. Yet it is the very failure of poetry to produce a definitive new *Hochsprache* on the basis of its generic superiority which will ultimately make it necessary to conceptualize a category of "literature" inclusive even of the novel. The same failure is the condition for the crisis-rhetoric which confronts the question of "what is poetry" not as a traditional problem of poetics but as a problem of linguistics, of poetry as a distinct language, the vernacular's own Latin.

If the prose genres continue to function paradigmatically to produce the standard vernacular, this does not mean that poetic diction is doomed to extinction as a peculiar written dialect which no one speaks. Coleridge understood very well that the life of this dialect was sustained by the schools, just as it was originally produced by the institutional lag between Latin and vernacular literacy. One cannot improve upon this analysis:

> this style of poetry which I have characterized above as translations of prose thoughts into poetic language had been kept up by, if it did not wholly arise from, the custom of writing Latin

verses and the great importance attached to these exercises in our public schools. Whatever might have been the case in the fifteenth century, when the use of the Latin tongue was so general among learned men that Erasmus is said to have forgotten his native language; yet in the present day it is not to be supposed that a youth can think in Latin, or that he can have any other reliance on the force or fitness of his phrases but the authority of the author. Consequently he must first prepare his thoughts and then pick out from Virgil, Horace, Ovid, or perhaps more compendiously, from his Gradus, halves and quarters of lines in which to embody them.[65]

Coleridge credits Wordsworth with suggesting this line of thought to him; and indeed, these remarks recover a genealogy of poetic diction far more accurate than the mythological narrative Wordsworth offers in his Appendix to *Lyrical Ballads,* and which backdates poetic diction to a prehistoric era. For whatever reasons, and no doubt they have their own interest, Wordsworth is not able in the Preface to acknowledge the institutional relations of the poet who is produced as a literate subject by the school; such a disavowal in its many subsequent forms has condemned literary history to misrecognize these relations as the mere taint of academicism clinging to lesser talents. In fact it does not seem possible to eradicate poetic diction so long as the poetic genres continue to claim generic superiority, and hence poetic diction can be resurrected as, for example, the inherent "difficulty" of modern poetry. In the same way the classroom practice of prose composition has now produced a prose diction in the form of an invidious distinction between the norms of writing and the norms of conversation. It is pointless at this date to deny that these linguistic effects are produced by anything other than the interaction of literary production with the pedagogy of the schools. The language of the school is always a *literary* language, the language produced by the formal study of canonical texts.

In retrospect we can say that the virtual indifference of poetic and prose diction in the earlier eighteenth century (Davie's ideal "purity of diction") represents a historically unique moment. Purity of diction requires the participation of nearly all writing genres in the forging of a standard vernacular, in other words, a linguistically homogeneous bourgeois public sphere. When the successful dissemination of the standard permits production in genres which have no canonical authorization, but which are nevertheless unimpeachable vehicles of polite speech, a canonical crisis arises in the form of an anxious discrimination of "serious" from "popular" writing. Wordsworth can conjure an apocalyptic scenario in which the works of Milton and Shakespeare are swallowed up in the sea of popular writing only because the distinction between serious and popular genres produces no corresponding linguistic differentiation within the reading public. The language of Radcliffe and Scott is as pure and correct as the language of the poets, but this condition does not obtain indefinitely. The division of literary production into "literature" and the genres which are by definition subliterary or nonliterary does eventually produce a corresponding linguistic distinction when genres are distributed by the curricula of the educational institution in order to separate them out according to the *levels* of the system. Already in the early nineteenth century certain "popular" works are relegated to the lower levels of the system, other "serious" works to the higher, and this sorting out across the vertical structure of the educational system, initially very modest, is gradually more marked over the succeeding century and a half.[66] As the school becomes the exclusive agent for the dissemination of High Canonical works, replacing the quasi-educational institutions, the coffeehouses, literary clubs, and salons of eighteenth-century literacy—the realm of the bourgeois public sphere— the prestige of literary works as cultural capital is assessed according to the *limit* of their dissemination, their relative exclusivity. When a finite set of genres becomes the supergenre of "literature," all canonical works can be regarded as exemplifying a language essentially different from the language spoken by "real men," namely, "literary language." But from the vantage of the *longue durée,* "literary language" is nothing other than the successor to poetic diction, the reduction of all literature to a written language which produces a difference in speech, a social distinction, among those who have access to this second language through the schools. The theory of "literary language" is indeed our poetics, even when that language appears in prose, as the "literariness" of literary prose. The fact that it is still possible to speak of the intrinsic difference between literary language and ordinary language is a measure of how successfully the conservators of literature have erased its origins even in the act of writing its history.

Chapter Three

Ideology and Canonical Form: The New Critical Canon

Doxa

The canons are falling
One by one
Including "le célèbre" of Pachelbel
The final movement of Franck's sonato for piano and violin.
How about a new kind of hermetic conservatism
And suffering withdrawal symptoms of same?
—JOHN ASHBERY, "The Tomb of Stuart Merrill"

In this chapter I would like to reconsider some consequences of the well-known revisionary judgments advanced in T. S. Eliot's criticism: his devaluation of Milton along with major Romantic and Victorian poets, and his revaluation of the seventeenth-century "metaphysical" poets. While it is obvious in historical retrospect that these judgments did not alter the canon nearly so definitively as might have seemed between the wars, Eliot's canonical reformation remains significant for having enabled both in England and in the United States the most important new literary pedagogies in the first half of the twentieth century, the first associated with the name of F. R. Leavis and *Scrutiny,* the second with the New Criticism. Despite the real differences between the more or less explicitly "ideological" tenets of these movements—Leavis's progressive but anti-Marxist critique of modernity, the New Critics' conservative advocacy of Christian, "agrarian" values—both set out from the same revisionist judgments about English literary history, for which the authority of Eliot as critical arbiter was constantly invoked.

The remarkable fact that the revaluation of certain figures in English literature could appear to legitimize politically incompatible doctrines confirms the position for which I have argued throughout this book, namely, that ideology cannot simply be read off from the "canon" itself, and that a positive or negative valuation of a work does not necessarily imply a corresponding affirmation or rejection of the "ideology" expressed in the work. The substantial area of agreement between the judgments of Leavis and the New Critics points to a deeper level of social determination underlying these judgments, a set of common social conditions. Viewed from this level, the two movements could be seen to provide different solutions to the same social or cultural problems. The surprising consensus about the necessity for a revaluation of established literary reputations in the years between the wars indicates not an ideological consensus per se, but the common perception of a crisis in the state of literary culture. Eliot's suggestion that traditional criticism had been seriously mistaken in its evaluative judgments displaced the perception of the crisis into the very *form* of the canon. I will argue that it was not any particular judgment which possessed the force of ideology, but (to use Eliot's own words) the "whole existing order" of the literary canon. It was the form of the canon in its totality which became the vehicle of "ideology" in critical discourse, since that totality could be made to signify either a certain perceived disorder of culture or (after the appropriate "revaluations") an alternative, more "ideal" order.

It is always a mistake, then, to read the history of canon formation as though individual acts of revaluation had specific and determinable ideological effects simply determined by the choice of authors revalued, as though the revaluation, say, of Donne, could somehow infuse literary culture with attitudes, beliefs, or values peculiar to Donne or his milieu. The question before us is rather how the revaluation of particular authors alters the set of terms by which literature as a whole, or what we now like to call the canon, is represented to its constituency, to literary culture, at a particular historical moment. The effects of ideology are generated around the conceptualization of literature itself, which is to say around the discursive/institutional form by means of which literary works are disseminated.

The reduction of ideology to doctrinal contents, and the attempt to read those contents into the particular canonical choices of literary critics such as Eliot, are mistakes which, as we have already seen, pervade current critiques of the canon. For that reason alone the ambitious reformation of the English literary canon between the wars should prove to be an interesting case study in the relation between ideology and the form of the canon. I shall be concerned in this chapter more with the New Criticism than with Leavis and the Leavisites; excellent case studies of the latter already exist by Francis Mulhern and Chris Baldick.[1] We may endorse at the outset of the present study Mulhern's and Baldick's insistence upon the Arnoldian derivation of the problem for which twentieth-century criticism attempted a solution. In Baldick's admirable formulation, "The general project of Arnold and his followers can be described as an attempt to replace the current dogmatic and explicit forms of ideological expression with the implicit and intuitive properties of literary sensibility" (228). This project, we may note in passing, was very different from the project of the vernacular canon in the century before Arnold's. As we saw in the last chapter, the revaluation of vernacular works in English as the equivalent of the Greek and Roman classics provided the emergent bourgeoisie with a means of emulating the cultural capital of the aristocratic and clerical estates. The project of installing a "literary sensibility" in the largest possible constituency was on the contrary intended to have the social function of neutralizing the very political ideologies which set the classes in opposition to one another. The literary sensibility was to unify the nation culturally just as Standard English was supposed to unify it linguistically. Of course the Arnoldian representation of literary culture could itself be construed as an "ideology," not least because the literary sensibility was always reappropriated in the schools as a means of enforcing the cultural distinction of the bourgeoisie. Nevertheless the fact that this ideology was deliberately opposed to "dogmatic and explicit forms of ideological expression" does not mean that its nature as ideology can be recovered simply by reducing literature itself to another form of dogmatic expression, as though literary works themselves expressed directly the interests of a class. To make this claim would be to misrecognize the specificity of literature as an ideological form, namely, its capacity in concrete institutional contexts to produce ideological effects *through form*. In that sense the example of literature tells against all notions of ideology which reduce it to positive statements of political content; indeed the major tradition in the theory of ideology has been concerned to develop just this point.

Arnold's tendency to regard literature as a substitute for religion thus needs to be read in the full recognition of how complex such a substitution was to be: literary *sensibility* takes the place of religious *belief*. Eliot pulls the Arnoldian project only slightly out of shape when he remarks in his later criticism that he "wants a literature that should be *unconsciously*, rather than deliberately and defiantly, Christian."[2] Such a statement coyly presupposes a society in which Christianity is so pervasive and dominant a belief-system as to require no explicit advocacy on the part of authors. I should like to characterize the relation between doctrine and literature in this (hypothetical) situation with reference to what Bourdieu calls "doxa," a state of belief preexistent both to orthodoxy and to heterodoxy:

[I]n the extreme case, that is to say, when there is a quasi-perfect correspondence between the objective order and the subjective principles of organization (as in ancient societies) the natural and social world appears as self-evident. This experience we shall call *doxa,* so as to distinguish it from an orthodox or heterodox belief implying awareness and recognition of the possibility of different or antagonistic beliefs.[3]

What is the relation between this complex of notions and the concept of ideology? It will be clear upon reflection that all ideology aspires to the condition of doxa but that doxa is condemned in the real world to complex relations with both orthodoxy and heterodoxy; the latter appears precisely to the extent that a society fails to achieve the universality of belief supposedly defining only primitive cultures. Not even feudal culture managed to establish Christianity as doxa, else there would have been no heresy in the Middle Ages. Bourdieu says that "the dominant classes have an interest in defending the integrity of doxa or, short of this, of establishing in its place the necessarily imperfect substitute, *orthodoxy*" (169). But the very difficulty which Bourdieu admits of drawing a line between the "field of opinion" and the "field of doxa" (as Bourdieu knows, "opinion" is one credible translation of doxa) guarantees the simultaneous emergence of both orthodoxy and heterodoxy; the latter always implies the "imperfection" of the former's capacity to substitute for doxa. If "ideology" can be located in the scheme of this analysis, it must refer to the noncoincident relation between doxa and orthodoxy, to the fact that what is *unquestioned* in the social-discursive realm does not correspond *exactly* to the doctrine or "opinion" that the dominant seek to impose upon the whole social order. Orthodoxy "aims, without ever entirely succeeding, at restoring the primal state of innocence of doxa," because it "exists only in the objective relationship which opposes it to heterodoxy" (169).

If these terms suggest a way of describing the Arnoldian project, they foreground within that project the difficult "substitutive" relation between "sensibility" and "belief." Were it possible simply to reduce sensibility to belief, then literature would indeed enter the "field of opinion" as orthodoxy. The fact that it does not suggests that this relation must be otherwise understood. Eliot's desire for a literature that is "unconsciously Christian" obviously places Christian belief in the position of doxa. If literature is unconsciously Christian, it serves no *dogmatic* function. It is merely redundant with respect to Christian belief. As a historical substitute for doxa, however, literature seems to stand in a relation of orthodoxy to beliefs that are *no longer dominant,* that is, literature stands as a testament to the absence of doxa. In this situation, the literary sensibility is free-floating, curiously deracinated in its relation to beliefs. Or—and we shall here propose another way of looking at the same situation—literature itself can be installed as a sensibility that performs the social function of doxa—producing a state of cultural homogeneity, of unquestioned belief—without ever requiring the "imperfect" supplement of orthodoxy, without specifying directly what these beliefs are. Precisely because sensibility is not the same thing as belief, it is never subject to decay into mere orthodoxy. What is required, however, in order for sensibility to serve the purpose of cultural unification is a means of exhibiting the fact that sensibility is really unanimous; and this was the meaning of that attempt between the wars to develop a consensus around the revaluation of certain writers in English literary history.

While such a consensus was never perfect, it was successful enough to support both Leavis's movement in England and the New Criticism in the United States. In retrospect the substitution of sensibility for belief appeared to replace the orthodoxy/heterodoxy complex of "ideological expressions" with a culture that would restore a social condition *like* doxa, but not consisting of specifiable "beliefs." The success of this replacement even depended upon how thoroughly literature could be made to resist translation into doctrine, a translation Cleanth Brooks called, in a revealing shibboleth of the New Criticism, the "heresy of paraphrase." It was only the thesis that this resistance itself constituted an orthodoxy of sorts (of a special sort) that brought sensibility into the "field of opinion," and thus called into question (*as* orthodoxy) the canonical reformations of both Leavis and the New Critics. But contestation of New Critical orthodoxy in the 1950s or later did not necessarily amount to a critique of New Criticism as an "ideology"; these responses were often restricted to disputing the particular value judgments of the New Critics, or to reasserting the doctrinal contents of literary works. Neither of these modes of contestation explains the *discrepancy* between the doxa-like "sensibility" exhibited by a new consensus of judgment and the manifest political opinions of the New Critics themselves, the fact that the ideological efficacy of the New Criticism did *not* lie in the actual dissemination of these opinions. Hence the New Critics' revaluation of the canon could be registered in its time as politically ambiguous; it was difficult at best to assign a progressive or reactionary coefficient to particular judgments about particular authors. Only when such judgments are located within critical discourse as the basis for a conception of the "whole existing order" of literature does the practice of the New Criticism acquire a social referent, a target of ideological effect.

That referent is literary culture and its institutions, which, so far from establishing a cultural doxa for the social order as a whole, or even establishing a potent "orthodoxy" on the basis of the literary canon, remained culturally *marginal* to the social formation of modernity.

The latter hypothesis can be briefly elaborated with reference to the account of F. R. Leavis's intellectual trajectory given in Francis Mulhern's *The Moment of Scrutiny*. For Mulhern the crucial document in this trajectory is *Mass Civilization and Minority Culture,* published in 1930, which argues for a certain antithetical historical relation between the two terms in the title.[4] It is well known that the evaluative terms of Leavis's criticism are entirely dependent on a narrative (derived from Eliot's theory of a "dissociation of sensibility") whose tendency is radically conservative. Until the seventeenth century, according to this narrative, the social order is divided into a "popular" majority culture and smaller "minority" culture of intellectuals; the function of the latter is to mediate the cultural achievements of the past, and thus to insure that the level of general culture does not degenerate. The important point for Leavis is not so much the elite status of the minority culture as it is intellectual culture's total integration into the life of the community. The premodern social order was thought to be, in the favored trope of Leavis's day, "organic." For a variety of reasons this community began to disintegrate in the seventeenth century (Shakespeare and Elizabethan English are for Leavis its last cultural achievements), and that fragmentation produced a divorce between minority and popular culture, a divorce we recognize in such distinctions as that between "highbrow" and "lowbrow." Whatever validity this narrative may possess, its capacity to provoke revisionary judgments of the English literary tradition can scarcely be underestimated. What needs to be remarked additionally is that for Leavis the transformation of minority culture into a rootless highbrow elite culminated in the settling of this elite into the university system. In Leavis's view university professors failed to offer any resistance to the emergence of a degraded "mass civilization" (in the U.S. we would say "mass culture"). They are excoriated for complicity with this "civilization"; by contrast Leavis hoped to inaugurate a new oppositional "minority culture" which would operate outside the academy, by means of a "committed journalism" (76). There it would set out to recover an authentic tradition of authors who would constitute an "impalpable metacommunity" exactly correspondent to the status of minority culture itself. But like the church of Luther, or like the soul of Donne's "Extasie," Leavis's "disinterested clerisy capable of guiding the moral life of an aberrant society" (306) had to descend into an institutional body, and this body could only be the school (where the Leavisian clerisy had considerable success).

Given the terms of Leavis's adversarial critique, the institutional success of his movement posed a problem his theory could not resolve. We can state this problem briefly as follows: The failure to install a doxa-like "sensibility" outside of the minority culture, which was compelled to claim its victory in the schools and not in the domain of "mass civilization," oriented the representation of literature in Leavis's discourse toward a permanent *heterodoxy*. A literary work was supposed to embody a kind of heterodox or critical relation to modernity; if it did not, it could on that basis be "excluded" from the canon. The assimilation of Leavis's "minority culture" into the school as another orthodoxy of opinion removed precisedly the *ground* of its adversarial critique.

In the case of the New Criticism, we shall be able to demonstrate that just the opposite eventuality prevailed: The failure of its practice to establish a doxa-like sensibility in the cultural mass was not accompanied by an adversarial relation to the academy. On the contrary, the New Critics saw the university as the necessary site of adversarial culture. For that reason the New Criticism's doxical failure and institutional success oriented its representation of literature toward *orthodoxy,* toward an increased investment in the university as an institution taking over some of the cultural functions of the church. Just as with the Leavisites, the status of literature seemed to correspond exactly to the status of the minority literary culture itself, at once adversarial in relation to mass culture and at the same time institutionally dominant. But the problem for the New Criticism was how to express the orthodoxy of literature without representing the university as an institution *too* like the church, within which literature would express its orthodoxy directly as doctrine (Christianity, agrarianism, etc.). The solution to this problem was "paradoxical." It involved detecting in certain formal aspects of literariness a *covert* thematic of orthodoxy. Where Leavis was committed at least to the possibility of a minority culture independent of the university, the New Critics found in the university a place exterior to "mass civilization" itself, a place in which "orthodoxy" was expressed by the form of literature.

Here we can register the significant difference between Leavis's and the New Critics' readings of Eliot in their respective extrapolations from Eliot's most distinctive trope of judgment—the revaluation of minor poets. As I shall demonstrate presently, the revaluation of "minor" poetry in direct opposition to major reputations is the most consistent principle underlying Eliot's revisionary stance. Leavis translates that revisionary trope of minority into his concept of "minority culture." Brooks and the New Critics eventually find in the traditional canon of "major" authors exactly what Eliot finds in his canon of minor poets—the *reserve* of orthodoxy—but only after a period during which they polemicize unsuccessfully for the narrow version of Eliot's canon. Hence the moment of institutional victory for the New Criticism is marked by a strategic reaffirmation of the traditional canon of major authors, reread according to a pedagogic strategy—"close reading"—that refinds in these authors what is well hidden there, what requires very close reading in order to be discovered at all: the same orthodoxy of opinion Eliot found only in the "minor" tradition. Leavis on the other hand was compelled by his orientation toward heterodoxy to maintain the severity of his canonical judgments to the end, and indeed, to maintain *judgment* as the essentially critical act. For the New Critics, the reaffirmation of major authors coincided with the moment of their institutional success, when a practice of *interpretation* came to define literary pedagogy. As we shall see, this practice does not imply the necessity of making strict evaluative distinctions among the canonical authors so much as between literature and mass culture. At the moment of its success, the New Criticism was at once unfaithful to Eliot's specific revisionary judgments and more deeply faithful to the *principle* of his judgment than Leavis ever was. But in order to see why this is the case, we shall have to examine first Eliot's systematic valorization of minor poetry, and then Cleanth Brooks's transformation of that evaluative principle into a technique of interpretation.

Orthodoxy

Longinus was strangled by that unbreakable chain, the tradition of mediocrity. Is that tradition perhaps the strongest support of literary continuity?
—ERNST ROBERT CURTIUS, *European Literature
and the Latin Middle Ages*

The leitmotif of Eliot's exercises in revisionary judgment appears most conspicuously when he compares a major to a less major reputation, as in the following judicious assessment from the essay on "John Dryden," on the respective projects of Milton and Dryden: "The great advantage of Dryden over Milton is that while the former is always in control of his ascent, and can rise or fall at will . . . the latter has elected a perch from which he cannot afford to fall, and from which he is in danger of slipping" (SE, 270). The apparent simplicity of Eliot's point is belied by the fact that the comparison is drawn between the "perches" from which composition ("flight") is undertaken, and not between the actual works themselves. What principle of judgment, or rather prejudgment, is adumbrated here? We know, of course, that Eliot already finds Dryden more congenial than Milton on doctrinal grounds, and it would be easy to explain Eliot's preference on these grounds alone. But a quick resort to "ideological" explanation leaves unexplained the principle of judgment Eliot seems to be invoking. In other words, what is the relation between the doctrinal allegiances of Milton and Dryden and the formal features of their respective poetic practices? This relation does not seem to be in any sense "necessary"; otherwise we should be able to demonstrate that Dryden's more "Catholic" affinity is responsible for the modesty of his poetic stance, just as Milton's Puritan commitments would have to produce his epic ambition.

Elsewhere in the essay on "John Dryden" the adjudication between Milton and Dryden is expressed in terms that possess a strategic vagueness: "[Dryden's] powers were, we believe, wider, but no greater, than Milton's; he was confined by boundaries as impassable, though less strait" (SE, 273). The Johnsonian balance of such a statement is entirely deceptive. Does it mean that Dryden's powers were *as* great *and* wider than Milton's? The effect of Eliot's rhetoric is very deliberately to displace the axis of evaluative tropes from the vertical—greatness, height—to the horizontal—width, breadth. While it is unclear from the context of this quotation what exactly constitutes the "impassable" boundaries of poetic ambition (unless these boundaries define the absolute limit of any ambition), the language of commensuration has the peculiar effect of cathecting these same boundaries, of valuing positively a stance of resignation to these unspecified limits. The cathexis of limitation itself is apparent when Dryden's poetry is described as an art "of mak[ing] the small into the great" (SE, 269). Eliot's discrimination gestures toward the conventional distinction within the literary canon between "major" and "minor" figures, and at the same time reverses the polarity of value. This does not mean, then, that Dryden is really a major poet, and Milton really minor, but that Dryden's peculiar value consists precisely in his minority.

The historical moment which makes possible and necessary the discrimination between Dryden and Milton is not coincidentally the moment of Eliot's "dissociation of sensibility," the mid-seventeenth century. We shall presently be able to acknowledge the full force of that narrative as it determines from a distance the various moves in Eliot's revisionary polemic. Meanwhile, we may set before us the text which immediately determines Eliot's conception of the "limit" or "boundary" which confronts every literary ambition. That boundary is nothing other than the established *order* of literature, insofar as that order is complete, insofar as it resists the assimilation of any "new work." The *locus classicus* is of course the famous statement from "Tradition and the Individual Talent," which, perhaps more than any other of Eliot's critical pronouncements, lies behind every subsequent reflection on tradition in twentieth-century criticism, and even behind our own discourse of canon critique:

> The existing monuments form an ideal order among themselves, which is modified by the introduction of the new (the really new) work of art among them. The existing order is complete before the new work arrives; for order to persist after the supervention of novelty, the *whole* existing order must be, if ever so slightly, altered; and so the relations, proportions, values of each work of art toward the whole are readjusted; and this is conformity between the old and the new.[5]

I shall not comment here on what it is about this text which calls forth such a volume of commentary; nor shall it be my concern to give an account of this commentary. I would like rather to notice how Eliot's heightened sense of the "simultaneous order" of literature (SW, 49), expressed here as an "ideal order," enjoins a strategic modesty upon practicing poets. The idealization of the very order of the monuments means that what the new poet threatens is disorder; the new poet must present himself or herself with a demeanor of conformity if there is to be any chance of altering the existing order of monuments, that is, of joining the company of canonical writers. The emphasis thus falls upon the minuteness of the readjustment, the "ever so slightly" of the alteration. The polemic develops predictably along the lines determined by the antithesis between a transhistorical tradition and a historical "individual talent"; hence the necessity for what Eliot calls the poet's "continual self-sacrifice, a continual extinction of personality," elaborate gestures of modesty before the existing monuments. The self-limiting stance is equivalent tropologically to the "perch" Eliot so unequivocally approves in Dryden, who might be said as a consequence not to have disturbed the order of literature but to have altered that order "ever so slightly." If Milton on the other hand declined the strategic modesty demanded by tradition, his greatness, his canonicity, should only signify as such in a kind of parallel literary universe, where the existing monuments form not an order but a *disorder*. In this way the evaluative schema of "Tradition and the Individual Talent" is folded back upon an implicit historical narrative of "dissociation," an alternative literary history in which the very perception of which writers constitute the legitimate tradition is mistaken.

The macroanalysis of tradition as an "order" is repeated in the microanalysis of the individual poem: "The other aspect of this impersonal theory of poetry is the relation of the poem to its author" (SW, 53). As it happens, the poet has the same relation to tradition as to the individual poem, a relation explicated in Eliot's essay by the analogy of the catalyst, the shred of platinum which catalyzes the fusion of two gases without itself entering into the product of the reaction process: "The mind of the poet is the shred of platinum." The potency of the analogy is hardly mitigated by an inherent confusion in its terms. For elsewhere (in the next paragraph) the poet's mind is "a receptacle for seizing and storing up numberless feelings, phrases, images, which remain there until all the particles which can unite to form a new compound are present together." The curious ambiguity which makes the poet's mind a kind of content (the shred of platinum) in relation to form, and a form (the receptacle) in relation to content, is the result of a conception of poetic form which is as yet inexplicit, which only begins to translate "order" into "form," in such expressions as the "conformity between the old and the new." Eliot wants to find in the form of any properly composed poem (any poem in which personality is properly sublimated) a kind of hologrammic image of the order of literature itself. The proof of this order is the very absence of the personality of the poet from the poem as product, an absence that would be analogous to the modesty of the minor poet's stance in relation to tradition. If this argument seems rather obscure in its analogical contortions, we have only to substitute great ideas for great personalities in order to understand its implications. What may seem to be an overinvestment in the concept of "order" in "Tradition and the Individual Talent" carries forward a project that virtually defines the historical presuppositions of Eliot's criticism; for that order was always a particular *historical* order, an order that is somehow doubled and confirmed by the order of the poetic tradition, or by the form of the poem. Eliot's polemic is offered on behalf of this order, an order which looks rather like form without content, but in which content is signified by the heightened valuation of order itself—the *idea* of order.

Having elaborated this schema *in abstracto* in "Tradition and the Individual Talent," Eliot can give a specific example in the companion essay, "The Possibility of a Poetic Drama," of a form whose function is precisely to ensure as well as to measure the viability of tradition. For some reason the poetic drama is uniquely capable in Eliot's view of conforming to the form of tradition, and in the wake of its demise a certain disorder becomes manifest: "Nevertheless, the drama is perhaps the most permanent, is capable of greater variation and of expressing more varied types of society, than any other. It varied considerably in England alone; but when one day it was discovered lifeless, subsequent forms which had enjoyed a transitory life were dead too" (SW, 61).[6] The momentary resort to narrative conjures something like a murder, a very British murder mystery. The identity of the murderer is withheld, however. Instead Eliot goes on to suggest, quite surprisingly, that the form of the drama renders tradition irrelevant: "The

Elizabethan Age in England was able to absorb a great quantity of new thoughts and images, *almost dispensing with tradition,* because it had this great form of its own which imposed itself on everything that came to it" (SW, 62; emphasis mine). How are we to reconcile this view of tradition with that of "Tradition and the Individual Talent"? The contradiction is perhaps only apparent. According to Eliot, the Elizabethan freedom from the necessity of conforming to the form of tradition is the gift mainly of one form, the blank-verse drama, and this fact implies conversely that tradition in the more famous essay compensates for the *absence* of living forms. What this means in effect is that tradition itself only emerges as the guarantor of form *after* a certain historical juncture, when the culture no longer produces forms of its own, when it must turn instead to the practice of conforming to the form of tradition. It is only at this point that the "extinction of personality" is required, a certain discipline that consists of resisting the temptation to invent form out of one's head, out of the supposed "greatness" of one's own ideas. For the Elizabethans no such extinction of personality was necessary, because they were presumably not tempted to assert personality at all. This is Eliot's understanding of what makes Shakespeare possible; he is not so much a great poet as he is the guild-like practitioner of a currently available form: "We should see then just how *little* each poet had to do; only so much as would make a play his, only what was really essential to make it different from anyone else's. When there is this economy of effort it is possible to have several, even many, good poets at once. The great ages did not perhaps *produce* much more talent than ours; but less talent was wasted" (SW, 64).

In the very next paragraph Eliot deduces from his analysis of form a conclusion about the fortunes of minor poetry—but who was speaking of minor poetry? The relation between the two subjects of form and minor poetry is profound, because it is through the tradition of minor poetry that form is developed and transmitted:

> Now in a formless age there is very little hope for the minor poet to do anything worth doing; and when I say minor I mean very good poets indeed: such as filled the Greek anthology and the Elizabethan song-books; even a Herrick; but not merely second-rate poets, for Denham and Waller have quite another importance, occupying points in the development of a major form. When everything is set out for the minor poet to do, he may quite frequently come upon some *trouvaille,* even in the drama: Peele and Brome are examples. Under the present conditions, the minor poet has too much to do. (SW, 64)

Eliot is saying that a "formless age" is one in which minor poetry is all but impossible; but does this not imply conversely that in such an age poetry must be "major" or nothing at all? And does the charge of *formlessness* then not extend to major poetry? The situation of the minor poet has somehow been taken as normative, even ideal; in the most desirable of historical circumstances, the individual poet has less and less to do, the form more and more. Ideally all poets are minor in a world of major form. While the mystery of the death of poetic drama remains unsolved, then, the serious consequences of its demise can be identified: English literary history continues to produce major poets while undergoing a simultaneous atrophy of form. Revisionist history seeks the traces of form in minor poets: "The poet must be very conscious of the main current, which does not flow invariably through the most distinguished reputations" (SW, 51).

At this point it would be relatively easy to extrapolate the specific judgments Eliot produced during his critical career from the trope of minority—his preference for the Metaphysical poets and Dryden over Spenser and Milton, for the Jacobean dramatists over Shakespeare, and his low opinion of much Romantic and Victorian poetry. The valuation of the minor stance paradoxically subtends a critical revisionism which would otherwise seem merely personal, merely the erection of personal preference into edicts of judgment: "From time to time, every hundred years or so, it is desirable that some critic shall appear to review the past of our literature, and set the poems in a new order." While Eliot goes on to say in this text from *The Use of Poetry and the Use of Criticism* that "This task is not one of revolution but of readjustment," the allusion to the more famous passage from "Tradition and the Individual Talent" only underscores the curiously reciprocal relation between the minor poet and the *great* critic.[7] The latter figure does not adjust the existing order "ever so slightly," but inaugurates a "new order" radically different from the old. This difference is more than apparent when the "monuments" of the existing order are toppled by the tribe of minor poets, who possess a sophisticated verbal weaponry for which the steroid rhetoric of the great poets is no match:

> This virtue of wit is not a peculiar quality of minor poets, or of the minor poets of one age or one school; it is an intellectual quality which perhaps only becomes noticeable by itself, in the work of lesser poets. Furthermore it is absent from the work of Wordsworth, Shelley, and Keats, on whose poetry nineteenth-century criticism has unconsciously been based. (SE, 262)

The tendentious logic of Eliot's argument culminates in the essay entitled "What Is Minor Poetry?" in which he writes that "What I am concerned to dispel is any derogatory association connected with the term 'minor poetry,' together with the suggestion that minor poetry is easier to read, or less worth while to read, than 'major poetry'" (OPP, 34). But this logic always exceeds its stated objective of redeeming minor poetry from the charge that it is "failed great poetry," and moves on to undermine the criteria by which great poetry is defined as such.[8] This is the context in which we must understand the polemic against Milton, which does not simply argue that in this one case a "great poet" has been overrated. The issue is always the mutually exclusive relation between great poetry and minor poetry:

> There is a large class of persons, including some who appear in print as critics, who regard any censure upon a "great" poet as a breach of the peace, as an act of wanton iconoclasm, or even hoodlumism. The kind of derogatory criticism that I have to make upon Milton is not intended for such persons, who cannot understand that it is more important, in some vital respects, to be a *good* poet than to be a *great* poet. (OPP, 157)

The same point is more explicitly elaborated in the second essay on Milton:

> There are two kinds of poet who can ordinarily be of use to other poets. There are those who suggest, to one or another of their successors, something which they have not done themselves, or who provoke a different way of doing the same thing: these are likely to be not the greatest, but smaller, imperfect poets with whom later poets discover an affinity. And there are the great poets from whom we can learn negative rules: no poet can teach another to write well, but some great poets can teach others some of the things to avoid. (OPP, 176)

We may concede the usefulness of looking at the history of poetry from the point of view of the practicing poet (this is the consistent feint of Eliot's critical prose) while still maintaining that the implicit evaluation of these two kinds of poets exceeds the requirements of his argument. If it were only a question of poetic practice, Eliot's particular judgments would not have had anything like the force they possessed in critical discourse between the wars.

But let us consider briefly what difference it makes to the status of those judgments after we acknowledge that the appearance in Eliot's criticism of a shadowy, alternative "tradition" of minor poets has a good deal to do with the legitimation of his poetic practice, with the emergence (somewhat belatedly in relation to the other arts) of a "modernist" poetic. The status of Eliot's "canon" (if it can be called that) corresponds exactly to the status of a minority *within* literary culture, that minority of poets and writers who can be associated with the practices of Eliot and Pound, and who are at the time Eliot's essays are written still relatively marginal to literary culture, a coterie whose work will only later come to define modernism in poetry. The question before us now is how Eliot's conception of an alternative "tradition" of minor poets represents imaginarily both the situation of literary culture in his own time and the situation of his coterie within that culture. In order to conceptualize his break with the poetic practice of his immediate predecessors, Eliot was forced to return to the moment of "dissociation of sensibility" in order to traverse that earlier rupture *in the other direction*. This is the meaning of his replacement of one precedent for English literary "tradition" (Victorian and Edwardian poetry) with another (the Jacobean dramatists, the Metaphysical poets, Dryden). The names of these poets thus function as quasi-allegorical counters in a critical game whose meaning, I shall argue, is finally only partially available to Eliot himself. This fact requires a double register of interpretation: we will have to understand first exactly what Eliot means by such names as "Dryden" or "Milton," what domains of significance are governed by these names for him. But beyond that, we shall have to understand what the revisionary *project* itself means, that is to say, what status it has as an ideological discourse.

Eliot's sense of the rupture constituted by the poetic practice of his coterie is inseparable from a narrative literary history in which the names of Dryden and Milton contend for a dominant position within that history. At certain moments, Eliot seems rather confident that in some sense the influence of Dryden was greater than that of Milton: "No one, in the whole history of English literature, has dominated that literature so long, or so completely. And even in the nineteenth century the language was still the language of Dryden, as it is today."[9] Elsewhere the claim for Dryden's benign influence is even more emphatic:

> Far below Shakespeare, and even below Milton, as we must put him, he yet has, just by reason of his precise degree of inferiority, a kind of importance which neither Shakespeare nor Milton has—the importance of his *influence*. . . . It was Dryden, more than any other individual, who formed a language possible for mediocrity, and yet possible for later great writers to do great things with.[10]

More usually, however, it is the influence of Milton which concerns Eliot:

Many people will agree that a man may be a great artist, and yet have a bad influence. There is more of Milton's influence in the badness of the bad verse of the eighteenth century than of anybody's else. . . . Milton's bad influence may be traced much farther than the eighteenth century, and much farther than upon bad poets: if we say that it was an influence against which we still have to struggle. (OPP, 156–57)

The surprising contemporaneity of both Dryden's and Milton's influences suggests that in neither case can Eliot's argument be taken quite literally, that these names are indeed *figures*, the allegorical representatives of benign and malign influence respectively. Their very historical distance allows a certain ease in the manipulation of their names, their transformation into narrative figures. When Eliot considers more recent poetic predecessors, however, his control over the allegorical significance of the names of the poets is less sure, a fact we may now demonstrate using the example of Tennyson.

The essay to be considered here is "*In Memoriam,*" written in 1936; but the reader of Eliot's criticism will recall that in "The Possibility of a Poetic Drama" (1920), Tennyson is described as a "master of minor forms," who "took to turning out large patterns on a machine." This early opinion is partially retracted, but the praise of the later essay is reserved almost entirely for *In Memoriam,* while other works by Tennyson are found deficient. The essay's rather ambivalent evaluation of Tennyson's oeuvre transparently recapitulates aspects of Eliot's own career, since Tennyson's elegy provides Eliot with the occasion of a displaced commentary upon the critical reception of *The Waste Land:*

> Apparently Tennyson's contemporaries, once they accepted *In Memoriam,* regarded it as a message of hope and reassurance to their rather fading Christian faith. It happens now and then that a poet by some strange accident expresses the mood of his generation, at the same time that he is expressing a mood of his own which is quite remote from his generation. (SE, 291)

The Waste Land was believed (mistakenly, according to Eliot) to express the "despair" or "disillusion" of a generation, and it is in that sense a peculiar mirror image of *In Memoriam.* Just as Eliot's own contemporaries were mistaken in their reading of *The Waste Land,* so Tennyson's contemporaries were mistaken in their understanding of his elegy. Eliot wants to argue that in fact Tennyson never recovered from his moment of disillusion, and that his elegy does not recover the "rather fading Christian faith" of his contemporaries but expresses the same loss of faith. The real Tennyson is said to be "more interesting and tragic" than his contemporaries knew (SE, 292). When *In Memoriam's* project of recovery fails, this failure broadens, spreads out into all of Tennyson's work; it marks the failure of his later work as the failure of *faith:*

> Tennyson seems to have reached the end of his spiritual development with *In Memoriam:* there followed no reconciliation, no resolution.
>
> > *And now no sacred staff shall break in blossom,*
> > *No choral salutation lure to light*
> > *A spirit sick with perfume and sweet night,*
>
> or rather with twilight, for Tennyson faced neither the darkness nor the light in his later years. The genius, the technical power, persisted to the end, but the spirit had surrendered. (SE, 295)

The quotation from Swinburne hints at the old world of religious faith and miracle, but this crypto-allusion to what in the most banal historical terms goes by the name of "secularization" is curiously shrouded in the pall of "decadence," a cultural milieu with which the early Eliot, as the poet of twilight (the "violet hour") stands in a relation of demonstrable continuity. The assertion of a rupture with that milieu always overextends itself historically, undoing both moments of secularization, the one early modern, the other late Victorian, recrossing the divide in the other direction. As a cryptic recapitulation of Eliot's own career, the essay on Tennyson thus argues that Eliot did recover from the despair his contemporaries believed to have been expressed in *The Waste Land,* did recover a religious faith denied in the end to Tennyson, a recovery Eliot would like to see from his retrospective point of view (1936) as *enabling* poetic production (we may wish to see it otherwise). The point, however, is deceptively simple: Eliot would like to see "Christian faith" as enabling poetic production in general. This conviction is responsible for his tendency to backdate his own religious inclinations, and thus to dispute the reading of *The Waste Land* in which it stands as a modernist document of "disillusion."

What emerges from the essay on *In Memoriam* is thus another attempt to understand the name of a poet in terms of a historical allegory, in this case to read the crisis of Tennyson's career as another version of the "dissociation of sensibility." But that allegory is interrupted by Eliot's *identification* with Tennyson, which gives him the occasion of his most plangent self-portrait: "Tennyson is not only a minor Virgil, he is also with Virgil as

Dante saw him, a Virgil among the Shades, the saddest of all English poets, among the Great in Limbo, the most instinctive rebel against the society in which he was the most perfect conformist" (SE, 295).[11] While it would be easy enough to see that it is Eliot himself who is the "minor Virgil," the reappearance of the figure of the minor poet at this moment represents Eliot's conceptualization (in a somewhat narcissistic mode) of the social conditions which govern the relation of literary culture to culture in general. The horizon of the problem for which the figure of the minor poet provided a historical solution was never less than culture in general. If this culture is capable only of bringing forth a "minor Virgil," what conditions would have to obtain in order for the thing itself, a major poet, to appear? Elsewhere, in "What is a Classic?" Eliot argues quite consistently that English literature has no classic poet such as Virgil or Dante, because it is not founded upon a universality or consensus of belief, a universality Eliot contrasts with what he calls "the provincial." Inconsistently, however, Eliot argues that English culture approached most nearly to such a condition in the eighteenth century, but even then the culture's "restriction of religious sensibility itself produces a kind of provinciality: the provinciality which indicates the disintegration of Christendom, the decay of a common belief and a common culture" (OPP, 137). The example of the eighteenth century is an interesting slip indeed, since it postdates the "dissociation of sensibility" of Eliot's earlier narrative. The slippage here is precisely that between doxa and orthodoxy, since the "associated" sensibility would presumably have functioned as a kind of doxa, the "common culture" in which the truths of Christian faith would not have been subject to questioning, and thus would not have had to be established as an "orthodoxy" in contention with a "heterodoxy." (Again, whether this condition ever actually prevailed is not our concern.) In another sense Eliot's example of the eighteenth century is quite appropriate: for the exclusion of Catholics and Dissenters from various privileges of English social life after the Restoration established "orthodoxy" in precisely Bourdieu's sense, as the exclusion of heterodoxy. If this condition was inadequate to constitute the social basis for the emergence of a "classic" or major poet (in Eliot's view major poets tended thereafter to "heretical" posturing) it was still sufficient for the cultivation of a "minor" tradition, which would have the function of investing the forms of the literary tradition with the intensity of its fidelity to a fragile religious orthodoxy: "The continuity of literature is essential to its greatness; it is very largely the function of secondary writers to preserve this continuity, and to provide a body of writings which is not necessarily read by posterity, but which plays a great part in forming the link between those writers who continue to be read."[12] Such statements, as usual, empty out the category of majority on behalf of a claim for the more essential cultural function of minor writers.

The tendency of Eliot's later criticism is finally to identify "tradition" with "orthodoxy," an identification which is made explicit in *After Strange Gods,* when Eliot declares that he is now rewriting "Tradition and the Individual Talent" by substituting the concept of "orthodoxy" for "tradition."[13] In the same gesture, Eliot can retranslate orthodoxy as "right tradition," thus deliberately conflating a literary with a doctrinal concept. The point of this conflation, however, is not to reduce literary work to the function of merely disseminating orthodox truths, but rather to insure its *conformity* to "right tradition," and especially to see in the discipline of that conformity the fact of its being "*unconsciously* Christian," the enabling condition of "greatness." It is at this point too that Eliot's critical prose begins to take the form of general cultural and social criticism, most of which proceeds by indulging a certain fantasy: the reinstitution of a "Christian society." This fantasy always falls somewhat short of depicting with any persuasiveness the condition of doxa, and hence it continually returns to the repressive invocation of orthodoxy: "A Christian education would primarily train people to think in Christian categories and would not impose the necessity for insincere profession of belief. What the rulers believed would be less important than the beliefs to which they would be obliged to conform."[14] The fact that Eliot imagines his Christian ruling class along the lines of a Stalinist *nomenklatura* is proof enough that the fantasy is fed by more than his nostalgia, or his religious faith. The very *excessiveness* of Eliot's fantasy of a Christian society suggests that the meaning of the fantasy is not entirely available to him, and that its inaccessiblity is just the evidence of its "ideological" status. The influence of Eliot's poetry and criticism need not be measured, then, by their capacity to persuade their audience of the need to reestablish a "Christian society"; that was never within the realm of possibility. Eliot's polemic always misses that target but hits another, namely, literary culture itself, which hears in his criticism a fantasy of power, a fantasy acted out by Eliot himself when he dictates with unself-conscious pomposity a new (or old) order to society on the basis of his authority as a *literary* figure. The most profound assumption of that fantasy was always that literary culture is the site at which the most socially important beliefs and attitudes are produced, the site at which those beliefs and attitudes are generated which *unify* the culture. When we state the basis of Eliot's social criticism in these terms, is it not obvious that this remains the wish-fulfillment fantasy of literary culture, that it is still what we would like to believe *about* that culture? Or from another point of view, that the ideology of literary culture consists in its claim to occupy the most important place of ideological production in the social order?

The historical narrative which we must now confront is in some ways all too familiar. The substitution of "literary sensibility" for "religious belief" always implied the substitution of literary culture for the *clergy*. But the very uneasiness with which we have to contemplate this conventional historical motif betrays how inappropriate are the terms by means of which that substitution has been apprehended. For it is not a case of simple substitution, for the same reason that the substitution of sensibility for belief was not simple (and could not be simplified by letting "tradition" stand surreptitiously for "orthodoxy"). The relation of literary culture to the social order as a whole *cannot* be the same as the relation of the clergy to that order—in what sense, then, a substitution? This is the kind of question for which Gramsci's analysis of intellectuals provides a hypothetical solution, since what is at issue here is the difference between Gramsci's "organic" and "traditional" intellectuals. If the clergy may be said to have been the organic intellectuals of the feudal order, their displacement by literary culture in the early modern period never represented the simple displacement of one set of organic intellectuals by another. For literary culture only very slowly distinguished itself from the clergy and, what is more, continued to form its pedagogic institutions and professional self-representations on the clerical model. Even in the period of its greatest dominance in modern culture, coincident with the emergence of the bourgeois public sphere in the eighteenth century, literary culture continued to *imagine* itself in clerical terms, a residual identification which determined the ambiguous status of literature as the vehicle of both *sensibility*—what Bourdieu calls the "habitus" and which consists of all those norms of "cultivation" and linguistic facility to which I have drawn attention in previous chapters—and *doctrine,* a set of truths which would have the status of orthodoxy. The decline of the public sphere in the nineteenth century transforms the agents of literary culture into exclusively traditional intellectuals who nevertheless continue to imagine their relation to the social order as organic on the clerical model.[15] The ruptures characterizing this historical narrative reappear openly in Eliot's later criticism when he moves away from the "dissociation of sensibility" hypothesis in order to attribute dissociation directly to the decline of the clergy as a unifying force within society. The literary phenomenon of dissociation was only the consequence of the protracted divorce of church and state: "a state secularized, a community turned into a mob, and a clergy disintegrated."[16] This narrative receives a kind of allegorical treatment in *Murder in the Cathedral,* where the rift between

Thomas and Henry is the premonitory instance of every subsequent rupture: in the social realm between church and state, in the literary realm between Dryden and Milton, in the realm of sensibility between thought and feeling. It equally informs Eliot's late polemic against Arnold's substitution of poetry for religion, which for Eliot now is a relation that can and must be stated in the most reactionary terms: as the necessary subordination of poetry to dogma, as the enabling relation of belief to sensibility: "The artistic sensibility is impoverished by its divorce from the religious sensibility, the religious by its separation from the artistic."[17]

If such a relation can exist only where the clergy has the power to establish an orthodoxy of belief, and no such social conditions obtain in the modern era, that fact is just what propels Eliot's social criticism into the realm of fantasy. In this fantasy the clergy disappears as an actual historical group, and reappears in the mystified form of an *incognito* community:

> We need therefore what I have called "the community of Christians," by which I mean, not local groups, and not the Church in any one of its senses, unless we call it "the Church within the Church." These will be the consciously and thoughtfully practising Christians, especially those of intellectual and spiritual superiority.[18]

The obvious analogy between Eliot's "Church within the Church" and F. R. Leavis's "disinterested clerisy" (which for Leavis *is* literary culture) suggests that it would be a mistake to take Eliot's statement literally, or conversely to take the analogy between the clergy and literary culture as merely casual. The sense in which most criticism remains, as Edward Said has argued, "religious criticism," is by no means simple or easy to explain, because the element of the "religious" occupies a realm of social fantasy, which yet testifies to a certain reality about literary culture.[19] When Eliot finally translates "tradition" into "orthodoxy," he makes uncomfortably evident what is really already implicit in the concept of tradition. If the reduction of tradition to orthodoxy remains unavailable in the general discourse of criticism, because that orthodoxy would be meaningless without such doctrinal contents as Christian belief (or some other belief) would provide, this is not to say that tradition does not continue to bear the burden of responding to the social demand for shared belief, for a "common culture." The literary canon continues to be regarded as the embodiment of such doctrine and such culture (is this not what the debate about the canon simply assumes?) and Eliot's revaluation of minor poetry was only one of many such attempts to refind in literary tradition the ground of a *total* culture, inclusive of belief. As we shall see in the case of the New Criticism, the social inhibition that disallows literary culture from making doctrinal claims of the "orthodox" sort drives these claims back into the refuge of literary form.

Paradoxy

All that is solid melts into air, all that is holy is profaned. . . .
—MARX AND ENGELS, *Manifesto of the Communist Party*

It has long been a received idea that the New Criticism depoliticized the study of literature by rejecting the significance of overtly political or philosophical ideas for the evaluation or interpretation of literary works, and by restricting the object of criticism to the text itself, supplemented by only so much contextual information as would enable the proper understanding of topical references or archaic usages. The received idea has been definitively revised by Gerald Graff's recent *Professing Literature,* which reconstructs the institutional history of criticism in the American university, within which the New Criticism established hegemony by the 1950s.[20] Graff emphasizes the fact that "the New Critics were originally neither aesthetes nor pure explicators but culture critics with a considerable 'axe to grind' against the technocratic tendencies of modern mass civilization" (149). In Graff's useful mapping of the literary academy in the 1930s and 40s, the New Critics represent a splinter group within the category of what Graff calls the "Generalists," those critics who saw the objectives of literary study as immediately social and edifying. These descendants of the bourgeois public sphere cohabited uneasily in the university with the philological specialists, who were likely to define their practice more narrowly as the accumulation of a specific kind of knowledge. Graff points out quite rightly that the emergence of the "literary critic" within the generalist faction did not imply a simple repudiation of the disciplinary style of the philologist, but rather the development of a more or less rigorous countermethodology of "interpretation" which could be put in the service of "Generalist" aims, the aims of cultural criticism. Therein lies the answer to the puzzle of the received idea, the sense in which it is both correct and seriously inaccurate; for the New Critics, "the point was to define these social and moral functions as they operated within the internal structure of literary works themselves" (148). This agenda is already implicit in Eliot's fetishizing of form, but as with Eliot it is difficult to see how form or "internal structure" can convey a critique of modernity unless it is in some way *read* as adversarial. The inability of form to express its own adversarial meaning is betrayed in Eliot's deliberate translation of tradition (fidelity to form) into orthodoxy (fidelity to doctrine).

Graff's analysis of how the New Criticism solved this problem argues initially for the implicitly critical nature of literary form: "These critics' very insistence on the disinterested nature of poetic experience was an implicit rejection of a utilitarian culture and thus a powerfully 'utilitarian' and 'interested' gesture" (149). Now this hypothesis converges in an interesting way upon a left critique of modernity such as we might find in Adorno, a convergence which is immediately suspicious. Granted that modernism produced both left and right critiques of modernity, does the difference between these critiques make no difference? We may suppose that if the New Critics ever passed through a pristine moment of faith in the social effects of disinterestedness per se, they would never have had to explicate the meaning of form in other than formal terms. But there is much evidence to suggest, as Graff goes on to insist, that literature was never entrusted to make its point by itself: "First generation New Critical explications of literature were rarely explications only: they were cultural and philosophical essays in which texts like 'The Canonization,' 'Sailing to Byzantium,' and the poems of Poe became allegorical statements about the dissociation of sensibility, technical rationality, the collapse of the Old South, or some other equally large theme" (150). After a certain point, however, the "allegory" tended to drop away, and "the argument that the politics of literature should be seen as part of its form modulated subtly into the idea that literature had no politics, except as an irrelevant extrinsic concern" (150). Presumably it is only at this point that the received idea becomes true, but true in a rather paradoxical sense. For is it not also a constituent of the received idea that the purging of the political from the study of literature has a tendentially conservative effect, conservative by default? What did it matter, then, when the "allegory" dropped away from the practice of New Critical reading if *in any case* that reading proved tendentially conservative?

Graff's historical account of the New Criticism raises an interesting question about the moment at which the allegory drops away (Graff dates it precisely to 1951, with the publication of Reuben Brower's *Fields of Light*), since that moment coincides with the triumph of the New Criticism in the university (150). It is also the moment (the decade following the war) when modernist poetry is irrevocably established in the curriculum (in our terminology, "canonized'). The connection between these several triumphs is extremely intimate, because a large part of the adversarial agenda of the New Criticism in the thirties and forties was expressed as a direct extension of Eliot's revisionary literary history, in the form of a double polemic on behalf of modernist poets and the metaphysicals. Graff observes that by the time Cleanth Brooks publishes *The Well Wrought Urn* (1947), it is no longer necessary for the New Critics to polemicize further on behalf of Eliot's or their own earlier revisionary judgments of English literary history. The same qualities that Eliot found primarily or only in minor poetry are now found in the works of the established literary canon. Eliot's narrative of English literary history as the story of a split between an orthodox minor tradition and a heterodox major line is thus displaced into allegorical explications of the "internal structures" of the canonical texts, which all exhibit the features of paradox, irony, or ambiguity formerly attributed specifically to the metaphysicals and the moderns. The question of what difference it makes when the larger historical allegory drops away is thus a question about the "moment" of the reassimilation of the alternative or "minor" tradition into the established canon, and about the effectiveness of that reassimilation in establishing a new institutional hegemony for the New Criticism. It is a question of how the socioinstitutional conditions of literary criticsm itself are registered in the allegorical reading of literary structure. We can put this question in more concrete terms, terms that recognize the peculiar significance of *The Well Wrought Urn* as a text which defines the moment in question. If that text discovers that all canonical literature (or literature per se) speaks the "language of paradox," it still reads paradox as the evidence of a "unity of experience" no longer available to dissociated moderns, though we moderns may continue to contemplate what we have lost in the experience of the literary artifact. What circumstances, then, will cause that historico-political meaning of paradox to disappear, while the thesis that poetic language is intrinsically paradoxical succeeds so spectacularly? I should like to argue that we will not be able to understand how paradox "modulates" (Graff's term) into an implicitly apolitical (*purely* formal) concept without recognizing that Brooks's concept is "ideological" in the sense I have already indicated, namely, that the explicit political significance of his concept of paradox cannot account for its political effects, a fact which is proven by the very ease with which the explicit political meaning drops away in the 1950s. The ideological effect rather inheres in the discrepancy between the level of doxa (what is unquestioned, *impensé*) and what is openly adovcated, an "orthodoxy." What needs to be explained then, is not simply the relation of the poem to particular beliefs, political or otherwise, but the institutional status of literary criticism in relation to the socioeconomic conditions of modernity.

Let us recall, then, that in 1939, in the chapter of *Modern Poetry and the Tradition* entitled "Notes toward a Revised History of English Literature," Brooks can still reproduce almost exactly the judgments implicit in Eliot's criticism, an indebtedness Brooks later acknowledged in these terms:

I was particularly stimulated by two paragraphs in one of his essays on the metaphysical poets. In this brief passage, he suggested that the metaphysical poets were not to be regarded as a rather peculiar offshoot of English poetry, but had a deep, hidden connection with its central line of development. This, to me [was a] new way of looking at the tradition of English poetry.[21]

The hiddenness of that connection, the peculiar centrality of a tradition which is perceived to be marginal—these are of course motifs with which we are very familiar. Yet it would be a mistake to find in Brooks's criticism only a replication of Eliot's literary historical motifs, as such a replication would not have sufficed in the 1930s to ground a new literary *pedagogy*. The pressure to produce such a pedagogic method is simply institutional. Eliot's cultural criticism presumes as its site of enunciation the "workshop" of the poet, or the journal of the authoritarian cultural critic. The New Criticism develops in the 1930s in competition with other pedagogic methods to which it also owes a considerable debt, chief among these the methodology developed by I. A. Richards. For Richards had already, in the 1920s, confronted the fact of modern "dissociation," and had produced a form of critical pedagogy more or less reconciled to the secularity presumed to characterize modernity. As we know, this pedagogy sought to place criticism on scientific grounds, a project whose immediate context is the logical positivism emergent between the wars. These circumstances are worth recollecting (if all too cursorily) because they suggest the heavy polemical burden initially borne by the New Criticism, the burden of a double antagonist: both modernity and the particular *accommodations* to modernity competing for hegemony in literary culture. We may invoke these antagonists by way of accounting for Brooks's rewriting of Eliot's literary history in *Modern Poetry and the Tradition* in order to demonize science: "We have argued . . . that the critical revolution in the seventeenth century which brought metaphysical poetry to an end was intimately bound up with the beginnings of the New Science."[22] This hypothesis was unnecessary to Eliot's narrative, but it is quite crucial to Brooks's. Aside from betraying the large epistemological anxieties to which literature has been periodically subject, it gives Brooks a way of apparently emptying the doctrinal content from every literary work, as a prolegomenon to the *reading* of the work. Hence the "heresy of paraphrase," as defined in *The Well Wrought Urn:*

> The position developed in earlier pages obviously seeks to take the poem out of competition with scientific, historical, and philosophical propositions. The poem, it has been argued, does

not properly eventuate in a proposition: we can only *abstract* statements from the poem, and in the process of abstraction we necessarily distort the poem itself.

This position is oddly enough very close to Richards's, in that it seems to regard every "proposition" with pretension to truth value as by definition a scientific proposition. If there exists any other kind of truth, it cannot by definition be expressed in the *form* of a proposition. Brooks's theory concedes a very great deal to the epistemological tyranny of science (really, to the positivist "philosophy of science" regnant between the wars), but only because that concession is strategic, because scientific truth has already been stigmatized as the origin of our dissociated modernity. The important point to note here is that when the "proposition" is conflated with the claim to scientific truth, then *any* proposition one might be tempted to derive from a poem can be stigmatized as putatively "scientific," as subject to the norms of scientific verification. It is not surprising, then, that *all* statements of *any* kind derived from a poem fall under the heading of "paraphrase."

Clearly the object of this strategy is not simply to remove the poem from competition with scientific truth, but to remove certain other truths from that competition. These truths are no longer expressed as propositions or statements but are rather embodied in the form of the poem, in the very antagonism between poetry (or literature) and the epistemological bully whose name is science. This strategic indirection of an alternative non-scientific truth commits the poem to a kind of gestural aphasia, an aphasia repeated in the process of reading the poem. The teacher or interpreter of the poem can only point to the truth which must not be spoken, but the very unspokenness of that truth elevates it to a status vastly greater than that of scientific truth, which always falls to the level of mere fact. Perhaps even more important, the interpretive method enjoined by this theory can safely bypass what looks like statement in a poem, secure in the knowledge that its truth lies elsewhere, in certain aspects of its *form*, in what Brooks calls "paradox." If this form, the form of paradox, can then be given a certain meaning, we shall see that this meaning is curiously self-reflective: it is that paradox names the very condition by which the poem does not *name* the truth to which it nevertheless gestures. The condition of paradox is precisely the fact that a certain truth (*doxa*) stands alongside (*para*) the poem itself. We shall further see that this condition characterizes what was once a mode of *historical existence*, a relation to truth that is for Brooks premodern, but which now survives only in the structure of the literary artifact. In this way the paradox specific to any given poem recapitulates the historical narrative that subtends New Critical practice, making possible the "allegory" Graff describes as characteristic of early New Critical readings. Insofar as every successful poem achieves the condition of paradox, it annuls the specific statements which may appear to be asserted in the poem, and becomes a kind of hologrammic image of literature as a whole.

We may now demonstrate this hologrammic effect by considering at greater length Brooks's reading of a particular poem, "The Canonization," which also happens to be the poem he offers as exemplifying the principle of paradox in the chapter of *The Well Wrought Urn* entitled "The Language of Paradox." The subsequent history of criticism has transformed the title of the poem into a pun intended neither by Donne nor by Brooks; but the pun is a fortunate contingency, since what is at issue in the reading of "The Canonization" is nothing less than the reintegration of the "metaphysical" poets into the "central stream of the tradition": "One was to attempt to see, in terms of this approach, what the masterpieces had in common rather than to see how the poems of different historical periods differed—and in particular to see whether they had anything in common with the metaphysicals and with the moderns" (WWU, 193).[23]

The definition of paradox in this first chapter of *The Well Wrought Urn* entails, to begin with, the usual distinction between poetry and science: "There is a sense in which paradox is the language appropriate and inevitable to poetry. It is the scientist whose truth requires a language purged of every trace of paradox" (WWU, 3). This tells us not so much what paradox is, only that it is a sort of language antithetical to the sort of language science employs; yet we are also told that paradox is "intellectual" and "hard" and that it is not usually thought of as the "language of the soul." In taking over some of the characteristics of scientific language, paradox is already paradoxical; it already refuses to be defined as either the language of thought or the language of feeling. If paradox then coyly implies what Eliot would have considered to be the linguistic expression of an "associated sensibility," it can only embody a state of dissociation which has already set in, after "thought" and "feeling" are perceived as antithetical. The reconciliation of these two antitheses, which has rather a long pedigree in the Romantic tradition, and which communicates distantly with other contemporary notions of alienation, gives us the first *historical* meaning of paradox. But this sense of paradox can be further generalized along purely formal lines, as the reconciliation of any apparent antitheses. The latter concept underlies all three major tropes defining the rhetorical lexicon of the New Criticism:

> One perhaps does not need to point out that the importance assigned to the resolution of apparently antithetical attitudes

accounts for the emphasis in earlier pages on (1) wit, as an awareness of the multiplicity of possible attitudes to be taken toward a given situation; on (2) paradox, as a device for contrasting the conventional view of a situation, or limited and special view of it such as those taken in practical and scientific discourse, with a more inclusive view; and on (3) irony, as a device for definition of attitudes by qualification (WWU, 257)

It would seem, given this set of definitions, that wit and irony are only versions of paradox, and that paradox thus bears the ideological weight of the New Critical agenda, its generalization from the reading of one poem to the reading of every poem (the canon), and from the canon to the larger historical and political field.

When we come to the example of Donne's "The Canonization," the antitheses in question are defined more narrowly in one sense, since they engage a theme specific to Donne's poem, but equally broadly in another sense, since this thematic concerns "the world":

> The basic metaphor which underlies the poem (and which is reflected in the title) involves a sort of paradox. For the poet daringly treats profane love as if it were divine love. The canonization is not that of a pair of holy anchorites who have renounced the world and the flesh. The hermitage of each is the other's body; but they do renounce the world, and so their title to sainthood is cunningly argued. The poem is then a parody of Christian sainthood; but it is an intensely serious parody of a sort that modern man, habituated as he is to an easy yes or no, can hardly understand. (WWU, 11)

No one would deny that the distinction between the sacred and the profane constitutes the thematic infrastructure of the poem, or that the technique of "sacred parody" is characteristic of "metaphysical" lyric. But the easy translation of parody into *paradox* is occasioned by Brooks's interest, entirely on the surface here, of contrasting the experience related in the poem to the cruder experience of "modern man." It is worth underscoring the fact that what Graff calls the "allegorical" level of New Critical interpretation requires no effort at all to recover, is in fact too easy to recover. That level of interpretation is "ideological," but in the rather obvious sense in which television commercials make hyperbolic or irrelevant claims about the effects of their products which everyone recognizes as a *design* upon his or her desire. Yet it is by no means evident that recognizing this design completely annuls the effectiveness of the advertisement, since there may well be other effects which operate elsewhere than at the level of overt claims, at the level of aesthetic "form." In a similar way, one might say that Brooks's too obvious intention to make an invidious contrast between the modern world and the world of the metaphysicals distracts one from a certain kind of work which is being done at another level of the reading. And this discrepancy between the overt claim made for the experience of the poem and that other "level" of the reading recapitulates the very distinction which founds the reading, between the "statements" in the poem and the "paradox" which supposedly defines its structure.

Let us pursue the Brooksian allegory a little further: "To use the metaphor on which the poem is built, the friend represents the secular world which the lovers have renounced" (WWU, 11). In this statement the distinction between sacred and profane is rewritten as the distinction between sacred and *secular*. The latter concept introduces a distinction which is again patently evocative of historical processes, of "secularization" as a phenomenon which postdates the period of the poem: "What happens to Donne's lovers if we consider them 'scientifically', without benefit of the supernaturalism which the poet confers on them?" (WWU, 18). The concept of the "secular" governing the intrusion of a "scientific" perspective here is not exactly equivalent to the concept of the profane (the word "secular" in fact does not signify in Donne's time what it does today, since it suggests an entire world from which the sacred has been evacuated). While one may construe the relation between the sacred and the profane as in some sense paradoxical in the poem, it is difficult to see how that paradox could operate where one of its terms is simply absent. In Donne's world there is profane space, but that world is not in our sense secular. Hence there is no question of a paradox in which the sacred and the secular are reconciled: "The lovers in becoming hermits, find that they have not lost the world, but have gained the world in each other, now a more intense, more meaningful world. The unworldly lovers thus become the most 'worldly' of all" (WWU, 15). If it is a question of *secularization,* of the "worldly" in our sense, how could there be any possibility of reconciliation between what are in fact two worlds, not two spaces within the world? The space of the profane always presumes the space of the sacred, else it is simply meaningless. The secular world, if that world is "modern," presumes rather the *absence,* or at least the marginalization, of the sacred. We would have to say, then, that the paradox overshoots its target, that it can at most extend to the antithesis between the sacred and the profane in Donne's world.

For Brooks the relation between two spaces in the poem can be signified unequivocally by the concepts of the sacred and the profane, or secondarily by the sacred and the secular. Even though the former distinction describes a certain aspect of Donne's world, it still may not be the primary referent in the poem, given the fact that the motif of sacred parody is not introduced until the penultimate stanza. Until that moment the spaces in the poem are organized by the distinction between *public* and *private*, the difference between the social space the speaker presently occupies and the social space from which he has withdrawn, the space of politics, business, war, etc. If this distinction is truly the organizing "antithesis" of the poem, one must concede as a matter of historical fact that in Donne's world the public space is indisputably valorized over the private, and that it is the very indisputability of this hierarchy which the poem takes as socially given. The wit of the poem then consists in its mobilizing the assymetrical hierarchy of the sacred and the profane in a surprising way, by aligning the sacred with the private and the profane with the public. Such an alignment is not exactly paradoxical, since it does not argue that the antitheses are in any way reconciled; it rather reverses one hierarchical opposition, between the public and the private, by transposing upon it another, the profane and the sacred. The question confronting the reader at this point is whether to understand the valorization of private experience in the poem as straightforward or ironic. It is no small irony of Brooks's reading that it must assume that valorization to be *unironic*, a point made by Arthur Marotti in his recent *John Donne, Coterie Poet,* in direct response to long-standing New Critical or formalist interpretations of the poem:

> In its original context, however, "The Canonization" communicated a very different message [than the one argued by Brooks]. Donne's readers knew that he was expressing his personal longing for the public world he pretended to scorn in this lyric and they would have read the poem as a more ironic, hence more aesthetically complex, work than the one the formalist critics and scholars utilizing literary and intellectual history have interpreted.[24]

In Marotti's reading the irony of the poem is at the expense of the speaker, who overcompensates for his withdrawal from the public world by hyperbolic claims for an erotic relationship. The sacred parody which Brooks reads as conveying an ironic superiority toward the "friend," and by extension toward the "modern" reader, is in this "contextual" interpretation a hyperbole which renders the poem "more ironic" when the site of ironized understanding is displaced to the "context." We need not pause here over the well-worn methodological issues raised by Marotti's distinction (between "formalist" and "anti-formalist" interpretation) in order to recognize the peculiar weakness of Brooks's allegory as an interpretation of the poem, an interpretation which violates a cardinal principle of New Critical reading by taking at face value what the speaker of the poem says, even by proposing an identification of the reader with that speaker. This depletion of the poem's irony nevertheless does not in the slightest vitiate the persuasiveness in historical context of Brooks's essay, the context of *The Well Wrought Urn's* programmatic rereading of the English literary tradition. This persuasiveness inheres not so much in the essay's generalizations about history, or about the desiccated secularity of modern life, as it does in its generalization of paradox as the "language of poetry." A second allegory emerges from behind, or is carried forward by the first, in which "The Canonization" somehow inscribes the essential condition of the poetic or the literary.

In the second allegory the historical thesis can indeed drop away, once it has done the work of transferring the epithet "sacred" from a historical period to the poem itself. The aura of the sacred is then transferred again to a certain *social space* accessible only in the reading of the poem. As we shall see, this social space replicates the space figured in the poem itself as a "hermitage," the space of religious withdrawal, or more narrowly as a "room":

> And if no peece of Chronicle wee prove,
> We'll build in sonnets pretty roomes;
> As well a well wrought urne becomes
> The greatest ashes, as halfe-acre tombes,
> And by these hymnes, all shall approve
> Us *Canoniz'd* for Love:

Brooks explicates this passage as follows:

> The poem is an instance of the doctrine which it asserts; it is both the assertion and the realization of the assertion. The poet has actually before our eyes built within the song the "pretty room" with which he says the lovers can be content. The poem itself is the well-wrought urn which can hold the lovers' ashes and which will not suffer in comparison with the prince's "halfe-acre tomb." (WWU, 17)

It is a measure of just how effective this moment has been for the subsequent history of literary criticism that the great inconsistency of Brooks's attributing to the poem a "doctrine" which it unequivocally "asserts" has been forgiven, if it has even been noticed. The point is not simply that the poem is an artifact, or that as an *aesthetic* utterance it excludes the kind of political assertion one would associate with the prince, with the social space of the political. The literary critical doctrine which the poem asserts, by virtue of the second allegory, really achieves its effect *only* by having followed so directly from the first; in this way the distinction between the sacred and the secular is carried over into a characterization, respectively, of the social space of literature and some other, antithetical social space.

If that other social space is thus to be defined as "secular," it would have to include in Brooks's terms virtually everything within the experience of modern life, the space which is perceived to be inherently hostile to literature. Conversely the space of literature is obviously not the *same* space as that of religious withdrawal—the "hermitage" of which Donne speaks— such as actually may survive in the modern world, and which secular culture suffers to exist because it is no longer significant enough to extinguish. Just as the sacred parody defined the space of erotic withdrawal in Donne's poem, so it defines the social space of the *reading of the poem* in the second allegory. This space is unmistakably institutional—it is where literature is read, the site of Brooks's address to the professors of literature: "The urns are not meant for memorial purposes only, though that often seems to be their chief significance to the professors of literature" (WWU, 21). The addressee here is specifically the philologist, with whom the New Critic contended for hegemony in the university, and against whom Brooks directs a running polemic in *The Well Wrought Urn*. The effect of this polemic is not simply to rehearse once again the imaginary identification of literary culture with the clergy but to redefine the social space of literary culture as necessarily *institutional*. The school becomes the site at which the practice of reading can be cultivated in such a way as to preserve the cultural capital of literature (signified in the Brooksian allegory as a kind of *sacredness*), just because its social space can be conceived as a space of deliberate and strategic withdrawal, as the withdrawal of literary culture from "the world."

The aura of sacredness which is communicated first to the poem and then to the social space in which the poem is read defines that space not simply as an "elsewhere," but as transcendent, the latter because that space acquires the auratic properties of the sacred. In the same way the truth the poem communicates becomes transcendent, and its refusal to speak directly, to assert propositions, is the guarantor of its possession of that other kind of truth, a "paradoxical" truth. The truth of every poem thus retreats before the act of interpretation; our arrival in its pretty room discovers an empty shrine, but a shrine nevertheless. The poem enjoins upon us the recognition of the externality of dogma and conceals from us the fact that we are already within its truth, that its truth *is* this externality: the poem as paradogmatic text. In this sense every poem becomes an image of the very institutional space in which it is read, a perfect mirror in the imaginary of that space, alerting the company of professional readers that the retreat of literary culture into the university can be understood as a kind of transcendence of the cultural conditions of modernity. This is Brooks's solution to the same problem which Leavis hoped to solve by reconstructing literary culture as an incognito clergy—but a very different solution.

It is also a solution fraught with contradictions, the most important of which is registered by the very ambiguity of the "urn" as a figure for the poem. While that figure does convey straightforwardly both the artifactual nature of the poem and its sacred aura, it offers a much less straightforward figure for the paradogmatic status of the literary work. If the urn were merely empty, that would suggest that its contents (its doctrine) were elsewhere, in a relation of transcendence to the (secular, scientific) doctrines which circulate as truth in the modern world. But the urn contains the ashes of something no longer living, and thus the figure stumbles unwittingly on the very social conditions for which it attempted to compensate: the perceived decline in the cultural significance of literature itself, the perceived marginality of literary culture to the modern social order. It would not do for Brooks to represent the truth toward which literature gestures as, in the terms of his allegory, mere ashes. Brooks is sufficiently aware of this implication of his allegory to attempt a conflation of Donne's "well wrought urn" with the urn in Shakespeare's "The Phoenix and the Turtle," which urn, as it happens, contains the ashes of a *phoenix:* "The urn to which we are summoned, the urn which holds the ashes of the phoenix, is like the well-wrought urn of Donne's 'Canonization' which holds the phoenix-lovers' ashes: it is the poem itself" (WWU, 21). Paradox has a doctrinal content after all, and Brooks cannot quite resist hinting at the doctrine he has in mind by offering as his privileged examples of paradox two biblical citations: "He who would save his life, must lose it," and "The last shall be first" (WWU, 18). Here again, however, the hint is too blatant to be effective in its own terms, and the truth of the paradoxes in question beg to be read otherwise, perhaps as: "he who would save the truth claims of literature must give them up"; and "literary culture, though it may appear to be marginal, has now found a site at which it can exercise renewed power." The rebirth of the phoenix thus signifies the Eliot-like wish-fulfillment fantasy of a return to Christian orthodoxy; but that wish drops away virtually as soon as it is expressed and the phoenix rises instead as the figure for a resurgent literary culture, a "new criticism" which establishes hegemony in the university by displacing the philologists, whose relation to literature was merely "memorial," merely the preservation of the ashes of literary culture.

Doxy

With someone like you, a pal good and true
I'd like to leave it all behind, and go and find
Some place that's known to God alone,
Just a spot to call our own.
We'll find perfect peace, where joys never cease,
Out there beneath a kindly sky,
We'll build a sweet little nest, somewhere in the West,
And let the rest of the world go by.
      —J. KEIRN BRENNAN, "Let the Rest of the World Go By"

It remains to be seen whether the retreat of literary culture to the university was really strategic. I would argue that Brooks betrays considerable ambivalence about the strategic withdrawal of literary culture to the confines of the academy whenever he reverts to Eliot's revisionary narrative of literary history: "A history of poetry from Dryden's time to our own might bear as its subtitle 'The Half-Hearted Phoenix'." (WWU, 20). What could this possibly mean if not that one implication of the reading of "The Canonization" is that much of English literature after Dryden is defective in terms of wit, ambiguity, paradox? The history of English literature is the history of the decline of literary culture itself. The momentary reassertion of the radically revisionist construction of the English literary canon thus stands in uneasy relation to the programmatic agenda of reading the major canonical poets "as one has learned to read Donne and the moderns" (WWU, 193).[25] If the revisionist canon was the basis for a cultural jeremiad against modernity, a jeremiad in which the authority of literary culture was pitted against competing modern cultural authorities (whatever these may be), the programmatic attempt to demonstrate the continuity of every canonical English writer with the metaphysicals on the one hand, and the moderns on the other, was the strategic imperative of a more narrowly institutional campaign, a campaign for hegemony within the university.

Surely one of the more widely accepted received ideas about New Critical pedagogy has been that its success in the university was in part an effect of its suitability for the new, postwar university constituency of college students. Graff remarks, for example, that in addition to its larger ambition of counteracting the effects of "cultural fragmentation,"

> putting the emphasis on the literary text itself had a more
> humble advantage: it seemed a tactic ideally suited to a new,
> mass student body that could not be depended on to bring to

the university any common cultural background—and not just the student body but the new professors as well, who might often be only marginally ahead of the students. The explicative method made it possible for literature to be taught efficiently to students who took for granted little history. (173)

This is carefully worded and does not claim for New Critical pedagogy much more than its being at the right place at the right time. It would be a mistake to conclude on the basis of its resounding success that the technique of close reading was *designed* with the "mass student body" in view. Brooks and Warren's *Understanding Poetry,* for example, was first published in 1938, at a time when the university was still a very exclusive institution, when one could still assume the relative cultural and class homogeneity of its constituency. There is no reason to assume that the basic principles of New Critical pedagogy were not formulated in a context highly sympathetic to elitist notions of High Culture. The version of formalism espoused by the New Critics never assumed that the readers of literature should be other than very well educated, else it would be difficult to see how these readers could follow the historical allegory continually being invoked in early New Critical interpretive essays. Even as late as *The Well Wrought Urn,* Brooks remarks that an apparently accessible poem such as Gray's *Elegy* is not so intelligible to modern readers as it may seem, because so much of the poem's meaning depends on allusions to work which is no longer familiar: "How important they [allusions] are may be judged by the response to the poem made by an audience which is *really* completely unaware of them: our public school system, it may be said, is rapidly providing such an audience for the purposes of making such a test" (WWU, 107). If the technique of close reading proved so congenial to the graduates of this same public school system, this fact presents a historical problem which is on the face of it not easy to explain.

Let us first of all acknowledge that for the New Critics the language of poetry, and of literature in general, was intrinsically *difficult.* This was not a difficulty which could be removed by the glossing of sources, or by recourse to information about the author's life or beliefs; it was a difficulty which did not disappear in the process of interpretation so much as it was confirmed. One may go further than this and say that difficulty itself was positively valued in New Critical practice, that it was a form of cultural capital, just by virtue of imparting to cultural objects a certain kind of *rarity,* the very difficulty of apprehending them. How, then, could this notion of difficulty survive the transformation of the New Criticism into a pedagogy which was disseminated far beyond the university, which penetrated even into the high schools and the grammar schools? The success of the New

Criticism in the school system did not entail discarding the notion of poetry's difficulty for the contrary notion of its simplicity; rather, it was the notion of difficulty itself which became capable of wide dissemination, which became in a certain sense "popular."

If "difficulty" names the condition of poetic language more specifically signified by the terms "paradox," "ambiguity," or "wit," the valorization of difficulty as the general quality of poetic language was always an integral part of the New Critical agenda of canonizing the modernist poets. This project was not easy to accomplish, precisely because the notion of difficulty circulated between the wars as a negative criterion of judgment, as the basis for the resistance to modernist poetry. It was difficulty itself which had to be rehabilitated by invoking the precedent of the metaphysicals. The revaluation of difficulty on behalf of both metaphysicals and moderns is a consistent objective of *The Well Wrought Urn*, from which I extract the following exemplary polemical statements:

> The question of what poetry communicates, if anything, has been largely forced upon us by the advent of "modern" poetry. Some of that poetry is admittedly highly difficult—a great deal of it is bound to *appear* difficult to the reader of conventional reading habits, even in spite of the fact—actually, in many cases, *because* of the fact—that he is a professor of literature.
>
> For this reason, the difficult moderns are often represented as untraditional and generally irresponsible. . . .
>
> The question, however, allows only one honest answer: modern poetry (if it is really poetry, and, at its best, it is really poetry), communicates whatever any other poetry communicates. (WWU, 67)

> Much modern poetry is difficult. Some of it may be difficult because the poet is snobbish and definitely wants to restrict his audience, though this is a strange vanity and much rarer than Mr. Eastman would have us think. Some modern poetry is difficult because it is bad. . . . Some modern poetry is difficult because of the special problems of our civilization. But a great deal of modern poetry is difficult for the reader simply because so few people, relatively speaking, are accustomed to reading *poetry as poetry.* . . .
>
> Now the modern poet has, for better or worse, thrown the weight of the responsibility upon the reader. The reader must be on the alert for shifts of tone, for ironic statement. He must be prepared to accept a method of indirection. He is further ex-

pected to be reasonably well acquainted with the general
tradition—literary, political, phiolsophical, for he is reading a
poet who comes at the end of a long tradition. . . . (WWU, 76)

It would be disingenuous not to admit that in some respects this polemic is
as viable now as it was when Brooks and the New Critics first advanced it;
but this is not to say that the polemic is incapable of being read in historical
context. The question before us is not whether difficulty should be a positive or negative criterion of value—one assumes that difficulty justifies itself, like anything else, in the specificity of its circumstances—but what
difficulty *means* in a given context of its deployment as a concept. I have
quoted Brooks's polemic at length in order to appreciate the sliding status
of difficulty as a quality at once peculiar to the practice of modernist poetry
and yet somehow characteristic of poetry in general, of "poetry as poetry."
I would suggest that in possessing this (paradoxical?) quality of peculiarity
and generality, the concept of difficulty corresponds to the waffling in
Brooks's judgment between the narrow canon of metaphysicals and moderns authorized by Eliot, and the much larger "traditional" canon, which
is identical to the established literary curriculum in the university. The very
difficulty of demonstrating the difficulty of much "traditional" poetry accounts for the strenuous polemic of *The Well Wrought Urn,* since Brooks
must convince his readers both that the difficulty of modernist poetry is
justified and that all poetry is inherently difficult—the former proposition
by means of the latter.[26]

The literary historical context of Brooks's valorization of difficulty has
been persuasively established in a recent article by Craig S. Abbott entitled
"Modern American Poetry: Anthologies, Classrooms, and Canons," whose
conclusions I here incorporate.[27] Abbott reminds us that there already existed by the 1920s a fairly well established canon of "modern" American
poets, whose works were extensively anthologized, as well as taught in the
high schools and colleges. These figures were not the familiar titans of
modernism but rather "such poets as Vachel Lindsay, Amy Lowell, Edgar
Lee Masters, and Carl Sandburg—poets not thought especially difficult
then or now" (209). The point of recollecting these names here is neither to
emphasize once again the contingency of the process of canon formation,
nor to defend the modernist canon which prevailed in the end, but rather to
understand the basis for the *resistance* to the kind of modernism espoused
by the New Critics. For the poets who were so consistently anthologized in
the 1920s and 1930s, as well as taught in the schools, were perceived to be
in every way *modern.* That modernity was characterized, however, by its
affirmative quality, by its embrace of a culture which it regarded opti-

mistically as progressive, democratic, and "popular" in an entirely positive sense. Such a relation to modernity demanded of cultural works themselves that they be generally accessible, and therefore that they not be difficult. It was on the basis of this "popular" modernism that the work of Eliot, Pound, or Stevens could be dismissed precisely for its quality of difficulty.

The conflict between a "popular" and a "high" modernism engages issues rather larger than can be treated here, and hence I will be content with making a somewhat more limited point: The meaning of simplicity and difficulty as qualities of poetic language cannot be resolved into unambiguous political oppositions. Popular modernism's affirmation of the "democratic" was also, at least in its American version, intensely chauvinistic, as well as complicitous with aspects of mass culture whose effects tended toward the domination of what Adorno and Horkheimer called the "culture industry." Conversely the reactionary elitism of so much high modernism could stimulate the production of genuinely adversarial cultural forms, an ambiguity that tends to obscure the differences between left and right versions of modernism at the *level of form*. If this ambiguity is only too familiar now, as the occasion of an interminable analysis of "modernism," we need not adjudicate the positions within this debate in order to recognize that the very existence of a "popular" literary modernism testified to a temporary blurring of the cultural capital embodied by literature and by the artifacts of mass culture. Hence the anthologies of the period, as Abbott points out, included as representative modern poems works such as Joyce Kilmer's "Trees," or even Katherine Lee Bates's "America the Beautiful" (216, 218)—works which it is difficult to regard now as anything other than kitsch, perhaps the least interesting "popular" artifacts of the twentieth century.

One might hypothesize that literature and mass culture could converge in this way in part because the linguistic capital traditionally acquired by the study of literature—Standard English—really was by the period in question very efficiently distributed at the lower levels of the school system to a very large percentage of the population. In other words, when Standard English (as the capital conveyed by a literary curriculum) became the possession of nearly everyone with a grade-school education, it coincided in the scope of its distribution with mass culture itself. In that circumstance the redundancy of the literary curriculum at the level of the university could become the occasion of a struggle over what kind of cultural capital was to be produced by literary study at that level. The argument for the linguistic simplicity of literature became a losing argument in that context just because it could not establish a sufficiently marked difference between the literary curriculum of the university and the curriculum at the lower levels of the school system. The argument for the linguistic difficulty of literature, on the other hand, revalued literature as the cultural capital of the university by reading it in a new way, as the embodiment of a language distinct in its difficulty, and thus by implication providing a different kind of linguistic capital from that conveyed by the literary curriculum at the lower levels of the school system. If this fact is hard to see in historical retrospect, that is because the valuation of difficulty in New Critical practice never had to be expressed, and could not be expressed, as the devaluation of Standard English itself. These two languages were not antithetical but rather coexisted as languages which were cultivated in different institutional spaces, at different levels of the school system. There was no question of any opposition between these languages, because one was spoken while the other was more or less exclusively written, a language embodied in literature as the New Critics defined it, a language which required *interpretation*. The valorization of difficulty thus entailed no derogation of Standard English but rather a renewed and intensified attack upon mass culture, precisely in order to distinguish the capital embodied in literary texts from the literary simulacra circulating as "popular modernism." As a result of the New Criticism's success in installing a modernist canon of difficult poets the works of popular modernism fell precipitously to the level of mass culture.

This effect could be achieved without advertising literature itself as the exclusive capital of an elite class, even if in practice the university was open only to a very small group within the society. It is worth recalling, then, that while the protocols of New Critical reading were established long before the universities opened their doors to a somewhat larger constituency after the Second World War, these protocols were not substantially altered by the increased size and diversity of that constituency. In discovering that literature was intrinsically difficult, these new students also discovered at the same moment why it needed to be studied *in the university*. The intrinsic difficulty of literary language marked precisely the distinction between High Cultural artifacts and mass cultural artifacts, but the important point here is that this distinction also defined the social spaces appropriate to the consumption of these cultural artifacts. This is the reason why the crypto-religious polemic of the New Critics against the secularity of modern life could drop away in the 1950s: that polemic could be received as a polemic against mass culture per se. The features of this polemic are not difficult to recover in such a text as *The Well Wrought Urn*, since the properties of "secularity" are confused throughout that text with the denigration of mass culture. But in an appendix refuting the "cultural relativism" of Frederick Pottle's recently published *Idiom of Poetry*, Brooks develops a longer and more explicit polemic against the depravity of mass culture. Pottle's cautious entertainment of a skepticism about the possibility of grounding the value judgments which distinguish High Culture from Low provokes in Brooks the sense of an imminent crisis in the humanities: "The issue is nothing less than a defense of the Humanities in the hard days that lie ahead" (WWU, 235). So far from eschewing judgment, then, Brooks presents the agenda of the New Criticism as expressly evaluative: "For critical relativism wins its simplicity and objectivity only at the sacrifice of the whole concept of literature as we know it. For what is the sensibility of our age? Is there any one sensibility? Do we respond to T. S. Eliot, Dashiell Hammett, Mary Roberts Rinehart, or Tiffany Thayer?" (WWU, 232). The necessity of judgment here is not the necessity of making discriminations within the canon of literature (such discriminations as Eliot's criticism continually advanced). Literature rather presents a united front, in the form of its intrinsic *difficulty,* against the artifacts of mass culture, and it is along this front that a defensive posture must be maintained: "Tied in with language may be a way of apprehending reality, a philosophy, a whole worldview" (WWU, 236). Not to maintain the distinction of poetic language would be tantamount to crediting the sensibility, in Brooks's sensational example, of the "young lady who confesses to raptures over her confessions magazine" (WWU, 233). While it is unlikely that the young lady in question ever bothered to compare her confession magazines with the great works of literature, the fact that Brooks must do so, and must arrive at the obvious conclusion about the respective values of these artifacts, suggests that he is really responding to a certain stage in the development of mass culture, a stage in which such a rapprochement of literature with mass culture as that embodied in "popular modernism" is no longer desirable for literary culture.

If she had been asked, the reader of the confession magazines would no doubt have conceded the cultural superiority of literature, whether or not she ever felt inclined to read any works so designated. Therein lies the peculiar power of mass culture, since the waning cultural centrality of literary works in the face of new mass cultural forms never entailed a denial of the nominally superior value of literature. In this context one may appreciate the historical irony of the later reappearance of "The Canonization" as an exemplary text for explication in the fourth edition of *Understanding Poetry* (1976). There Donne's poem is contrasted not with secular, scientific culture, its antagonist in *The Well Wrought Urn,* but with a lyric from Tin Pan Alley called "Let the Rest of the World Go By." The choice of a "popular song from the 1920s" may reflect a certain High Cultural disconnection from popular culture, but it is more likely that the song is standing in rather coyly for more recent music, whose lyrics would only make the comparison with "The Canonization" more embarrassing: "The reader may question the propriety of comparing this massive poem with the flimsy little lyric from Tin Pan Alley quoted above on page 130. Surely one does not need to bring up a howitzer in order to annihilate a gnat."[28] There follows nevertheless a rather painstaking demonstration of the superiority of Donne's poem to the gnat-like popular song. The very belatedness of this polemic attests, however, to the persistence of the gnat, which is only a gnat in the hopeful perspective of its determined opponents, those who, as Brooks writes in *The Well Wrought Urn,* resist rather than give in to "the spirit of the age" (WWU, 235).

In its immense capaciousness, the mass culture of modernity never coveted the institutional space to which literary culture retreated. In that space a polemic against mass culture could be developed and blandly received by a generation of university students who willingly credited the cultural capital of literature, who learned to recognize the superiority of literature to mass cultural artifacts, but who continued to consume both kinds of artifacts in the distinct spheres of their consumption. It may be said that "minority culture" came to be identified with the social space of the school, but it would be more accurate to say that it was internalized as a *mode of consumption* in the graduate of the university. The capacity to experience the social space of the schools and the social space of mass culture as disjunct effectively institutionalized two modes of consumption, one consequence of which was to make literary works more difficult to consume outside the school.[29] The polemic on behalf of the difficulty of literary language, and against the degraded simplicity of mass culture, did not have to be aimed at an audience of the socially elite, only university students, whoever they might be. It was even possible, after its triumph in the university, for New Critical pedagogy to be disseminated at the lower levels of the school system, since it was only necessary, in order to maintain the cultural capital of the literary curriculum, for the constitutive difficulty of literary language to be asserted there as well. We may fairly describe the effect of New Critical pedagogy as "paradoxical," since its most strenuous effort to impose a divorce between literary culture and mass culture produced in the end a curious kind of rapprochement. If this cultural detente does not represent an "association of sensibility," its submission to a certain cultural logic of inclusiveness renders unintentionally ironic such Brooksian attempts to characterize modernity as the following:

> But if Donne could have it both ways, most of us, in this latter day, cannot. We are disciplined in the tradition of either-or, and lack the mental agility—to say nothing of the maturity of

attitude—which would allow us to indulge in the finer distinctions and the more subtle reservations permitted by the tradition of both-and. Flesh *or* spirit, merely a doxy or purely a goddess (or alternately, one and then the other), is more easily managed in our poetry, and probably, for that matter, in our private lives. But the greater poems of our tradition are more ambitious in this matter: as a consequence, they come perhaps nearer the truth than we do with our ordinary hand-to-mouth insights. (WWU, 81)

When the choice is between literary culture and mass culture, however, there is no question of "both-and." There is no question of which might be represented as a goddess, which by the doxy; the example of the woman absorbed in her confession magazines confirms that. If mass culture can be stigmatized by association with the lurid taste of the female consumer, literary culture on the other hand becomes the site of a certain kind of worship, not of a goddess, but of its own version of transcendence, the experience to be found only in reading "the greater poems of our tradition." How very ironic, then, that neither the polemic against secularity nor the polemic on behalf of Eliot's canonical choices proved capable of imposing Brooks's "either-or" upon the generation of postwar readers. The effect of New Critical pedagogy was rather to produce a kind of recusant literary culture, at once faithful to the quasi-sacred authority of literature but paying tribute at the same time to the secular authority of a derogated mass culture. For the recusants the artifacts of mass culture might be consumed with a certain guilt, or a certain relief; but for those whose allegiance was sworn to the secular authority, that culture provided everything there was to consume.

Chapter Four

Literature after Theory:
The Lesson of Paul de Man

The Canon and Symptom of Theory

The movement to open the literary canon to works by minority authors has been paralleled in the last twenty-five years by an opening of the canon in another direction: The emergence of theory in the 1960s breached the disciplinary fortifications between literary texts and texts derived from other discourses, such as the linguistic, the psychoanalytic, the philosophical. These texts are sufficiently well identified now as to constitute what may be called the "canon of theory." While we would want to say, in retrospect, that there must have been some relation between these parallel challenges to the perceived closure of the literary canon, the nature of that relation is still far from obvious. In practice it has been possible for the two movements to maintain considerable distance from one another, and even to skirmish over such questions as the political efficacy of their respective agendas. Thus Paul de Man in his later work could echo the language of the anticanonical critique in arguing that theory "displaces or even transcends the traditional barriers of literary and presumably non-literary uses of language and liberates the corpus from the secular weight of textual canonization" (RT 9).[1] Theory's suspension of the category of the literary, institutionalized as the inclusion of nonliterary works in its syllabus, might seem in a narrow sense more radical than a movement to open the canon to minority works that remain, after all, literary works. Nevertheless the apparent detachment of much theory from overtly political questions has been the occasion of considerable uneasiness on the part of theorists, an uneasiness expressed recently, for example, in Barbara Johnson's determination to force a belated confrontation between deconstruction and feminism in order to interrogate, by means of theory itself, "the literary canon, particularly in terms of its sexual and racial exclusions and effacements."[2]

The emergence in recent years of a sophisticated antitheoretical position, "neo-pragmatist" in orientation, suggests that it may be possible now
to attempt at least a preliminary historical retrospect on the age of
theory—in the recognition, of course, that theory is an enterprise that will
continue in some form. To speak of an "age of theory" is to recognize first
of all the enormous significance of the *word* "theory," as the unifying name
of manifestly heterogeneous critical practices. I shall not offer here anything like a definition of theory in general, much less a survey of its various
forms, but rather an initial engagement with the name of theory, as a sign
both defining and defined by a syllabus of texts. These texts include the
master theorists themselves, along with the historical writers—Nietzsche,
Saussure, Freud, Heidegger, etc.—whose works are retroactively constructed as the *canon* of theory. This canon has emerged in the graduate
schools alongside the literary canon, not only (or even most importantly)
as a new area of specialization, but as the means by which to practice the
criticism of literary texts in a new way. Again we may quote a statement
from de Man's oeuvre as exemplary of this project: "There is absolutely no
reason why analyses of the kind here suggested for Proust would not be
applicable, with proper modifications of technique, to Milton or Dante or
to Hölderlin. This will in fact be the task of literary criticism in the coming
years" (AR 17).

De Man's explicit injunction to apply the lessons of theory to the whole
of literature locates the practice of theory squarely within the discipline of
literary criticism. From this statement we may infer that while the texts that
constitute the canon of theory are not ordinarily literary texts, it is in *relation* to the literary syllabus that they can be constructed as the syllabus of
"theory." This fact is indisputable, but its significance has been missed
because that significance is, precisely, *symptomatic*.[3] The Continental
(mostly French) provenance of theory in the several discourses of anthropology, philosophy, linguistics, criticism, or political analysis restricts the
practice of theory to no single discipline, and that circumstance has made
the signifier "theory" perhaps less institutionally significant in the country
of theory's origin than in the United States. On the Continent, moreover,
particular movements (structuralism, poststructuralism) tended to produce interdisciplinary coalitions which never really emerged on this side of
the Atlantic. The syllabus of theory has even now conquered only minor
territories in disciplines other than literary criticism, and the agency for the
dissemination of theory has remained departments of literature; for that
reason the emergence of theory remains indissolubly linked to the discipline of literary criticism, and thus to the literary curriculum. Theory is
last, if not first, *literary* theory.

How then should one understand the determination of theory as literary theory? Let us consider another "symptomatic" fact: the circulation of the name "deconstruction" as *another name* for theory.[4] Now the equation of theory with deconstruction will seem obviously inaccurate, given that one can speak of "Marxist" theory, or "psychoanalytic" theory, or "feminist" theory. Surely it is only in the popular media, in the somewhat hysterical minds of the journalists, that deconstruction and theory are interchangeable terms. But once again, to dismiss such a fact as merely hysterical or ill-informed is to miss its symptomatic significance. We need look no further than de Man's essay, "The Resistance to Theory," to find a text within theory in which deconstruction and theory are indeed *identified*. For de Man does not mean by his title the resistance to Marxist theory or feminist theory; he means the resistance to deconstructive theory, and even more specifically to the version of deconstruction he calls "rhetorical reading." If deconstruction can *stand for* theory in his argument, this does not imply that all theory is deconstructive but that deconstruction stands in a peculiarly representative or symptomatic relation to all theory. To read deconstruction—or the oeuvre of de Man—as symptomatic, then, is to understand something about the way in which particular writers and writings, of whatever discursive affiliation, can circulate as representatives of "literary theory" in a specific institutional and disciplinary context, a context defined, as we shall see, by the symptomatic significance of the writing and position of Paul de Man.

A reading, then, of the symptomatic significance of de Manian deconstruction as "literary theory"—as a certain expression of the relation between literature and theory—need make no case for the objective preeminence of de Manian doctrine within the profession. It will not matter to this argument to what extent, or for how long, de Manian deconstruction dominated the critical scene. On the contrary the "resistance to (de Manian) theory" will prove to be a measure of its symptomatic significance even greater than the capacity of de Man to seed the profession with his disciples. The immense symptomatic significance of the *figure* of de Man has been indisputably confirmed by the paroxysm which passed through the entire critical profession in the wake of the revelations concerning de Man's wartime journalism. It would not have been necessary for so many theorists and antitheorists, de Manians and anti–de Manians, to "respond" to these revelations if *theory itself* were not perceived to be implicated in the figure of de Man. The easy condemnation in the media of theory along with de Man only confirmed a symbolic equation already present in the professional imaginary. A symptomatic reading of the de Manian corpus will elucidate this equation along the axis of imaginary identification: theory-deconstruction-de Man. Such a reading will entail a close examination of the text of de Man, not in order to discover there the contradictions or lapses that will disprove the argument of deconstruction, but in order to discover what problem within the discipline of literary criticism becomes manifest as the symptomatology of the de Manian oeuvre.

A first level of symptomatology is spectacularly betrayed by the scandal of the wartime journalism: That scandal reveals, over and above the revelations about de Man himself, the fact that the charismatic persona of the master theorist is the vehicle for the dissemination of theory; otherwise the status of deconstructive theory could not rise or fall with the reputation of its master. Furthermore, even the most cursory survey of the theoretical field discloses how intimately the fortunes of theory are dependent upon the capacity of the master theorists to produce disciples. This does not mean, of course, that one must be a disciple of a given teacher in order to recognize that teacher as a master theorist, but that the title of theorist is attributed retroactively to a writer (even dead writers, even writers whom one knows only as a body of writing) by the company of disciples. There is no master without disciples. The effect of discipleship is not confined to the seminar (though it has its origin there), but communicates itself through the medium of the master's writing, insofar as that writing counts as "theory," as the discourse of a master. Here we can make two preliminary points about the argument to follow, one very general, the other specific to de Man: First, discipleship is an effect of all teaching, and theory only magnifies this effect by objectifying the charisma of the master teacher as a methodology. While charisma may first appear in the seminar as a personal quality, it passes into the disciplinary field as a certain effect of *style,* an imitable effect. Second, the value of a symptomatic reading of de Man in this context inheres in recognizing the renowned intensity of his charismatic teaching, its power to intensify the effects of discipleship. Again, this is not an argument about the actual effects of de Manian discipleship, but about its representative relation to the conditions governing the dissemination of theory.

The articulation of the first level of symptomatology is incomplete, as it only brings to light the most *obvious* of symptoms—de Manian discipleship. The second level of analysis concerns the theory itself, "rhetorical reading" or "deconstruction." The question we shall ask again, is not how this theory is typical or dominant but how it is symptomatic. Here we can adduce an additional term from the Althusserian lexicon, and ask what *problematic* underlies rhetorical reading. The answer is undoubtedly the problematic of literature, of its definition. To this question de Man gives an unequivocal answer, reiterated throughout his work: "I would not hesitate to equate the rhetorical, figural potentiality of language with literature it-self" (AR 10). The equation of literature with rhetoric is not exclusive to de Manian deconstruction; it rather describes an identification which is more or less accepted within most versions of literary theory. It is by means of a shift onto the terrain of rhetoric that theory opens the literary syllabus to nonliterary works: theory discovers the "rhetorical" in these works and in finding rhetoric it *refinds literature*. By referring all language to rhetoric the literary critic can read anything, but in practice this has meant reading non-literary texts *as literary*, according to the protocols of "literary theory." Hence Derrida has quite rightly recognized in the distorting mirror of American deconstruction the appearance of what he calls "rhetoricism," and which he condemns as yet another logocentrism. Be that as it may, we can recognize in "rhetoricism" something like an epistemic feature of liter-ary theory. Let us take, for example, a certain familiar discursive regu-larity: the emergence of "metaphor" and "metonymy" as a ubiquitous terminological binarism within theory. It is obvious that this binarism gov-erns the assimilation of Saussurean linguistics into literary theory, by way of translating the linguistic motifs of contiguity and substitution into their supposedly correspondent rhetorical tropes. It also governs the assimila-tion of psychoanalytic terminology, by way of foregrounding the signifi-cance of condensation and displacement in the dreamwork. And it has even been possible to find in the tropological binarism a rhetorical basis of *marxisant* ideology-critique, by way of identifying metaphor with ideolog-ical mystification, and metonymy with the deconstruction of those mysti-fications. Whatever the local interest of such rhetoricism, I will suggest in the following argument that rhetoricism itself, the equation of literature with rhetoric, is the ideology of theory. But what is that ideology's pur-pose? Althusser suggests that a symptomatic reading of a text reveals that the text provides an answer to a question which does not itself apear in the text. In the case of de Man, the question which *does* appear in the text is "What is literature?" But this is not the question for which rhetoricism provides the answer. The real question, the invisible question, is "What shall replace literary criticism as it was formerly practiced, as the apprecia-tive interpretation of the syllabus of 'literary' works?" Literary theory as a version of rhetoricism defends literature from its half-perceived and half-acknowledged social marginality. But this marginality, which must be un-derstood in relation to the social and institutional conditions of the teach-ing of literature, is not finally overcome by the revival of rhetoric alone. No theory, least of all "rhetorical reading," can alter the social conditions of critical practice without first recognizing the real nature of these condi-tions.

The adjustment of critical practice to new socioinstitutional conditions of literary pedagogy is registered symptomatically within theory by its tendency to model the intellectual work of the theorist on the new social form of intellectual work, the technobureaucratic labor of the new professional-managerial class. It is for that reason that the turn to rhetoric not only gestures beyond the narrow confines of the literary syllabus but also resurrects the ancient art of rhetoric as a *technical* practice, quite unlike either the "art" of interpretation or the even more intuitive exercise of judgment or taste, the art of appreciation. This point brings us to a third level of symptomatology, inhering in theory's characterization of its own methodological procedures. Here the de Manian oeuvre is again supremely symptomatic, since perhaps more than any other literary theorist, de Man insisted on the technical quality of theoretically enlightened readings, a quality he designated by the term "rigor." In the final section of this chapter I will argue that "rigor" has the symptomatic function of characterizing both the master theorist (*his* rigor) and the methodology (*its* rigor). Here we can also begin to understand the relation between the first and second levels of symptomatology, since rigor stands both for what constitutes the charisma of de Man, as well as the iterability of his teaching. At this level the symptomatology must be read in the immediate context of its institutional conditions, since what functions as "rigor" in the idealized self-representation of rhetorical reading translates in practice into the *routinization* of charisma, the "political" problem the disciples recognize (and misrecognize) as the "institutionalization" of de Man's putatively radical teaching. I will attempt to read this problem as the failure of de Manian theory (and theory in general) to function as anything other than an interim, imaginary solution to the new conditions of intellectual labor, conditions that will certainly require a thorough rethinking of what it is that literary critics do in the classroom and in their writing. In the meanwhile we can say that the reconstruction of criticism as a "technical" practice revealed the intrinsic inadequacy of the literary syllabus as the object of that intellectual labor; hence the "rigor" of theory had to be embodied not in literary works but in the philosophical or other nonliterary texts supplementing that syllabus. It is these works, the "canon of theory," which *signify rigor.* Insofar as all theory aspires to the condition of rigor, the de Manian oeuvre does indeed represent the symptom of a crisis in the nature of the intellectual work performed by the teachers and critics of literature.

The Transmission of Theory, or Transference Transferred

I suspected that I found in him the educator and philosopher whom I had sought for so long. It is true that I only found a book, and that was a great lack. And thus I made all the more effort to see beyond the book and to picture the man who promised to make only those his heirs who wished to be and were capable of being more than just his readers: namely, his sons and pupils.

—NIETZSCHE, "Schopenhauer as Educator"

"He never sought followers"

To begin, we may concede that there is in theory "absolutely no reason" why deconstructive practice should not be disseminated much *farther* than Milton or Dante or Hölderlin. What could possibly retard its dissemination, or keep it close to the syllabus of de Man's own teaching, as though close to home? The injunction quoted above tacitly names the problem of deconstruction's limit by assuming a nameless addressee; for "the task of criticism in the coming years" was really the task of the disciples; it was only for them that the sentence could be received as an imperative. It was the disciples who were to produce "analyses of the kind here suggested" of Milton or Dante or Hölderlin. The analysis upon which I embark here is not a description of the charismatic per se, but of the social relation between the teacher and the student. If the institutional locus of canon formation is the school, and its instrumentality the syllabus, the social relation between teacher and student oddly effaces its institutional conditions in producing nothing less than a kind of love: first the love of the disciple for the master, and then the love for what the master teaches, his "teaching," and beyond that, as we shall see, a love for the very texts the master loves.

That the relation between teacher and student is "erotic" is perhaps the least surprising statement one might make about it, nearly the oldest news in Western writing. I would suggest nevertheless that the voluminous testimony to the truth of Plato's argument in the *Symposium* does not necessarily amount to a good analysis of the pedagogic relation. For reasons of decorum the analysis of that relation has usually been conducted elsewhere than in the classroom, or called something else, in order not to have it interfere with the love that reproduces reproduction itself, and which can be made visible only in testimony, in anecdote. Such testimony circulates *alongside* the doctrine the disciple reproduces, but not in immediate logical relation to that doctrine, which constitutes itself as a love object by a devious pathology. Consider, then, the following anecdote of discipleship, in which love declares itself, loudly, but at the same time with a certain reticence:

> In the face of his imminent death, there was once again the passion: as we sat in a New Haven café, as we had sat in so many other cafés in Paris, Zurich, New York, he asked me, "What are

you working on next?" and I said I had begun to take a real
interest in James—*The Portrait, The Princess*. His clear delight
broke out—"I *love* Henry James."[5]

One would not like to deny the author, Juliet Flower MacCannel, the pleasure of repeating this anecdote, which itself conveys so emphatically the
pleasure of a certain repetition. The teacher, like the scene, is reassuringly
the same in Paris, Zurich, New York, or New Haven. Nor does the conversation cease to recur with the death of de Man, since the narrative fixes the
scene of the conversation in a loop of eternal recurrence, exemplary of what
Freud called "the inappreciation of time characteristic of the unconscious."
It is indeed the *transference* which denies that the object of its love can
change or be killed, least of all "in effigy."[6] In the face of de Man's imminent death, the transference love is forced, as always, into a strategic indirection. What makes de Man's love for Henry James a necessary fact to
relate in this context is not simply the love that exists between the disciple
and the teacher, but the way in which the two "faces" are mutually averted
from the fact between them. Only for this reason can de Man's love for
James, upon which the anecdote insists, mean to the disciple, "I love *you,*"
in the sense that it retroactively endows the disciple's interest in James with
the semantic surcharge of the love for the teacher. This love has no place at
all in whatever reading of James might eventuate from it, and it is paradoxically not "expressed" there at all. Hence the efflux of delight when it can
"break out" in what is merely anecdote, testimony that has conversely
nothing to do intrinsically with Henry James, but which endorses James as
the object of study.

It would be difficult indeed to open the phenomenon of discipleship to
analysis without invoking the concept of the transference, however carefully and even decisively we may wish to distinguish the analytic scene from
the pedagogic. The necessity of such a distinction arises from the fact that
the evidence at hand about this relation is anecdotal, the evidence of the
café and not of the seminar room. The "erotics" of discipleship surround
the classroom with the constant chatter of testimony, with declarations of
love and hate that fall silent at the threshold of the seminar. Freud argues
that in some institutions, in contrast to the institution of psychoanalysis,
the transference has no "inhibitory effect" in relation to the cure, precisely
because it is "decorously glossed over." In psychoanalysis the transference
is ruthlessly exposed as "resistance," but also encouraged as the primary
means of access to the unconscious. From the anecdote of the disciple we
might guess already that an erotic relation which is so "decorously glossed
over" as to be foreclosed from discussion is not less complex than its vol-

uble cousin in analysis; as a consequence it hardly suffices to say that the love of the child for the parent is simply transferred to the teacher, as it is to the analyst, positively or negatively. The possibility of transference exists in any relation between unequal partners, and we do not need the evidence of the café to posit this love. What concerns us is the capacity of the sentence, "I love Henry James" to mean in the anecdote both "I [the student] love you [the teacher]," as well as "I [the teacher] love you [the student]." The fact that the transference operates under the same injunction to indirection on both sides of the relation inserts both parties into the antecedent position of the pronouns. The double proposition does not tell us that the disciple loves Henry James only because the master does, although this love frequently enough has its origin there too, as another disciple attests: "If he said in an aside one day that we ought to read Hegel's *Aesthetics*, we read them, in order to understand why we must read them. If he said that the first draft of Rousseau's *Social Contract* was more interesting than the second and more polished draft, we spent weeks comparing them" (YFS, 11). What is said "in an aside," like the protestation of love for James, is that the transference is transferred, and must be transferred, because it cannot express itself in any other way. The very intensity of the transferred cathexis—"I *love* Henry James"—gestures emphatically to the inexpressive decorum of the inexpressible "I love you."

One might have guessed that the death of de Man in 1983 would have demolished that decorum which obstructs the transference from expressing itself immediately in the place of its origin, and in relation to its object, as "love." Of the love expressed in grief, there can be no question; the reality of that love is not at issue. Its mode of expression, however, on the occasion of the eulogies later published by *Yale French Studies* as "The Lesson of Paul de Man," only raises a larger and somewhat more distressing question about the possibility of overcoming that very decorum. The "lesson" that emerges with entire unanimity among the disciples is that the erotics of the transference was always a delusion, in de Manian terms an *epistemological* delusion, and that it was always disdained by the master, even that his teaching was *about* the delusion of the transference. Hence the "I love you" of the transference submits to a prior restraint, which it must nevertheless transgress in a troubled speech that recoils from every lapse into erotic expression to praise instead the more austere discipline of the *counter*transference:

> Paul disclaimed his own authority, yet none had more authority than him. He did not seek leadership, yet he was naturally at once an intellectual leader and a human guide. (YFS, 8)

The last thing he probably would have wanted to be was a moral and pedagogical—rather than merely intellectual—example for generations of students and colleagues, yet it was precisely his way of *not* seeking those roles that made him so irreplaceably an exception, and such an inspiration. He never sought followers; people followed him in droves. He was ironic toward discipleship; the country is dotted with his disciples. (YFS, 10)

His care was all the more eagerly sought by his students because it hid no suspect pity, voyeuristic kindness, or self-love; he did not need to care about us personally because he cared about us professionally. . . . His detachment, and our fascination with it, made it possible for us to profit practically from his teaching too. But while he was able so to divest himself of personal claims as to become an entirely effective teacher in these practical ways, the real *tour de force* was in the way he unmasked our fascination, explaining in the dryest and most impersonal manner, why his own detachment was necessary. (YFS, 11)

Those who learned the lesson he had to teach learned not to read like *him* but like him to *read*. (YFS, 13)

The disciples are after all well aware that the love expressed in discipleship is transference-love, and this admirable self-knowledge cannot fail to be troubled by the convergence of the eulogy's imperative to speak extravagantly upon the never less than hyperbolic language of the transference. There is no way to render the disciples' love as "impersonal" or "detached" in the context of eulogy. It would seem that the master has set his disciples an impossible task: to distinguish the "merely intellectual" in him from the "moral and pedagogical," that is, to refine the love they bear him until nothing remains of the transference. Would that be, in the end, nothing at all? Presumably such a refined eros would take as its object the "lesson" of Paul de Man, or would love him only *for* his lesson: "[W]e must divest ourselves of our personal investments, our studenthood, if we wished to understand him" (YFS, 12). Let us take due note of this thesis, because much will depend upon it. By transferring the eros of the transference to the lesson, the transference itself will disappear; it will be terminated. One will learn to read not like de Man, "but like him to *read*." And this is to say that nothing will remain of de Man in the lesson, that loving the lesson is not, finally, the same as loving de Man.

If the project of transferring the transference in order to destroy it, in order to read as impersonally as de Man taught, seems on the face of it difficult, it is no more difficult than the project of loving de Man in the first place. The delusion of the transference is the belief that the eros it generates is directed entirely toward the man who is Paul de Man. The student, as subject of the transference, is not pleased with the notion that he or she might really love the teacher only *as teacher,* that the transference-love really has no other object than the teacher as teacher. Hence the disciple will seek to distinguish the man from his "role" in order to love him for himself, a distinction the disciple will then attribute to the master ("yet it was precisely his *not* seeking those roles") as a motive of the countertransference, as though his detachment were, incredibly, detachment from his role. If the latter were possible, then there would in fact be no question of discipleship; there is no lesson without a teacher. The "exceptional" detachment beheld with such wonder is quite otherwise, not a cutting off of the transference at the point of its origin, but its *occasion:* "his detachment and our fascination with it." The disciples quoted above are unequivocal on this point, although it is presented as a mystery, an improbable failure of the very strategy designed to frustrate the transference. In this account the disciples seem to forget what they surely must know, namely, the first thing about the transference: nothing succeeds so well as detachment to produce fascination, provided that detachment can be made to speak, as in the silence of the analyst. For it is precisely by disappearing as Paul de Man, by disappearing *into* the place and function of the teacher, that the transference is allowed the fullest play, is allowed the delusion that it has gotten behind the function, the role, to love the *person.*

It is not a question, then, of the master's real indifference to his disciples but of how his hypothetical "detachment" is expressed, of how it declares itself. The argument of the countertransference is not "I do not love you," but "I do not care if you do not love me." The former statement, if it were true, need never be uttered; but the latter must speak all the time, and in such a way that it might be interpreted. For example, as follows: "He did not care about us personally, we thought, because he cared about us professionally." Just as the transference sought to distinguish the person from the teacher, the countertransference distinguishes the person from the student, but not in order to declare love for the person. On the contrary, this transference is "counter" because it is determined to limit the object of its eros to the objectified role of the student, even to refine this eros until nothing remains, until every student is indifferently just another student: "The issues were entirely pragmatic: how was a student to find the money to continue his or her studies? Which would be the proper place to send his letter of recommendation . . . ?" (YFS, 11). If nothing of the "person" survives in the student as object of transference, then the teacher's transference also is terminated in the sheer impersonality of an objectified relation. Needless to say, this state of affairs is never accepted by the disciple, who takes up the master's "I do not care if you do not love love me" as a gauntlet cast down on the path of desire. The challenge inaugurates the scenario of the student's clamorous demand to be regarded as different from the others, as the one for whom the teacher *does* care. Because the argument of the countertransference is *expressed,* it always leaves open the possibility of its potential retraction, its meaning at some time, "He loves me," just as it can glance darkly at the countertruth, "He does not love me." Either statement will do to maintain the transference, or rather we should say the transference is just the oscillation between the two.

"long before Freud"

The transference therefore depends on the disciple's taking at face value the argument of the countertransference, that the master has no desire with respect to his disciples. This proposition must be "believed" in order to enter into the state of fascination, where it then becomes possible to undertake the project of awakening the master's desire, as a slumbering leviathan. On this aspect of the transference, it is worth invoking Lacan, as the transference's master theorist and practitioner. In Lacan's Seminar XI, *The Four Fundamental Concepts of Psychoanalysis,* the concept of the transference has a rather special place; it is the subject to which Lacan is always returning, the seminar's unfinished business. It is occasionally introduced by invoking Plato's *Symposium,* the text in which "long before Freud" the transference was "perfectly articulated."[7] There, of course, it is a question of Socrates not having sex with Alcibiades; but for our purposes much more crucial than the descent of eros into the body is the fact that Lacan returns the scene of the transference to an origin in pedagogy. Socrates, we know, loves Alcibiades and that is what *The Symposium* does not evade at the level of the thematic. Neither does psychoanalysis evade the subject of eros, although too simple a reading of the transference would recognize only the desire of the patient. Likewise, it is entirely too simple a reading of the pedagogic relation to recognize only the desire of the student, especially when that desire is banished as a thematic from the seminar. The hypothesis that the teacher has no desire produces in the student a "transference-neurosis" the teacher has no occasion, as does the analyst, of addressing. In the context of analysis, Lacan quite rightly rejects the notion of the countertransference as evading what truly is " the pivotal point . . . *the desire of the psycho-analyst"* (231). Nevertheless he does not want to say, again too simply, that the desire of the analyst is, like that of the patient, *to be loved*. Rather the desire of the analyst manifests itself as "not wanting to desire": "The whole of analytic experience . . . shows us that not to want to desire and to desire are the same thing. To desire involves a defensive phase that makes it identical with not wanting to desire. Not wanting to desire is wanting not to desire." (235).

If this desire is the very pivot of analysis, as well as of the transference in pedagogy, what prevents it from taking the shorter path to satisfaction and expressing itself directly as the desire to be loved? We know that such an embarrassing short circuit can occur in both the analyst's office and in the classroom. The Stoic discipline of the desire not to desire—Lacan remarks from time to time on the "echo" between the "ethic of analysis" and the "Stoic ethic" (254)—is certainly the more complex case of desire itself. It may well be a theoretical advance to locate in the reality of this desire the mechanism of the cure (in Lacan's sense), the beautiful stratagem by which the analysand is forced by the silence of the analyst to enter into a dialogue with himself or herself, and thus to manifest the "discourse of the Other." However theoretically necessary it is to recognize in the transference the "affirmation of the link between the desire of the analyst and the desire of the patient," Lacan rather coyly will do no more than foreground that desire: "I will not say that I have named the analyst's desire, for how can one name a desire?"(254). At the end of the seminar, he argues, in the process of showing how analysis can be terminated without "liquidating" the transference, that the analyst's desire "remains an x," that is, it remains (274). After the dissolution of the Ecole Freudienne it would be easy to say that the desire of at least one analyst, of Lacan himself, was in some sense implicated in the preservation of the transference, although this statement does not yet name the desire or its object. In Monique David-Menard's excellent account of the collapse of the Lacanian school, she confronts squarely the circumstance that Lacan "unleashed the transference without being able to assure it would remain analyzable." But unleashed it for what purpose? Leaving Paris the day before the famous vote on the dissolution of the Ecole Freudienne, Lacan remarked, "It will interest me to see what happens when my presence is not there to screen what I teach. Perhaps my 'matheme' will be the better for it." About which David-Menard comments: "A curious remark for an analyst who founded his work on the art of linking his teaching and its institution to the transference! Is not this appeal to 'mathemes' just an avoidance of the task at hand, an attempt to free the transmission of his teaching from the effects of the transference upon which it was built?"[8] The transference in question here is not the erotics of analysis but of the *seminar*. How indeed was the transference to be analyzable there? The conflation of the analytic and the pedagogic is the institutional consequence of that theoretical rejection of the "liquidation" of the transference in Seminar XI. Lacan goes very far in this direction, so far as to dissolve the Ecole in order to maintain the transference *where he wanted it to be,* onto the "matheme," the knowledge which he transmits extra-analytically, in his seminar. It is a mistake to see this version of the transference as simply a transference onto the person of Lacan. Rather the transference is transferred: "It is my good fortune to have followers. Thus the discourse has a chance." How troublesome it was in the end, if the followers saw their transference differently, since, as Lacan knew, the undissevered erotic bond of the transference, with its necessary ambivalence, proved to be the greatest threat to the preservation of this doctrine. In this context we might grant to Lacan's severest critic, François Roustang, the ferocity of his insight into the difference between transference and transference transferred:

> As long as one transfers onto Lacan, for example, making him the "subject who is is supposed to know," anyone who is able to penetrate the obscurities of individuals and who can even illuminate the misunderstandings of a culture may think about the role played by this man, about the role others give him. If one believes, however, that Lacan has revealed the logic of the real, of the science of the unconscious, or even more extreme, if one sees in him the one and only theoretician and, what is more, justifies this uniqueness through pseudotheory, one's transference onto Lacan is effaced and transferred onto his theory, which prohibits understanding anything about the transference. For theory then becomes the starting point for thinking in general and thus a system in which one is caught. Theory becomes a symptom or a system of defense.[9]

Yet one may wonder whether the transference is ever entirely transferred, whether transference transferred does not entrust the desire of the analyst to the illusion of the *perfect* transmissibility of theory. One need not, perhaps, follow Roustang in the full of measure of his severity with the father by denying the transmissibility of theory except as an unrecognized delusional discourse. Nevertheless the problem has been posed: the transference transferred.

What is at stake in the distinction between the transference and the transference transferred is indicated throughout Seminar XI by the thematic of the difference between religion and science, or the question raised in the introductory "Excommunication" of "whether psychoanalysis is a science" (11). If the question is not capable of being answered, that is because any affirmative runs up against its negation in the *unconscious* desire of the analyst, the same desire on whose basis Lacan claims "we have a right to ask the question of the desire that lies behind modern science" (160). The possible indistinction between religion and science at the level of the unconscious is the achievement of psychoanalysis to have discovered, but at the (possible) cost of its own scientificity, if science itself is to fall from its heaven of reason. To put this in other thematic terms, we have a right to ask what the (master) analyst wants, science or religion. For Lacan the question is answered unequivocally in the "Letter of Dissolution": "One knows what price was paid for Freud's having permitted the psychoanalytic group to win out over discourse, to become a Church."[10] The "Letter" testifies to how far Lacan finally moved away from the fine equivocation of Seminar XI.

"Teaching is not an intersubjective relationship"
The foregoing excursus on the transference in Lacan returns us to de Man with a problem. It may not matter to the transference of the disciple whether the desire of the master "remains an x" or whether its existence is denied altogether. The susceptibility of de Manian discipleship to analysis in analytic terms is all too obvious, and it is difficult to see how another theory might better explain the facts of the case. One is not surprised that the disciples take literally the proposition of the countertransference, that the master has no desire, even if each one knows secretly that he or she is beloved. Nor should one be surprised to find the proposition of the countertransference expressed by the master with the utmost subtlety and effectiveness in the cafés and in the classrooms, in the psycho-pedagogy of everyday life. What does always surprise the reader of de Man is the unequivocal rejection of desire itself as a concept at all material to the practice or analysis of pedagogy. This rejection is the opening thesis of "The Resistance to Theory":

> Overfacile opinion notwithstanding, teaching is not primarily
> an intersubjective relationship between people but a cognitive
> process in which self and other are only tangentially involved.
> The only teaching worthy of the name is scholarly, not per-
> sonal; analogies between teaching and various aspects of show
> business or guidance counseling are, more often than not, ex-
> cuses for having abdicated the task. (RT, 4)

I shall attempt to disburden this passage of its anxieties as fully as possible, savoring first the affect of its dismissal of the "personal." I would name the affect *testiness*, a certain irritation which is already a reaction to the response de Man imagines his statement will provoke. The name of the response is obviously "resistance," but from what quarter? The assertion of the impersonality of teaching asserts nothing more than the ideal image of pedagogic decorum ("the only teaching worthy of the name"), an ideality everyone knows to be an illusion and for which psychoanalysis attempts an explanation in the dynamics of the transference. "Overfacile opinion notwithstanding" registers the very readiness-to-hand of an analytic terminology, but reduces that opinion to the supposedly degraded mass cultural forms of show business and guidance counseling. We must surmise on the contrary that it is psychoanalysis and not these mass cultural forms that provides an "analogy" for teaching; else the essay could not have inaugurated its meditation on pedagogy by invoking the analytic concept of "resistance." Show business and guidance counseling are rather the debunking analogies *for* psychoanalysis.

That de Man nowhere openly contrasts psychoanalysis to rhetorical reading has been taken to evince the subtlety of the relation between them, the bloodless coup by which the Freudian terminology is made to serve in a new theoretical order.[11] The presumed interlinear dialogue with psychoanalysis, into which we must look more closely, is without doubt of considerable interest; but I would characterize this relation as something other than dialogical, as a strenuous repudiation or foreclosure of the very possibility of such a dialogue. The announcement that "teaching is not an intersubjective relationship between people" declares at the outset the absolute irrelevance of psychoanalysis to the discussion of pedagogy. If psychoanalytic terms nevertheless pervade the essay (in ephemeral comparisons of literature to "jokes . . . and even dreams," in offhand allusions to "repression," to "psychic and political depths," to "overdetermination," to "displaced symptoms," all in continuous proximity to the concept of resistance), this terminological pervasion has nothing to do with a return of the repressed, but results from the threatening public prestige of psychoanalysis. There is no attempt here to refute what might be an analytic account of the vicissitudes of theory's transmission, or of pedagogy in general, but rather a displacement of psychoanalysis that takes the form of de Man's virtual *identification* with the figure of the analyst. Whatever work an analytic theory might do, that work is simply taken over by another terminology, and presumably done better. Elsewhere in de Man's oeuvre, the process of displacement is offered as programmatic; the following statement, for example, is as definitive a formulation of this thesis as it is possible to find:

Far from seeing language as an instrument in the service of a psychic energy, the possibility now arises that the entire construction of drives, substitutions, repressions, and representations, is the aberrant, metaphorical correlative of the absolute randomness of language, prior to any figuration or meaning. (AR, 299)

The "entire construction" of psychoanalysis is a "correlative" of a certain fact about language, but an aberrant correlative, a displacement. A more accurate terminology, which at least escapes the condition of ignorance about its own metaphoricity (if it cannot escape another ignorance, about its referentiality), would necessarily be linguistic; but it would be a terminology which names in *other words* the same process of aberration. This terminology can be recovered by retracing (backwards, as it were) the original aberration of terms from the linguistic to the psychological. Hence de Man can speak more casually at times of "translating back from a subject centered vocabulary of intent and desire to a more linguistic terminology," where "translating back" means displacing the displacement backwards (BI, 276). The labor of constructing an alternative linguistic terminology (which would also be a theory or pedagogy of reading) therefore does not dispense with a concept of displacement; such a theory insists rather that displacement or aberration is a linguistic and not a psychological occurrence.

The hostility of the takeover might be gauged if we were to ask the hypothetical question, "If teaching is not an intersubjective relation, what is?" The answer obviously is that there is no intersubjective relation:

in seeking to interpret intentions, he suggested, we are avoiding the question of whether intentions are determined by subjects, or by language as figures in texts. The stake of such a doubt was subjectivity, and subjectivity included the moral trait of detachment that we ascribed to him. We found the source of our fascination, his power to speak truth, dismissed by him as a strategy of our self-love. Our fascination was but one of the illusions he was systematically undoing. We wanted to attribute to him an authority equal to the knowledge that he brought us, an authority from which he was always, with irony, with a shrug of his shoulders, detaching himself. (YFS, 12)

We shall have occasion to note presently the consequences for the disciples of that *resemblance* between the person of de Man and the truth of his teaching. But perhaps the repudiation of all intersubjective relations still falls short in the above formulation of an explicit repudiation of psychoanalysis, if de Man only intends by his statement in "The Resistance to Theory" to shuffle off once again, as he had in the preceding decades, the language of phenomenology (what de Man repudiates in the foreword to the revised edition of *Blindness and Insight*, as "the thematic vocabulary of consciousness and temporality" [xii]). What is not necessarily implied by that vocabulary of subjectivity (consider Sartre on this question) is Freud's particular discovery, the unconscious. As we shall see, the subject or self in de Man continues throughout his work to mean the phenomenological self of *self-reflection,* and not the Freudian subject, which is primordially split along quite another axis of division.[12] That difference is established by the time of *Blindness and Insight,* if not earlier: "it follows from the rhetorical nature of literary language that the cognitive function resides in the language and not in the subject. The question as to whether the author himself is or is not blinded [that is, the question of the unconscious] is to some extent irrelevant" (BI, 137). De Man's asseveration operates most powerfully as a foreclosure of the Freudian subject just by *not* raising the problem of the unconscious along with the notion of an intersubjective relation, by arguing instead that teaching is a "cognitive process." It may be possible to entertain the illusion that teaching is *not* a cognitive process (thus, that it involves transference), but this illusion is not itself determined by the "unconscious." It is rather a *cognitive* error, merely an "overfacile opinion." What de Man gains tactically by reducing all intersubjective relations to the possibility of cognitive (that is, linguistic) error is the total obliteration of the transference from the terrain of the discussion. The crater that remains is so very large, however, that one is led to wonder whether all of the surplus megatonnage has been necessary to demolish this one target. How is one to read the very intensity of the denial of intersubjective relationship in the specific context of that denial, the context of teaching? What de Man has no patience for at all, not even the patience to name, is the notion of transference, which his argument implicitly condemns in absentia as an error about subjectivity.

If one objects that, after all, the unconscious is itself a cognitive concept—*das Unbewusste,* what one does not know—the necessity for the foreclosure of that concept only becomes all the more apparent. For the *place* of the Freudian unconscious is effectively occupied by the concept of "error," the centrality of which in de Manian deconstruction needs no demonstration. To continue the above quotation from *Blindness and Insight,* the question of whether the author is blinded "can only be asked heuristically, as a means to accede to the true question: whether his language is or is not blind to its own statement." The continuity between the latter statement and the following, from *Allegories of Reading,* is beyond question: "The entire assumption of a non-verbal realm governed by needs may well be a speculative hypothesis that exists only, to put it in all too intentional terms, *for the sake of* language" (AR, 210). The speculative hypothesis is an error, but of the de Manian sort, an unavoidable error: "The error is not within the reader; language itself dissociates the cognition from the act" (AR, 227). The concept of error, then, as a linguistic concept, takes the place of the concept of the unconscious only by transferring an unconscious agency to language itself, in its privileged linguistic forms such as literature, rhetoric, or the text. This sentence of course only restates a central de Manian thesis which, for those who believe it to be true, must represent a theoretical advance over the Freudian concept of the subject. Nevertheless the relocation of agency implied by the tacit derogation of psychoanalytic terminology to an aberrant correlative of the linguistic is not simply the necessary effect of that terminological displacement; it is in a sense the *project* of that displacement. The very ease with which the displacement is effected measures the force of a disavowal, a struggle which leaves as its trace the *absence* of reference to the psychoanalytic correlative of error, the concept of the unconscious.

The "transference" of the self or its agency into language is finally the means by which all the relevant psychoanalytic concepts—displacement, resistance, substitution, the unconscious—are replicated within rhetorical reading, at the cost (or benefit) of preserving the phenomenological self of self-reflection. In contemplating its own lack of agency, that self becomes the vehicle for a certain pathos, a familiar affect whose descent from the versions of Romantic melancholy seems apparent. The one analytic concept which cannot be named within this displaced terminology is transference itself, which orchestrates the severance of affect from agency. The relevance of the latter fact emerges with spectacular irony in the context of pedagogy, where the foreclosure of transference is effected by the very same transference of the "self" into language, or the displacement of an "intersubjective relationship" by a "cognitive process." If we object that, just as the unconscious could be conceived as a cognitive concept, so might it be conceived as a linguistic one, the example of Lacan is at hand: "The unconscious is the sum of the effects of speech on a subject, at the level at which the subject constitutes himself out of the effects of the signifier."[13] Without endorsing this formula at all, we may at least conclude that the validity of analytic thought cannot be impugned by charging that psychoanalysis has neglected the issue of language. But the utility of that foreclosure is more than evident to the master teacher who may wish to deny the very possibility that the unconscious desire of the disciple is addressed to the unconscious desire of the master: "We wanted to attribute to him an authority equal to the knowledge that he brought us, an authority from which he was always, with irony, with a shrug of his shoulders, detaching himself" (YFS, 12). In contrast to such more than Socratic irony, Lacan's very stagey insistence upon the desire of the analyst is in no sense incompatible with the "insistence [*Instanz,* agency] of the letter in the unconscious." I bring Lacan back into the discussion at this point in order to witness an interesting scenario of mutual exclusion. From the perspective of the choice here enjoined upon us by "The Resistance to Theory," we observe that Lacan and de Man appear to set off resolutely in opposite theoretical directions, but that they end up in the same place, the place of the "the subject who is supposed to know." The ineradicability of this subject for the disciples is evidence of how difficult it is for them to learn de Man's lesson. But that is because their transference is an unconscious replication of psychoanalysis's transference transferred, and hence it displaces the desire of the disciple to a *nowhere* by reducing it to a pathos which is only "tangentially involved" (epi-phenomenologically, we might say) in the cognitive process of teaching. The disciples cannot possibly know what to do with their affect because the transference it signifies is supposed to correspond to nothing in the teacher, since he has no "desire." In his "impersonality" he rather resembles language itself, or more accurately, he resembles his *teaching about language.*

To return now to the argument of "The Resistance to Theory," we can see in retrospect that the disavowal of "intersubjective relationship" in the context of teaching is for de Man a necessary consequence of the "advent of theory, which occurs with the introduction of linguistic terminology in the metalanguage about literature" (RT, 8). While such a terminology is privileged for the literary theorist, it is by no means necessary that this privilege be universally recognized, as the prevalence of a "resistance to theory" proves. De Man is not especially concerned to refute, much less to eradicate, this form of resistance, which is simply a resistance to the doctrine of a privileged linguistic terminology, "a resistance to the use of language about language" (RT, 12). What troubles the argument much more interestingly is the possibility that even the acceptance of this doctrine does not guarantee its accurate dissemination. What would account for such a failure in transmission, if teaching is in fact "impersonal," if it is a matter of the transmission of a certain *knowledge*? According to the logic of the argument, de Man must give an account of the necessity of this error without recourse to an explanation on the grounds of the transference. And as we would expect, whatever necessary failures are detected to occur in the cognitive process of teaching must be derived from the cognitive process itself, from theory itself, or ultimately from language itself, as the place within which resides the *agency* of resistance:

> It may well be, however, that the development of literary theory is itself overdetermined by complications inherent in its very project and unsettling with regard to its status as a scientific discipline. Resistance may be a built-in constituent of its discourse, in a manner that would be inconceivable in the natural sciences and unmentionable in the social sciences. It may well be, in other words, that the polemical opposition, the systematic non-understanding and misrepresentation, the unsubstantial but eternally recurrent objections, are the displaced symptoms of a resistance inherent in the theoretical enterprise itself. (RT, 12)

The crowding of the passage with psychoanalytic terms is rather more revelatory than the doctrine's restatement in the essay's final paragraph, where the terms of the argument are coaxed into a condition of paradox preemptively defensive against refutation on any grounds: "[Rhetorical readings] are theory and not theory at the same time, the universal theory of the impossibility of theory. To the extent that they are theory, that is to say, teachable, generalizable, and highly responsive to systematization, rhetorical readings, like other kinds, still resist the readings they advocate. Nothing can overcome the resistance to theory since theory is itself this resistance" (RT, 19). The resistance to theory which *is* theory is finally indistinguishable from the actual production of "technically correct" rhetorical readings. If they are indeed the same thing, then resistance itself must signify a "fall" (de Man's term) into the reception of theory as a positive knowledge. But there is no other context for this paradoxical reception than pedagogy, the site of theory's transmission. It scarcely matters in this context that the knowledge conveyed by theory is a kind of nonknowledge, "an unreliable process of knowledge production." What matters is that the formal model of "unreliability" is *exactly replicable* ("teachable, generalizable"), and that its exact replication can be mistaken by the disciple for knowledge in a supposedly simpler, positive sense, knowledge about an entity such as "language." De Man may insist upon the nonscience of his teaching; but such protestations of epistemological modesty are never received by the disciples as anything but the authentication of the master theorist's privileged position with respect to knowledge itself. What confronts us here is a moment and a question exactly parallel to the Lacanian question about the scientific status of psychoanalysis, a fortuitous conjunction in that we might set Lacan's equivocation about the science of the unconscious alongside de Man's unequivocal but oxymoronic propositions about the nonscience of rhetorical reading. Like psychoanalysis, de Manian deconstruction has the *form* of a science, but this "responsiveness to systematization" has in the terms of the theory nothing to do with the desire of the theorist. It has to do, rather, with the tendency of an error to repeat itself, an error in and of language. Nor does it have to do with the desire of the disciples, who merely learn well in learning to produce rhetorical readings which are "technically correct." If they mistake this certifiable method for knowledge, that mistake is something de Man would call *theory's* resistance to theory, but it is not *their* resistance. They do not resist at all. In fact, they cannot yield *enough* to the lessons of rhetorical reading.

We are in a position now to give some account of what de Man means when he says that the "resistance to theory" which takes the form of a simple rejection of rhetorical reading is a "displaced symptom" of a resistance internal to the theoretical enterprise itself. It is a displaced symptom of something the master actually encounters in his disciples, namely, *no resistance at all,* a boundless receptivity to the transmission of his doctrine as a positive knowledge. Of course such a frictionless medium of transmission is not what the master wants, if indeed he has no desire at all. This is what theory wants, what language wants, the proliferation of a knowledge which carries the aboriginal virus of error, and whose consequence is the continuous conversion of nonscience into science. Having granted to this scenario the pathos of the de Manian narrative, I would suggest that nothing is produced (beyond the effect of pathos) by "transferring" the agencies in this narrative out of the language of intersubjectivity into a purely "linguistic" terminology except a more complex state of ignorance: the peculiar circumstance in which one might, as the writer or reader of "The Resistance to Theory," fail to recall that transference in the analytic scene *is* the manifestation of resistance, the transference-resistance (*Übertragungswiderstand*). What "The Resistance to Theory" produces as its own unconscious, on behalf of "decorously glossing over" the desires of teacher and student, is a displaced enactment of a fully psychoanalytic logic: the (transference)resistance (on)to theory.

If the concept of the transference is foreclosed, it will not be possible to see that the resistance to theory is identical to the transference onto theory. For where would that transference have been from? And a transference of what? Surely no de Manian argument has been more mystifying or attractive than the one which concludes "The Resistance to Theory"; but it is scarcely illuminated by being taken at face value. De Man knows at some level that it is on the question of his teaching as a positive knowledge that the question of discipleship is articulated, even if that question is immediately translated into the thesis of the *self*-resistance of theory. Werner Hamacher divines the centrality of this question, with which he inaugurates his reading of de Man: "It is not certain that there can be a science of literature" (RDR, 171). It is certain, however, that there can be a *discipline* of literature. The foreclosure of transference from the displaced analytic logic of "The Resistance to Theory" is simultaneously the foreclosure of the disciplinary context, its effectual conflation with an autonomous agency of theory, or the agency of language itself. Theoretically, we ought not to have been able to see that transference was what language was "up to"; but that cognitive blindness was entirely artificially induced, an effect of the privileging of the linguistic terminology.

Let us for the sake of argument "displace" this terminology into the Lacanian problematic of the transference, not in order to credit that language with the privilege it too seeks, but in order to glance at the same problem from that other scenic overlook. We recall that Lacan expresses the problem of psychoanalytic theory's transmission as the thematic of the distinction between science and religion. What the theorist wants (but this is not yet equivalent to the "desire of the analyst") is the transmission of theory, that is, the solution to a problem in pedagogy. Whether or not a theory carries with it a claim to scientificity, its transmission would be better assured by its organization in the form of a science, or more simply, by its systematization; hence the "matheme." In the context of the pedagogic objective, discipleship is simply instrumental (as Lacan says) and no transference which took as its final object the person of the master theorist would be adequate to the task of transmission. Such a transference would presumably give rise to the institutional form of a church; yet the transference operative in this form never fails to proceed to the reception of the master's truth. Transference transferred is the form of transference *in general.* How would this transference, formally speaking, be different from the transmission of a science? We are forced to conclude that it would not, that the desire for one's works to be received as science is not distinguishable from the desire for discipleship, for the *form* of a church. The very intensity of this desire, which manifests itself on the surface as the most "impersonal" concern that one's theory be gotten right, measures precisely the intensity of the desire to produce transference.

"highly responsive to systematization"
The forms of discipleship are multiple, as Roustang has shown. I will not discuss here the case of the disciple who struggles heretically with the mas-

ter, or the vexing case of the disciple who extrapolates just ahead of the master's thought. From the master's point of view, the heretical pupil is simply the one who enacts a negative transference. The history of discipleship provides more than enough documentation of the transference in these forms. Lacan, for example, chastizes two of his pupils for attempting to correct one of his formulas: "Heavens, I am not so touchy, I leave everyone to go his own way *in the way I point out*" (217; emphasis mine). For the master there is no more certain testimony of the transference-love than the willingness of the disciple to repeat exactly what the master says. But does the circumstance of such a repetition mean that the master has got what he wants? The master's desire falls short of gratification at just this point, an impasse which locates the general problem of pedagogical desire in the experience of an ambivalent fixation: It may be very annoying indeed when the pupil does not get it right, but it is equally annoying, and in a different, profounder way, when the pupil gets it *exactly* right. The distress arising from the latter circumstance appears unmistakably at the outset of the "The Resistance to Theory," but redirected toward the *concept* identifying that anxiety, the "overfacile opinion" that construes pedagogy as the scene of transference. The affect of the countertransference is turned around in de Man's essay into its opposite, the signature affect or "pathos" of serene resignation to the triumphant or tragic circumstance that theory is the resistance to theory (that is, the transference onto theory).

Let us look a little more closely now at the self-discipline of the disciples, the mechanism by which theory is reproduced with an exactitude which then becomes the object of the master's ambivalent fixation. The following sentences by several of the disciples are juxtaposed to sentences written by de Man himself (in italics), by way of exemplifying the process of replication at the micro-level of style—as we shall see, the actual mechanism of replication:

> *There seems to be no limit to what tropes can get away with.*
> (AR, 62)
> . . . for when it is a question of metaphor, there is no telling where it may lead (RDR, 112)
>
> *All that will be represented in such an allegory will deflect from the act of reading and block access to its understanding. The allegory of reading narrates the impossibility of reading.* (AR, 77)
> These figures are merely the incomplete narrative, or allegories, of a purely nonfigurative occurrence that remains beyond them

and their pseudomovement, and when they are read, such figures always and again tell the story of their impossibility to occur historically. (RDR, 134)

What remains impossible to decide is whether this flourishing is
a triumph or a fall. (RT, 20)
The fall into uncertainty cannot even be certain that it is a fall.
(RDR, 142)

Reading is a praxis that thematizes its own thesis about the im-
possibility of thematization and this makes it unavoidable,
though hardly legitimate, for allegories to be interpreted in the-
matic terms. (AR, 209)
It remains undecidable whether discourse about the rhetoricity
of all discourse can be read referentially or not. (YFS, 130)

The precision of verbal replication should not obscure the more general
point that, well-intentioned protestations to the contrary, such repetition is
the immediate object of the master's desire. Nor is it the case that any
knowledge can be transmitted without, on the student's part, the exercise
of imitation, whether induced by love or the rod. If one nevertheless finds
the examples quoted above unusual in their imitative precision, this precision is a measure of how successful the pedagogy of de Man happens to
have been, a fact about which we have no lack of testimony. But the exqui-
site precision of the sentences quoted above also indicates how intimately
the knowledge conveyed in the systematization of rhetorical reading is related to a reflection on pedagogy. This thought is easy enough to put into
psychoanalytic terms: it is the proposition that in pedagogy no dissolution
of the transference occurs. For this reason Freud tends to associate pedagogy with hypnosis, in other words, with the most extreme form of mastery:

> The doctor has no difficulty, of course, in making him [the pa-
> tient] a supporter of some particular theory and in thus making
> him share some possible error of his own. In this respect the pa-
> tient is behaving like anyone else—like a pupil—but this only
> affects his intelligence, not his illness. After all, his conflicts will
> only be successfully solved and his resistances overcome if the
> anticipatory ideas he is given tally with what is real in him.[14]

Whether or not the theoretical problem posed by the relation between pedagogy and hypnosis in Freud's corpus is ever overcome, the passage unmistakably correlates the historical break between analysis and hypnosis with
the *theoretical* distinction between analysis and pedagogy. The important

point for our argument, then, is not that de Manian discipleship is anomalous in permanently fixing the transference, but that pedagogy itself is a social relation constituted by a transference which tends toward permanent fixation. It is in that sense rather more like hypnosis—what Freud calls "thought-transference"—than like analysis. Discipleship is an inescapable pathology, then, but not like the "artificial neurosis" of the transference. The transference in pedagogy is least likely to be dissolved when the thought is transmitted in the "impersonal" form of a science.

The latter question is crucial because it allows us to assess the consequences of the distinction between the avowed nonscience of rhetorical reading and its transmission in the "technical" form of a science. Clearly the desire of the master finds an object in this *form,* for which the master is even willing to exchange the claim to pure scientificity of doctrine. The presumed iterability of doctrine is essential to the gratification of desire. In the same way the desire of the disciple takes as its object the form of the doctrine, which it will then conflate with knowledge itself. What then does the de Manian disciple imitate in the transference onto theory? Not quite the doctrine itself, the truth of which is always expressed in the self-canceling mode of the perpetuation of error. What is imitated rather is the form of the doctrine's iteration, in other words, its style. Now it may seem rather unhelpful at this point to equate style with the form of a science, but that is exactly the equation operative to an extraordinary degree in de Manian discipleship. Nothing else can explain the precision of the imitations quoted above, which produce "technically correct rhetorical readings" by virtue of having replicated so precisely the master's style.

The style of the master's writing thus has the same relation to its knowledge-content as the form of the knowledge's transmission has to knowledge. That form, the fact of its being "teachable, generalizable, and highly responsive to systematization" (RT), represents nothing other than the imitability of a style. Such imitation is not categorically different from any other expression of the transference, such as the imitation of personal traits or mannerisms. For this reason the transference onto theory always misses its object, the positive content of theory, by cathecting in and behind that object the image of the master. Theory is cathected because it is the theory of the master, a circumstance which always renders its truth merely axiomatic, and therefore secondary. The problem of imitation is given a very concise, if in retrospect ironic, statement in Andrejz Warminski's remark, quoted above: "Those who learned the lesson he had to teach learned not to read like *him* but like him to *read.*" The possibility of this distinction has already been written off by de Man's preemptive resignation to the resistance of just those who have "learned his lesson," that is, who have transferred their transference onto theory. It is for them that reading will always mean reading "like *him,*" that is, replicating the style of his written readings.

The intersecting trajectories of these two desires, the master's and the disciples', is perhaps more obvious in the fate of the Lacanian matheme, which is entirely parallel to that of rhetorical reading. Nothing seems more evident in the aftermath of the Lacanian school's dissolution than the fact that it was the matheme which conveyed the desire of the master; what "remained an x" in the scene of analysis colluded in the seminar with the "algorithm," the quasi-mathematical formula. In Lacan's own terms, the desire that theory be a science was always identical to the desire that the disciples form a church. At the intersection of the master's and the disciple's desires, something like an interference pattern emerged, an area of cognitive emptiness. For the matheme went, so to speak, over the heads of the disciples. Its formulaic propositions could be reproduced, the science transmitted, without depending upon the intervention of the disciple's understanding. By reducing transmission to a rote process the doctrine was supposed to escape a certain contingency of the transference, its constitutive ambvialence, its love-hate. But the reception of the matheme marked a greater investment in the transference than ever before, even as both master and disciple deferred to the impersonal form of the algorithm. (It was Jacques-Alain Miller who ardently promoted the matheme while insisting at the same time upon the necessity of experiencing "the master's rod.") If the matheme was finally, as David Macey has recently argued, a *metaphor* of scientificity,[15] then it expressed in effect the furthest development of the idiosyncratic Lacanian style and not an epistemological break with a prescientific psychoanalysis. There was finally no distinction between that style and the discourse's systematization as a scientific knowledge.

The indistinction of style and doctrine nevertheless falls short of invalidating the doctrine's truth. For the present I am concerned only with the circumstance that the teaching of both de Man and Lacan attempts to account and compensate for the vicissitudes of transmission by attributing those vicissitudes to an epistemological defect of language, or by refusing in principle the possibility of the dissolution of the transference. The two positions amount in practice to the same thing. If we must now stop short of addressing the question of science itself, of that form of knowledge which does admit of mathematization, we are nevertheless well over the threshold of the general scene of pedagogy, the general problem of knowledge transmission. All pedagogy tends in a necessary and banal way to the formulaic, and for this reason the scene of pedagogy is not confined to the classroom. Its extension beyond that context is identical to the invention of a style, a form of notation or writing that serves as the "technical" instrument of knowledge transmission (even mathematical notation does not fail to serve as a vehicle of style, as mathematicians know). Discipleship has never for that reason been contingent on the actual presence of the master, only on the condition that he exist somewhere, or once existed, and that his presence as "the one who is supposed to know" can be projected in imagination out of the signature of style. Without claiming too much for this effect, we may insist upon the relation between the iterable technicalities of style (as the instance of some particular writing, a way of handling the *stylus*) and the structure of the transference in pedagogy.

With this principle in mind we can offer a preliminary conjecture about the meaning of the theory-canon, about the emergence of this particular organization of texts. For what unifies the syllabus which includes (among others) Derrida, Foucault, Lacan, Lyotard, Kristeva, or Nietzsche, Freud, Saussure, and Heidegger, is the fact that these oeuvres can be taken to embody a *discourse of mastery,* which is always by definition an imitable discourse. Now this fact may seem simply obvious, but its significance has yet to be appreciated either by those who defend theory or by those who dismiss it. The names which circulate as "theory" in this canonical sense are actually very few in number, much more restricted a list than that which constitutes "canonical" literary work. Furthermore the very canonical organization of these texts, their recategorization as "theory," has the effect of neutralizing the generic, disciplinary, and ideological differences between them in much the same way that the literary canon tends to define all canonical literary texts as the embodiment of a single quality of "literariness." The discursive homogenizing of theory permits different theoretical methods to be "applied" more or less indifferently to the same literary texts—however uneasy those who do theory seriously may happen to be with this consequence of its iterability. The larger question, for which I shall attempt to provide a properly sociological analysis in the latter part of this chapter, is why the literary critical profession should now require a canon which signifies in its totality a discourse of mastery, in addition to the traditional "literary" canon, whose significance, as we shall see, is considerably altered by its interrelation with the theory-canon.

The transference onto the syllabus is not essentially different, then, from the transference onto method; it is expressed as a set of choices whose necessity only *seems* more arbitrary than the cathexis of theoretical propositions. The relation between theory and textual choices is quite interestingly hinted in the Preface to *Allegories of Reading,* where de Man informs us that:

The choice of Proust and of Rilke as examples is partly due to chance, but since the ostensible pathos of their tone and depth of their statement make them particularly resistant to a reading that is no longer entirely thematic, one could argue that if *their* work yields to such a rhetorical scheme, the same would necessarily be true for writers whose rhetorical strategies are less hidden behind the seductive powers of identification. (AR, ix)

The explanation for these choices invokes on the one hand, chance, and on the other, the exemplary value of Proust's and Rilke's (ultimately failed) resistance to a rhetorical reading. But on no account is the choice of these writers attributed to "the seductive powers of identification" in the sense in which the texts themselves might have been seductive to a particular reader, to Paul de Man. It is difficult to conceive what is meant by the pathos specific to Proust or Rilke (as opposed to which other writers?), unless that pathos names just the contingent attraction of de Man to these authors. What could "seductive powers" otherwise signify? While the disciples return with conspicuous fidelity, as if along hidden lines of force, to the syllabus of de Manian reading, even to specific passages within works, the determination of those choices seems to lie beyond analysis; hence de Man's invocation of "chance." But what is in truth unanalyzed is a mode of determination, the transference.

De Man's allusions to pathos, resistance, and identification in the above passage from the Preface to *Allegories of Reading* displace the determination of textual choices to the terminological context of psychoanalytic discourse, without however acknowledging that displacement. The problem is indeed one of "identification," but the latter makes its appearance in the pedagogic scene as a result of the nature of the transference as an erotic relation, namely, that it must be transferred. The object of the transference is from the beginning unattainable, a lost object, and the perpetual mourning of the disciple thus gives rise to the familiar narcissistic identification with the master. Yet the development of the transference into identification concerns the master only insofar as he is necessarily and ambivalently fixated on the effect of *imitation*. The disciple's imitation, although it takes the primary form of a transference onto theory, eludes the desire of the master precisely by reflecting his *image* in the mirror of discipleship. For this reason it would not be correct to say that the transmission of theory is encumbered by unfortunate instances of stylistic imitation, which might with some effort be eradicated from the process of transmission—not if imitation *constitutes* that process. De Man is reported to have "winced" at the effects of mimicry occasioned by his teaching.[16] The affect expressed in "wincing" is quite exact: it is a shrinking back from the image of *oneself*. The flattened, empty, but animated image of the master in the mirror of the disciple's imitation proves to be intolerable, even hateful. It has all the chthonic force of the imaginary, like the photograph with which the anthropologist robs the soul of the primitive.

It follows from this argument that the injunction to transfer the transference onto theory, *and onto the syllabus of theory,* will always entail a contempt for the very discipleship which is the mechanism of theory's transmission. And this is in fact what we find thoughout de Man's later work. We should add, however, that such contempt is not specific to de Man but is inevitably cultivated by the master theorists, as the inevitable accompaniment to the cultivation of disciples. The severity of the critique of discipleship is thus exactly commensurate with the intensity of discipleship, a circumstance which insures the paradoxical consequence that the de Manian disciples are compelled to take that critique at face value, as the "lesson" of Paul de Man. If the question of discipleship was always a concern of de Man's criticism, from *Blindness and Insight* onwards, asides on the subject become even more frequent in such later essays as "Aesthetic Formalization in Kleist," where the form of pedagogy is supposed to produce aesthetic effects incompatible with the merely cognitive process of pedagogy itself; or in "Sign and Symbol in Hegel's Aesthetics," where Hegel's *Lectures on Aesthetics* are said to suffer "from the the stylistic infelicities of magisterial lecture courses recorded by overloyal disciples."[17] In both of these essays, de Man worries the question of the relation between the master's style and his doctrine. The effect of style (called "grace" in the Kleist essay) is stigmatized as an instance of the aesthetic; it raises the possibility of a seductive identification with the teacher. The critique of discipleship implicit in these essays is pervasive in *The Resistance to Theory,* perhaps its real subject. The critique underlies the interrogation of Riffaterre's pedagogically oriented theory in "Hypogram and Inscription," and breaks the surface of "Reading and History" as the sharply drawn contrast between Jauss's modest position in the Konstanz school ("a participant on a team") and the ubiquity of discipleship cults: "In the field of literary theory, the existence of such groups is not an unusual occurrence. They are, at times, centered on a single, dominating personality and take on all the exalted exclusiveness of a secret society, with its rituals of initiation, exclusion, and hero-worship" (RT, 54). Such comments can of course be read easily enough to refer obliquely to the fact of de Manian discipleship; but we should also perhaps entertain the hypothesis that de Man did not actually regard his favored disciples in this light. For it will always be possible to exempt oneself from the consequences of mastery by distinguishing the good disciples from the bad; or in a more theoretically sophisticated gesture, by making oneself disappear as master, as the "subject who is supposed to know." In any case, the problem of a specifically de Manian mastery is foreclosed and can only be considered by proxy in discussions of Riffaterre, Jauss, or preeminently, Bakhtin, whose posthumous resurrection as a theorist raises the vexed question for de Man of "why the notion of dialogism can be so enthusiastically received by theoreticians of very diverse persuasion, and made to appear as a valid way out of many of the quandaries that have plagued us for so long" (RT, 107). In his essay on Bakhtin, "Dialogue and Dialogism," the critique of discipleship is pushed to its furthest possible conclusion, the proscription of imitation: "To imitate or to apply Bakhtin, to read him by engaging him in a dialogue, betrays what is most valid in his work" (RT, 114). The fine blade of this critique cuts cleanly between Bakhtin and his disciples.

"Dialogue and Dialogism" in fact opens with de Man's severest gesture of foreclosure: "Literary theory, and especially theory of narrative, a rather barren area of endeavor constantly threatened by the tedium of its techniques as well as the magnitude of its issues, offers poor soil for the heroes and the hero-worship that it rather desperately needs" (RT, 106). Once again the construction of pedagogy as intersubjective relation is reduced to a low cultural correlative—"hero-worship"—which has the same pejorative status as "show business" in "The Resistance to Theory." That literary theory "desperately needs" such heroes argues the sublime audacity of a foreclosure which erases de Man himself as master. Such a gesture is not at all ironic, since it counterposes quite seriously the ascesis of literary theory (a figurative desert, a "barren area" and "poor soil" out of which no prophet has emerged) to Bakhtin's seductiveness, which has produced the discipleship de Man is so eager to condemn:

> the circulation of more or less clandestine class or seminar notes by initiated disciples or, even more symptomatic, the rumored (and often confirmed) existence of unpublished manuscripts made available only to an enterprising or privileged researcher and which will decisively seal one mode of interpretation at the expense of all rival modes—at least until one of the rivals will, in his turn, discover the real or imaginary countermanuscript on which to base his counterclaim. What in the context of our topic interests us primarily in this situation is that it is bound to engender a community tied together by the common task of decrypting the repressed message hidden in the public utterance. As the sole retainers of an esoteric knowledge,

this community is bound to be small, self-selective, and likely to consider itself a chosen elite. (RT, 108)

De Man's contempt for Bakhtinian discipleship is so completely without irony as to constitute the purest form of negation, a simulacrum of irony, as in the following statement: "The last thing I wish to do here is to dispute or dispel this enthusiasm [of the Bakhtinians]" (RT, 107). It is entirely obvious that the *first thing* de Man sets out to do is to "dispel" the enthusiasm of the disciples, which enthusiasm is always implicitly represented as a kind of "spell," thought-transference, or hypnosis. By merely venting a contempt for discipleship as imitation, de Man is forced to simplify its psychodynamic, to reproduce as a critique of Bakhtin the caricature of de Manian discipleship which already circulates as gossip. In his struggles with competing master theorists, the theorist who established his own claim to mastery in *Blindness and Insight* with a virtuoso rereading of other master theorists confirms the symptomatic status of his oeuvre. The doctrinal insight into the "linguistic predicament" needs to be read at every moment as symptomatically blind to the *necessary* relation between theory and discipleship.

Rhetorical Reading, or the Thematization of Rhetoric

. . . the apparent relationship between prophecy and its audience must be reversed: the religious or political prophet always preaches to the converted and follows his disciples at least as much as they follow him, since his lessons are listened to and heard only by agents who, by everything they are, have objectively mandated him to give them lessons.
                        —BOURDIEU AND PASSERON, *Reproduction*

"if one wants to conserve the term 'literature'"
The situation of rhetorical reading in the wake of its dissemination has been characterized by Jonathan Culler in a recent essay as follows: "In the hands of its best practitioners, such as Paul de Man or Barbara Johnson, deconstruction is an interpretive mode of unusual power and subtlety. In other hands there is always the danger that it will become a process of interpretation which seeks to identify particular themes, making undecidability, or the problem of writing, or the relationship between performative and constative, privileged themes of literary works." [18] The peculiar circumstance that deconstruction can be disseminated as a mode of thematic criticism calls attention to the fact that a large part of its agenda was to replace thematic criticism with a specifically *rhetorical* methodology. Deconstruction shares this agenda with nearly all theory, which rediscovered rhetoric

in the course of its reflection on language. The valorization of rhetoric belongs to a long-standing episteme of literary theory, but the meaning of that valorization has to do, as we shall see, with a certain exhaustion in the discourse of literature itself. The return of rhetoric is the discursive precondition of rhetorical reading, and therefore the precondition of its effects of discipleship. In moving now from the psychodynamic to the discursive terrain of theory, we will be able to confirm Bourdieu and Passeron's point, quoted above, that the master theorist commands discipleship only on the condition that the disciples are already prepared to hear what he is prepared to teach. De Man's version of deconstructive theory is in this sense a symptomatic discourse of "rhetoricism" as well as a symptomatic practice of mastery.

The antithesis between the rhetorical and the thematic is forcefully asserted in the Foreword to the revised edition of *Blindness and Insight:*

> With the deliberate emphasis on rhetorical terminology, it augurs what seems to me to be a change, not only in terminology and tone but in substance. This terminology is still uncomfortably intertwined with the thematic vocabulary of consciousness and temporality that was current at the time, but it signals a turn that, at least for me, has proven to be productive. (BI, xii)

Whether or not the appearance of a new terminology represents a change in substance will no doubt continue to be debated in accounts of de Man's career. If not for its substance, the shift to a rhetorical terminology is decisive for its enabling pedagogic effects. The rhetorical terminology becomes, in the Preface to *Allegories of Reading,* the basis for a methodology called "deconstruction," the name of a school, of a relation between masters and disciples. For the literary critical profession, this name is so definitive that it can stand, as we have seen, in virtually synonymous relation to theory itself. Such an equation is not merely the effect of dissemination but the argument of "The Resistance to Theory": "The advent of theory, the break that is now so often deplored and that sets it aside from literary history and literary criticism occurs with the introduction of linguistic terminology in the metalanguage of literature" (RT, 8). It can hardly be denied that other theories and other terminologies than that of rhetorical reading circulate in the discourse milieu of criticism, but such theories are dismissed by de Man as only versions of thematic criticism. If his writing tends toward the conflation of theory with a *specific* linguistic terminology, the rhetorical, then we would do well now to look more closely at how this terminology produces certain discursive effects. These effects are (1) the conflation of linguistics with rhetoric; (2) the equation of literature with rhetoric; and (3) the reduction of rhetoric to trope.

1. *The conflation of linguistics with rhetoric.* Let us consider first what is implied in general by a linguistic terminology. Not initially, not even for de Man, a taxonomy of rhetorical figures: "By linguistic terminology is meant a terminology that designates reference prior to designating the referent, and takes into account, in the consideration of the world, the referential function of language, or, to be more specific, that considers reference as a function of language and not necessarily as an intuition" (RT, 8). While the allusion here is to Saussure, who is invoked several sentences later as the originator of the problematic of linguistic reference, very little archaeological work is needed to uncover a phenomenological problematic of "consciousness and temporality" sedimented in the linguistic. The latter is completely transparent to the former, and it declares its presence in the concept of "intuition": "Intuition implies perception, consciousness, experience, and leads at once into the world of logic and of understanding with all its correlatives, among which aesthetics occupies a prominent place" (RT, 8). The operation of reference is unsurprisingly displaced from the phenomenological realm to the linguistic, where it suffers an initial disabling blow at the hands of a familiar linguistic agency. We know that the name of this agency is "trope," but we will not find tropes of particular interest to Saussure, or to linguistics in general. Twentieth-century linguistics is rather more often concerned with grammatical structures, which it does not necessarily have to conceive as exclusive of semiotic questions (although it sometimes has). In order to arrive at the concept of trope as the elementary unit of a "linguistic terminology," de Man must overleap linguistics to recover the relation between grammar and rhetoric that obtained in the medieval trivium of grammar, rhetoric, and logic, a system he calls "the most familiar and general of all linguistic models" (RT, 13). Whatever the ultimate pertinence of rhetoric to linguistic science (one may well concede that the omission of rhetoric is a conspicuous deficiency of linguistics, as well as perhaps its constitutive moment), it must be acknowledged that de Man does not come by his linguistic terminology in the domain of Saussurean linguistics.

In subsequent paragraphs of "The Resistance to Theory" another term, "literary language," or "literariness," must supervene upon the discussion in order to facilitate the return to the trivium: "The linguistics of semiology and of literature apparently have something in common that only their shared perspective can detect and that pertains distinctively to them. The definition of this something, often referred to as literariness, has become the object of literary theory" (RT, 9). But if rhetoric is in fact largely absent from linguistic terminology, how could it be what linguistics and literature have in common? And if rhetoric can be introduced into linguistic science only by doubling back upon the latter's discursive precursor, why does de

Man need to insist at all that his terminology is a *linguistic* terminology? Would it not be possible to say that rhetoric has to do with language but that it does not have to do with it in the same way as linguistics? The reason for the equation between the linguistic and the rhetorical is not difficult to see, however; it is determined by the proposition that the rhetorical is the foundational instance of language per se: "Tropes, *unlike grammar,* pertain primordially to language" (RT, 15; emphasis mine). In the immediately following sentence de Man goes on to set up the conditions for a mutual antagonism between rhetoric and linguistics by removing grammar, as the matter proper to linguistics, to a position partially exterior to language itself: "They [tropes] are text-generating functions that are not necessarily patterned on a nonverbal entity, whereas grammar is by definition capable of extra-linguistic generalization." The expulsion of grammar from the inner sanctum of the linguistic is intended to make room for rhetoric as the defining instance of language, and thus as the substance of any properly "linguistic" terminology.

The exterior relation of grammar to rhetoric/language is nevertheless not a non-relation. It is a relation of *subordination,* to invoke a term from the lexicon of grammar. Grammar is retained within a reconstituted linguistic terminology as the name for the referential function formerly located in the trivium's "logic," but more nearly located in an "intuitional" or phenomenological problematic. In that sense the antithesis of rhetoric and grammar restages the move from a phenomenological to a "linguistic" terminology within the *terms* of the latter terminology. What de Man calls "logic" is assimilated to the logic of the medieval trivium so as to counterpose rhetoric to an amalgamation of both grammar and logic: "And this is the point at which literariness, the use of language that foregrounds the rhetorical over the grammatical and the logical function, intervenes as a decisive but unsettling element which in a variety of modes and aspects, disrupts the inner balance of the model, and consequently, its outward extension to the non-verbal world as well" (RT, 14). The logic of which de Man speaks here has perhaps little to do with its medieval antecedent (also known as "dialectics"), but it is absolutely essential to the construction of his linguistic terminology, since this terminology sets itself squarely athwart any definition of linguistics as the descriptive analysis of grammatical structure. Hence the emphatic dismissal of Greimas (representing twentieth-century linguistics), because he attempts to define the "semiotic project" as the construction of a general grammar: "It is clear that for Greimas, as for the entire tradition to which he belongs, the grammatical and the logical functions of language are co-extensive. Grammar is an isotope of logic" (RT, 14). What is the relation, then, between rhetoric and linguistics? In retrospect the only possible point of convergence between rhetoric and twentieth-century linguistics is a tacit conflation of the referentially disruptive trope with the Saussurean signifier; there is no more universal donnée of criticism than the concept of the signifier, which, as we know, sets aside the question of reference by specifying the arbitrariness of its relation to the purely ideational "signified." An equation of the trope with the signifier is nowhere proposed in Saussure, but such an equation is one effect of the Jakobsonian fusion of the rhetorical terminology with the linguistic in the episteme of critical theory. De Man's "linguistic terminology" locates itself opportunistically within the general field of Saussurean/ Jakobsonian linguistics, and thus casually conflates the arbitrary signifier with the polysemy of trope: "The rhetorical character of literary language opens up the possibility of the archetypal error: the confusion of sign and substance" (BI, 136). The Saussurean signifier is always a precondition for de Man's "confusion of sign and substance," and the means by which, in the episteme of theory, the trope becomes the paradigmatic instance of the signifier.

De Man's "linguistic terminology" forms the basis for a theory of language as the "latent tension between rhetoric and grammar" (RT, 15), where the term "grammar" incorporates a disabled but necessary referential function whose name was heretofore "logic." The reconstruction of the medieval syllabus as a theory of language corresponds programmatically to the dissemination of that theory in the form of a privileged terminology, one which systematically displaces *another* terminology, also claiming to be "linguistic": "The tendency to replace a rhetorical by a grammatical terminology (to speak of hypotaxis, for instance, to designate anamorphic or metonymic tropes) is part of an explicit program, a program that is highly admirable in its intent, since it tends toward the mastering and the clarification of meaning. . . . The argument can be made, however, that no grammatical decoding, however refined, could claim to reach the figural dimensions of a text" (RT, 15). The "replacement" of a rhetorical by a grammatical terminology corresponds to no current position within linguistics, however, unless de Man means only to say that linguists have their own terminology, which they prefer to use. The truth is rather the opposite, that de Man raises the possibility of systematically replacing the grammatical terminology of the linguists with a rhetorical one. The grammatical terminology, like the psychoanalytic, is another "aberrant correlative" of the rhetorical, and the effect of the subordination of grammar to rhetoric is to empty it of its terminological copia (phonology, syntax, semantics, etc.) and to impose upon it the quasi-allegorical function of being the disciplinary antagonist of rhetoric.

2. *The equation of literature with rhetoric.* It is important to recognize, then, that the insistence upon rhetoric as a "linguistic terminology" is a move against linguistics itself. The consequent emergence of a de Manian theory of language is one moment in the systematization of his teaching, but it is not the only moment. It is interfused with another and equally important discursive operation, already implicit in the texts quoted above, namely, the equation of rhetoric with *literariness.* Nothing might seem at this date less surprising—more epistemic—than such an equation, but it is by no means obvious or necessary. In the classical world, rhetoric is a socially restricted linguistic practice, an oral art *(techne)* with a specific social locus: the forum. The "art" is of course the art of persuasion, a motive de Man assimilates into his reconstruction of rhetoric by means of a homology with the grammatical/logical function. The relation between rhetoric and literature can be given a historical account, such as has already been sketched in Chapter 1; but as soon as such an account is proposed, it must confront de Man's principled objection to any possible history of rhetoric: "rhetoric is not in itself an historical but an epistemological discipline"(EM, 26). If rhetoric is truly a "dimension of language" (RT, 17), the defining instance of the linguistic, its theorization is necessarily prior to any historical consideration: "One would have to conceive of a rhetoric of history prior to attempting a history of rhetoric or of literature or of literary criticism" (EM, 26). How then would one describe the relation between this rhetoric and the institutionalized practice of the classical and medieval educational systems? While it may well be possible to regard the rhetoric of the ancient world as embodying in a set of social-institutional practices an implicit theory of language, a theory which does not know itself as such, the extension of this claim to literature in the sentence just quoted reopens the question of the historical in a troubling way. For if literature is also to be defined as a "dimension of language," much more follows from this fact than the epistemological inadequacy of literary history, with its concepts of period and genre.

As I have already noted at the beginning of this chapter, such an extension of the category of the literary removes any logical grounds for distinguishing between literature and any use of language whatsoever. De Man's relative lack of interest in this consequence of his theorizing has given rise posthumously to such compromise formulations as that by Werner Hamacher, quoted earlier, or J. Hillis Miller: "Canonical works can now be seen as especially concentrated forms of universal features of language."[19] Such qualifications do not simply represent a practice that contradicts its theoretical presuppositions. On the contrary, the restriction of the literary to specific (and canonical) uses of language is a theoretical necessity, since literariness continues to be defined by de Man in conventionally Jakobsonian terms as "the use of language that foregrounds the rhetorical over the grammatical and logical function." The contradiction is installed at the level of theoretical formulation. The difference between "language" in general and a particular "use of language" is the difference between a purely theoretical and a historical account of the literary. If literature foregrounds the rhetorical dimension of language, it follows that not every use of language will be characterized by such an objective. Once the literary is conceived in this fashion, its existence must without question be regarded as historically determinate, and it cannot ipso facto be identified with rhetoric as a universal dimension of language.

What is at stake in the noncoincidence of literature and rhetoric is the historical relation between them. The identification of literature with rhetoric is conditional upon the appearance of the category of "literature" in the later eighteenth century as a set of genres both segregated from, and elevated above, the general field of writing. Not until that moment (as I argued in Chapter 2) were the various genres of writing capable of being easily distinguished as literary or nonliterary on the basis of such distinctions as that between fictive (or "imaginative") and nonfictive writing. We have seen that such a distinction makes it conventional now to include Henry Fielding within a history of literature, but not David Hume, whose corpus belongs to philosophy, a categorization that would have been exactly reversed earlier in the eighteenth century, when Hume had a distinguished literary career and Fielding could be dismissed as a mere writer of "novels." The distinction between fictive and nonfictive writing is not without discursive precedent, however, since it is already implicit in the assimilation of classical rhetoric by medieval and Renaissance treatises of *poetics*. Puttenham's *Arte of English Poesie,* for example, recycles the system of classical rhetoric entirely *as* poetics, with all of the traditional rhetorical devices transposed from speech to writing. The matter of rhetoric is assimilated in this new context (within which the identification of rhetoric with oratory is no longer dominant) under the category of "ornament"—a concept which relegated many poetic/rhetorical devices to a position external to, though not necessarily in conflict with, the "truth" of the work. The development in the early modern period of new discourses of truth (the scientific) occasioned, in a sequence of events whose narrative is well known, if still controverted, the epistemological bracketing of the poetic genres as "fiction," and the identification of ornament as defining the linguistic difference of those genres. Over the long term, new discourses of knowledge undermined the classical curriculum of rhetorical study and, in turn, the classical system of genres. It was no longer possible by the latter half of the eighteenth century to deny the cultural force of the distinction between fictive and nonfictive writing, and the category of the "literary" could then be restricted to the fictional genres. The new generic system had to develop a conception of truth proper to its form and the theorization of this truth describes in the largest sense the project of "Romantic" criticism, as it struggles with the largest possible generic distinction between a *Geisteswissenschaft* and a *Naturwissenschaft*.[20]

Now it is apparent in retrospect not only that de Man's emphasis on the cognitive status of rhetoric locates his concerns entirely within this project, but also that his theorizing of rhetoric elides the historical conditions that produced the category of the literary out of the very obsolescence of poetics and rhetorics in the school system. To be sure, we are always prepared for another rehearsal of the quarrel between poetry and philosophy—and deconstruction has not been averse to celebrating the recurrence of the quarrel—but it remains a historically determinate fact that, for us, the question of this relation can only be posed *after science*. The existence of a scientific discourse and practice has irrevocably altered the terms of the quarrel, which cannot now trace its unbroken lineage to Plato's archrepudiation of the poets. It is only after the discursive rupture of early modern science that rhetoric can be consigned to the same epistemological status as the poetic. The "pre-rhetorical" terminology of *Blindness and Insight* functions entirely within the post-Renaissance discursive regime, that is, within the conventional bracketing of literary genres as "fictional": "The truth emerges in the foreknowledge we possess of the true nature of literature when we refer to it as *fiction*" (BI, 17). If de Man then initiates a break with the thematic vocabulary of *Blindness and Insight* by positing rhetoric as literature's transhistorical essence, he can only effect this break because, prior to the historical emergence of the category of literature, poetics had effectively assimilated rhetoric to its domain. The "turn" to rhetoric unwittingly recovers as the essence of literature its historical *precondition*, the early modern integration of rhetoric into poetics.

The subsequent decline of rhetoric in the eighteenth and nineteenth centuries is a historical circumstance that must be suppressed in order for theory to assign rhetoric a new function in relation to literature. Without resorting here to a full historical account, which would have to acknowledge the significance for the theoretical episteme of the convergence (via Jakobson) of Saussurean linguistics with the reflections of Russian formalism on the idea of "literariness," we can at least affirm that it is by means of a return to rhetoric that the *generic* distinction between literary and non-literary texts can be reconceptualized as a *linguistic* distinction, the problem of "literary language." The reduction of literature to the expression of "literary language" in turn effects a disruption of the canonically based "literary" syllabus, specifically its extension to include philosophical texts: "We are entitled to generalize in working our way toward a definition by giving Rousseau exemplary value and calling 'literary', in the full sense of the term, any text that implicitly or explicitly signifies its own rhetorical mode and pre-figures its own misunderstanding as the correlative of its rhetorical nature; that is, of its rhetoricity" (BI, 136). Of course de Man does not acknowledge here that Rousseau's work would never have been considered in the eighteenth century as anything but "literature," in the sense of "polite letters." It is only the subsequent emergence of literature in the restricted sense which enjoins a distinction between literature and philosophy, and which removes Rousseau's discursive works from the domain of literature. A footnote to the passage from *Blindness and Insight* spells out the implications of the rhetorical turn with regard to the syllabus of literary study by insisting that a "discursive or philosophical text is not more or less literary than a poetic text." Let us say, however, that the truth of this statement is *historical* rather than *ontological*. At any rate we can draw a preliminary conclusion with regard to the de Manian syllabus, whose content is partially but not entirely determined by de Man's own affective choices, and thus by the psychodynamic of the transference. The constitution of this syllabus is also determined by a complex and evolving development within the episteme of theory, a development which can be indicated briefly by the de Manian formula: literature=literary language=rhetoric.

The transitive implication of this equation, literature=rhetoric, has the effect of removing the ground for the traditional syllabus of literary study without at the same time moving beyond the category of the literary. The aporia between the *object* of rhetorical reading—the unit of rhetoric, the trope—and its syllabus of "literary" texts, remains, so to speak, untheorized, the unconscious of rhetorical reading. The symptomatic status of this aporia is betrayed in de Man's own formulations by a repeated moment of heightened anxiety (indicated with emphases) at the threshold of the transitive equation:

> And although it would perhaps be somewhat more remote from common usage, I *would not hesitate* to equate the rhetorical, figural potentiality of language with literature itself. (AR, 10)

> The key to this critique of metaphysics, which is a recurrent gesture throughout the history of thought, is the rhetorical model of the trope or, *if one prefers to call it that,* literature. (AR, 15)

215

The key to Nietzsche's critique of metaphysics . . . lies in the rhetorical model of the trope or, *if one prefers to call it that way,* in literature as the language most explicitly grounded in rhetoric. (AR, 109)

And since, if one wants to conserve the term "literature," *one should not hestitate* to assimilate it with rhetoric. (AR, 131)

The undeniable hesitation betrayed in so emphatic a refusal to hesitate traces through de Man's corpus the unjoined seam of a theoretical patchwork, a conceptual catachresis. Nevertheless, because the syllabus of de Manian reading has considerable stability in its institutional context, because it comprises a relatively fixed group of literary and philosophical texts, the discrepancy between its stability and its theoretical groundlessness need never be examined. The disciples can always fall back in practice upon the transference transferred to the texts de Man chooses "by chance" to read, namely, a very select set of texts within the Romantic tradition. This more limited "transferential" syllabus can be reinforced by returning periodically to the same passages of those texts de Man himself has already read, and which thereby acquire the status of "touchstones" in the practice of rhetorical reading.

3. *The reduction of rhetoric to trope.* The third discursive operation is not the least violent of the de Manian catachreses, as it is in the area of the trope that de Man locates the provocation of resistance: "The resistance to theory is a resistance to the rhetorical *or tropological* dimension of language" (RT, 17). As we have seen, the program of reduction is not complete with the reduction of rhetoric to trope but goes on to equate language itself (implicitly the *signifier*) with the trope: "tropes pertain primordially to language." Elsewhere in *Allegories of Reading,* these formulations are elaborated in the context of paraphrasing Nietzsche's early writings on rhetoric, which give de Man the authoritative antecedent for his major thesis, that "the trope is not a derived, marginal, or aberrant form of language but the linguistic paradigm par excellence. The figurative structure is not one linguistic mode among others but it characterizes language as such" (AR, 105). Nietzsche does remark that "with respect to their meanings, all words are tropes in themselves, and from the beginning"—a proposition he argues by analogizing meaning to synecdoche in the sense that "language never expresses something completely, but only characteristics which appear to be prominent to it."[21] De Man quotes Nietzsche's further argument to the effect that "There is no difference between the correct rules of eloquence [*Rede*] and the so-called

rhetorical figures. Actually, all that is generally called eloquence is figural language." In so reducing "eloquence" to figuration, Nietzsche appears to accede to a version of the "tropological reduction" Genette has demonstrated to have been in force throughout the nineteenth century, at least since the publication of Fontanier's *Commentaire raisonné des tropes* (1818), a treatise in which even the traditional distinction between "figures" and "tropes" is discarded, and rhetoric is reduced to a taxonomy of tropes.[22] Whether or not the reduction of *eloquence* to trope is the same as the reduction of rhetoric to trope (I will defer discussion of this point), de Man argues that Nietzsche makes a distinction between rhetoric as a "system of tropes" and "rhetoric as having to do with the skills of persuasion" in order to "contemptuously dismiss the popular meaning of rhetoric as eloquence and concentrate instead on the complex and philosophically challenging epistemology of tropes" (AR, 130).

Elsewhere de Man remarks that "the study of tropes and figures" is "how the term *rhetoric* is used here, and not in the derived sense of comment or eloquence or persuasion" (AR, 6). It is a question of *derivation:* the reduction of eloquence to trope argues the exteriority of eloquence or persuasion to rhetoric itself. When the trope is asserted to be an underived form of language, it becomes possible to argue conversely that the "rhetoric" of persuasion is *simply* derived from this primordial form. Nevertheless persuasion retains an important function in the de Manian scheme, in the same way that grammar is not simply translated into rhetoric but subordinated to its terminological priority. The distinction between trope and persuasion is also maintained in the deconstructive system by correlation with the Austinian distinction between the constative and the performative; but that correlation also requires no history of rhetoric. On the contrary, rhetoric is defined tautologically as the "eternally recurrent" question that "coincides with the term 'rhetoric' itself" (AR, 131)—perhaps on that ground a unique terminology, a "system" incapable of translation into any other terminology or system. Since the "performance" signified by persuasion is always deconstructed by trope, the concept of persuasion can be retained in another of the hierarchical binarisms that structure the system of rhetorical reading.

De Man retains the concept of persuasion, then, as the antithesis of trope *within rhetoric.* Persuasion finds itself an internal exile in the domain of rhetoric, and for this reason it governs no territory of that domain. Within a post-Romantic discourse of rhetoric in which rhetoric is routinely reduced to trope, it may be difficult to appreciate exactly how much of what rhetoric once was disappears with the "motive of persuasion." It will be useful for comparison here to set before us a schematic outline of the "art of rhetoric," as that art was typically practiced in antiquity. The text is Cicero's *De Inventione* (I, vii, 8):

> The parts of [rhetoric], as most authorities have stated, are Invention, Arrangement, Expression, Memory, Delivery. Invention is the discovery of valid or seemingly valid arguments to render one's cause plausible. Arrangement is the distribution of arguments thus discovered in the proper order. Expression is the fitting of the proper language to the invented matter and words. Memory is the firm mental grasp of matter and words. Delivery is the control of voice and body in a manner suitable to the dignity of the subject and the style.

Of these categories, only the third, expression (*elocutio*), concerns what we now call rhetoric, that is, figurative language. (The sentence of Nietzsche's quoted above by de Man is scrupulous in reducing only *elocutio* and not *rhetoric* as a whole to trope.) The point of locating trope in this fashion within the general scheme of classical rhetoric is not to diminish its linguistic importance—contemporary theory is entitled to the grandest of theoretical formulations about tropes—but to foreground the *historical* fact of the reduction of rhetoric to the binarism of trope and persuasion. The conditions for such a reduction are obviously contingent; we may note, immediately, that the category of "delivery" is irrelevant to polemical writing. For Cicero the art of rhetoric is still the art of oral performance, and its scene is still a public forum, the law court or the senate. The force of de Man's binarism will depend in effect upon whether or not it is possible to reduce all the parts of rhetoric to trope, so that persuasion stands clearly isolated from the taxonomy of trope as the "derived" complement of that taxonomy. It is not my intention here to prove that such a reduction is not possible, only that it has not been demonstrated. De Man is much more concerned, so far as demonstration goes, with the problem posed by the existence of a competitive *grammatical* terminology; the existence of a terminology generated by the other "parts" of rhetoric in the classical system concerns him not at all.

The dependence of de Manian rhetoric on the *post*rhetorical tradition that extends from Fontanier to Nietzsche is obvious as soon as we look more closely into any treatise of classical rhetoric. Invention, for example, "the finding of arguments," generates an enormous and theoretically illimitable list of what Aristotle called topics (*topoi*) which are in turn subject to various schematic divisions and subdivisions. The topics form a sufficiently large part of rhetoric to require separate treatises by Aristotle, Cicero, and others. Aristotle defines topics as "dialectical and rhetorical syllogisms" (*Rhetoric* I, ii, 21). The first example given in the *Rhetoric* is fairly typical: "If war is responsible for the present evils, one must repair them with the aid of peace." The relation of cause and effect in this proposition, or the question of "whether one opposite is predicable of the other," is difficult to distinguish, except by context, from a question in logic. The place in which the "probable" suffices is public; the place in which a "dialectical" proof is requisite is private, the coterie of Plato, or Aristotle's academe. Topics are otherwise rather closer to a form of propositional logic (in Aristotle, the enthymeme) than to trope, and their significance in rhetoric is that argument is no less the vehicle of persuasion than trope, scheme, or style. But even to put the distinction in this fashion (as though logic and rhetoric were *opposed* practices), is to misrepresent the relation between the parts of rhetoric, since that relation is not determined by an epistemological concern but by the exigent social circumstances of rhetorical practice. Within this context, topics are not conceived as incompatible with tropes, but neither can they be assimilated to tropes. It is only *as* logic that they are part *of* rhetoric.

The position of the topics within classical rhetoric could not be deduced on the basis of the binarism of trope and persuasion, according to which the motive of persuasion is associated with trope rather than with logic or dialectic. In the metanarrative of deconstruction, tropes are said to have seductive powers of persuasion but never fail, by virtue of their cognitive dimension, to deconstruct their own persuasive performances. But that narrative achieves its compelling form only because the reduction of rhetoric to trope can assume without question a model of the trope based epistemologically on the relation of the signifier to the signified, or alternatively the word to the referent. We may note in passing here that the intersection of linguistics with epistemology can be otherwise described, and has been: as the question of the "proposition" in analytic philosophy, or of "discourse" in Foucault or Pêcheux. Let us recall here Foucault's agenda in "The Order of Discourse": "to question our will to truth; to restore to discourse its character as an event; to abolish the sovereignty of the signifier." For Foucault the epistemological question does not enter at the level of the signifier but rather at the level of certain kinds of social predication, what he calls "discourse." De Man's insistence that epistemology belongs to the field of the trope-as-signifier produces many familiar effects, but the most interesting of these is a certain anachronistic assumption about the relation of trope to *scientific* discourse. De Man characterizes scientific discourse entirely conventionally as the discourse with the largest epistemological claims, but he would also like to argue that these claims are undermined by

the presence of trope: "Philosophers of science like Bachelard or Wittgenstein are notoriously dependent on the aberrations of the poets" (AR, 17).
But why is such dependence "notorious"? There is no reason to assume
that the expunging of trope forms any part of the epistemological agenda of
either Bachelard or Wittgenstein, or of scientists in general (the mathematization of science has assured that its verbal language is nothing but trope).
The fact that de Man can represent science in the way he does marks rhetorical reading as the latest development of an *anti*rhetorical epistemology
firmly grounded in the discourses of early modernism, when a polemic
against trope was indeed a programmatic feature of scientific discourse formation. Rhetorical reading recovers rhetoric from its refuge in literature in
order to discover it as the defining instance of the linguistic, even while it
continues to regard it, in early modern fashion, as a contaminant of language with respect to language's referential function (what Hamacher calls
"de Man's imperative"). But if argument is never other than rhetorical (in
the sense, say, of Feyerabend), if propositions persuade or fail to persuade
in context, then it will not be necessary to extend the domain of rhetoric to
argument; the historical irony of such an extension is striking, since it returns rhetoric to its original function of persuasion, but only after its
nineteenth-century reduction to trope. The disappearance of the "topics"
from the terminological domain of rhetoric thus facilitates the deployment
of a rhetoric which effaces its own history, and is even incapable on theoretical grounds of admitting to any historical determination.

Having granted epistemological status to the trope-as-signifier, according to a post-Saussurean linguistics of the signifier, rhetorical reading can
then revert to an early modern epistemology by extending the domain of
rhetoric to argument in the sense that argument is *also* tropological, that is,
in the sense that it look like what we call literature: "All philosophy is condemned, to the extent that it is dependent on figuration, to be literary, and
as the depository of this very problem, all literature is to some extent, philosophical" (EM, 28).[23] The return of rhetoric is the return of literature, the
rehearsal in the mode of linguistic generalization of literature's *historical*
differentiation from other early modern discourses, among them the scientific and the philosophical. At a later point, it will be possible to assess
some of the institutional consequences of this return; for the present it will
at least be evident that in declining the question of *discourse,* of literature as
a historical discourse, for the "epistemological" question of the trope-as-
signifier, the agenda of rhetorical reading is determined in an occult process
by the same syllabus of literary works it has the illusion of overcoming. The
addition of philosophical texts to the syllabus of rhetorical reading is in no
way threatening to the discursive boundary between philosophy and litera-

ture, since the reading of philosophical texts is always determined by the formula derived from the discourse and discipline of literature: literature=literary language=rhetoric=trope. Wherever trope is found, there is literature.

As Suzanne Gearhart has persuasively shown, de Man's investment in the category of literature is the most persistent tendency in his work, and that tendency remains dominant through the turn to a rhetorical terminology.[24] But in this regard de Man's thought is not unique; the revival of rhetoric by theory is in the *interest* of literature, in the interest of the literary critical discipline, even when rhetoric is presented as the supersession of the category of literature. The rhetorical terminology becomes the basis for claims as exalted in their way as the most aggrandizing of such claims within the humanist tradition: "Literature as well as criticism—the difference between them being delusive—is condemned (or privileged) to be the most rigorous and, consequently, the most unreliable language in terms of which man names and transforms himself" (AR, 19). The reconstitution of literature as the most rhetorically (tropologically) sophisticated of languages and therefore the privileged discourse by which "man names and transforms himself" advertises literature to its students in the most explicitly *thematic* terms, as the pedagogue's repository of truths about the human condition. What these truths are we shall now be able to demonstrate, by recognizing the rhetorical terminology in de Man as a covert thematic.

"the whole of literature would respond in similar fashion"

For de Man the two most privileged tropes with respect to the epistemological status of literature happen to be metaphor and metonymy, a suspiciously unsurprising binarism.[25] These two tropes also represent, respectively, the systems of rhetoric and grammar, for reasons that we shall now be able to demonstrate. The exemplary argument here is de Man's discussion of the scene of reading in Proust's *À la recherche du temps perdu*. I shall not be concerned directly with the validity of this reading. The interest of de Man's commentary is rather its exemplarity, its thematization of rhetorical reading's rhetoric. The passage from Proust's novel follows, in de Man's translation:

> I had stretched out on my bed, with a book, in my room which sheltered, tremblingly, its transparent and fragile coolness from the afternoon sun, behind the almost closed blinds through which a glimmer of daylight had nevertheless managed to push its yellow wings, remaining motionless between the wood and the glass, in a corner, poised like a butterfly. It was hardly light enough to read, and the sensation of the light's splendor was

given me only by the noise of Camus . . . hammering dusty crates; resounding in the sonorous atmosphere that is peculiar to hot weather, they seemed to spark off scarlet stars; and also by the flies executing their little concert, the chamber music of summer: evocative not in the manner of a human tune that, heard perchance during the summer, afterwards reminds you of it but connected to summer by a more necessary link: born from beautiful days, resurrecting only when they return, containing some of their essence, it does not only awaken their image in our memory; it guarantees their return, their actual persistent, unmediated presence.

The dark coolness of my room related to the full sunlight of the street as the shadow relates to the ray of light, that is to say it was just as luminous and it gave my imagination the total spectacle of the summer, whereas my senses, if I had been on a walk, could only have enjoyed it by fragments; it matched my repose which (thanks to the adventures told by my book and stirring my tranquility) supported like the quiet of a motionless hand in the middle of a running brook the shock and the motion of a torrent of activity. (AR, 13–14)

The reading of the passage is initiated by a reflection on what de Man sees as a metaphor substituting inside for outside in the activity of the young Marcel's reading (the same metaphor is said to govern theorizations of reading). Let us assume for the sake of argument that the representation of metaphor is at least in this context legitimate; the scene in which Marcel's indoor reading is asserted to be as good (in several senses) as enjoying the summer outdoors is presumed on these grounds to be "about" metaphor itself, or "metafigural." The argument is as follows:

> [The passage] contrasts two ways of evoking the natural experience of summer and unambiguously states its preference for one of these ways over the other: the "necessary link" that unites the buzzing of the flies to the summer makes it a much more effective symbol than the tune heard "perchance" during the summer. The preference is expressed by means of a distinction that corresponds to the difference between metaphor and metonymy, necessity and chance being a legitimate way to distinguish between analogy and contiguity. The inference of identity and totality that is constitutive of metaphor is lacking in the purely relational metonymic contact: an element of truth is involved in taking Achilles for a lion but none in taking Mr. Ford

for a motor car. The passage is *about* the aesthetic superiority of metaphor over metonymy, but this aesthetic claim is made by means of categories that are the ontological ground of the metaphysical system that allows for the aesthetic to come into being as a category. (AR, 14)

We might begin by pointing out how quickly and to what a remarkable extent the rhetorical binarism yields a corresponding conceptual polarity. The distinction of metaphor from metonymy orders up from the general stock of Jakobsonian poetics the terms "analogy" and "contiguity," which in turn suggest the philosophical distinction between necessity and contingency. Metaphor is also said to imply claims of "identity and totality," a metaphysical pretension presumably undermined by the nonidentical or nontotalizing aspects of metonymy. In the more elaborated version of the reading (AR, 57ff), metaphor is assigned the function of representing rhetoric: "Structures and relays of this kind, in which properties are substituted and exchanged, characterize tropological systems, as being, at least in part, paradigmatic or metaphorical systems" (AR, 62). If trope is conceptualized as an operation of substitution (x for y), then it is not surprising that metaphor stands here, as it does generally in theories of trope, for all tropes. The point of such a reduction in de Man is presumably to demonstrate that the system of rhetoric does in fact deconstruct itself as a consequence of the mutual interaction of metaphor and metonymy. What seems unpredictable in this argument, if perhaps also ineluctable, is that the binarism imposes upon a trope, metonymy, the task of representing *grammar*. Trope operates on both sides of the antithesis between rhetoric and grammar, one side of which *is* trope, rhetoric:

> By passing from a paradigmatic structure based on substitution, such as metaphor, to a syntagmatic structure based on contingent association, such as metonymy, the mechanical, repetitive aspect of grammatical forms is shown to be operative in a passage that seemed at first sight to celebrate the self-willed and autonomous inventiveness of a subject. Figures are assumed to be inventions, the products of a highly particularized individualized talent, whereas no one can claim credit for the programmed pattern of grammar. Yet, our reading of the Proust passage shows that precisely when the highest claims are being made for the unifying power of metaphor, these very images rely in fact on the deceptive uses of semi-automatic grammatical patterns. (AR, 15)

De Man goes on to describe the process articulated here as the "grammatization of rhetoric," which is also called the "metonymization of metaphor." The sequence of binaries can now be represented as follows:

metaphor vs. metonymy
analogy vs. contiguity
necessity vs. contingency
rhetoric vs. grammar

The schema is curious not simply for positing trope on both sides of its antitheses—the evacuation of the grammatical terminology necessitates the double duty of trope—but also for the more or less casual assumption that the equation of metaphor with rhetoric is sufficiently grounded in the concept of paradigmatic substitution. The semantic operation of trope is as capable of being conceptualized as *displacement* as it is of being conceptualized as substitution, and in that sense metonymy might just as well have been taken to represent rhetoric (as in Lacanian tropology). The appropriateness of such an assignment of metonymy to ur-tropological status would on the face of it accord with the overarching conceptualization of rhetoric as productive of an effect of linguistic indeterminacy, an effect which puts into question the necessity of defining the metaphysical pretensions of metaphor. What logic, then, governs the assignment of metaphor to rhetoric, and metonymy to grammar?

The above schema suggests that de Man generates his major concepts out of an analysis of tropes themselves; but let us consider the possibility that the logic of the argument moves in exactly the opposite direction. What if the role assigned to the Jakobsonian tropes were determined from the first by the concepts of necessity and contingency, and tropes were being employed simply as the "technical" rhetorical names for these thematic notions? At this point we must look more closely at the two tropes of metaphor and metonymy as de Man identifies them in Proust's text. The metaphor, we are told, is established by the link between the music of the flies and summer; but this trope does not look at first glance like a metaphor at all since the music of the flies does not substitute for the summer in its absence. The music is not *like* the summer; it is as much a part of the summer as the quality of the light, or renewed vegetation. The relationship is associative rather than analogical, and the form of association is specifically synecdochic in that "summer" names the sum of the constituents enumerated by Proust. But the relation is also conventionally metonymic, in that the music of the flies enacts a reversal of cause and effect: the chamber music is an effect of summer days, but is said to "guarantee" their return. How, then, does de Man identify the trope as a metaphor? In this way:

The "necessary link" that unites flies and summer is natural, genetic, unbreakable; although the flies are only one minute part of the total event designated by "summer,"they neverthe-less partake of its most specific and total essence. The synec-doche that substitutes part for whole and whole for part is in fact a metaphor, powerful enough to transform a temporal con-tiguity into an infinite duration: "Born of the sunny days . . ." (AR, 63)

The terminological difficulty involved in reconstructing the synecdoche as a metaphor is acknowledged in a footnote, which returns to the problem of the rhetorical terminology qua terminology:

> Classical rhetoric generally classifies synecdoche as metonymy, which leads to difficulties characteristic of all attempts at estab-lishing a taxonomy of tropes; tropes are transformational sys-tems rather than grids. The relationship between part and whole can be understood metaphorically, as is the case, for ex-ample, in the organic metaphors dear to Goethe. Synecdoche is one of the borderline figures that create an ambivalent zone be-tween metaphor and metonymy and that, by its spatial nature, creates the illusion of a synthesis by totalization. (AR, 63)

The massive superstructure of the argument is balanced delicately on this slender note, which argues, by invoking the precedent of Romantic organi-cism, that synecdoche can be "understood" metaphorically. Whether or not it has been *generally* understood in this fashion, or specifically by Proust, the distinction de Man makes between a "transformational sys-tem" and a "grid" is immediately withdrawn by locating synecdoche in an ambiguous "zone" betwen metaphor and metonymy, in other words, on a grid of tropes. It is simply at de Man's own discretion whether to as-similate synecdoche to metonymy or to metaphor, and the grounds for the choice have little to do with how tropes actually work. Synecdoche is moved across the border into the domain of metaphor only because the concepts of identity, totality, and necessity have already been imputed to metaphor as its defining attributes. Because Proust's synecdoche is allied to these thematic motifs, it too must be assimilated to metaphor. But the concepts of "identity" and "necessity" do not describe in any general way the properties of metaphor; they are rather derived directly from the the-matic motifs foregrounded in Proust's text. The concept which permits their assimilation to metaphor is (via Jakobson) analogy: "necessity and chance being a legitimate way to distinguish between analogy and contiguity." On the one side, then, is the solid ground of the "grammatical" concept—analogy—and on the other side, the equally weighty metaphysical concept of necessity. Between the two concepts is nothing at all, an abyss bridged by the interpolation of the rhetorical term: analogy= [metaphor]=necessity.

The same strategic interpolation authorizes the identification of metonymy in the Proust passage. De Man argues that if the text asserts the superiority of metaphor over metonymy, "it owes its persuasive power to the use of metonymic structures" (AR, 15). The "metonymic structure" occurs in the admittedly metaphoric expression "torrent of activity," which de Man argues is "not simply metaphorical" but "doubly metonymic," first because "the coupling of the two terms ["torrent" and "activity"] is not governed by the 'necessary link' of resemblance . . . but dictated by a mere habit of proximity," and second, "because the reanimation of the numbed figure takes place by means of a statement ('running brook') which happens to be close to it, without however this proximity being determined by a necessity that would exist on the level of transcendental meaning" (AR, 66). One certainly has no difficulty accepting the effects of syntactic contiguity on signification, and hence that the dead metaphor is reanimated by proximity to a living one. But, in the example, *there is no metonymy*, unless the actual syntax of the sentence, without which no sentence could exist, is being conflated with the trope of metonymy. Such a conflation has in fact already been posited earlier with the identification of metonymy with the "mechanical, repetitive aspect of grammatical forms," in other words, with grammar itself (AR, 15).

The passage that "explicitly asserts the superior efficacy of metaphor over that of metonymy" therefore contrasts not a metaphor and a metonymy but a metonymy (or synecdoche) "understood" as a metaphor and a metaphor "understood" as a metonymy. I have taken the trouble to sort out these terminological difficulties not in order to argue for one taxonomy over another but to demonstrate how very detached the names of the tropes are in de Man's reading from their conventional significations in rhetoric. The terms which really govern the meaning of "tropes" clearly emerge at the end of the reading:

> . . . persuasion is achieved by a figural play in which contingent figures of *chance* masquerade deceptively as figures of *necessity*. A literal and thematic reading that takes at face value assertions of the text at their word would have to favor metaphor over metonymy as a means to satisfy a desire all the more tempting since it is paradoxical: the desire for a secluded reading that sat-

isfies the ethical demands of action more effectively than actual deeds. Such a reading is put into question if one takes the rhetorical structure of the text into account. (AR, 67; emphasis mine)

The status of this passage as an epitome of rhetorical reading can hardly be overestimated. But the practice it displays and enjoins is not founded upon an account of rhetorical structure at all, but rather upon the reduction of tropes to themes. Nothing is changed in the logic of the argument if "figures of chance" and "figures of necessity" are rendered as "themes of chance" and "themes of necessity." What de Man called the "metafigural" level of the text was never anything other than a preexistent thematic, now superimposed upon the figural language of the text. This is not to say that the invocation of tropes is merely superfluous, however; the names of the tropes are essential to the methodology of rhetorical reading because they permit the methodology to advertise itself as rigorously rhetorical or nonthematic, and therefore to displace its thematic to the unconscious of its own terminology.

The thematic of chance and necessity in fact pervades *Allegories of Reading* through its final pages, which read the Marion episode in Rousseau's *Confessions* as a "fiction" in which the " 'necessary link' of the metaphor has been metonymized beyond the point of catachresis" (AR, 292). In the latter statement, as everywhere else, metaphor and metonymy *mean* necessity and chance. The contradiction overtaking the argument at this moment—the denial of the thematic is asserted at exactly the point at which the thematic governs the rhetorical taxonomy—need never be confronted. In this way rhetorical reading can proceed directly to the stigmatizing of metaphor and the valorization of metonymy, a topos now habitual in the dissemination of theory itself, and taking the form of a rather easy assimilation of metaphor to all forms of linguistic mystification, even the ideological. The fact that tropes can be forced into an epistemological hierarchy is only possible because the thematic which governs the tropology is already so structured: The "metaphysical" concepts of identity, totality, or necessity are deconstructed (effectively devalued) by valorizing the theme of chance. The taxonomy of tropes exists for the sake of that thematic binarism.

Once this point has been acknowledged, it is easy to see that the purpose of the thematic is to carry over, under cover of the rhetorical terminology, the phenomenological problematic of "temporality and consciousness" supposedly superseded by that terminology. Specifically the new thematic reinscribes the problem of *agency*. Here we must quote again the relevant statement from *Allegories of Reading:* "the mechanical, repetitive aspect of grammatical forms is shown to be operative in a passage that seemed at first sight to celebrate *the self-willed and autonomous inventiveness of a subject*" (AR, 15). What is at stake, always, is the locus of agency, or the illusion of the determination of language by an autonomous subject or person.[26] Such determination of the object by the subject is nothing but the philosopher's "freedom of the will," to which de Man alludes in the phrase, "the self-willed and autonomous inventiveness of a subject." The metaphysical "necessity" coupled to the concept of analogy thus names in conventional philosophical terms the metaphysical freedom of the subject, its power to determine an object, a power negated by the very language positing the subject as agent: "The deconstruction of metaphor and of all rhetorical patterns such as mimesis, paranomasia, or personification that use resemblance as a way to disguise differences, takes us back to the *impersonal precision* of grammar and of a semiology derived from grammatical patterns." (AR, 16; italics mine) The deconstruction of metaphor is an effect of the "latent tension between rhetoric and grammar," but this grammar *redivivus* is not the grammar of the linguists; it only appears at all as the equivalent of a trope, metonymy, and as the name of another kind of necessity than the "metaphysical," a necessity embodied in the inexorability of grammatical patterns. "Grammar" has the narrowly allegorical function of naming the "impersonal precision" correspondent to an impersonal linguistic agency. Grammar evinces the fact that tropes are the names of the merely mechanical operations of language: "thus conceived, tropes certainly acquire machinelike, mechanical predictability" (RR, 288).

The "semiology" which emerges from rhetorical reading at this point ("the semiological moment can be described as the metonymic deconstruction from necessity into contingency" AR, 122) finally reconstructs contingency as another kind of necessity, one that is not metaphysical but simply *physical,* a determinate indeterminacy in which the process of signification is subject to the random causality of chance. Like a throw of the dice, such causality yields a pattern at once determined by the laws of physics and radically contingent in the sense that the value on the upturned faces of the dice is related by mere contingency to the physical forces which yield that value. Shall we now say that the thematic of chance and necessity has led de Man to a version of *materialism*? For that is indeed, as we shall see, how his theory of language has been interpreted by the disciples themselves, who regard that materialism as the emergence of a de Manian ideology-critique (on this point I shall comment more fully later). The thematic of necessity and chance does in fact yield in a very late essay on Kant to the binarism of "phenomenality and materiality": "the bottom line, in Kant as well as in Hegel, is the prosaic materiality of the letter and no degree of obfuscation or of ideology can transform this materiality into the phenomenal cognition of aesthetic judgment."[27] One can scarcely overestimate the power of such a formulation to circulate authoritatively in the episteme of literary theory, which also speaks casually and ubiquitously of the materiality of the signifier. This is not to say that signifiers are not in some sense "material"; but it is also a fact of contemporary critical discourse that the concept of the materiality of the signifier has produced no supporting analysis of the concept of materiality itself, *except* as that concept is associated with the notion of the signifier. In the absence of such an analysis, "materiality" is nothing more than the "matter" of vulgar materialism, a literalization whose consequence will concern us presently.

Nothing in the articulation of these categories prevents the further collapse of the materiality of the signifier into the simple determinism of physical causality, that is, into the literalization of a metaphor.[28] Yet for reasons that we are only at the threshold of considering, it is precisely the determinism of this metaphor that is received as the deep truth of linguistic thought. It is worth distinguishing such a concept of materiality from that of historical materialism, for which it may be said that the world is the totality of relations, not things.[29] To forget this fact is to forget why materialism names the critique of idealism, as it is only *within idealism* that matter and spirit constitute a binary opposition. The question, then, is not whether the signifier is material, but whether or not the concept of "materiality" in literary theory is sufficiently defined by the concept of matter.

The materialism now subtending the principle of the materiality of the signifier easily passes over into a *subjectless determinism* which is only the obverse of idealism's transcendental subject. Hence when de Man speaks of the "human subject" in Shelley's "The Triumph of Life" as "standing within the pathos of its indetermination" (RR, 118), this very indetermination has the status of a fate, an implacable determinism (the fatedness of Shelley's accidental death, an accident to which every event of signification also submits). The pathos whose roots are driven all the way down into the bedrock of Western mythology is evoked not by the arbitrary intervention of a divine Atropos into human lives but by an *animus ex machina,* the ghost in the linguistic machine; the word as material object is invested with the same numinous agency evacuated from the subject. The linguistic Atropos cutting the thread of Shelley's text produces the pathos of indetermination (accident) out of the simple determinism of a material causality (in this case, bad weather). The latter causality is always the determinant of the former, and for this reason the concept of indeterminacy is empty in the discourse of rhetorical reading; that concept never signifies indetermination *tout court* but always determinate indeterminacy, the determinism of chance.[30]

In the same fashion tropes are removed from the "transformational system" to which de Man wished to assign them and repositioned in a "grid" or thematic hierarchy. They always mean exactly what their thematic equivalents specify, and these thematizations have no remainder, no "residue of indetermination." Nothing is more obvious in de Man's reading of the Proust passage than the fact that the antithesis of metaphor and metonymy is exhaustive: metaphor is nothing more than necessity; metonymy is nothing more than chance. The tropes themselves have in effect disappeared from the argument, and "rhetorical structure" is what rhetorical reading must take no account of at all. For that reason the function of rhetoric can be specified by the conclusion of de Man's reading of Proust as nothing less than the discovery of a thematic which governs the "whole of literature":

> The further text of Proust's novel, for example, responds perfectly to an extended application of this pattern: not only can similar gestures be repeated throughout the novel, at all the crucial articulations or all passages where large aesthetic and metaphysical claims are being made . . . but a vast *thematic and semiotic network* is revealed that structures the entire narrative and that remained invisible to a reader caught in naive metaphorical mystification. *The whole of literature would respond in similar fashion,* although the techniques and patterns would have to vary considerably from author to author. (AR, 16; emphasis mine)

In retrospect we can say that de Manian deconstruction brought to a moment of completion the "rhetoricism" of the twentieth-century critical episteme, its enduring attempt to define the *essence* of literature by reference to figurative language. Yet theory's embrace of rhetoric paradoxically reaffirmed literature as the expression of a coherent thematic; it reaffirmed the canonical form itself, the sublation of individual works into the ideological homogeneity of "the canon." What remains of great interest is the fact that while the project of theory was to produce such a thematic sublation of literature, this project could be accomplished only by supplementing the literary canon with another set of texts whose function was to reflect precisely the *identity* of literature. The question of why the literary canon was not sufficient to define itself requires a rather different explanatory context, one which will discover yet another function for the canon of theory.

De Rigueur, or the Charisma of Routinization

The condemnation which prophets and creators, and, with them, all
would-be prophets and creators, have levelled through the ages at
professorial or priestly ritualization of the original prophecy or original work (cf. the anathemas, themselves doomed to become classic,
against the "fossilizing" or "embalming" of the classics) draw their
inspiration from the artificialist illusion that the Work of Schooling
could escape bearing the mark of the institutional conditions of its
exercise. All school culture is necessarily standardized and ritualized,
i.e. "routinized" by and for the routine of the Work of Schooling, i.e.
by and for exercises of repetition and reconstitution which must be
sufficiently stereotyped to be repeated ad infinitum. . . . (58–59)
—Bourdieu and Passeron, *Reproduction*

"the truly political mode of discourse"
While the concept of indeterminacy names the effect of trope in general, the
determinism of rhetorical reading's thematic of fate is reproduced at another level, as the "rigor" of the methodology, which is thus overstructured
into narrative form. That narrative is now very familiar: it is the story of the
disappearance, death, fall of a subject, and it drives toward a reiterated effect of pathos. What strikes one in retrospect about this narrative is not its
ubiquity—de Man is very well aware that the method of rhetorical reading
produces in every instance an "allegory of reading," that is, a narrative.
The important point is rather that for de Man the pathos of the narrative is
entirely distinct from the desire of the reader, like a dream in which no wish
is fulfilled. The rigor of deconstruction is always certified by the predetermination of its conclusion; but the conclusion itself is neither desired nor
desirable. It is a matter of indifference to the rigorously rhetorical reader:
"What makes a reading more or less true is simply the predictability, the
necessity of its occurrence, regardless of the reader or of the author's
wishes. . . . Reading is an argument (which is not necessarily the same as a
polemic) because it has to go against the grain of what one would want to
happen in the name of what has to happen" (CW, 221–22). In practice,
deconstruction construes the desire of the reader, as it innocently confronts
the text, as a desire for some other conclusion than the one to which rhetorical reading is inexorably driven. In Barbara Johnson's description of this
scenario of reading, "the impossible but necessary task of the reader is to
set herself up to be surprised."[31] But the uncanny effect of writing criticism
in the pluperfect tense is an effect of narrative, of *knowing the story*. Let us
consider the possibility that nothing is more desirable than that the conclusion of the reading be known in advance, that such knowledge is itself an
object of desire, what one "wants to happen." It scarcely matters to this

narrative whether the name of the conclusion is "indeterminacy," not if the same conclusion (or knowledge) is always produced by adhering in the practice of reading to what is already known about the nature of language itself. The rigor of rhetorical reading is not by any means the rigor of an argument in which the knowledge produced at its conclusion can actually take the reader by surprise. On the contrary, the thematization of trope assures us that the effects of rhetoric, if indeterminate or undecidable with respect to signification, are always predictable with respect to the conclusion of the reading. The rigor of rhetorical reading is thus more rigor than a science requires: it is the rigor of a prescience, a foreknowledge. Such foreknowledge is prophetic; it is authorized by the one who is supposed to know, and who did know, and it aspires to be disseminated without aberration, without heterodoxy. It is the same knowledge in the disciple as in the master, equally "impersonal." Indeed, we may venture to speculate that no knowledge can be cathected with greater intensity than a foreknowledge, the knowledge of what *must* happen. For this reason it is of the essence that the determinism of rhetorical reading ("the necessity of its occurrence") must appear as the rigor of an unassailable *method:* "Technically correct rhetorical readings are . . . irrefutable." The determinism attributed to linguistic structures by virtue of their "prosaic materiality" is reproduced as the very *logic* of rhetorical reading. In retrospect, we can see that the thematic of fate is insufficiently "technical" to signify the "necessity" of rhetorical reading's methodology, and that this task is given over to rhetoric precisely because it is a *technical* terminology.

The valorization of the technical, however, means nothing outside the context of certain institutional practices. De Man insists throughout his later work upon rhetorical reading's technical character; for example, he will praise the work of a disciple as "technical rather than aesthetically pleasing" (CW, 121), by which he means that it achieves the condition of rigor. It will be my contention that just as the rhetorical terminology exists for the sake of the determinist thematic, that thematic in turn offers a means of recharacterizing the rhetorical terminology as technical or rigorous in *contemporary* terms. The ancients meant by *technē rhetorikē*, the *art* of rhetoric. It is important to acknowledge at the outset that rhetorical reading thematizes rigor as the means of characterizing its technical terminology, because critics of deconstruction (and of theory in general) have not often understood the relation between the theme of rigor and what they see as the typical determinism of deconstruction, a determinism they read as implying a politics of apathy or conservatism. By failing to consider separately the metathematic of technicality or rigor, the debate about the politics of rhetorical reading mistakes its object from the very beginning; it fails to recognize the complexity of that object. I will question the adequacy of hypothesizing any political effects of deconstructive criticism without first specifying the relation of that discourse to its institutional conditions. Hence I shall be attempting to locate the political effects of deconstruction initially in the conditions of *intellectual work,* the labor specific to the literary academic. It is in the latter context that the fetishization of "rigor" has particular force, where rigor signifies less the fatedness of human beings in general as it does the nature of the intellectual work of theory.

If the concept of rigor has not frequently raised the question of the political, that question has been raised for one reader of de Man by the term with which rigor is mysteriously allied in his writing, *pathos.* Here I would like to follow up the important argument of Neil Hertz's "Lurid Figures" in order to lay the groundwork for an analysis of the institutional context of both the term "rigor," as the metathematic signifier of the technical methodology, and the term "pathos," which Hertz rightly observes to be inextricably associated with the concept of rigor. He describes this relation generally as

> a characteristic—and characteristically unsettling—aspect of Paul de Man's writing, his particular way of combining analysis and pathos, of blending technical arguments about operations of rhetoric (often presented in an abstract, seemingly affectless idiom) with language—his own and that of the texts he cites— whose recurrent figures are strongly marked and whose themes are emotively charged, not to say melodramatic. (RDR, 82)

"Lurid Figures" is not directly concerned with the institutional relations of deconstruction, but it is very much concerned with the politics of deconstructive discourse. As we shall see, the latter is virtually the only entry into the former. As a consequence we shall have to question a good deal of what is currently said about the "politics of deconstruction" in order to see the actual political valence of its metathematic of rigor. Hertz's suspicion that political questions are raised by the status of pathos in de Man's language eventually turns up a difficulty with *gender,* specifically the question of why, in de Man's reading of the "Marion" episode of Rousseau's *Confessions,* the pathos of Marion's situation is evacuated from the text (along with, presumably, the motive of a feminist reading) on behalf of another pathos, the "pathos of uncertain agency." If the theoretical position asserted by de Man sems to shut the door irrevocably on a reading in which pathos is attached to a subject (with attributes such as gender), the very hyperbole or sexual luridness of the tropes of pathos (Hertz cites among others, beheading, castration, and most luridly, matricide) permits Hertz to argue that on this basis "questions of sexual difference, desire, and misogyny come back into play" (RDR, 102). I take this to mean that Hertz believes the de Manian tropes of pathos produce an excess of affect (luridness) over the pathos that can possibly be elicited by an essentially "linguistic predicament." Such an excess would then have to be read in other terms than those to which de Man restricts himself, terms (and questions) toward which de Man maintains a studied indifference (an indifference, as Hertz says, "he liked to call rigor"). Of course de Man might insist that since these other questions are simply derivative of the linguistic situation, no affect appropriate to them is inappropriate to the situation from which they derive. But de Man himself, as Hertz points out, seems to draw attention to the inadequacy of such an argument in warning his readers to "avoid the pathos of an imagery of bodily mutilation and not forget that we are dealing with textual models" (RR, 289). For our purposes it is rather crucial that de Man could just as easily have said that pathos is to be avoided when we are dealing with *technical* models; the note of the technical is never absent from such formulations. It is finally a question, then, of determining whether the de Manian tropes are truly excessive or "lurid," as only in that case would they be readable in terms other than those already designated by de Man as adequate and rigorous, namely, the "seemingly affectless" technical terminology of rhetoric.

"Lurid Figures" reads de Man both with and against the force of his rigor, which is to say that Hertz is willing to locate the de Manian pathos in its linguistic region or provenance, but also (and at the same time) in a "drama of subjectivity" where a psychoanalytic (and perhaps also a political) discourse would prefer to locate it. What is at stake throughout the essay is clearly the perceived incompatibility between psychoanalytic and deconstructive methodologies: "I have exaggerated the salience (and the immediate pertinence) of a psychoanalytic reading in order to point out the brief appearance of a drama of subjectivity within a discourse, de Man's, which is committed to questioning its privilege as an interpretive category" (RDR, 85). To the extent that a confrontation of opposed methodologies structures the argument, Hertz's reading of de Man introduces a thin wedge of heterodoxy into the de Manian system, after which it is perhaps not possible to recover its dogmatic integrity. Nowhere is this heterodoxy more apparent than in the analysis and defense of de Man's "forcing" of texts, those moments, of some notoriety, when the allegorical narrative overrides what appears to be the plain or indisputable sense of a text. If de Man's theory of language truly constitutes a knowledge of the "prestructure of language" (Hamacher), then such moments of forcing count for little in the ultimate project of deconstructive reading; they might even be recuperated according to Hertz as evidence of an always necessary "estrangement between subject and utterance" (AR, 289), of the very truth they make manifest by means of a failed close reading. But the moments of forcing also happen to be nearly allied to the appearance of lurid figuration, and such proximity raises questions about the rigorousness of rigor; for what if the trajectory of the argument were being determined by the effect of pathos itself—that is, a *narrative* effect—and not by the argument's unassailable logic, its "technical arguments about operations of rhetoric"? In such a circumstance, one would have to say that the argument possessed no rigor at all, only the persuasive force of its sensational tropes.

It is at this point that Hertz diverges from de Man, but not too openly; he seeks only to reconstruct the argument that forces an incorrect reading (in this case, on a passage of Shelley's "The Triumph of Life") by way of proving, with de Man, "why readers cannot help forcing their texts" (RDR, 95). The gesture of recuperation is not without its own aberrant interest: "I can't hope to reproduce either the analytic care or the persuasive force of that argument, but I need to roughly indicate its path and some of its turns, for it is backward along that path that what de Man would call the disfiguring figure of drowning is communicated from Shelley to the shape" (RDR, 93). The Hertzian difference is produced here as a failure to *reproduce* de Man, to occupy the subject position of the disciple. The antithesis of rigor and pathos is thus rewritten in terms sufficiently heterodox to indicate just what difference there is between a de Manian and a Hertzian reading. For Hertz, reading is a matter not of "rigor" but of "care," as in: de Man may not care about getting the passage from Shelley right; or he may not care about Marion, about feminism, about questions conventionally called "political." And of course, what Hertz will not (rather than cannot) reproduce is precisely the "persuasive *force*" of de Man's argument since the problem was with forcing the text to begin with. If Hertz seems at this point the Ferenczi to de Man's Freud, the question of "care" need not be conceived as in any way a sentimental concern. The difference between "analytic care" (at this moment probably a displaced signifier for psychoanalysis) and "persuasive force" (the de Manian rigor) is implicitly the difference between two ways of reading the determinism of the phrase "cannot help" in "why readers cannot help forcing their texts." This difference rehearses the difference between a "linguistic" determinism, the "effet machinal" of *Allegories of Reading,* and the "overdetermination" of psychoanalyisis, a rather different sort of determinism.

In retrospect the tension between deconstruction and psychoanalysis so clearly discerned by Hertz as a subtext of de Man's work must be understood as a struggle over the discursive prize of a concept of causality grounded in the linguistic domain but ultimately operative in the realm of the *social*. For that reason one has to take quite seriously de Man's claim in his later writing that rhetorical reading is a political discourse: "In the description of the structure of political society, the 'definition' of a text as the contradictory interference of the grammatical with the figural field emerges in its most systematic form" (AR, 270). And similarly: "literature is condemned to being the truly political mode of discourse" (AR, 157). The pathos of literature's "condemnation" is only in a trivial sense the expression of a political fatalism, itself the obverse of a liberal voluntarism more or less the consensus of the American academy. The inherent attractiveness of the former affect in the general context of political reaction is obvious enough; but the recurrent defense of deconstruction as a genuinely political discourse on the grounds that political questions are derivative of linguistic ones argues that no theory of literature has discursive force in the current social/institutional context if it is not also capable of reducing the social field to its own mode of determination or necessity. The entire theoretical apparatus grounded in the "prosaic materiality of the letter" can now be seen as existing for the sake of the signifier which itself does no work within rhetorical reading but is nevertheless its most crucially overdetermined concept: rigor. It is not the least irony of that term's circulation within the discourse that it signifies an implacable necessity (a good rhetorical reading is one in which "we do openly what we have no choice but to do anyway" CW, 222), which lends to the technicalities of deconstructive method the aura of a fate, the *same* fate to which the social order submits by virtue of its identity with an "effet machinal" of language. In this way the positing of a universal linguistic mechanism of random causality opens a pathway for the imaginary identification of the trope with the mechanism of causality in the social, and hence for grasping the social within the terms of literariness, as the occasion of a pathos-effect: "Literature is *condemned* to being the truly political mode of discourse." As rhetorical reading's most overdetermined concept, rigor facilitates an imaginary reduction of the social totality to the structure of the trope, and it thus permits rhetorical reading to function as a political theory just by virtue of being *no more than* a theory of literature.

"politico-institutional debates"

If de Manian deconstruction authorizes no specific political practice, as its critics have been eager to claim, that is beside the point. We should do better to ask why a theory of literature (much less of trope) *should* imply a political practice. What is the origin of such a demand? At the moment we are only able to observe that the demand is not actually generated from within the discourse of rhetorical reading but that it confronts literary criticism generally, as a question about the relation between literary pedagogy and political practice. Deconstruction's response to that demand is a response to the present disciplinary conditions of critical practice. It seems highly unlikely that a theory of political practice can be generated out of the terms of any particular academic discipline or discourse. The hypertrophic demand upon literary criticism to adumbrate such a practice is clearly not capable of being satisfied by the literary curriculum alone. It is only a certain kind of pressure exerted from without the discipline of criticism that can impose upon the discourse and syllabus of criticism such a task of political articulation. Provisionally we can say that deconstruction responded to this demand by imposing a *limit* to curricular revision, a limit intended to preserve theory as *literary* theory. For the thematization of the political always falls short of satisfying political demand just by being confined to the literary syllabus. The same disciplinary constraint has determined the reception of all theory, whatever the discourse of its origin, as some version of literary criticism, new ways of reading old texts. In the absence of a "politics of deconstruction," which would in any case descend to the usual emptied-out routines of postmodern democracy, rhetorical reading projects upon the screen of the literary syllabus an immediately apprehensible image of the social totality, an imaginary reduction of the social to an instance of the linguistic. The pathos of that image allows its subjects to apprehend the secret mechanism of causality in the realm of the social without ever transgressing the decorum of literary study. The force of the imaginary reduction resides not only in the strategy of extending the domain of trope to society as a whole, but just as much in the discretion of that strategy, its very reticence. That reticence can be dramatically contrasted now with the concurrent movement to "open the canon," the *indiscreet* correlative of deconstruction's own imaginary grasp of the social totality. For the demand that the syllabus somehow represent the actual constitution of society is a response to the same demand which confronted literary criticism generally.

In his later essays de Man acknowledges the emergence of an "indiscreet" political antagonist of rhetorical reading not only by reasserting his alliance with Derrida's sometimes more explicitly political "deconstruction," but more interestingly by claiming for the tactic of discretion itself a political force, the effect of "subversion": "To the extent that Derrida has this classical discipline in him, his subversion is particularly effective, much more so, I think, than somebody like Foucault, who directly addresses political issues, but without an awareness of the textual complexities that lead up to it" (RT, 117). We should not expect to learn, however, in what sphere the announced political effects are operative, since de Man is at this moment responding to the pressure of his indiscreet antagonist in resorting to a popular concept of "subversion." The significance of the quoted statement is rather that rhetorical reading's discreet image of the social totality is intended to have the effect of detotalizing all other totalizations, that is, all other totalizing claims except the rhetorical. In Rodolphe Gasché's version of this position, de Man's thought constitutes a "consistent, relentless attempt at debunking totalities, totalizing gestures, and ideologies in danger of turning totalitarian."[32] On this basis the avatars of deconstruction have responded to the indictment of its political credentials with the retroactive counterclaim that it has all along been nothing but a political discourse, "nothing but a sustained, relentless meditation on history and the political."[33] And this political discourse consists at the same time of nothing but the rigorous adherence to a rhetorical terminology: "Those apparently 'extrinsic' relations [of literature] themselves require a rhetorical analysis, for example a clear understanding of the various figures of speech always necessary in one form or another to talk about the relation of a work of literature to its 'context': 'reflection,' which is metaphor; 'context,' which is metonymy; 'ideology,' which is anamorphosis, and so on."[34] While such a "translating back" of political into rhetorical terms must seem at this date a last resort, it is authorized by what was all along a powerful implicit "totalization" of rhetorical reading's terminology, otherwise known as its "rigor." Theoretically, no concept at all should resist translation into its rhetorical correlative.

But having made this point, I would also insist that the targeting of supposed "totalizations" for a subversive deconstructive critique is itself the signature of an "ideological" discourse, and not simply because that strategy has in practice responded to critiques from the left (supposedly "totalitarian" discourse). More fundamentally the rhetoric of "totalization" projects as the object of deconstruction's critique its own imaginary totalizations in the discreet reduction of the social totality to the linguistic instance of trope. The "debunking" of totalities is so much shadow boxing, then, but of a sort determined by the present political and institutional conditions of literary criticism, since it characterizes not only rhetorical reading but virtually all critical theory. The reconstruction of rhetorical reading as a "political" discourse represents, as we will now be able to demonstrate, the subordination of de Manian theory to the agenda of a specifically American institutional apparatus. That apparatus effects the retrodetermination of de Man's teaching by the demand of his American disciples. These disciples were neither world-weary European expatriates, nor the younger sons of the *haute bourgeoisie* who formerly constituted the American professoriate. They were middle-class liberals who entered graduate school during or after the Vietnam War, and who wanted to believe that their "technical" discourse was also, however discreetly, a "political" discourse.

If de Man seems to have been quite aware of an unfavorable change in the climate of theory, he clearly hoped to preempt the second wave of "left" reaction to deconstruction by admitting the term "ideology" into the theoretical language of rhetorical reading. In his later critique of "aesthetic ideology" the concept of the aesthetic is virtually identified with that indiscretion of "directly addressing political issues": "It is because we teach literature as an aesthetic function that we can move so easily from literature to its apparent prolongations in the spheres of self-knowledge, of religion, of politics" (RT, 25). When de Man signals in a late interview that, having achieved a "certain control" over linguistic questions, he is now ready to address questions of ideology, a good sense of how the critique of "aesthetic ideology" might maintain its literary decorum is conveyed by Andrew Parker in his introductory comment on de Man's essay "Hegel on the Sublime": "Any consideration of the political now must pass through a preliminary consideration of the aesthetic; more oblique in that the irresolvable complications of the aesthetic call into question the very assurance of any such passage."[35] In retrospect it would appear that the defile of the trope, the impasse of reference, has been refunctioned as the defile of the aesthetic, or the impasse of politics itself. The later Derrida, who may or may not be an avatar of de Manian or "American" deconstruction, provides an interesting account of what de Man's discretion accomplishes as a politics of the defile, which Derrida locates in an institutional context:

> Every reading proposed by Paul de Man, and recently rendered more and more explicitly, says something about institutional structures and the political stakes of hermeneutic conflicts. The characteristics of these readings are most often discreet, but always clear and incisive, and directed not so much against the profession or the institution, but against the academisms of the right and the left, against the conservatism that apolitical traditionalists and activists share in common. The introduction to "Hegel on the Sublime" describes these "symmetrical gestures." "Reactionaries" and "political activists" in truth misunderstand, in order to protect themselves, the political stake and structure of the text, the political allegory of the literary text, no less than the allegorical and literary structure of the political text. More and more Paul de Man publicly took part in

the politico-institutional debates surrounding deconstruction. The positions he took do not have the coded simplicity of well known oppositions, of predictable and unpardonably tiresome predications.[36]

If the subsequent revelations of de Man's wartime collaboration have rendered this politics suspicious for some, these revelations have also disabled any genuine ideology-critique of deconstruction by reducing the discussion to the relatively trivial question of "de Man's politics."[37] Concerning that politics, it is worth noting only that it is easy to document de Man's consistent (generally liberal) opposition to Marxism, but that in no context after the academic purges of the 1950s would such a position be remarkable. It would simply have been assumed. The "politics of deconstruction," insofar as it eschews "unpardonably tiresome predications" of the left or the right passes through a comfortably broad defile, the very American multilane highway betwen the two margins of "reactionaries" and "political activists." In the last two decades such a politics of the center has been played out in the mass media as the Trojan horse of a reactionary revolution, for which the Sinons of the media might reasonably be held in part accountable. It is not clear, however, that an academic posture of disdain for extremism has quite the same function or effect as its media correlative, since the academic "center" is rather to the left of the analogous fulcrum of public opinion. De Man's essays of the 1950s, which address political questions more directly than his deconstructive work, suggest that his aversion to activist intellectuals of the Sartrean type expressed a complexly motivated repudiation of the entire European political ethos; but that ethos is irrelevant to the situation of American academics, for whom Marxism has not been a *political* force in many decades. For that reason the tacit centrism of deconstruction's passage through the defile of politics is much less interesting, because much less consequential, than its implicit claim to have achieved a certain privileged exterior vantage upon the political itself, a position at once "subversive" but not conventionally leftist.

Such an exterior vantage is made possible, according to de Man, by the peculiar nature of the American educational institution. De Man is fortunately very explicit in pronouncing upon this difference, as in the following comment from his 1983 interview with Stephano Rosso: "[I]n Europe one is much closer to ideological and political quesions, while, on the contrary, in the States, one is much closer to professional questions." De Man goes on to link this institutional difference to the discreet subversiveness of deconstructive discourse, as though the discourse were uniquely constructed to take advantage of the very political marginality of the university, its cultural irrelevance:

So, personally, I don't have a bad conscience when I'm being told that, to the extent that it is didactic, my work is academic or even, as it is used as a supreme insult, just more New Criticism. I can live with that very easily, because I think that only what is, in a sense, classically didactic, can be really and effectively subversive. And I think the same applies there to Derrida. Which doesn't mean that there are not essential differences: Derrida feels compelled to say more about the institution of the university, but that is more understandable within the European context, where the university has such a predominating cultural function, whereas in the United States it has no cultural function at all, here it is not inscribed in the genuine cultural tensions of the nation. . . . (RT, 117)

No proposition could be more blind to its own meaning than the claim that the American university has no "cultural function." A claim of this sort would hardly be credible about any social institution. Yet this is not to say that de Man's assertion has no basis whatsoever. At an earlier point in the interview he remarks that he "found it difficult in Europe to be teaching material that was so separated from the actual professional use that students, who were mostly destined to teach in secondary school, would make use of." In this country, by contrast, "one teaches future colleagues, one has a very direct professional relationship with them—which however, has its own ideologies, and its own politics, which are the politics of the profession, the relationship of the academic profession to the American political world and society" (RT, 116). The "politics of the profession" is grounded as a politics in the cultural defunctioning of the university, but more specifically in the unique position of the graduate schools in the university system. It is in the graduate schools that university teachers of literature address other, future university teachers, and thus confirm an institutional autonomy constituting the domain of professional credentialization. How one moves across the gap between the "politics of the profession" to the "American political world" is difficult to say. Derrida is rather more circumspect in delimiting the field of this politics to the academic institution itself: "More and more de Man took part in the politico-institutional debates surrounding deconstruction." The place of this politics is at once a separate place, a place with no "function" and therefore politically irrelevant, and at the same time the place of a *politics,* even a politics more real, more subversive than might be practiced elsewhere.

Of what, then, does this politics consist? The "politico-institutional debates surrounding deconstruction" concern nothing other than "the resistance to theory," a resistance which is invariably attributed to the *institution* of literary criticism. The occurrence of such an institutional resistance is the basis for the positing of subversive effects inherent in the discourse of deconstruction; resistance evinces subversion. The same claim entails conversely the proposition that the "institutionalization" of deconstruction marks the limit of its subversion, the neutralizing of its politics. The argument that such an itinerary describes the institutional fate of deconstruction (as of any "subversive" discourse) is so pervasive as scarcely to require citation. But I should like to subject several examples to scrutiny here, in order to demonstrate how entirely mistaken this assumption is. Here, first, is a summary statement by Peggy Kamuf, with reference to de Man's "Resistance to Theory":

> On the one hand, that the "main theoretical interest [of literary theory] consists in the impossibility of its definition" will continue to manifest itself in institutional resistance. And, on the other hand, because the institutionalization of literary theory in this country has tended to follow the way in which it can be made to serve an overarching pedagogical program and because literary theory, when it pursues its main theoretical interest, has to question the defining limits of any such program when applied to literary language; institutionalization can be made to appear in its effects—the marks it has left—on the movement of thematic thought. "The Resistance to Theory" inauspiciously resists this program and thus bears the mark of a certain institutional closure. (RDR, 140)

The allusion in the final sentence is to the Modern Language Association's refusal to accept "The Resistance to Theory" in a collective volume on scholarship in various fields; that refusal is often cited as the exemplary occurrence of an institutional resistance which then testifies to the subversiveness of de Man's essay. I belabor the obviousness of this point for the sake of appreciating the magnitude of its error. For what could the "institutionalization" of such a discourse mean in this context, if the place of its production is never elsewhere than an institutional place? If the site of the discourse's production is the Comparative Literature department of Yale University, what trick of ideological optics eclipses this institution with so weak an institutional antagonist as the MLA? Deconstruction is always and from the first "institutionalized," as it has no other locus of practice, dissemination, or resistance than university literature departments. Nevertheless the motif of "institutionalization" has large discursive effects because it allows deconstruction to occupy, at the moment of its origin, an imaginary locus *exterior* to the institution. Thus Geoffrey Hartman writes:

"The spirit of criticism embodied by de Man threatens the institutionalization of criticism itself. . . . Those who oppose deconstruction as obscuran-
tist, and those who espouse it as intellectually necessary, agree that it
pushes against the limits of the academic" (RDR, 11). The privileged exteriority of the university to the political order is thus reproduced in the
"politico-institutional" debate about deconstruction as the subversive exteriority of deconstructive discourse to the *institution itself*. The same removal of deconstructive discourse to a position of privileged exteriority
characterizes the even more extreme claim of Christopher Norris, that "de
Man's work cannot easily be classified in terms laid down by the standard
academic division of labor."[38] It is not merely a *façon de parler* that represents the hypothetical subversiveness of an academic discourse as a subversion of the very conditions of institutional existence, such conditions as the
division between departments. There are compelling reasons, which we
may now elucidate, why resistance to deconstruction *within* the university
must be equated with subversion *of* the academic institution itself.

The survival of that institution with all its faculties intact bequeaths to
the disciples the very problem of the waning of deconstruction's "subversive" effects. Here is Barbara Johnson's description of this problem in an
essay that foregrounds the paradox of institutionalization in its title,
"Nothing Fails Like Success":

> As soon as any radically innovative thought becomes an *ism*, its
> specific ground-breaking force diminishes, its historical noto-
> riety increases, and its disciples tend to become more simplistic,
> more dogmatic, and ultimately more conservative, at which
> time its power becomes institutional rather than analytical. The
> fact that what is loosely called deconstructionism is now being
> widely institutionalized in the United States seems to me both
> intriguing and paradoxical, but also a bit unsettling, although
> not for the reasons advanced by most of its opponents.[39]

Johnson moves the argument about institutionalization a little further
along its blind path by linking the motif of institutionalization to the problem of discipleship itself. The disciples are enjoined to recover the "vital,
subversive power" of deconstructive discourse by recovering the state of
"surprise" precedent to the congealing of deconstruction into a methodology. And this they can only do by unlearning the very lessons they assimilated as a positive knowledge. Yet it is difficult to see how such unlearning is
to be produced, especially if the methodology is itself cathected as the truth
of the master teacher. Because the problem *is* discipleship, it is the problem
of transference transferred. The wish to recapture the moment of "sur-

prise" is only a wish to experience once again the first and freshest moment of the transference. It is that moment which seems in retrospect to have no relation to the "institution," to exist entirely in a private space between the master and the disciple, and therefore to be subversive of institutionality per se. Yet the desire to repeat that moment of quasi-exteriority to the institution is hardly incompatible with the institution of a methodology: it *is* methodology, the transference in its formal aspect of repetition.

The equation of institutionalization with both discipleship and the standardization of methodology acquires its own narrative pathos in more recent accounts of deconstruction's institutional career by Lindsay Waters and Howard Felperin:

> It was unfortunate that he became such an academic institution. It is not, however, as if he did not work toward that goal. He did. But he became in a way the victim of his own success. His ideas and procedures with all their avant-gardiste characteristics . . . got turned into a set of academic techniques, rules for the Mechanical Operations of the Spirit. (CW, lxi)

> Deconstruction is indeed proving thoroughly amenable to routinization at the hands of the institution to whose authority it once seemed to pose such a challenge of incompatibility. More than that, it has all but become the institution, as its life and activity rapidly become indistinguishable from the life and activity of the institution at large. . . . [40]

Felperin goes on to invoke the Weberian concept of the "routinization of charisma" as a paradigm for comprehending the institutional fate of deconstructive discipleship, but that paradigm has been everywhere implicit in the narrative of dissemination. Here it is worth recalling Weber's precise formulation: "Charisma . . . by its very nature . . . is not an 'institutional' and permanent structure, but rather where its 'pure type' is at work, it is the very opposite of the institutionally permanent."[41] The question of the pure type is not simple, however; Weber generates his ideal types of charisma and institution out of the history of religion, where the career of the prophet gives way to the institution of a church. The transposition of these concepts to the context of the educational institution constitutes a remarkably unconsidered recourse to sociology in the current narrative of deconstruction's dissemination, within which the Weberian motif of the "routinization of charisma" has been tacitly assumed. The historical fact that the charismatic authority of de Man was never exclusive of, nor incompatible with, his institutional authority suggests that an account of deconstruction's institutionalization will not advance very far if its divergence from the Weberian "ideal type" is not acknowledged at the outset. It would be more accurate to say that deconstruction has been "routinized" rather than instititutionalized. The failure to distinguish these terms means that the representation of de Man's authority as charismatic (in Weber's sense of the term) will always entail the unquestioned assumption that such charismatic authority can *only* be conceived as anti-institutional. This is the way deconstruction becomes a "politics": by opposing its charismatic authority to the very institutional *conditions* of that authority. The status of such a politics can always be confirmed for the disciples, then, by the appearance of any resistance whatsoever, from whatever quarter of the institution. Such resistance is always instantly converted into "institutional" resistance, just as the charismatic authority of de Man is instantly converted by the appearance of resistance into the "subversive effects" of his methodology.

"the madness of authority"

Discussions of the "politics of deconstruction" are usually forced to construe deconstruction as a political allegory—either the allegory of the evasion of the political, according to its detractors, or the allegory of its secret subversiveness, according to its defenders. I will pursue here an analysis along quite different lines, by addressing directly the institutional dilemma of deconstruction—not resistance but discipleship (transference-resistance), and the routinization effects at once produced and lamented by the disciples. This is to say that what theory responds to is not immediately politics, but the conditions of institutional life, the everyday life of the professors of literature. The larger theoretical question engaged by such an analysis is the nature of *intellectual labor,* but that question is confronted in the very specific context of contemporary literary pedagogy. Hence the necessity of beginning with the scene of the transference in pedagogy, which the "politics of deconstruction" converts into the scene first of a subversive, anti-institutional charisma, and then into the narrative of the institutionalization of that politics. The invocation of Weber already betrays the fact that charisma requires a sociological and not immediately a political context of interpretation, because the immediate task of the university is to produce a certain segment of the work force, its "intellectual" laborers. The larger question that arises here concerns the nature of the intellectual labor that takes place within, and is produced by, the university; the narrower concerns the nature of deconstruction (and theory in general) as a self-described "technical" labor.[42]

The disciples have found it all too easy to invoke the Weberian commonplace in preference to the analytic concept of the transference, in accordance with de Man's own foreclosing of a psychoanalysis of pedagogy. The invocation of Weber has produced a satisfying narrative of rhetorical reading's institutional fate, but at the cost of simply and uselessly stigmatizing the "institution" which is the inescapable context of rhetorical reading. Such a narrative offers no analysis of the specific institutional apparatus in question, in its historical time and place. Interestingly, de Man is rather careful to distance himself from the Weberian theme. In his interview with Stephano Rosso, in the passage from which I have already quoted, de Man goes so far as to reject implicitly the Weberian scenario:

> It is often said—and this is true to some extent—that whatever is audacious, whatever is really subversive and incisive in Derrida's text and in his work is being taken out by academizing, by making him just one other method by means of which literature can be taught. . . . As far as I'm concerned, I'm often mentioned as one who is much responsible for that, since my work is, in a sense, more pedagogical than philosophical; it has always started from the pedagogical or the didactic assignment of reading specific texts rather than, as is the case in Derrida, from the pressure of general philosophical issues. I can see some merit to that statement, except for the fact that I don't think it is possible, in Derrida, to separate the classical didactic pedagogical element, which is undeniably there, from the subversive aspect of his work. (RT, 116–117)

The preemptive strategy of identifying the subversive effect with the very "academizing" of the discourse already acknowledges the compatibility of rhetorical reading with the institutional structures of the school. What are we to make, then, of the surprising contradiction between de Man's investment in the academic institution and his disciples' recourse to an anti-institutional narrative? For the disciples, the stigmatizing of "academization" was always a way of reinstating the authority of charisma, of attributing to that charisma an effect of "subversiveness" by imagining its locus as somehow exterior to the academic institution.

We are now prepared to appreciate the significance of de Man's assumption that rhetorical reading is nothing if not "academic"; it is for him "mere reading," merely performing one's "didactic assignment." So far from "subverting" the institution itself, it is quite clear that rhetorical reading is conceived by de Man as the fulfillment of purely institutional requisites, even as the refusal of any demand emanating from without the institution. But this lesson is very hard to learn indeed, since it requires that the methodology of rhetorical reading be *identified* (how closely, we shall see) with the institution and its strictly institutional agenda. This is the point finally of de Man's response to Walter Jackson Bate's attack on what Bate regards as the overspecialization of literary study. So far from inhabiting a space exterior to the institution, de Man proposes that fully implementing a deconstructive pedagogy would transform "departments of English from being large organizations in the service of everything except their own subject matter into much smaller units, dedicated to the professional specialization that Professor Bate deplores" (RT, 25–26). Such a statement is rather typical in its capacity to frustrate a political analysis, since the position of Bate in the argument could easily have been occupied by a leftist (or Sartrean) intellectual-at-large. For de Man, any determination of the political function of the literary critic, either from the left or from the right, is incompatible with the *institutional autonomy* of criticism. If de Man also concedes that "The institutional resistances to such a move, however, are probably insurmountable," this does not mean that he takes Bate to be arguing on behalf of the institution against a discourse subversive of its basic structures. On the contrary, de Man's argument is that departments of literature have denied their institutional identity *as departments;* they have constructed an institutional self-image which devalues their own purely institutional functions. Against such institutionalized anti-institutionalism de Man proposes a thorough reinvestment in the *form* of the department, as the basic structural unit of the university. Once we are able to acknowledge this fact we can recognize how misleading is such a claim as Christopher Norris's, that de Man's work "cannot easily be classified in terms laid down by the standard academic division of labor." De Man expresses a very strong investment in precisely this division of labor.

It might be possible at this point to assimilate de Man's argument to the aggressively "professionalist" polemic which has apparently succeeded the "politico-institutional debate" about deconstruction. But such a thesis would be premature, as well as inaccurate. I have already suggested that professionalism names an ideological discourse, the ego-ideal of the professoriate, and not simply an institutional practice. The profession has its specific institutional arrangements—conferences, journals, and the like— but these are almost entirely dependent upon the material infrastructure of the universities. In the passages quoted above, de Man does not yet resort to the current form of the professionalist argument (such as that advanced by Fish)[43] against Bate's anti-professionalism, but he does insist upon the structural preeminence of the department even to the extent of proposing its division into "much smaller units." The moment of investment in the principle of *division itself*—of departmentality—moves in a direction apparently opposite to the present ideology of professionalism, which imagines the profession as an autonomous collectivity transcending the institutional constraints of the particular schools and departments by which the professors are employed. The cathexis of the department, on the other hand, reinvests in the basic unit of bureaucratic structure, the "bureau." The division into departments or "bureaux" defines the very logic of institutional structure and development.

As with the term "charisma," I would insist upon the necessity of returning to the precise formulations of Weberian sociology. As it happens the terms "charisma" and "bureaucracy" are crucially linked in Weber's work. They are the historical and structural antipodes of his sociology: "The bureaucratic structure is everywhere a late product of historical development. The further back we trace our steps, the more typical is the absence of bureaucracy and of officialdom in general. Since bureaucracy has a 'rational' character, with rules, means-ends calculus and matter-of-factness predominating, its rise and expansion has everywhere had 'revolutionary' results . . . as had the advance of *rationalism* in general."[44] Charisma is thus transformed into bureaucracy, the institutional embodiment of that "rationalization" Weber sees as defining modernity. As a social relation, bureaucracy is a form of status hierarchy; it defines the structure of nearly all our institutions, including the school. As Cornelius Castoriadis argues in his discussion of the bureaucratic form in modernity, "At a certain stage, bureaucratization (i.e. the management of activity by hierarchized apparatuses) becomes the very logic of this society, its response to everything."[45] The question for us, then, is not whether, but to what extent the bureaucratic form now determines the structure and procedures of educational institutions, since these institutions likewise exhibit an increasingly differentiated organization of specialized functions, along with the complex status hierarchies defining the historical work-form of the "career." It is along this path of analysis that we will be able to relate de Man's cathexis of the departmental structure, on the one hand to the phenomenon of discipleship, and on the other to the internal protocols of his discourse, its "rigor."

Let us look, then, a little more closely at the implications of Weber's proposition, that "charismatic domination is the very opposite of bureaucratic domination."[46] According to this formulation, it should be impossible for charismatic authority to appear within bureaucratic institutions at all. Truly bureaucractic authority dissolves charisma and replaces it with a cathexis of the office rather than the person: "It is decisive for the specific nature of modern loyalty to an office that, in its pure type, it does not establish a relationship to a *person*, like the vassal's or disciple's faith in feudal or patrimonial relations of authority. Modern loyalty is devoted to impersonal and functional purposes" (69). The existence of such a pure type raises an interesting problem for the articulation of a psychological with a sociological analysis. Weber's analysis appears to be devised to explain the effective operation of bureaucracy in the absence of any positive affective attachment to superior officeholders (and bureaucracy does in that sense "work"); but Weber's ideal-type analysis goes on to conceive of bureaucratic authority as though the officeholder were in fact anonymous, impersonal in that purely ideal sense. Of course there is no functional office without an officeholder, and thus the affect which binds to the office is premised upon the complex and necessarily continuous process of distinguishing the office from the officeholder. The rigorous enforcement of such a distinction cannot simply be assumed to characterize any actually functioning bureaucratic apparatus, however—only its ideal type.

The absence of a psychodynamic account of bureaucratic loyalty has in fact been the major theoretical problem in the history of the analysis of bureaucracy. The best current account of this problem, by Claude Lefort,[47] returns to Marx's critique of Hegel on just this point: Hegel's conception of bureaucracy in his *Philosophy of Right* anticipates Weber's in representing the bureaucratic functionary as the bearer of a general interest, that is, as personally disinterested. In his critique of Hegel, Marx rejects this construction as an idealization of the bureaucracy's own interests (ultimately also, the interests of the bourgeoisie, as the class claiming to represent the universal interest): "Bureaucracy must therefore safeguard the *imaginary* universality of the particular interests . . . in order to safeguard the *imaginary* particularity of the universal interest."[48] Clearly Weber's conception of bureacracy is in accord with certain aspects of Hegel's, though Weber does not necessarily idealize the disinterestedness of the bureaucrat; he takes the impersonality of the bureaucratic structure as itself the problem, the "iron cage" of modernity.[49] Marx emphasizes, in contrast to Hegel, the typical incompetence of the bureaucracy, an incompetence derived from a deep irrationality in the bureaucratic form of social relation. Where Hegel and Weber see the bureaucratic function as impersonal, Marx sees an entirely different social form, a cult of authority: "the principle of its knowledge is therefore authority, and its patriotism is the adulation of authority" (108). Office and function always mask interpersonal struggles (in the form of "a hunt for promotion, of careerism"), which are ultimately disconnected from the express function of the bureaucracy as a whole: "The aims of the state are transformed into the aims of the bureaux and the aims of the bureaux into the aims of the state." In such an institutional context, charismatic authority is not extirpated but rather acquires a rhetorical mask of impersonality, and a jargon in which social relations can always be translated into the language describing purely formal relations between offices or ranks. Hence the emergence of *factions* within a bureaucracy cannot be predicted on the basis of the purely formal structure of a bureaucratic organization; rather, factional networks are superimposed in an indeterminate way upon the official structure, the ends of which are continually deformed by the pressure of these struggles. To quote Lefort's analysis, "behind the mask of rules and impersonal relations lies the proliferation of unproductive functions, the play of personal contacts and the madness of authority" (109). We may assume that familiarity with such madness is virtually universal, but the point of Lefort's analysis is not simply to denounce bureaucracy but to analyze it, to give the reason of its unreason. It is not enough merely to expose the "madness of authority" behind the stenciled doors of the bureaux. It is the intimate and mutually determining relation between the charismatic and the bureaucratic which stands in need of analysis, and which disallows the displacement of the one term by the other.

I would appropriate two further points of Lefort's analysis, both relevant to the specific question of the relation of the bureaucratic form to the charismatic authority of the master teacher. Lefort adopts, with certain qualifications, a Weberian thesis about the relative autonomy of bureaucratic institutions: "The bureaucracy is essentially indifferent to the interests and values defended by a political regime. It is an organ in the service of dominant groups, situated, as it were, between those who dominate and those who are dominated" (98). This formulation captures the self-preservative and opportunistic drive of bureaucratic institutions without failing to emphasize the real subordination of bureaucracies to larger sociopolitical determinations. The concept of "relative autonomy," which is indispensable to characterize a broad range of social institutions, signals the impossibility of any *absolute* autonomy within the realm of the social, or the fact that extrainstitutional "interests" can be expressed within a given relatively autonomous institution only as they are mediated by the self-interests of that institution. Of few institutions is the assertion of autonomy closer to absolute than the school, but for this very reason it has posed a particular problem for the analysis of the bureaucratic form. The second point I would appropriate form Lefort's discussion is thus his observation that, although "the position of the teacher [Lefort's example is, like de Man's, the French secondary school teacher] corresponds exactly to that which Weber attributed to the bureaucrat," the teacher is also atypical of the bureaucratic funtionary. "[T]he content of his activity is only very partially determined by ministerial decisions. This professional activity has its own goal which should not be confused with the objective goal immanent in the ministerial organization; it is an activity oriented towards a transformation of its object and this alone can provide it with a sufficient justification" (102). The degree of bureaucratization, or what I will call "heteronomy"—the degree to which one's work is prescribed by superiors in the bureaucratic hierarchy—exists in a certain ratio to the degree of "professional activity," a realm of more autonomous behavior, defined for teachers both by the privacy of the classroom and by the academic freedom of discourse among colleagues in a field.[50] In the American educational system, the realm of "professional activity," in the sense of work autonomy, has in practice been more and more confined to the universities, while the "content" of teaching at the primary and secondary levels is almost entirely dictated by a bureaucratic policy which has in effect "proletarianized" teachers. At the same time, universities (both public and private) have developed large bureaucratic apparatuses to which teachers belong as one level of the bureaucracy itself (increasingly so, since the growth of administration has been paralleled by an increase in the burden of administrative tasks imposed upon teachers). University teachers, then, at once occupy the classroom and the office, simultaneously moving within the relatively autonomous realm of the seminar or their professional research projects, and pursuing bureaucratically structured careers within the elaborately graded status hierarchy of the educational institution.

I have already alluded in Chapter 1 to the significance of the relative autonomy of pedagogic practice in the context of appropriating Bourdieu and Passeron's contention that "by ignoring all demands other than that of its own reproduction, the school most effectively contributes to the reproduction of the social order." The question before us now is somewhat more complex. Bourdieu and Passeron insist in *Reproduction* on the theoretical distinctiveness of the "autonomy" specific to the educational system, and they are thus resistant to any reduction of pedagogic action to a species of the bureaucratic. They object in particular to the argument of Michel Crozier in *The Bureaucratic Phenomenon* that "we should find, in the French educational system, the main characteristic patterns of the bureaucratic system of organization," a thesis they regard as construing the formal features of the educational institution merely as reflections of the dominant mode of social organization:

> Thus, for example, Crozier is only able to grasp characteristic features of the school institution, such as the ritualization of pedagogic action or the distance between master and pupil, insofar as he recognizes in them manifestations of the logic of bu-

reaucracy, i.e. fails to recognize what is specifically scholastic about them, in that it expresses tendencies or requirements proper to all institutionalized educational systems, even when scarcely or not at all bureaucratized: the tendency toward "routinization" of pedagogic work, which is expressed in, among other things, the production of intellectual and material instruments devised by and for the School, manuals, corpuses, topics, etc., appears, alongside the first signs of institutionalization, in traditional schools like the rhetoric and philosophy schools of Antiquity or the Koran schools, which exhibit none of the features of bureaucratic organization. (190)

The argument of *Reproduction* is explicitly here, as it is implicitly throughout, a description of the transhistorical structure of the educational institution, and in the terms of this project, the concept of autonomy emerges as the single most significant concept defining the transhistorical identity of the school as an institution. The routinization effect exhibited in the school's formal procedures is thus only accidentally congruent with the historical form of bureaucracy, which is a mode of social relation specifically *modern:*

> when Crozier sees in the institutional guarantees of university "independence" no more than a form of the guarantees statutorily written into the bureaucratic definition of official posts, he lumps together two facts as irreducible to one another as the systems of relations to which they belong, on the one hand the autonomy which teachers have claimed and obtained as civil servants subject to the common legislation of a Government department, and on the other hand, the pedagogic autonomy inherited from the medieval corporation. (190–91)

The distinction drawn by Bourdieu and Passeron between bureaucratic and pedagogic autonomy is indeed the crucial one, but that does not mean that in practice, in the pedagogic imaginary, the two forms of autonomy are not actually *confused*. It is not a question of "lumping together" the two autonomies, when they are "irreducible to one another," much less of reducing the pedagogic to the bureaucratic, but of acknowledging the overdetermination of the concept of "autonomy" in the contemporary school by the complex interaction of the two relative autonomies, the pedagogic and the bureaucratic. In the situation of the bureaucratized educational institution, pedagogic autonomy must defend itself against the heteronomous pressure of the *educational institution itself*, insofar as it bureaucratically administers pedagogy, and not only against the pressures that seek to constrain or determine pedagogy from outside the school. The defense of pedagogic autonomy has taken the form of an aggressive defense of "professionalism," whose social function we can now identify as an attempt to compensate for the bureaucratic constraints upon pedagogic autonomy. In these circumstances, the career of the college professor is increasingly structured as a mimesis of the bureaucratic career (even sometimes, as a movement "up" from teaching to administration). It would not otherwise be possible to explain the subordination of even the most rarefied intellectual inquiry to norms of "productivity" which usually determine the trajectory of the bureaucratic career.[51]

The larger question of the relation between the professional and the bureaucratic has been addressed recently in an excellent study by Magali Scarfatti Larson, *The Rise of Professionalism*.[52] Larson points out that while the profession has always been represented as "the antithesis of bureaucracy," all professions are now "bureaucratized to a greater or lesser extent" (xvii), and further, "in a bureaucratized world, professions can no longer be interpreted as inherently anti-bureaucratic" (199). While a greater measure of "work autonomy" can still be said to define the professional mode of work organization, a condition which characterizes such institutions as "the medical clinic, the graduate school, the large legal or accounting firm, large architectural offices, and research instititutes," the existence of common standards of "technical competence" governing all the "professional bureaucracies" suggests that bureaucracy and profession can be regarded as "two subtypes of a larger category—that of rational administration" (191). This proposition may seem at first glance only to reassert a Weberian thesis, but its implications are profound. Larson argues finally that "the alleged conflict between bureaucracy and profession as modes of work organization is not so much a conflict between two structures as it is a contrast between the structure of bureaucratic organizations and an ideology promoted by some of their members" (219). In the case of the university teacher, the claim to professional autonomy can thus be asserted *against the school itself*, despite the fact that accomplishments in the professional field are compensated by the usual rewards only a bureaucratically organized institution can offer. In reality, then, the "personal talent and charisma" of the professor, though they are established in the seminar or in the professional field, are never entirely distinguishable from the status hierarchy of the institution:

> The more incorporated into heteronomous organizations a profession is, the more its members' prestige is determined by

the organization: thus, the pattern of academic mobility—by "horizontal upward displacement" from campus to more prestigious campus—appears *prima facie* to replicate the pattern of the careers of executives in the private or public sector, or across both.

However, the individualization of organizational prestige is different in consulting or academic professions from what it is in technobureaucratic careers. The fact that achievements in the former are personalized seems to allow for an ideological blending of personal and organizational *prestige*. (205)

Such "ideological blending" is paradoxical in that bureaucratic organizations like the modern university tend to encourage the very professionalist ideology that denies the subordination of professional activity to merely bureaucratic ends. Professionalism is thus lodged within bureaucracy as the affirmation of the principle antithetical to bureaucracy itself, the principle Weber called "charisma" and which Larson recognizes as a form of "individualism":

Typically, professions maintain indeterminate and untestable cognitive areas in order to assert, collectively, the uniqueness of *individual* capacities. Collectively they solicit trust in *individual* professionals and *individual* freedom from external controls. . . .

This individualism is, I believe, one the powerful factors that make professions continue to appear, in the eyes of the public and of most social scientists, as the "anti-bureaucracy." (206)

At the least Larson's argument implies that discussions of the academic "profession" which do not acknowledge its incorporation into a heteronomous bureaucracy simply disseminate an *ideology* of professionalism and not an analysis of its real institutional conditions. It is just such an ideology which has subtended the claims for the subversiveness of literary theory, and rhetorical reading in particular, by naming the "institution" as the object of subversive teaching by charismatic master theorists. Such charisma is always a "blending of personal and organizational prestige." Yet within the ideology of professionalism, the charisma of the master theorist appears to constitute a realm of *absolute* autonomy, and therefore, as we have noted, an "other scene" of politics.

Nothing confirms this point more certainly than the mutation of the master theorists in the 1980s into "superstars," into the free agents of pure charisma. It is not difficult to see that the deployment of this category was driven by the interests of competitive university administrations, for whom the content of theory, subversive or otherwise, was largely irrelevant. What mattered was that the charisma of the master theorists could be converted into bureaucratic prestige. The social horizon circumscribing and conditioning the emergence of the academic superstar is thus nothing less than the total socioeconomic order, within which the pervasive mass-cultural form of the celebrity system is directly (but at the same time invisibly) correlated to the disappearance of "work autonomy" at every level and in every sphere of the work force. For the professoriate, it is only in the superstar as a form of *celebrity* that autonomy or free agency truly resides, an autonomy ratified by "horizontal upward mobility." Such mobility signifies an imaginary transcendence of institutional heteronomy by means of *professionalism itself*, by the deliberate cultivation of charismatic authority.[53] But the figure in whom so large an imaginary investment is deposited, so far from representing a real autonomy, is the site of the maximum determination of the university teacher's "professional activity" by external social forces, namely (as everyone also knows) the forces of the market. The invisible hand which gives the charismatic celebrity "mobility" is thus the same hand which makes a given commodity irresistible in a given time and place, especially when that commodity signifies (as so many commodities do) autonomy itself.

"the task of literary criticism"

The foregoing argument confirms, if it needs confirming, that the institutional position of the master theorist, as the person in whom institutional and personal prestige is "blended," and in whom the concept of "autonomy" is maximally overdetermined, was always a condition for the emergence of theory. In the case of de Man, his institutional affiliation was never merely incidental, it was essential to the propagation of rhetorical reading as a school, and therefore also to the construction of his personal "charisma." The same circumstances explain why the waning of deconstruction was a consequence not of its successful refutation, but of its successful dissemination, the transference onto the methodology. Theory itself is burdened with the task of "subverting" the very institutional conditions that permit it to construct itself as the vehicle of an anti-institutional, charismatic authority. This paradox is only intelligible from the point of view of a sociological analysis: as the pedagogic transference moves out of the seminar into the larger institutional field, it produces the phenomenon of *factions,* the internecine bureaucratic conflict that is misrecognized as "institutional resistance" to deconstruction. Hence deconstructive theory is vulnerable, as the object of transference transferred, to the same bureaucratic and market forces the theorist experiences in his or her career. This point has been underscored in the wake of the scandal of de Man's wartime collaboration, since the scandal itself has absurdly but inevitably discredited deconstructive theory, as though the theory and the theorist were the same.

More consequential than the decline of deconstruction, however, is the current "crisis" of theory itself,[54] with which the name "deconstruction" is inseparably entangled. So far from recognizing here only the supposedly "journalistic" misapprehensions about a monolithic theory, [55] we must insist again that de Man himself always endorsed deconstruction's claim to be the most exemplary of theories ("always in theory, the most elastic theoretical and dialectical model to end all models"), in other words, that theory in which the name of theory is at stake. The resistance to theory was never anything other than the resistance to deconstruction. Are not the consequences of this gamble still with us? Why else should the fortunes of theory itself rise or fall *after deconstruction*? I do not imagine that any challenge to the authority of a monolithic "theory" (on behalf of, for example, a neorelativism or neopragmatism) would have the slightest chance of succeeding if theory itself were not capable of being experienced *as* monolithic, even by its advocates. There is no answer, then, to the question "What is theory?" because the concept of theory inhabits (like the concept of rigor), the pedagogic imaginary, where it does indeed mean *one thing,* however different that thing may be to different factions within the profession. If deconstruction no longer establishes the terms by which certain texts, of whatever provenance, can be integrated into the corpus of literary theory, that is preeminently because it no longer offers to the pedagogic imaginary a resolution to the problem of professional autonomy, a resolution which begins to fail in rhetorical reading as soon as the problem itself becomes visible in de Man's later essays as an uneasy reflection on pedagogy, on the dilemma of discipleship. To the demonstration of this point we now turn.

The nature of this problem has been well described by Bourdieu: "Intellectual labour carried out collectively, within technically and socially differentiated production units, can no longer surround itself with the charismatic aura attaching to traditional independent production."[56] The increasingly technobureaucratic organization of the professional field of literary criticism was a condition for the emergence of theory, which we can understand in retrospect as the reassertion of charismatic authority in the face of that technobureaucratic domination. In the graduate schools of the last quarter-century, a *contradiction* appeared to open up between an enlarged sphere of intellectual autonomy—a kind of extra-institutional space occupied by the master theorists—and the bureaucratization of professional life. The deconstructive resolution to this contradiction was to model the work of theory on bureaucratic work, and thus to reproduce *as theory* the mutual nonrecognition of the bureaucratic and the charismatic. It was of the essence of this theory that its dissemination could be attributed to a "cognitive process" and not to the effects of the transference, the "madness of authority," for only by means of such a formalization of its method could theoretical discourse be disseminated beyond the immediate institutional sphere of charismatic authority, the graduate seminar. Theory's constitutive "impersonality" was achieved not simply by the deconstruction of illusions of autonomous agency but by the transformation of the work of reading into an *unconscious mimesis* of the form of bureaucratic labor: "Technically correct rhetorical readings may be boring, monotonous, predictable, and unpleasant, but they are irrefutable" (RT, 19). There is no lack of overdetermination in this sentence; it characterizes rhetorical reading as "technical" in a quasi-scientific sense of "rigorous," but also as a specific kind of *work*, the work of the office. For the disciples, the transference is transferred not only onto the methodology of rhetorical reading, but onto the sheer "technicality" of that method, its iterability, which can then take on the properties of routinized labor in the bureaucratic sphere.[57] In this way the transference finds what appears to be the same object to cathect in both the intellectual and the bureaucratic fields, the routinization-effect it knows as "rigor." Only in this way can boredom, monotony, predictability, and unpleasantness be revalued as *positive* qualities of rhetorical reading, as the objects of a psychic investment. And the question of "boring to whom" is of course not the issue at all, since the referent of these terms is not some real, experiential boredom but the "technical" iterability of rhetorical reading. Just as transference transferred in the pedagogic sphere imparts to "rigor" the eros, the sexiness, of the master teacher, so in the bureaucratic sphere it signifies a *charisma of routinization,* the cathexis of routine.

To return to the lexicon of deconstructive terms, we can easily give a de Manian equivalent for the "charisma of routinization": it is the *pathos of rigor.* The puzzle of Hertz's "lurid figures" is solved by reading the terms "pathos" and "rigor" as equally overdetermined, provided we recognize that the concept of the "lurid" or the "pathetic" governs not only its spectacular instances—beheading, castration, and the like—but most of all the "pathos" of the method, its boredom, its predictability, its unpleasantness, the "tedium of its techniques" (RT, 106). At this point we may go on to contextualize the entire de Manian thematic by turning it inside out, as it were, by correlating the terms which are internal to its discourse with the terms defining the conditions of its institutional practice:

rhetoric vs. grammar
metaphor vs. metonymy
necessity vs. chance
pathos vs. rigor
↓
literary texts vs. philosophical texts
↓
charisma vs. routine
profession vs. bureaucracy
autonomy vs. heteronomy

By means of this diagram we can see that the development of a dual syllabus of literary and philosophical texts served as a kind of hinge between the rhetorical/thematic terminology, internal to the discourse of rhetorical reading, and its institutional conditions, the conditions of intellectual labor for literary critics in general. Our analysis has already revealed that the terms on the left-hand side of the diagram are entirely governed by the terms on the right: just as agency is deconstructed by the "effet machinal" of language, just as metaphor is "metonymized," just as metaphysical necessity is displaced by the mechanical causality of chance, so pathos is determined to be nothing other than the effect of rigor, the inexorable rigor of the deconstructive method. It is crucial nevertheless that what does not and cannot appear within deconstructive discourse is the *meaning* of these terms in their institutional context, what the lower half of the diagram reveals: the subversion of charisma, of the claims to professional autonomy, by the heteronomous organization of the school. Such heteronomy rather appears within rhetorical reading only as a symptomatic doctrine: the *linguistic determinism* which somehow determines, without the intervention of any authoritative agent, of any "intersubjective relation," the protocols of rhetorical reading as a disciplinary practice: "But there is absolutely no reason why analyses of the kind here suggested for Proust would not be applicable, with proper modifications of technique, to Milton or to Dante or to Hölderlin. This will in fact be the task of literary criticism in the coming years" (AR, 17). The supreme confidence with which this prophecy is offered as a fact is staked on nothing other than a "blending" of personal and institutional authority in the figure of de Man; but that hindsight observation scarcely begins to confront the statement's rhetorical mode. By the latter term, I do not mean that these artfully dry sentences perform the same deconstruction to which all of canonical literature is to be submitted. The rhetorical mode of the passage is rather more homely and familiar: it resonates with the style of the *memo*, the humblest text of bureaucracy. It reports on the future *productivity* of rhetorical reading. But to whom is the memo addressed? It is as though de Man were merely reporting, as though he were merely passing on instructions from somewhere higher or deeper within the institution itself, and not setting an agenda for his disciples, for the school (and faction) of rhetorical reading. The denial of the master theorist's charismatic authority, his reabsorption into the company of nameless critical laborers, is enacted in the erasure of any agency, any higher authority, directing "the task of criticism." No one can claim credit for the setting of this agenda, not even de Man.

If the mask of impersonality conceals the "madness of authority," that is no more than what is to expected of bureaucratic domination. The denial of the charismatic network (and its factions) belongs to the official ideology of the bureaucratic organization, to its language of "impersonal" relations and merely "technical" standards of competence; and it is under cover of this ideology that charismatic authority can be cultivated to an extreme degree, can be given the maximum field of play. At the same time, the transferential dynamic can only be unofficially acknowledged, reduced to the language of gossip, which dominates everyday working life and is like talk about the weather, at once tedious and compelling. At this point we can offer a summary reading of the de Manian oeuvre as a *symptomatic* discourse, a discourse that registers at the heart of its terminology the historical moment of the fusion of the university teacher's autonomous "professional activity" with the technobureaucratic organization of intellectual labor. Within the larger discourse of "theory," rhetorical reading has the important symptomatic function of figuring a rapprochement with the institutional conditions of criticism, by acknowledging the loss of intellectual autonomy as a theory of linguistic determinism—at the same time that autonomy is continually reinvested in the figure of the master theorist. But this is an autonomy which exists only on the imaginary *outside* of the institution, as an "anti-institutional" charisma.[58]

We are now prepared to take an even longer view of the moment of theory, and the symptomatic role of rhetorical reading in that moment. For what we have attempted to understand is a historically specific routinization effect—the "rigor" of rhetorical reading—that was always articulated on the preexisting routinization effects of literary education, the most important of which is the literary curriculum itself. On the syllabus as routinization effect, Bourdieu and Passeron have commented: "Because sacerdotal practice can never so entirely escape stereotyping as can pedagogic practice (the manipulation of secularized goods), priestly charisma can never rest so entirely as teacherly charisma on the technique of ritual deritualization, the juggling with the syllabus that is implicitly *on* the syllabus" (66–67). Rhetorical reading has vigorously endorsed the "scheduled improvisation" of theory, its "juggling" with the syllabus, and at the same time tacitly returned in its practice to the syllabus of literature. The latter motive is expressed without apology in de Man's injunction to "apply" the techniques of rhetorical reading to "the whole of literature" (AR, 16). As I have already argued, the theory of rhetorical reading can provide no rationale for limiting the syllabus to works of literature, and no rationale is available in de Man for the deconstructive reading of nonliterary texts, except by extending the quality of "literariness" to those texts. While departmental inertia may ultimately limit the extent of curricular "improvisation," the larger context of a general and well publicized curricular crisis of the "humanities" suggests that the ambivalence of theory with respect to the literary syllabus is itself related to long-term developments in the educational institution. For the "canon of theory" introduces into the institutional context of literary pedagogy (the graduate seminar) a syllabus whose symptomatic function is to signify precisely methodological "rigor," rather than the taste or discrimination which for so long determined the ideological protocols of literary criticsim. In no other circumstance would it have been possible for deconstruction to circulate as the other *name* of theory, the name given by de Man himself in the Preface to *Allegories of Reading*. At a certain moment, then, the syllabus of literary texts, constituting the traditional "routinization" of literary education, could be perceived as inadequate to support a practice that possessed "rigor"; and that inadequacy could only be compensated by another syllabus, one which in effect signified rigor.

Those authors or texts designated as "theoretical" are now increasingly capable of being introduced to students in traditional routinized forms, even by means of anthologies. It is difficult to imagine how graduate education could proceed at the present moment without recourse to a relatively standardized set of theoretical texts, which are employed not only in the context of "application" to works of literature, but also in the seminar on theory. These arrangements are hardly to be deplored in themselves. The routinization of theory does not necessarily represent, as Gerald Graff worries, only the rise of another specialization within literature: "It is largely the institutionalization of literary theory as a special field that lends truth to the complaint that literary theory has become a private enclave in which theorists only talk to one another."[59] Graff points out that theory is no more specialized than any other specialization in a period or an author, and he recommends that it become more like work on a set of problems that concern all critics. But I would suggest that theory has already become just that, with the qualification that the problem which is negotiated (unconsciously) in the language of theory, its language of "rigor," *is* the problem of "specialization," or the effects of the technobureaucratic organization of intellectual labor on the discipline of criticism. The interesting historical question remains what institutional conditions produced the secondary routinization effect by which theory was constituted as a syllabus both supplementary to the literary syllabus and in a necessarily pendant relation to that syllabus.

We can emphasize, to begin with, that it is only in the graduate seminar that theory can emerge as such, as a distinctive "canon" of writers and texts. The institutional conditions for the emergence of literary theory are therefore related to the institutional distinction between the graduate and undergraduate levels of the educational system. The signal feature of that distinction will already have been apparent: the relatively greater autonomy of the graduate teacher, which is in turn the condition for the transferential cathexes necessary for the propagation of theory. The relative nondetermination of the graduate syllabus by any higher administrative power is the sine qua non of theory, and for that reason theory itself is the vehicle of a claim to autonomy; it is the discursive field in which that autonomy can be negotiated, even when it is negotiated ideologically, as the perennial theoretical problem of the relation between language and the agency of the subject. The development of theory was always premised on the inviolability of the graduate seminar, the site of an autonomy not possible at the undergraduate level, where the syllabus of literature was subject to much greater oversight. At the same time it seems unlikely that theory would have been permitted to achieve so extensively routinized a form in the graduate schools if an exclusively literary curriculum were still the norm at the graduate level. The indifference of university administrators to the graduate curriculum reflects less their respect for the traditional autonomy of the graduate teacher as it does an accurate estimation of the diminished significance of the literary curriculum in the context of the university's perceived social function, the perceived demand for the knowledges it disseminates.

The ultimate social horizon of the latter development is the hegemony of that technobureaucratic organization of intellectual life which has rendered the literary curriculum socially marginal by transforming the university into the institution designed to produce a new class of technical/managerial specialists possessed of purely technical/managerial knowledge. It is in this context that we shall have to understand the ambivalent position of literary theory with respect to literature, since theory is both indissolubly bound to that curriculum and yet opposed to reproducing it as the vehicle of universal "humanist values" constituting a knowledge of a nonspecialist nature. The project of literary theory in its premier deconstructive form was therefore to discard one ideological rationale for the literary curriculum, and then immediately to install another in its place. Rhetorical reading identified this rationale with the practice of *rhetoric*, but the invocation of that premodern discipline should not disguise the function of rhetoric as an ideological discourse when it is deployed as the means of transforming the method of reading into a rigorously iterable *technical* procedure. The refunctioning of rhetoric's *techne* as a kind of technology directly incorporated into the protocols of rhetorical reading a mimesis of the technobureaucratic itself. Deconstructive literary theory testified to the obsolescence of the "humanist" rationale of literary study not only, then, by attacking that rationale directly, but by reproducing in the form of its practice the form of that hegemonic rationality which had *already* rendered the traditional ideological rationale of the literary curriculum obsolete. The failure of deconstructive theory to produce a new rationale for the literary curriculum accounts for the tenacity of the concept of the "literary" in its discourse, the fact that its syllabus was in practice confined to a specific set of literary and philosophical texts selected for their capacity to foreground (or thematize) rhetorical reading's ideological motifs and methodological procedures.

The absence of a rationale for the literary curriculum has up to this point meant nothing but the absence of an *ideological* rationale. This is necessarily so because the syllabus of literary works always demanded an essentialist concept of literature to ground it. Theory replaced the "humanistic" thematic of literature with an equally universalizing, if antihumanistic, thematic of *language;* the important point is that theory belongs to the long-term historical project of providing a rationale for the literary curriculum that would effectively establish a syllabus of study. Can essentializing concepts of literature be discarded without resorting to the kind of ideological debunking of literary works sometimes characterizing the critique of the canon? Perhaps it is time to reconsider the implications of Raymond Williams's "cultural materialist" critique of literature, a critique which is opposed both to the traditionalist ideological defense of literature and to the rhetoricism of theory: "It is in a way surprising that the specialized concept of 'literature,' developed in precise forms of correspondence with a particular social class, a particular technology of print, should be so often invoked in retrospective, nostalgic, or reactionary moods, as a form of opposition to what is correctly seen as a new phase of civilization."[60] Yet the progressive critical movements of the 1980s took as the object of their critique not the historical category of literature but "the canon." We are in a position now to recognize that the career of theory had everything to do with the status of literature in "a new phase of civilization."

A preliminary attempt at reconsidering the category of literature might begin with the observation that while the original ideological rationale of literature justified the social project of producing a standard vernacular by presenting literature as the repository of the most universal truths of the human condition, this project was always belied by the actual structure of the educational system. The contradiction between the politico-administrative requirement of linguistic homogeneity and the socioeconomic necessity of distributing unequally every form of cultural capital (including Standard English) burdened the educational system throughout its modern history with the impossible task of at once democratizing the distribution of knowledges and maintaining class distinctions. This contradiction marks in familiar ways the complex interrelations between public and private schools, and between the various levels of the educational system. At the present moment, the nation-state still requires a relatively homogeneous language to administer its citizenry, but it no longer requires that a distinctive practice of that language identify a culturally homogeneous bourgeoisie. That class has long since been replaced by a culturally heterogeneous New Class, which has in turn been fully integrated into mass culture, a media culture mediating the desires of every class and group. In this "new phase of civilization," the historical function of the literary curriculum—to produce at the lower levels of the educational system a practice of Standard English, and at the higher levels a more refined bourgeois language, a "literary" English—is no longer crucially important to the social order. We might even speculate that it is the *absence* of such a crucial social function which the professors of literature experience as powerlessness in the face of a political entity—the state—which they misrecognize as the source of disempowerment. For the same reason the absence of a central social function for the literary curriculum has become the occasion of an anxious thematizing of the political in literary critical discourse, as well as the occasion of an undervaluation of the field in which teachers do possess agency, namely, the school itself. What appears to be a politically significant fact from the point of view of a "cultural materialism" may be something rather different than the question of which social groups are represented in the canon: for example, the fact that the function of producing in a segment of the populace a minimal degree of linguistic uniformity (in ideological terms, "competence") has been given over to the field of composition, which has developed a nonfictional prose syllabus specific to its function, a syllabus which seems to have no necessary relation to the study of literature. As we have seen in Chapter 1, the new institutional significance of composition marks the appearance of a new social function for the university, the task of providing the future technobureaucratic elite with precisely and only the linguistic competence necessary for the performance of its specialized functions.

The study of literature has taken its place in the undergraduate curriculum, then, as one apparent specialization among many others, but a specialization without a rationale specific to its syllabus. It is still a specialization with a *universalist* rationale, and this was true even of rhetorical reading, which expressed this contradiction as the discrepancy between its mimetically technobureaucatic methodology and its universalist theory of language, a theory which rediscovered in works of literature an expression of the universal human condition. If deconstructive theory did not provide an enduring new rationale for literary study, that was in part because it was incapable of seeing the relation between its practice of *supplementing* the literary syllabus at the level of the graduate school, and composition's practice of *displacing* it at the entry level of university study. Rhetorical reading was entirely symptomatic of theory in general in its incapacity to rationalize its syllabus, except by falling back upon the textual preferences of de Man himself, or by generalizing the concept of literariness to a particular set of philosophical texts. The weakness of this rationalization was only too apparent when it had to confront the demand from other factions of the profession to "open the canon." But the diminished significance of the literary syllabus in the university is in reality a systemic institutional effect, and not the result of a deconstructive (or any other) attack upon the universality of the values supposed to be expressed in the literary canon. Here, then, is a new "political" question: What is the systemic relation between the syllabus of composition and the syllabus of theory? Both of these practices have invoked in highly charged ideological contexts the precedent of rhetoric, and both have refunctioned rhetoric in practices which are overdetermined by the technobureaucratic conditions themselves responsible for the social marginality of the literary curriculum.[61] What de Man considered to be the cultural irrelevance of the university describes a real condition, perhaps, not of the university but of the literary curriculum, a condition which has given rise, among other things, to the canon of theory.

The difficulty of imagining what might succeed the curricular forms of literature and theory is well indicated in the following comment of John Frow, from his *Marxism and Literary History:*

> The whole weight of recent literary theory has been on the *constitutive* status of language, on the impossibility of linguistic

transparency, on the agonistic rhetorical strategies of discourse, and on the shaping of language by the forces of power and desire. The effect of this emphasis should be in the first place to redefine the traditional objects of literary knowledge, and in particular the forms of valorization of writing which have prevailed in most forms of literary study.[62]

Frow recommends a "general poetics" or "general rhetoric" which would not be addressed exclusively to the traditional canon of literary texts but would take as its object noncanonical genres and forms, including popular romances, journalism, film, television, scientific discourses, and even "everyday language." But the recourse to "poetics" and "rhetoric" confirms once again how nearly impossible it is to imagine what lies beyond the rhetoricism of literary theory, and hence beyond the problematic of literariness. It is not yet clear whether a "cultural studies" curriculum has been conceived which does not replicate the theoretical and hermeneutic paradigms of literary interpretation. There is also evidence to suggest that cultural studies' new "opening" of the syllabus to popular or mass cultural works has been accompanied by a closure of the syllabus to the same High Cultural philosophical texts which were so important to the dissemination of theory. Such a cultural studies syllabus would certainly not be inclusive of cultural products generally.[63] If literary criticism is ever to conceptualize a new disciplinary domain, it will have to undertake first a much more thorough reflection on the historical category of literature; otherwise I suggest that new critical movements will continue to register their agendas symptomatically, by ritually overthrowing a continually resurgent literariness and literary canon. At the same time it is unquestionably the case that the several recent crises of the literary canon—its "opening" to philosophical works, to works by minorities, and now to popular and mass cultural works—amounts to a terminal crisis, more than sufficient evidence of the urgent need to reconceptualize the object of literary study. One may predict, without resorting to prophecy, that such reconceptualization will become "the task of literary criticism in the coming years."

Part Three
Aesthetics

Chapter Five

The Discourse of Value: From Adam Smith to Barbara Herrnstein Smith

Exit Aesthetics: The Contemporary Critique of Value

> The essential feature of materialist dialectics is not only that it grasps
> all the facts of social life in terms of a single method, but also that it
> leaves relatively autonomous the specificity of each domain.
> —MAX RAPHAEL, *Proudhon, Marx, Picasso*

The preliminary remarks on the question of value in Chapter 1 argue that
the process of canon formation cannot be reduced to acts of evaluation in
the simple sense of affirming or rejecting the specific values assumed to be
expressed in a literary work. Having granted the obvious fact that acts of
evaluation are always presupposed by the process of canon formation as a
necessary but not sufficient condition of that process, I then attempted to
demonstrate in the following chapters that the institution which is the historical site of these evaluative acts—the school—subordinates specific
values expressed in works to the social functions and institutional aims of
the school itself. It is only when presented as *canonical,* as the cultural capital of the schools, that individual literary works can be made to serve the
school's social function of regulating access to these forms of capital. The
canonicity of works is therefore another name for their institutional mode
of reception and reproduction, but it is the name by which the concrete
instrumentality of the syllabus in the formation of the transhistorical
canon is typically misrecognized.

If the socioinstitutional agenda of constituting and regulating the distribution of cultural capital is accomplished in part through the canonical
form itself, this fact does not mean that the selection of works is merely
arbitrary. Since the emergence of the vernacular canon in the eighteenth

century, however, literary works have been judged not only as expressions of approved social or moral values, but also for their specifically "aesthetic" value. The immense significance of the concept of the "aesthetic" to the institutions of canon formation can be suggested by noting that the expression of manifestly repugnant or socially obsolete values has not in itself been enough to disqualify a work for canonicity. Literary critics have long been aware of this circumstance (David Hume already remarks upon it in "The Standard of Taste," published in 1757),[1] and they have taken the problem itself as an occasion for developing a discourse of the aesthetic. In one form or another that discourse, as a discourse of the evaluation or judgment of cultural works, mediates the specific social values expressed within literary works; as "aesthetic" objects, cultural works are not so much the sum of the values they express as the effective transcendence of them, the embodiment of "aesthetic value."

It is scarcely surprising that a critique of canon formation which reduces that process to conspiratorial acts of evaluation is compelled to regard the discourse of the aesthetic as merely fraudulent, as a screen for the covert affirmation of hegemonic values which can be shown to be the real qualification for canonicity in the first place. For the same reason that such a critique sees the discourse of the aesthetic only as a mystification of the bias of judgment, it can ignore the mediating functions of the school, reducing that institution to a support for equally fraudulent claims to objectivity or expertise on the part of the judges, the gatekeepers of the canon. Just as they are supposed (until recent years) to have expressed directly the values of the hegemonic culture, and not their own interests as a professional group with complex relations to that culture, so canonical works in this view can always be represented as the direct expression of these same hegemonic values. Conversely, as we have seen in Chapter 1, noncanonical works can be represented as excluded from canonicity by virtue of expressing values of a nonhegemonic and even subversive nature. Such a critique does not really need to account for the effects of works in their discursive/institutional guise as the embodiments of aesthetic value, that is, as the representatives of the social value of aesthetic value, or what I have been calling cultural capital. For if the canonical work can in every instance be reduced to the "extra-aesthetic" values expressed within it, then the status of the aesthetic as a "value" can be dismissed altogether. Such a critique would argue that the aesthetic has the purely ideological function of concealing the fact that the canonization of a work is nothing but the affirmation of the social values expressed in the work.

It is just because the problem of canon formation has so often been reduced to the problem of *value judgment* that I propose now to revisit the latter concept. We might begin with Gayatri Chakravorty Spivak's suggestion in her essay "Scattered Speculations on Value," that the concept of value occupies a somewhat larger discursive domain than literary criticism, where "the issue of value surfaces . . . with reference to canon formation."[2] Spivak reminds us that the concept of value is of preeminent significance in the discourse of political economy; but literary critics are not generally disposed to consider the relation between these two disciplines. Even the critique of the canon for the most part proceeds as though the *concept* of value could be taken for granted. The problem is conceived rather to be the incompatibility of different values. The canonical critique argues, as we know, for the essential plurality of values, different values for different social groups. Such pluralism forms the basis for a critique of aesthetic discourse itself, inasmuch as that discourse appears to subsume the differences between different groups into the ideological "universality" of aesthetic value, the same universality which virtually founds aesthetics in Kant's *Critique of Judgment:* "[T]he judgment of taste, accompanied with the consciousness of separation from all interest, must claim validity for every man, without this universality depending on objects. That is, there must be bound up with it a title to subjective universality."[3]

The emergence of a critique of the aesthetic is, surprisingly, already in evidence by the twilight years of theory, specifically in Paul de Man's belated translation of rhetorical reading into the deconstruction of "aesthetic ideology." If the retooling of deconstruction as a critique of aesthetics was not enough to save it from its present fate, the thorough dismissal of the aesthetic as an "ideology" has nevertheless become a ubiquitous gesture in the contemporary critical scene. Progressive criticism can now proceed on the assumption that the validity of aesthetic discourse has been irrevocably called into question by the critique of the canon. The conflation of aesthetics *in toto* with a discredited concept of aesthetic *value* is nowhere more strenuously affirmed than in the text which, as I will argue in this chapter, is most representative of the new critical episteme of the 1990s, Barbara Herrnstein Smith's *Contingencies of Value* (appropriately subtitled *Alternative Perspectives for Critical Theory*). In this work, though by no means only in this work, the concept of aesthetic value is finally dismissed from critical discourse, where it had always masqueraded as the name of a uniquely privileged kind of value:

> Indeed, since there are no functions performed by artworks that may be specified as generically unique and also no way to distinguish the "rewards" provided by art-related experience or behavior from those provided by innumerable other kinds of

experience and behavior, any distinctions drawn between "aesthetic" and "non-aesthetic" (or "extra-aesthetic") value must be regarded as fundamentally problematic.[4]

The positing of "aesthetic value" is, in Herrnstein Smith's terms, a supreme example of "axiological" thinking, the attempt to ground some particular, local, or "contingent" value in a hypothetically universal realm of human experience or in an equally hypothetical realm of the logically axiomatic. Hence she can speak of the existence of something called "aesthetic axiology," a historical discourse descending with remarkable continuity from Hume and Kant, and remaining trapped throughout its history within the circle of an untenable pseudo-logic: "'aesthetic' comes to be roughly equivalent to 'relating to certain cognitive/sensory experiences, these being the ones elicited by objects that have certain formal properties, these being the ones that identify objects as artworks, these being the kinds of works that elicit certain cognitive/sensory experiences, these being . . . ,' and so forth round again" (35). Such an account "is a parody, but not by much." Indeed, by very little. In a footnote to the passage just quoted Smith admits of only two partial exceptions in the entire history of aesthetic discourse, Monroe Beardsley's "'instrumentalist' theory of aesthetic value" in *Aesthetics: Problems in the Philosophy of Criticism,* and Jan Mukarovsky's *Aesthetic Function, Norm and Value as Social Facts*—both arguments which, despite their subtlety, "do not altogether escape the confinements and circularities of formalist conceptions of, respectively, 'aesthetic experience' and 'aesthetic function'" (192). No aesthetic theory can escape the dubious logic of "aesthetic axiology" unless it discards as politically suspect the concept of the aesthetic itself. In this chapter I will argue that current critiques of aesthetics arrive at this conclusion just because they pose the question of the aesthetic as the question of aesthetic *value.* In retrospect, one can see that the critique of the canon opened up a privileged perspective upon the entire discourse of value, and it was thus the means by which that discourse, as a putatively absolutist or "axiological" discourse, could be opened to an antifoundational or relativist reorientation. The new relativist discourse of value could then be turned against the historical discourse of aesthetics, removing once and for all its axiological props. As we shall see, the important historical fact about this critique for literary critics is its emergence out of the canon debate. A critique of the concept of value setting out from some other starting point (such as the history of political economy) might not have yielded the same critique of value, or the same conclusions about aesthetic discourse.

It must be emphasized that literary theory's new discourse of value, whether or not it happens to be linked explicitly to a relativist or neopragmatist theoretical agenda, is usually "progressive," in whatever political senses that word can bear. This was true even of rhetorical reading in its later phase, and even though the de Manian critique of "aesthetic ideology" engaged the political at one remove, as an "epistemological" critique of aesthetic pleasure rather than aesthetic value. The effect of an openly progressive critique of aesthetics is to position the "aesthetic" and the "political" as the discursive antitheses of current critical thought, and thus to enjoin a choice between them. It would be embarrassing at this date to claim for aesthetics any privilege in relation to the political, as embarrassing as an argument for "absolute" or "transcendent" values—the dismal chorus of most reactionary thought. In the context of critical theory, however, it may be surprising to some that the concept of the aesthetic was never rejected within the Marxist tradition, the very body of theory which cultural conservatives are likely to blame for the current critique of aesthetics. It is only necessary to invoke Marx's famous comments on the transhistorical appeal of Greek art, from the introduction to the *Grundrisse,* to confirm that Marx himself scarcely reduced the work of art to "ideology"; and it would be easy to demonstrate that the theory of ideology in the Marxist tradition has nearly without exception attributed to the domain of the aesthetic the capacity to produce a critique of the capitalist social order analogous to, and not at all superseded by, the critique produced in such a text as *Capital*.[5] A rehearsal of this tradition, up to and beyond Althusser's theory of the work of art's "internal distanciation" from the operation of the ideological,[6] would confirm this fact; but in lieu of such a history it will be useful to set before us Adorno's valedictory comment in *Aesthetic Theory* on the refusal of the aesthetic, a comment characteristically both tart and dialectical:

> Take a look at the widespread inclination (which to this day has not been mitigated by education) to perceive art in terms of extra-aesthetic or pre-aesthetic criteria. This tendency is, on the one hand, a mark of atrocious backwardness or of the regressive consciousness of many people. On the other hand, there is no denying that the tendency is promoted by something in art itself. If art is perceived strictly in aesthetic terms, then it cannot be properly perceived in aesthetic terms.[7]

I would suggest that his statement is quite representative of the Marxist tradition, even of the most recent work of Terry Eagleton, Fredric Jameson, or Frank Lentricchia.[8] If this tradition can now be tacitly assimilated to the dismissal of aesthetic discourse, the arguments for dismissing the aesthetic do not derive from Marxist theory. One may conjecture that the very ease with which that tradition is misremembered, or spuriously rewritten, argues for the origin of the critique in an academic consensus much larger than the sphere of Marxist theory, and possessing the force of "axiology" for current critical practice.

The historical circumstance of Marxism's long-standing alliance with aesthetics has recently been drawn to our attention in an essay by a Marxist critic, Tony Bennett, entitled "Really Useless 'Knowledge': A Political Critique of Aesthetics," which argues that this alliance has indeed been an embarrassment to Marxist theory, and that "The time is long past . . . when the project of a Marxist aesthetic ought finally to have been laid to rest."[9] I shall briefly take note of Bennett's argument, before considering Herrnstein Smith at greater length in the next section of this chapter, in order to establish a basis for the point just proposed, that the refusal of the aesthetic is an epistemic feature of current critical practice, constituting a consensus powerful enough to enlist in an alliance of "left" critiques even the form of left critique—Marxist theory—historically sympathetic to aesthetics. What one would like to understand here is the nature of the consensus which produces, at the same historical moment, a thorough refusal of the aesthetic in left-liberal criticism, and a certain embarrassment within Marxist theory at the legacy of Marxism's long-standing alliance with aesthetic discourse.

Bennett acknowledges as a premise of his argument the importance of a distinction between aesthetic discourse, which "construes the aesthetic as a distinctive mode of the subject's mental relation to reality," and "discourses of value," the "much more numerous and heterogeneous array of discourses which regulate the social practice of valuing within different valuing communities" (35). More to the point, we should emphasize (Bennett does not) that there is a discourse of aesthetics long before there is any conception of "aesthetic value." This can be confirmed on philological grounds by the fact that the word "value" scarcely ever appears in *The Critique of Judgment,* or in the other texts cited as the ur-texts of aesthetics. The concept of value does appear quite prominently, however, in the central texts of political economy (Smith, Ricardo, Marx), but the current critique of value is not especially interested in these texts, and makes no reference to them. How, then, has the concept of the aesthetic come to be so indissolubly linked to a concept of value whose basic meaning can be taken for granted (however contested particular values may be), and without reference to the discourse of political economy? Bennett's argument traces the *problem* of aesthetic value (but not the concept, the *word*) to the central problem of Kantian aesthetics: an attempt to give the grounds or conditions for judgments of taste in the constitution of a perceiving subject—in the faculty of judgment—rather than in the properties of an aesthetic object. Kant argues typically in the first paragraph of *The Critique of Judgment* (the passage cited by Bennett):

> In order to distinguish whether anything is beautiful or not, we refer the representation, not by the understanding to the object for cognition, but by the imagination (perhaps in conjunction with understanding) to the subject and its feeling of pleasure or pain. The judgement of taste, therefore, is not a judgement of cognition, and is consequently not logical but aesthetical—which means that it is one whose determining ground can be *no other than subjective.* (37)

In quoting even this much of Kant, Bennett already recovers more of the history of aesthetics than is usually invoked in the current critique, since within the present consensus the fundamental thesis of aesthetic discourse is always abbreviated as the thesis of the transhistorical or transcendental value of the *object,* the work of art. Kant defines the problem of the aesthetic as the problem of demonstrating the conditions for the hypothetical universality and therefore "disinterestedness" of aesthetic judgment, adduced usually as the simple determination of a perception of the "beautiful" or the "sublime" (and for Kant the examples are usually adduced from nature, not from works of art). The problem of value, on the other hand, could not possibly enter into this problematic until two such objects of aesthetic perception are *compared.* It is only at this point, when judgments differ, that the universality of aesthetic perception is revealed to be restricted to certain individuals or social groups; and a little further analysis would reveal that the work of art rather than the object in nature will ordinarily provide the occasion for such a contradiction between the actual and the hypothetical universality of aesthetic judgment. It is relatively easy to read out of this contradiction another version of the narrative of a dominant social group's ideological universalization of its particular interests and historical situation, an ideology which we can be sure will be asserted along a variety of fronts, especially in the context of "values." (Herrnstein Smith similarly remarks on the "move to assign dominant status to the *particular* conditions and perspectives that happen to be relevant to or favored by that person, group, or class.") Bennett argues—and this point is worthy of emphasis—that aesthetic discourse is the peculiarly *exemplary* form of such ideological assertion. By contrast with most discourses of value, which "have effect solely within the limits of particular valuing communities," aesthetic discourse "is the form taken by discourses of value which

are hegemonic in ambition and, correspondingly, universalist in their pre-
scriptive ambit, and which have, as their zone of application, those practices nominated as aesthetic" (36). It would seem that it is primarily by
means of aesthetics that a concept of a "general" or "universal" subject can
be formulated for ideology. And thus one can see why it should have become important for recent critiques to call the claims of aesthetics into
question; for aesthetics appears on this account somehow to be the ideology of ideologies, the *source* of the ideological effect of subject-formation.

What Bennett discovers in casting a disillusioned glance at the obscure
origins of aesthetic discourse is the concealing of this universal subject in
claims about the value of the object: "Once this determining ground has
been universalized . . . aesthetic discourse tilts on its axis, as the properties
of the subject which guarantee the universality of aesthetic judgement are
transferred to the object. Value, transfixed in the singular gaze of the universal subject, solidifies and takes form as the property of the object" (38).
It should be pointed out, however, that the transference of aesthetic properties to the object was precisely what aesthetic discourse in its Kantian form
considered to be problematic, and what it therefore designated as a kind of
necessary error: Kant remarks that in the judgment of beauty, one "will
therefore speak of the beautiful as if beauty were a characteristic of the object and the judgment logical (constituting a cognition of the object by
means of concepts of it), although it is only aesthetical and involves merely
a reference of the representation of the object to the subject" (46). In spite
of such qualifications in the text of Kant, Herrnstein Smith too can dis-
patch, with no more ado than Bennett, Kant's fiction of "subjective universality" by referring casually to "objective—in the sense of universal
subjective—validity" (66). In other words Kant's "subjective universality"
is not the name of a theoretical *problem* but an overt-covert claim to objective validity, an assertion of the objective value of the aesthetic object. As a
fraudulent discourse of the subject, then, aesthetics as such can be discarded and replaced with an overt discourse of "subjects"—the true constituents of "valuing communities."

This is in fact what Bennett proposes as the inescapable conclusion of a
critique of aesthetics, and on behalf of a more "politically useful" discourse
which inaugurates its project as the choice between aesthetics and politics:

> The political utility of discourses of value, operating via the
> construction of an ideal of personality to which broadly based
> social aspirations can be articulated, is unquestionable.
> There is, however, no reason to suppose that such discourses
> must be hitched up to the sphere of universality in order to se-

cure their effectivity. To the contrary, given the configuration of today's political struggles, it is highly unlikely that an ideal of personality might be forged that would be of equal service in the multiple, intersecting but, equally, non-coincident foci of struggle constituted by black, gay, feminist, socialist and, in some contexts, national liberation politics. In particular conjunctures, to be sure, an ideal of personality may be forged which serves to integrate—but always temporarily—such forces into a provisional unity. But this is not the basis for a generalizable and universalisable cultural politics. Nor is this the time for such a politics. (49)

The critique of aesthetics always assumes a concept of value grounded in the notion of a "valuing community" or "communities." Yet insofar as Bennett represents such communities as constitutively "black, gay, feminist, socialist," etc., he opens the concept of the "valuing community" to the same logical objection cogently advanced by Mary Louise Pratt against similar notions of "subcommunities" proposed by linguists: "What the 'subcommunity' approach does not do, however, is see the dominated and dominant *in their relations with each other*—this is the limitation imposed by the imaginings of a community."[10] Such "imaginings" reinstate a kind of local "subjective universality," functioning with vigorous exclusivity in the various valuing communities to construct black values, or gay values, or feminist values; but also, for other communities, "American" values, and "fundamentalist Christian" values, and "white male" values, and "heterosexual" values. Any of these communities might also construct objects of value (let us say, "canons") which can only be properly valued within the respective community of the object's production. I have already suggested in Chapter 1, in considering Fish's notion of an "interpretive community," that such a logical contradiction fatally afflicts the critique of canon formation, and that in practice there is very little to arrest the disintegrative force breaking communities down into progressively smaller groups precisely in order to confirm a distinct, ideal, and homogeneous social identity as the basis of the solidarity, and thus the *values* of the community.

Herrnstein Smith is by contrast entirely aware of the temptation to regress to a theoretical position which construes valuing within local communities as "in effect" universalizing and exclusive by virtue of the homogeneity of experiences, beliefs, or "values" attributed to such communities, a problem she identifies with good reason in Richard Rorty's appeal to community as the only basis of a consistent pragmatism: "indeed, the current invocation of community as a replacement for 'objective reality' is not only a problematic gesture but an empty one" (168). If Herrnstein Smith nevertheless allows at a later point in her argument that there are certain purely conventional "norms and standards" (like units of measurement, or safety standards) which are functionally "unconditional and universal," and may thus be called "contingently absolute," or "contingently objective" (182), she understandably does not extend such objectivity to any cultural norms or standards of the kind which might include objects of "aesthetic value." Rather she is here, as elsewhere, intent to emphasize the fact that, so far as culture is concerned, "a community is never totally homogeneous, that its boundaries and borders are never altogether self-evident, that we cannot assume in advance that certain differences among its members are negligible or irrelevant, and that the conditions that produced the relative unconditionality, local universality, and contingent objectivity are themselves neither fixed forever nor totally stable now" (ibid.). In practice, however, a "valuing community" is impossible to conceive at all without recourse to the local universalization of its local values; such communities, once constituted, seldom refrain from policing differences within themselves as a logical consequence of the fact that they must exalt the difference of the community from other communities. For this reason, Herrnstein Smith's additional qualification, seconded by Bennett, to the effect that "each of us is a member of many, shifting communities, each of which establishes, for each of its members, multiple social identities" (Bennett speaks of "multiple, intersecting, but equally non-coincident foci of struggle") qualifies out of existence the concept of a community as the basis even of values which are "local, temporary, and conjunctural"—or rather reveals in the very insistence on "locality" that these notions of community have a surreptitiously *geographical* basis. The notion of community in the present discourse of value is always modeled unwittingly on the paradigm of the "primitive" community, geographically separate, autonomous, and long since nonexistent.

Clearly the debate has been lacking any concept of what Benedict Anderson calls an "imagined community," the precondition for which would have to be the development of "modernity" as the name of the social formation in which social groups are inhibited from forming really discrete communities or hermetic subcultures *except* imaginarily, as the projection of homogeneous subjecthood never actually realized anywhere. Subcultural formations within the social condition of modernity obviously do form imagined communities with real consequences for many individuals, but their "local, temporary, and conjunctural" acts of evaluation are the very cultural exhibits which prove the fact that "values" are never produced by an actually exclusive "local" consensus but always emerge in a determinate relation to the entire culture which holds in conflictual inter-relation every subcultural formation within it. The fact that communities do function as though they could legislate values within their borders, and not in response to the perceived values of other imagined communities, is the most definitive testimony to their imaginary status.

The grounding of value in discrete communities inaugurates a contra-dictory practice which moves back and forth between making separatist and universalist claims. This contradiction characterizes the practice of identity politics in America *on both the right and the left*. Nothing else can explain the alliance, for example, of antipornography feminists with con-servative Christians, on behalf of legislating (or universalizing) values emergent from avowedly different valuing communities. It is indeed re-markable that the same cultural objects—images of women—have some-how provoked the same recourse to law in social groups with otherwise incompatible interests; but the more interesting point is that the agenda of universalizing particular values as *law for everyone* really does have the ef-fect of confirming the two communities of antipornography feminists and fundamentalists in their *separate* identities.

The ambiguous logic of separatism/universalism is equally obvious in the response by certain "local communities" to the travelling exhibition of Robert Mapplethorpe's photographs in the spring and summer of 1990. The citizens of Cincinnati, who hoped to prosecute the exhibitors of the photographs for purveying pornography, also claimed to constitute a "val-uing community," just as much a community as those named by Tony Ben-nett. But even their relatively more grounded claim to such status (Cincin-nati is after all a real geographical locus) was finally spurious, since it was only the claim to legislate the values of some of Cincinnati's citizens (per-haps the majority) over others (perhaps the minority). Given the familiarity of very many people with the content of the photographs, there is good reason to question whether even geographical localities can form the basis for "community values." This does not mean that communities do not ex-ist at all—they obviously do—but that they are constantly embattled and that they have internalized their defensive positions in the supracultural formation of modernity as, precisely, *discourses of value*. The question of values, in the current sense, does not emerge at all except in the circum-stance of contestation.

It is no accident that the problem of a specifically "aesthetic value" should arise most urgently in the debate on pornography, for it is just in this context that the distinction between aesthetic discourse and the dis-course of value evinces the pretensions of both discourses to "universalize" within the boundaries of "local" communities a particular value. The defenders of the Mapplethorpe exhibit had in fact only one defense of his work—the aesthetic—by which they had to mean something like a refusal to reduce the work of art to its "contents," when the latter are conceived as constituent values (such as the affirmation of homosexuality, and so on). We cannot as yet even begin to address the problem that is opened up here—the question of content and its supposed antithesis, form—but we can suggest that the refusal of the category of the aesthetic fixes the relation between form and content prematurely and far too simply as the irrelevance of form, defined as the vehicle of the claim to a specifically aesthetic value, to the judgment of constituent values or contents. This position has been argued *ad absurdum* (but entirely consistently) by Suzanne Kappeler in *The Pornography of Representation*. Kappeler not only dismisses the aesthetic as merely the alibi of the pornographic, but makes the much larger claim that the same procedure of "objectification" which characterizes pornography also characterizes (and discredits) all representational forms. For Kappeler the aesthetic is the excuse by means of which the artist can "get rid of his responsibility toward the subject matter," and thus the choice between aesthetics and the discourse of value is the same as the choice between aesthetics and a progressive politics: "the concept of 'aesthetics' is fundamentally incompatible with feminist politics."[11] The interest of Kappeler's argument is not so much its extremity as its elucidation of the inexorable logic by which the aesthetic becomes the casualty of *any* discourse of value grounded in the concept of a valuing community, whether of the left or the right. The cultural separatism of some imagined communities, even those on the left, indulges at an unconscious level the desire for a community in which values are consensual and "universal" for that community. But no community, insofar as it projects its concept of social identity into an ideal of homogeneity, knows where to draw its boundaries. Let us recall that the "values" of the citizens of Cincinnati were in effect universalized by the National Endowment for the Arts, which succeeded in temporarily requiring an anti-obscenity pledge of its grant recipients. If such censorship is disastrous as a national policy, that is because there is *no* local community in which this censorship could be justified.

But lest the latter circumstances be read too simply as evidence for a cultural coup d'état of the American right, consider also what a prospective juror in the Cincinnati trial was telling us: "These people are in a different class. Evidently they get some type of satisfaction looking at it [art]. I don't understand art work. That stuff never interested me."[12] The citizen of Cincinnati does not seem to recognize that his daily life is pervaded by innumerable and various aesthetic expressions, from the clothing he wears to the situation comedies which entertain him in the evening. Yet the citizen is for some reason able to recognize a cultural production *as* aesthetic only when it takes the form of a certified work of art. The animus against Mapplethorpe was at some level, then, an animus against art as a social institution in which the abrogation of "traditional" values can be perceived as a content of art by a stratum of the middle and upper classes. The overdetermination of the refusal of the asethetic by, in this case, a kind of class *ressentiment* confirms not only the fact that, when aesthetic artifacts are certified as "works of art," they become the bearers of cultural capital, and as such are unequally distributed, but also that the aesthetic is not simply identical to the form of cultural capital embodied by the work of art. The importance of this distinction will escape the discourse of value grounded in the notion of a "valuing community," since that critique is forbidden in principle from recognizing anything in the work of art but the expression of a particular community's particular values. Such a critique also takes for granted that the question of the aesthetic concerns *only* works of art, and thus that the one question remaining, once aesthetics is discarded, is *which* works of art are to be approved and on the basis of *which* values. But the question of the relation of the aesthetic to the social institution of the work of art should not escape the project of a "Marxist aesthetic," for which that question was, after all, the founding problematic. The present discourse of value emerges out of a pluralist consensus which, in discarding aesthetics, excludes just the sort of question that might be raised by a Marxist aesthetic—the question of the relation of the aesthetic to other domains of the social.

The latter point bears directly on the familiar dilemma of the contemporary critique of the canon, which always has before it the theoretically suspect option of devaluing canonical works on the basis of disapprobated values expressed within them. It is significant in this context that throughout her book Kappeler attaches her antipornography argument to the critique of the canon (from which, one suspects, it derives its premises anyway), most explicitly by invoking Joanna Russ's *How to Suppress Women's Writing* as the parallel study to her own. From the latter text we may extract the following passage, virtually identical to Bennett's position:

> In everybody's present historical situation, there can be, I believe, no single center of value and hence no absolute standards. That does not mean that assignment of values must be arbitrary or self-serving. . . . It does mean that for the linear hierarchy of

good and bad it becomes necessary to substitute a multitude of
centers of value, each with its own periphery, some closer to
each other, some farther apart. The centers have been constructed by the historical facts of what it is to be female or black
or working class or what-have-you; when we all live in the same
culture, then it will be time for one literature. But that is not the
case now.[13]

The discourse of value operating with such epistemic force in left-liberal
criticism takes as its occasion disputed objects of aesthetic value such as
"noncanonical" literary works, which it must then revalue; yet these objects only express finally the self-affirmation of the subjects valuing these
objects. One can easily see that such an evaluative practice replicates in an
even more mystified fashion the same error which for Tony Bennett defines
aesthetic discourse, the error of "transferring the properties of the subject
to the object." If no subject is unequivocally the member of only one valuing community, neither is any cultural object the bearer of the values of
only one community. The value of a cultural object can least of all be expressed (in Bennett's words) as having "effect solely within the limits of particular valuing communities," since no concept of value circulates within
the intercultural conditions of modernity which is not the product of the
interrelation of all of the apparently subcultural forces constituting the social totality.

The concept of value, then, must be referred to that totality, even though
the latter is, strictly speaking, unimaginable *as a totality;* it is a totality of
conflict and not of consensus. Because the discourse of value always dreams
of consensus (conceived as a kind of separate peace) it must deny not so
much the reality of conflict as the *constitutive* nature of conflict for any discourse of value. The dismissal of aesthetics, as the discourse of "universal"
value believed to suppress differences, has thus had the paradoxical effect
of removing the basis for apprehending the work of art as the objectification not of subjects or communities but of the relations between subjects,
or the relations between groups. The aesthetic object has the same relation
to the discourse of "aesthetics" as the economy has to political economy or
the psychic to psychology or psychoanalysis. We should not expect that a
critique of aesthetic discourse in its historical forms can proceed by rejecting the category of the aesthetic any more than a critique of political economy would have to deny the reality or specificity of the economic domain.
We shall expect rather that aesthetic discourse is capable of being subjected
to critique to the extent that it, like economic discourse or any discourse, is
the vehicle of ideology, that is to say, an arena of social struggle.

Exit Political Economy: Barbara Herrnstein Smith's Contingencies of Value

The highest point reached by contemplative materialism, that is, materialism which does not comprehend sensuousness as practical activity, is the contemplation of single individuals and of civil society.

MARX, "Theses on Feuerbach," IX

A New, Improved Individualism

By rejecting the appeal to community as the consensual ground of value, Barbara Herrnstein Smith believes that she has avoided the logical contradiction into which the discourse of value has fallen. Her more-relativist-than-Rorty argument seeks to raise relativism itself to a new level of philosophical sophistication by awakening it from its dogmatic dream of community. In the colder light of her philosophical gaze, the community is regarded from a kind of imaginary exterior vantage, from which the emergence of apparently consensual values can be seen as a consequence of the fact that "a coincidence of contingencies among individual subjects who interact as members of some community will operate for them as noncontingency and be interpreted by them accordingly" (40). The real epistemological groundlessness of values can be made visible only by alienating the community *in thought*, since it is not possible to remove oneself in reality from the many communities within which one has no choice but to live. The problem of value is still very much the problem of community, then; but once alienated in thought, the community is defined as a "coincidence of contingencies" rather than as the epistemological guarantor of values. The fact that social forces determine any particular coincidence of contingencies can always be assumed, but particular social forces need not be enumerated in order to arrive at Smith's concept of community because the argument defines the general conditions for the existence of *any* community. This point is important to underscore: Smith's discursive orientation allows her to assert throughout her study the historical situatedness of values and evaluation without raising as a distinctly different question the situatedness of the *discourse* of value. At the cruising altitude of the philosophical critique, communities and their values succeed one another as the succession of one "coincidence of contingencies" by another. Within this problematic, evaluation is assumed to be a transhistorical feature of human social organization—which it no doubt is—*but so is the discourse of value*, or what Smith calls "axiology." The latter assumption is not correct, and its inaccuracy can be confirmed easily enough with reference to aesthetics, everyone's favorite example of an axiological discourse.

The discussion of Hume and Kant in *Contingencies of Value* as exemplary practitioners of aesthetics proceeds immediately to the refutation of their arguments, as though these arguments were produced yesterday. Hence Smith need not pause to consider what historical situatedness, even what particular "coincidence of contingencies" might have given rise to their arguments, a question of some interest in view of the fact that aesthetics as a *discourse* does not exist before the eighteenth century. When the critique of value is raised to the Cyclopean height of philosophical argument, it becomes possible to excise from its field of vision that discourse's own history and historicity, with what results we shall see.

Once she has rejected the notion of community as the epistemological ground of value, Smith is careful to argue that the contrary notion of the "contingency of value" cannot be reduced simply to the meaning of "subjective," in the sense of "personally whimsical, locked into the consciousness of individual subjects and/or without interest or value for other people" (11). Having overcome a false objectivism, it will not do to take up an equally false subjectivism. The problem of how to construe the relation between individual subjects and the community without lapsing into either objectivism or subjectivism is resolved in a formulation that is recurrent in *Contingencies of Value,* one version of which is cited here:

> a verbal judgment of "*the* value" of some entity—for example, an artwork, a work of literature, or any other kind of object, event, text, or *utterance*—cannot be a judgment of any independently determinate or, as we say, "objective" property of that entity. As we have seen, however, what it can be (and typically is) is a judgment of that entity's *contingent* value: that is, the speaker's observation or estimate of how the entity will figure in the economy of some limited population of subjects under some limited set of conditions. (94)

The admirable precision of this formulation permits one the more easily to draw out some of its implications. Let us bracket for the moment the fact Smith elsewhere acknowledges, that judgments of value are ordinarily produced out of the epistemologically deluded conviction of their non-contingency. In order to re-enable judgments of value on relativist grounds (or nongrounds) Smith must reinsert the conceptually alienated and nondeluded observer back into a particular community, although that community will no longer look the same to the observer as it does to someone who has not performed the exercise of alienating the community in thought. The community is now a speculative construct of the observer, who "observes" or "estimates" how a given object will be valued on the basis of what he or she believes to be a coincidence of contingencies in a "limited population." Nothing determines, in fact, how *small or large* these populations may be, provided they can be acknowledged as limited. The formulation as it stands thus does not disallow the observation of a set of contingencies "limited" to the entire human race (for example, death), since even the sum total of human beings living or dead still amounts to a limited population. (Some aesthetic theories—for example, Peter Fuller's—are founded on conditions of such a biological nature, "limited" to the human race as a whole.)[14] The full significance of this point will be apparent when we come to consider Smith's speculation about the possible "survival value" of the aesthetic disposition, as there it will be a question of the human race as such.

One can conclude from Smith's formulation that evaluation does not necessarily require that an individual subject be correct in identifying a certain limited population of subjects as a functional community, a real coincidence of contingencies. In fact, it is difficult to see how the existence of a real community could be confirmed except by the community's ex post facto confirmation of the individual subject's estimate of the value of an object to that community. In the case of an incorrect judgment, the act of evaluation would fall into a kind of social vacuum, since it would be without any observable effect. What we are not capable of describing in the terms of this theory is the effect of a value judgment which deliberately disputes the normative judgment of one's own community, unless we can posit at the same time some "limited population" which would affirm that disputative judgment. In other words, there is no place in Smith's formulation for describing the effects of a dissenting judgment *on the community whose judgment is disputed.* Within this theory we have no way of describing the effects of struggle in general. For a negative judgment must always be recuperated as consensual or valid by some other ad hoc community, or subcommunity. If this is so, then the philosophical exercise of alienating the community in thought could never have been undertaken for the sake of critique, but only in order to scope out, as it were, the particular population likely to affirm a particular judgment. It will be evident that while Smith refuses to invoke consensus, as pragmatism's candidate for the ground of evaluation, she reinstates a concept of community as the basis of the discourse of value by effectively displacing consensus to a prior "coincidence of contingencies"—prior, that is, to conscious or decisional behavior. The displacement guarantees that a kind of *unconscious* consensus will operate to constitute certain limited populations as communities, however ephemeral or enduring, small or large, such communities may be. Hence Smith is able to employ a descriptive rhetoric emphasizing the dynamic and conflictual contexts of value judgments without ever having to explain how conflict or dissensus might be constitutive of evaluative acts.

Within the present discourse of value, even within Smith's more sophisticated version of that discourse, value must always be represented as the effect of a relation between the individual subject and a discrete community. The question is: what relation? To this question there are only versions of the same answer, because the question itself is wrong. But the fundamental nature of this error will be clearer when we have before us an elaboration of what Smith means by "contingencies," since that word names her answer to the question of the relation between individual and community. Let us consider, to begin with, the following statement: "[O]ur experience of the "value of the work" is equivalent to *our experience of the work in relation to the total economy of our existence.* And the reason our estimates of its probable value for other people may be quite accurate is that the total economy of *their* existence may, in fact, be quite similar to our own" (16). The reinstatement of a concept of community is unmistakable when value judgments are said to require a coincidence of the *total* economy of subjects. The insistence on the coincidence of contingencies is crucial to Smith's argument, in that it neatly displaces all of the problems dismissed with the rejection of consensus. For example: Because Smith's formulation describes community as a *likeness* of individual subjects, a disagreement as to the value of an object will have to count as prima facie evidence that subjects who disagree belong in effect to different communities, that is, that their "total economies" are noncoincident. Conversely, there is no way within this schema to explain agreement between parties whose total economies manifestly diverge. Since no community can be conceived as anything other than a limited population of similar individual subjects, it would seem that we need no analysis of the relation between subjects other than a determination of whether they are *like* or *unlike*. Smith's theoretical armature is thus designed primarily for describing subjects, since, in order to have a functional community, one need only have two or more *similar* subjects. The coincidence of contingencies (or total economies) governing the successful assertion of value judgments always refers to the individual subject's *perception* of contingencies, rather than to those social conditions which structure the society as a whole, and which affect differently situated persons in their relations to one another's differences. Smith would perhaps respond to the latter point by arguing that if the same general social conditions are experienced differently by differently situated persons, then they are, in effect, different contingencies. But such a response would only betray the implicit subjectivism—or let us say, *individualism*—of her account of value; for the reality of experiential differences does not mean that differently situated persons will be unable to recognize that certain conditions—the capital-labor relation, the sex-gender system, racism, etc.—are the structuring conditions of the whole social order, and that they affect different social groups differently as a consequence of their very universality. On what other basis could one imagine a politics of coalition? But in this domain Smith's argument dutifully reproduces the aporia in contemporary left-liberal discourse between the supposed objectivism of traditional political or sociological analyses (Smith singles out Marxism as typical of such offensive objectivism) and the subjectivism of identity politics, with its preference for testimony and personal experience. Smith locates herself squarely within the latter discourse by taking as the initial occasion of her critique of value the history of her "personal" encounter with Shakespeare's sonnets.

If it were not possible to identify general social conditions, then all judgment could indeed be reduced to a report on the experience of the individual subject, or of a limited number of individual subjects with the *same* experience. And if the total economy or coincidence of contingencies is truly determinative of judgment, then judgment itself can express nothing more than a commonality of experience, not a perception of the ways in which different social groups respond to the general social conditions determining their relations to one another. But I do not expect that the latter concept of critique will escape the charge of "objectivism" for those who will in every instance look to reduce an *argument* to its supposed ground in *belief,* as though no thought could ever aspire to a reflection on itself, and as though no "individual" were ever capable of reflection on the social conditions of his or her thought. For what it is worth, we might follow up the thesis on Feuerbach quoted as the epigraph to this section, and propose that all analyses fixated on the relation between individuals and communities are vitiated by their failure to identify the forms of social structuration which do not in fact emerge from the experience of community. These forms of objective structuration would include the class structure itself, as well as the "discourses" about which Foucault writes, or the social institutions analyzed by Bourdieu. These structures may or may not be associated with communities of one sort or another, but the point is that they need not be. Hence one cannot extrapolate their real effects upon social life by construing them as "communities" composed of "individuals." Liberal pluralism remains trapped within this paradigm.

Turning back, then, from the dead end of liberal pluralist epistemology, let us ask another question of Smith's theory: How is an individual's "experience of the value of a work" related to those contingencies which Smith herself would locate in the sphere of social relations? What is a "contingency," in other words, such that it can exist prior to an experience, as what an experience is an experience *of*? The color of my eyes is a "contingency," to be sure, but what sense does it make to say that my *race* is likewise a "contingency"? It is only certain social relations that select certain contingencies as consequential. Here it is necessary to take note of an impoverishment in Smith's vocabulary of social relations, when compared to her analysis of the individual's experience, an impoverishment that is nowhere more pronounced than in the phrase by means of which she everywhere introduces the economic, the concept of the "personal economy":

> Like its price in the marketplace, the value of an entity to an individual subject is *also* the product of the dynamics of an economic system: specifically, the personal economy constituted by the subject's needs, interests, and resources—biological, psychological, material, experiential, and so forth. Like any other economy, moreover, this too is a continuously fluctuating or shifting system, for our individual needs, interests, and resources are themselves functions of our continuously changing states in relation to an environment that may be relatively stable but is never absolutely fixed. The two kinds of economic system described here are, it should be noted, not only analogous but also interactive and interdependent, for part of our environment *is* the market economy and, conversely, the market economy is composed, in part, of the diverse personal economies of individual producers, distributors, consumers, and so forth. (30–31)

We are led to suspect on the basis of this account that the concept of a market economy is simply extrapolated from the concept of the personal economy. Another way to register this short-circuiting of the supposed reciprocity of relation in Smith's argument is to recollect that for Smith the act of evaluation has two scenes, in the first of which one assesses the value of an object *for oneself,* in relation to one's own needs and desires; and in the second of which one assesses the value of an object to a hypothetical social group, defined by the likeness of its individual members' needs and desires to one's own. In this two-part scenario the concept of "economy" changes not at all as one moves from the personal to the collective: the "market economy" is just the multiplication of the personal economy by a factor greater than one.

If the personal economy determines *all* value, then what gives an object value within that personal economy? Valuation for Smith is defined as the act of determining an object's capacity to perform certain specific *functions* within the "total economy" of one's needs or desires. The capability of performing these functions is not of course attributed to the object as an intrinsic property, but is entirely the result of a "contingency," the particular circumstances of a particular encounter between an individual subject or subjects and a possible object of value:

> I would suggest, then, that what we may be doing—and, I think, often are doing—when we we make an explicit value judgment of a literary work is (a) articulating an estimate of how well that work will serve certain implicitly defined functions (b) for a specific implicitly defined audience, (c) who are conceived of as experiencing the work under certain implicitly defined conditions. (13)

These functions are specific but they are not as yet specified. For most objects, the specification of function would seem to mean the same thing as specifying the "use" of an object; but a moment's reflection yields the simple observation that use is defined contextually (the murder weapon was an ax). Theoretically, this condition should not be different for the work of art (as object) except that the discourse of aesthetics intervenes at this point to confuse the issue rather thoroughly. The functions attributed by aesthetics to works of art are extraordinarily numerous, if also distinguished by a certain vagueness; but they have in common the assumption that these functions are performed by no other objects than works of art. These functions would then constitute the specificity of the work of art, as they are, precisely, "aesthetic" functions. Surprisingly Smith is not averse to hypothesizing a specifically aesthetic function, but she locates it at the "biophysiological" level of human existence, an important qualification, as we shall see:

> [T]here is reason to believe that the experience of much that we call "aesthetic value" is, to some extent, a function of species-wide mechanisms of perception and cognition and, with regard to the value of literary works, a function of such mechanisms as they relate to what may be universals of verbal behavior. Nevertheless, such presumably biophysiological mechanisms will always operate differentially in different environments and interact with a broad range of other variables (historical, cultural, situational, etc.) and, therefore, the experience of literary and aesthetic value cannot be altogether accounted for, reduced to, or predicted by them. (15)

One might think that the hypothesis of specifically aesthetic "species-wide mechanisms of perception and cognition" would have to count as a proposition within aesthetic discourse, since the statement sounds very much like an anthropologically updated version of Kant (or more recently, of Peter Fuller), in that it locates the aesthetic at the level of the universal, on the face of it a difficult proposition to reconcile with the polemic against Kant's notion of "subjective universality." But Smith does not specify what biophysiological mechanisms are at issue, and the absence of their enumeration permits her to dissolve them immediately in the bubbling solvent of the social, where only differences obtain. There is a realm of aesthetic "perception and cognition," then, but it is curiously inaccessible to analysis, unavailable to any account of "aesthetic value" in actually existent human societies. All that remains of this ephemeral aesthetic is the proposition that the aesthetic has a *function,* which traditional Kantian aesthetics is taken by Smith to deny:

> To those for whom terms such as "utility," "effectiveness," and "function" suggest gross pragmatic instrumentality, crass material desires, and the satisfaction of animal needs, a concept such as use value will be seen as irrelevant to or clearly to be distinguished from aesthetic value. There is, however, no good reason to confine the domain of the utilitarian to objects that serve only immediate, specific, and unexalted ends or, for that matter, to assume that the value of artworks has altogether nothing to do with pragmatic instrumentality or animal needs. The recurrent impulse and effort to define aesthetic value by contradistinction to all forms of utility or as the negation of all other nameable sources of interest or forms of value—hedonic, practical, sentimental, ornamental, historical, ideological, and so forth—is, in effect, to define it out of existence; for when all such utilities, interests, and other particular sources of value have been subtracted, nothing remains. Or, to put this in other terms: the "essential value" of an artwork consists of everything from which it is usually distinguished. (33)

Here finally is an enumeration of functions, but an enumeration in which no function can be called specifically aesthetic, or specific to the object defined as a work of art (aesthetic pleasure as opposed to some other kind of pleasure). This point is even more explicitly stated on the following page: "there are no functions performed by artworks that may be specified as generically unique." Let us not underestimate the difficulty of arguing simultaneously that the aesthetic has a function, and that no function is specifically aesthetic; for in this contradiction Smith has only restated the problem of traditional aesthetics, well formulated by Mukarovsky as the proposition that "the work of art appears, in the final analysis, as an actual collection of extraesthetic values and nothing else."[15] Mukarovsky goes on to propose that the specifically "aesthetic value" of a work inheres in the "dynamic totality" of the interrelations between the constituent values of the work, a dynamism which may well have a "use" or "function" without being reducible to the use or function of the individual values of which the artwork is composed. This was perhaps the burden of Kant's problematic distinction between aesthetic pleasure and mere sensual "gratification"; but the distinction has proven to be a burden indeed, since it has enjoined a certain unfortunate interpretation of the famous formula, "purposefulness without purpose"—namely, no purpose at all. (Do we need to insist here that *Zweckmässigkeit ohne Zweck* is not the same thing as purposelessness?) For Smith the refutation of the traditional denial by aesthetics of the utility of the artwork is surprisingly simple: one only has to reassert the artwork's purpose or "use"; but that use turns out be nothing less than all the *uses* to which the work may be put as an object not generically different—with respect to use—from any other object. And of course, one cannot predict or limit the uses to which any object may be put. "The murder weapon was a blunt instrument, a small sculpture perhaps." Every object is in this sense a blunt instrument.

One begins to understand, then, why Smith wants to recover an "aesthetic" function at the "biophysiological" level, where function is associated with species survival:

> It may be relevantly noted here that human beings have evolved as distinctly opportunistic creatures and that our survival, both as individuals and as a species, continues to be enhanced by our ability and inclination to reclassify objects and to "realize" and "appreciate" novel and alternate functions for them. . . . (33)
> . . . although we may be individually motivated to engage in various ludic, aesthetic, or artistic activities only for the sake of the ongoing pleasure they provide . . . our doing so may nevertheless yield a long-term profit in enhanced cognitive development, behavioral flexibility, or other kinds of advantage for survival, and our general tendency to *find* pleasure in such activities may, accordingly, be the product or by-product of our evolutionary development. (34)

The problem traditional aesthetics identifies as the peculiar quality of aesthetic pleasure, its deferral of supposedly more immediate gratifications, is reconceived as an investment in the "long-term profit" of certain subjective self-improvements, which improvements have an "advantage for survival." Since survival, as a rather abstract temporal concept, is not in itself

pleasurable, but is rather the condition for the experience of all other pleasures, our "evolutionary development" cleverly allows us to experience as
pleasurable the *deferral* of pleasures. The experience of the aesthetic then
converges upon the experience of deferral per se (or what might, in some
other discourse, be called "sublimation"), but deferral redefined as the experience of a *generalized utility* rather than the particular use of a particular object:

> [W]hat is otherwise referred to as the "nonutilitarian" value of
> something or, in explicit opposition to utility or use value, as its
> "symbolic" or "aesthetic" (etc.) value, could readily be re-
> described as *itself a utility,* though perhaps, in the case of things
> such as art, play, gifts, souvenirs, friendship, or wilderness pres-
> ervation, one that happens to be especially diffuse, deferred, re-
> mote, subtle, complex, multiple, heterogeneous, and/or, for
> these or other reasons, difficult to measure or specify. (128)

What aesthetic theory understands as the work of art's deferral of immediate gratification is equated by Smith with the notion of "species survival,"
which likewise is supposed by her to involve a deferral of individual or immediate gratification on behalf of the species (actually it does not). But this
theory is, as the analytic philosophers say, nonfalsifiable, since the question
of the "survival" of the species is mooted by the fact that "natural selection" has long since ceased to operate for human beings in its pristine "natural" form. The "biophysiological" subject is impossible to isolate from
the social subject (because it is not a subject at all!), and this is why Smith
has to argue that the *aesthetic itself* is impossible to isolate in the social
world, that it has no specificity. Whatever the merits of Smith's theory, the
only major difference between it and traditional aesthetics is that it *confines* the aesthetic function to the biophysiological level, which operates
beneath and before the emergence of social organization (even if it persists
in a mysterious way within the social itself).

If aesthetic function seems to disappear from view at the level of the social, where it is dispersed into the multiple individual forms of "utility," no
one of which can be specified as exclusively aesthetic, this circumstance
seems to be oddly correlated with the fact that what does make its appearance *only* at the level of the social is the work of art, the hypothetical embodiment in traditional aesthetics of a specifically aesthetic function. It
should be obvious that the relation between the aesthetic and the work of
art cannot be defined as their absolute distinction any more than the experience of the aesthetic can be identified *exclusively* with the experience of
the work of art. But Smith's argument tends toward the first position as a

response to the second, to the reduction of aesthetics to the theory of the artwork. When Smith turns her attention, then, to the question of how works of art "survive," or the "mechanisms of cultural selection and transmission" (in other words, canon formation), she can present the artwork not as an object embodying a specifically aesthetic function, but as an object somehow embodying an individual's experience of a certain flexible and utilitarian relation towards objects—that is, an object which has somehow acquired the properties of the evolutionary *subject:* "These interactions are, in certain respects, analogous to those by virtue of which biological species evolve and survive and also analogous to those through which artistic choices evolve and are found 'fit' or fitting by the individual artist" (47). The biophysiological mechanisms of survival are transposed into the social realm not as the subject's aesthetic cognition or perception (as in Kant) but as nothing other than the process of canon formation conceived as the survival of the fittest *object*. But we can hardly be surprised at this point that Smith's aesthetic theory is generated out of the critique of canon formation, since it was the challenge to the canon which initiated this entire line of inquiry in the first place.

The apparent reasonableness, even inevitability, of the evolutionary analogy is undermined by its patent confusion of the subject and the object. The biophysiological subject's disposition to recognize the multiple utility of objects reappears in the work of art itself as the work's *objectification* of that quality of adaptability: "An object or artifact that performs certain desired/able functions particularly well at a given time for some community of subjects, being perhaps not only 'fit' but exemplary—that is, 'the best of its kind'—under those conditions, will have immediate survival advantage" (48). Smith is in this way able to spin out her evolutionary analogy into a full-scale theory of canon formation. Once canonized, a work tends to remain so if "it continues to perform *some* desired/able functions particularly well, even if not the same ones for which it was initially valued" (49). None of these functions need be specified in particular, nor can any of them be isolated as exclusively aesthetic, just because their very nonspecificity or multiplicity is operating at the biophysiological level as the only credibly "aesthetic" function, a function which is really performed by reflecting back to the evolutionary subject an image of the "adaptability" that makes possible the survival of that subject:

> The works that are differentially reproduced, therefore, will tend to be those that gratify the exercise of such competencies and engage interests of that kind: specifically, works that are structurally complex and, in the technical sense, information-

rich—and which, by virtue of those qualities, may be especially amenable to multiple reconfiguration, more likely to enter into relation with the emergent interests of various subjects, and thus more readily adaptable to emergent conditions. (51)

It is easy enough to see in this formulation that the evolutionary subject and the canonical work of art are simply identified with one another, and therefore that it is no longer a question of the actual *uses* to which works of art are put, but rather their status as the embodiment of "utility" per se.

From the point of view of the individual in society, then, the work of art is confronted as another object with a variety of possible functions, all of which are wholly contingent and historically situated; but from the biophysiological perspective the work of art looks just like a biological species attempting to "adapt" to different environments and changes in order to survive. For evolutionary biology, however, the fate of any one individual is immaterial: only the species is capable of "adapting" over time. The confusion between the work of art as object and the work as subject thus also confuses the individual with the species: is the work of art analogized to an individual or to a species? The confusion of adaptation with use, of the species with the individual, "explains" the transhistorical status of canonical works by naming canonical works as those which have the function of signifying the human disposition to multiply the uses of objects.

The confusion of subject and object follows not only from the conflation of adaptation with use, but also from the apparently unobjectionable identification of *function* with use. The confusion here can be brought out by making a more rigorous distinction between these two concepts. We may concede that the uses of any object are potentially infinite, because the possible contexts of relation between subjects and objects are potentially infinite. But it would be very helpful to understand function in a more limited sense, as the finite range of uses prescribed by the social classification of an object. Smith is certainly aware of the relation between classification and function, in the context of works of art, and she is careful to describe this relation as "interactive." But she typically regards the relation from the vantage of the individual subject's elective classification of an object: "we implicitly isolate and foreground certain of its possible functions" (32)— for example, those functions which are performed by the work when considered as a work of *art*. But it would be very curious if one were obliged to undertake this exercise in voluntary classification for every object claiming to be a work of art. The fact that one does not, means that the aesthetic "function" is not just one of many possible elective uses of an object but something that is socially determined as the *condition* of an object's production or reception. It is thus no refutation of the specificity of the aesthetic that a work of art might be used in some nonaesthetic context; or that an object not produced as a work of art can be so regarded in a later social context than the context of its production. The relevant consideration is the specific social functions of objects produced or received in a given historical context *as* works of art, since it is only as works so classified that they can have certain *other* social functions. Hence it is rather inaccurate to speak of the function of individual works as changing or adapting over time, with favorable or unfavorable consequences with regard to canonicity, as though these functions could have any explanatory force at all outside the context of the classification of the object. This is why it is so difficult to specify social function for an individual work of art (what is the "function" of *Macbeth*?), because social function inheres in the *category* of the object—in the function of a particular genre, or of literature, or of art. The process of classification is part of a social discourse which is a condition of individual agency, even of the most perverse or brilliant acts of reclassification associated with the historical avant-garde. The "aesthetic function" does not name one possible use of an object among many, contingent upon the "personal economy" of an individual subject, but the predetermination of social function by a classificatory discourse (this might be one moral of the Mapplethorpe fable), whatever "nonaesthetic" use an individual may wish to make of a work of art, even whatever "nonaesthetic" uses are institutionalized for canonical works of art. To consider only individual objects and the particular uses to which individuals put them is to ignore the detemination of the relation between objects and consumers by *discourse*. If Shakespeare's plays, for example, can be received or "used" as moral exempla for adolescent schoolchildren, as monuments of nationalist pride, as the cultural capital of the educated classes, they are only capable of these "nonaesthetic" uses *because* they are classified as (canonical) works of art.[16] As we shall see, the possibility of a sociology of art depends upon this complexity of consumption, the fact that "uses" are not simply chosen from amongst a potentially infinite number of equal possibilities (aesthetic, political, moral, hedonic) but are complexly articulated in nested hierarchies according to the relation between the specific domains of the social named by such categories as the aesthetic, the political, the moral, the hedonic.

A New, Improved Utilitarianism

Smith's dissolution of socially determinate functions into the potential infinity of individual uses yields an aesthetic theory in which the work of art is surprisingly privileged as the (potentially) most variously "useful" of objects—not intrinsically, of course, but as the object which happens to be chosen for such various use. This artwork is exactly the opposite of the essentially "useless" object traditional aesthetics had represented it to be. So redefined, the work of art can simply be assimilated to the realm of the economic—for is the economy not the realm of "use value"? Aesthetic value, Smith argues, is the "product of the dynamics of an economic system," the circulation of "use values." If traditional aesthetics always denied this fact, it is nevertheless "not surprising that the languages of aesthetics and economics . . . tend to drift toward each other, and that their segregation must be constantly patrolled." Even were we to grant, however, that traditional aesthetics' denial of use to the work of art is just a piece of ideology, we would still have to ask whether the strategy of inverting the axioms of aesthetics really tells us what the *economic* is. Perhaps the most interesting aspect of Smith's argument is just her strenuous effort throughout *Contingencies of Value* to construct a kind of utilitarian economics, or general economy, by systematically negating the propositions of aesthetics. In this project she enacts a demystificatory agenda essential to the project of contemporary liberal pluralist criticism, which rediscovers economic discourse as precisely what was formerly excluded from its domain. The discipline of criticism thus seems to overturn its own founding premise when it negates the proposition that "aesthetic value" is categorically different from the kinds of value circulating in the market economy:

> On the one hand there is the discourse of economic theory: money, commerce, technology, industry, production and consumption, workers and consumers; on the other hand, there is the discourse of aesthetic axiology: culture, art, genius, creation and appreciation, artists and connoisseurs. In the first discourse, events are explained in terms of calculation, preferences, costs, benefits, profits, prices, and utility. In the second, events are explained—or, rather (and this distinction/opposition is as crucial as any of the others), "justified"—in terms of inspiration, discrimination, taste (good taste, bad taste, no taste), the test of time, intrinsic value, and transcendent value. (127)

The universality of what Smith very elegantly goes on to call "the double discourse of value" need not be disputed. The question here is rather what status such concepts as "calculation, preferences, costs, benefits, profits, prices, and utility" have within Smith's discourse. To be sure, Smith has only contempt for those who repudiate the realm of the economic, for "the priest/humanist's struggle to chase the money-changers from the temple, to preserve the sacred objects from the merchant, and to name and isolate their value as absolutely different from and transcendent of exchange value and use value" (131). Yet one may begin to question this apparent embrace of economic discourse by noting that here, and throughout *Contingencies of Value*, Smith makes no distinction between "use value" and "exchange value." The one concept is interchangeable with the other:

> Viewed in this latter aspect, all human (and not only human) activity could be seen to consist of a continuous exchange or expenditure (whether as payment, donation, sacrifice, loss, or destruction) of goods of some (but any) kind, whereby goods of some other (but, again, any) kind are secured, enhanced, or produced. Thus, money or material provisions are expended whereby power is enlarged and status confirmed, sumptuary goods are donated or destroyed whereby social or symbolic value is marked and maintained, bodily comfort and life are sacrificed whereby exhilaration and glory are gained, "hours of dross" are sold to buy "terms divine," and so forth—and also, for *any* exchanges, vice versa: money is hoarded whereby status is risked, glory is forgone whereby comfort is secured, terms divine are sacrificed whereby hours of dross are gilded—everywhere, in every archaic tribe and "modern era," *endlessly.* (144–45)

Exchange may supersede even the concept of utility in this total vision of human (or any) existence, but only as a term representing the inescapable means toward the end of *use:* The acquisition of any object (broadly defined) for the purpose of its use requires that something be given up or exchanged, even if that something is only the minimal energy required to pluck the fruit from the trees in Paradise. Is there then some distinction between exchange and use worth remarking, perhaps of interest to economists?

In some respects Smith's conclusions converge quite remarkably with those of Georg Simmel in his seminal treatise of 1900, *The Philosophy of Money.* Simmel's work is only just being fully acknowledged for its crucial influence on Weber, Lukács, and many others, although Smith nowhere cites it. Simmel is very much closer to the discourse and problems of political economy than Smith, specifically to the corpus of Marx, and as a consequence he characterizes his project as the attempt to "construct a new storey beneath historical materialism."[17] To that end, the end of the new discourse of "sociology," he proposed in *The Philosophy of Money* to argue that "the fact that two people exchange their products is by no means simply an economic fact" (55). What economics excludes from the purview of its discourse is the *subjectivity* of the exchange relation: "There are two sides of our relationship to objects, which we call subjectively our desire and objectively their value" (75). Simmel's account of the exchange relation is rigorously subjectivist, not in the pejorative sense of lacking "objectivity," but rather in the sense that it concerns itself with the subjectivity of economic agents. This subjectivity is objectified in sociological discourse, which defines the subject as its object. Simmel's "subjectivist" analysis of economic exchange discovers every exchange relation to be founded on a kind of "sacrifice," an expenditure of subjective energies: "Sacrifice is not only the condition of specific values, but the condition of value as such" (85). From this perspective it makes no difference at all with whom or what the exchange is undertaken:

> Thus the isolated individual who sacrifices something in order to produce certain products, acts in exactly the same way as the subject who exchanges, the only difference being that his partner is not another subject but the natural order and regularity of things which, just like another human being, does not satisfy our desires without a sacrifice. (83)

Whether or not Simmel's theory succeeds in constructing a kind of "basement" for historical materialism, it is worth emphasizing that, as a consequence of its rigorous subjectivism, it need make no distinction between the scene in which objects are exhanged between persons, and the scene in which, as on Robinson Crusoe's island, the "exchange" of personal energy for the use of a product takes place in the absence of *any* other subject. Shall we then say, as Crusoe would have it, and Smith too, that the latter scene of exchange describes the operation of a "personal economy"? Only for Simmel, however, does the distinction between the two scenes of exchange mark the distinction between an economic and a *sociological* discourse. For that reason Simmel is careful to say of his theory of value that "Not a single line of these investigations is meant to be a statement about economics" (54). So it would appear that one may speak of exchange, or speak of use, without uttering a proposition about the economic; or alternatively, that one may speak of use or exchange without *yet* speaking of the economic.

 Let us inquire, then, whether Smith too may be speaking about exchange without making any statement about economics. Shall we say that her theory, like Simmel's, is sociological? If it is, it is not particularly troubled by the specificity of culture under capitalism—a specificity which the sociological tradition, from Simmel and Weber through Bourdieu, has been quite concerned to understand. But we know that in fact Smith's argument is oriented throughout by its affinity with current *philosophical* debates; hence a version of "relativism" is supposed to give us the answer to the puzzle of value. Before deciding, then, whether she has succeeded in reducing aesthetics to the terms of a general economy, we must try to grasp the specificity of the economic itself. This we cannot do if we represent exchange in the market—exchange between subjects—as not in any relevant way different from the subject's private expenditure of energy on behalf of acquiring some object for use—as though Robinson Crusoe were really the archetype of the economic subject. The real intersubjectivity of the market relation disappears altogether if all exchangeable objects are defined as valued objects or " 'goods' (that is, as profits, satisfactions, gains, benefits, etc.) *only in relation to a particular state of a particular agent's personal economy*" (145; emphasis mine). Even when the subject's "desires and resources" are in turn "understood as themselves the product of the continuous interaction between, and thus mutual production by, the agent and an environment that is itself *always* socially and culturally constituted," the social and cultural "interaction" to which Smith rightly refers is always already reduced to the "environment" of an individual subject, merely the occasion of a demand on the "personal economy." In this scenario it is precisely exchange in the *economic* sense—as what takes place only *between* subjects—that disappears. It is not when the fruit is plucked from the tree for one's private consumption but when it is exchanged between subjects as a quantifiable "value" that there exists something called the "economic." To collapse the latter into a special case of the former is finally to collapse all exchange value into a version of use value, in the same way that Smith's notion of community as a "coincidence of contingencies" is projected out of, and collapses back into, the experience of the individual subject.

The primacy of use value is fundamental for Smith, and never more so than when she discards the "hedonic calculus" of classic utilitarianism for what she calls the "scrappiness" of human behavior (148), by which she means the irreducibility of the utility of objects or the ends of action to any single measure of value. The criterion of use value resists any single calculus, to be sure, but the criterion of exchange value does not: *its* measure is money, as Smith well knows. But money enters her argument only as a concept analogous to the concept of a "good," the name the ordinary language of value gives to any object when it enters the personal economy, when, in the simplest terms, we *want* it:

> Indeed, it appears that "good" operates within the discourse of value as does money in a cash economy: *good* is the universal

value-form of value and its standard "measure"; it is that "in terms of which" all forms of value must be "expressed" for their commensurability to be calculated; and *good* is that *for* and *into* which any other name or form of value can—"on demand," we might say—be (ex)changed. (146)

Only for a literary critic well insulated from the actual history of economic discourse can the analogy of the "good" and "money" as universal equivalents have the status of a demystifying revelation. (Simmel was by contrast very much aware that something strange happened when the object of desire, the "good" in Smith's terms, is translated into the universal equivalent of money.) Economists have been impressed by something quite different from Smith's "good"—the fact that the economy is no respecter of persons, or personal economies, or any unquantified "good." The economy knows only "goods," that is, commodities, whose values in exchange, or money-prices, do not reflect *any* individual's actual estimation of their worth within a personal economy. The price of a commodity has nothing to do, in fact, with what any particular individual is willing to pay for it, since this is not what price measures at all. The desire of individual consumers will vary greatly for any commodity that appears on the market, but individuals will not be able to express the relative intensities of their desire or need for the "use" of an object in monetary terms. The commodity will appear before them already priced, a price they will either be willing (or able) to pay, or not. To construe the exchange relation otherwise is to take bartering as the paradigm of exchange (an easy theoretical error), rather than an exception to the rule of the market.

This fact goes a long way toward explaining why the discourse of political economy is founded in the eighteenth century on the *distinction* between use value and exchange value, as in Adam Smith's canonical definition of value in *The Wealth of Nations*:

The word VALUE, it is to be observed, has two different meanings, and sometimes expresses the utility of some particular object, and sometimes the power of purchasing other goods which the possession of that object conveys. The one may be called "value in use"; the other, "value in exchange." The things which have the greatest value in use have frequently little or no value in exchange; and on the contrary, those which have the greatest value in exchange have frequently little or no value in use. Nothing is more useful than water: but it will purchase scarce anything; scarce anything can be had in exchange for it. A diamond, on the contrary, has scarce any value in use; but a very great quantity of other goods may frequently be had in exchange for it.[18]

It is a historical fact that this distinction founds political economy, as such, as a discourse of exchange value rather than use value. By the time the discourse is formalized in Ricardo's *Principles of Political Economy*, the virtual irrelevance of use value to economic discourse can simply be assumed. Moving over the same definitional ground in the first pages of *Capital*, Marx too can argue, without yet disputing the basic claims of political economy, that by "value" is properly meant exchange value, even if the usefulness of an object must be considered an enabling condition of its exchange. When Baudrillard still later argues for discarding the concept of "use value" altogether, he is really arguing against an anthropology of human needs and desires which has continued to cling to political economy as the dried husk of its earliest incarnation, and which can only be gotten beyond by recognizing that "use value" is determined by a "logic of equivalence" identical to that of exchange value.[19] To put this in the simplest terms, the use of an object can be represented as a kind of "value" only if there is *already* a discourse of exchange values, that is, an economy of generalized commodity exchange.

Exchange value is thus the condition for the retroactive construction of the use of an object as an expression of its value. Yet the adequation of use and exchange as "values" is already belied at the foundational moment of political economy, in Adam Smith's frequently cited example comparing the use and exchange of water and diamonds, an example which conspicuously foregrounds the discrepancy between use value and exchange value. What this discrepancy means in effect is that the use of an object cannot be *expressed in,* or *measured by,* its exchange value, its money price in the market. In Ricardo's words, "Utility then is not the measure of exchangeable value, although it is absolutely essential to it."[20] For this reason political economy was forced to construct, as its first order of business, a theory of value, a hypothesis about what it was that was actually measured or expressed in the exchange value of an object. It is in response to this problem that earlier political economists were able to propose that the exchange value of an object expresses the quantum of labor expended to *produce* that object for the market (the "labor theory of value") and not the quantum of energy expended to *acquire* the object in the market. The question of the use of the object, or the desire of any individual for an object, does not enter into the equation of exchange value as a quantum, but is bracketed. There is in that sense no such thing as a "personal economy," no economy at all on Crusoe's island, because no such hypothetical "intrapersonal" exchange could be expressed as a quantum of value. What Barbara Herrn-stein Smith thinks of as "utilitarianism," of which she advocates a more latitudinarian version, is the long shadow of ideology cast by political economy, the sign of that discourse's inability to solve the problem of the relation between the individual subject and market society. Thus political economy relegates use value to a domain of subjectivity, which it cannot enter into the equation of exchange value. Conversely, the discourse of util-itarianism attempts to reduce the domain of the economic to the expression of the individual subject's needs or desires, and its individualism cannot account for the manifest independence of exchange value from determina-tion by the individual subject.

We may recollect that Marx attempted to solve this problem by intro-ducing the "dialectic" into the critique of political economy, but we need not go so far as to argue for the validity of his solution. That will not be necessary! We need only acknowledge here, in more au courant Baudrillar-dian terms, that the theory of value offered up by the most rigorous of recent relativisms only reinstates a utilitarianism with which political economy uneasily colluded in the course of its history. That utilitarianism served as political economy's ideology, just as use value, in Baudrillard's pithy trope, served as the "alibi" for exchange value. But the point of great-est interest to the present discussion is perhaps the larger question of dis-course itself, or the fact that literary critics such as Barbara Herrnstein Smith believe they have exposed the *real relation* between the aesthetic and the economic in the reduction of "aesthetic value" to economic "use value." All that is required to reveal this reality is the negation of the negation founding the discourse of aesthetics in Kant's *Critique of Judg-ment:* "That the satisfaction in an object, on account of which we call it beautiful, cannot rest on the representation of its utility is sufficiently ob-vious . . . because in that case it would not be an immediate satisfaction in the object, which is the essential condition of a judgement about beauty" (62). A closer examination of the historical record will reveal that, on the contrary, *both* aesthetics and economics were founded in contradistinction to the concept of "use value." To collapse exchange value into use value, then, is to *forget* political economy in the very gesture of reducing the aes-thetic to an expression of the "economic." If these two discourses diverge on the question of the relation between their two exemplary objects—the work of art and the commodity, or between "aesthetic value" and a sup-posedly antithetical "exchange value"—that divergence, the institution of Herrnstein Smith's "double discourse of value," postdates a suspiciously convergent origin. In fact, we shall see that a consideration of the texts, pre-texts, and contexts of Adam Smith and Kant reveals an original indistinction of aesthetics and political economy *as discourses*. Both of these discourses gestate in the body of what in the eighteenth century was called "moral philosophy," and they can be said, with only the slightest recourse to the grotesque, to have been separated at birth.

Reenter Political Economy: Adam Smith and the Origins of the Value-Concept

> Everything can be summed up in Aesthetics and Political Economy.
> —MALLARMÉ, "La Musique et les lettres"

The Problem of Moral Philosophy

The figure of gestation already hints that what is required at this point in the argument is, in the simplest term, a narrative. Such a narrative would recover the history of political economy's relation to aesthetics at the same time that it would call into question the critique of "aesthetic value," or value in general, as a perennial philosophical question, for which different thinkers have provided different solutions, subjectivist or objectivist, relativist or absolutist. The problem of "aesthetic value" is not in fact a perennial problem, but can be posed as such only after the divergence of aesthetics and political economy, and as a consequence of the repression of their convergent origin. What the following narrative will discover is that the practice of judging works of art need make no reference at all to the concept of value before the emergence of political economy. It was not even the case that a concept of aesthetic value operated *implicitly* in the nascent forms of critical discourse in the early modern period; the point is precisely that the comparison of authors or works to one another need not at that time be expressed as the comparison of their relative "aesthetic values," because neither the concept of the aesthetic, nor the concept of value, are as yet defined in such a way that they can be yoked together. The more surprising fact for us to consider in the context of the present debate about value is that the problem of aesthetic judgment was as essential to the formation of political economy as the problem of political economy was to the formation of aesthetics. But we shall not be able to see how these origins converge until we see that they belong to the history of a discourse, "moral philosophy," which is quite distinct from what we mean by "ethics," and which no longer exists.

We are fortunate at this moment in that the requisite narrative is already available in the superlative form of Howard Caygill's recent study, *Art of Judgement*, which describes the social conditions and discursive pretexts for Kant's *Critique of Judgment*.[21] The narrative I shall produce here is in large measure indebted to Caygill's study, with considerable condensation, as well as necessary emendations. I have in particular inflected the narrative in such a way as to foreground certain methodological issues important to the current interrogation of the concept of value. Caygill is interested in reading Kant philosophically without deracinating the text, without displacing it to the transhistorical realm of a conversation among the great philosophers on perennial questions. It is on behalf of this project that Kant's philosophical argument needs to be located firmly in the discursive tradition of "moral philosophy," as well as in relation to the discursive break between natural and moral philosophy. Hence the names of Hutcheson, Shaftesbury, Mandeville, Baumgarten, and Wolff are just as important as Locke or Hume or Leibniz.

The largest historical condition for the formation of a discourse of moral philosophy is the emergence in the seventeenth and eighteenth centuries of "civil society" as a distinct and relatively autonomous sector of the social order, the sector of economic competition, commerce, and production. That autonomy was established or won both as a result of violence (in the case of the English revolution), and as a consequence of the vastly increasing importance of commercial, and later industrial, activity to the modern nation-states. Without resorting here to any more detailed or controversial analyses of causes, we can say that the effect of such a large-scale transformation of the social order was to require a massive rethinking of the nature of that order, indeed, a new formulation of the question of "society." Such a rethinking was necessary because it was no longer possible to defer on questions of public policy to the authority of the monarchy or the noble estate, or for that matter to theological doctrine. In Caygill's summary formulation, "the burden of legitimation shifted toward the establishment of an autonomous civil society in which the moral policing of society by the state was considered unnecessary for the establishment of 'throne, religion, happiness, and peace'" (41). The manifest dependence of the welfare of the nation upon the sectors of trade and manufacture generated a set of policy problems for which no traditional discourse provided solutions; preeminent among these was the problem of to what extent the state was needed to intervene in the sectors of trade or commerce. It is of course a historical commonplace that the earliest economic debates—between the Physiocrats and the Mercantilists—were concerned with just these issues, and hence with constructing a theoretical basis for such policies as taxation. What requires a further effort of contextualization here is the fact that these issues were not always debated within a discourse of the economic per se, but could also be posed (and had to be posed) at a level of philosophical abstraction, as questions belonging to the field of moral philosophy, the discourse whose largest project was to relate "private interest" to "public good." This is the discourse to which the work of Locke belongs, but also *The Wealth of Nations*. If Adam Smith's treatise may be accounted the first work of political economy, it also remains a work of moral philosophy, of which Smith was after all a "professor."

When the structural transformation of the social order became the object of contemplation for the moral philosopher, the very rapidity with which civil society expanded seemed to pose a continual threat of disorder. But moral philosophy was the servant and the agent of civil society itself, and hence it attempted to resolve this problem by revealing the order that emerged with the very freedom of civil society from control by monarchical or clerical authority. Moral philosophy saw "civil society" as a collection of individuals, relatively unrestrained by the state in their competition with each other, each acting in his or her immediate interest. The problem was to deduce the principle of the manifest order of society from the apparent disorder of incompatible individual self-interests.

At the highest level of abstraction, the problem of describing the order, harmony, or proportion of society became the problem of describing the unity of a manifold; at a slightly lesser degree of abstraction, the problem seemed to be repeated within the individual subject as the relation between higher and lower faculties, cognition and judgment, or the intelligible and the sensible. It would be less correct to say that these terms simply expressed or reflected the relation of the state to civil society than that this relation could be negotiated through these philosophical terms. The problem of justifying the social order could thus be addressed directly in the texts of moral philosophy, and not relegated to the level of the repressed referent of philosophical abstractions. Once the order of society ceased to be legislated from the top, it ceased to be conceived as simply the execution of rationally prescribed principles (not, of course, that it ever had been). Rather the order, proportion, or harmony of the social totality could be represented as analogous to the order, proportion, or harmony of a work of art, or any object of beauty. It was an order of the sensible rather than the intelligible. The former species of order failed to yield its rational principle to inspection, but it could be detected in the exercise of taste, whose principle could be summed up paradoxically in the expression "je ne sais quoi." The analogy between the aesthetic and the social order is typified, as is well known, in the work of Shaftesbury, whose aestheticization of the social order as "beautiful" inaugurated a major topos of moral philosophy, variously developed by Hutcheson, Kames, Burke, and others. The aesthetic analogy was at this time deployed in the absence of a developed concept of "aesthetics" as a separate discourse or set of questions, and hence it tended to be elaborated as the narrower problem of "taste." The evident absence of verifiable principles of taste could be cited not as an embarrassment of theory but as just the circumstance which permitted an analogy for the harmony of the social order. Shaftesbury, of course, took the precaution of depositing these absent but not nonexistent principles in the safekeeping of a divine Providence, but this residually theological resort could be read as a weakness of the theory, and was so read by other moral philosophers, such as Mandeville, who proposed a rather darker view of individual self-interest. A good deal, then, was at stake in the analogical concept of taste in British moral philosophy, and for that reason Caygill is able to argue persuasively that "the theory of civil society was haunted by the problem of taste" (37).

On the Continent, by contrast, civil society was less well developed, and thus without as elaborated a defense as that provided by British moral philosophy. That it existed at all, however, raised the same question of the harmonizing principles of the social order which stimulated the discourse of moral philosophy in England; but Continental absolutism called for the elaboration of a corresponding discursive form—*Polizeiwissenschaft,* what Caygill calls the "theory of the police-state." This theoretical tradition culminates in Hegel's philosophical system, wherein the concept of civil society is first clearly formulated (in *The Philosophy of Right*) and where it is opposed to the state—for Hegel the ultimate and legitimate source of the power to order society. At an earlier moment in the history of this theory, the logic of the social order could be expressed analogically as the relation of a higher to a lower faculty, in Baumgarten's seminal formulation the faculty of the "aesthetic." Such a faculty had its own logic or "science," but it was strictly inferior; it was not privileged in the peculiar way in which British moral philosophy privileged the concept of taste.

From this point on, we will not be concerned to record the permutations of the debate within British moral philosophy, or between British and Continental theories. We will follow instead one aspect of the problem: the specificity of the domain of practice to which both "taste" and the "aesthetic" refer. For civil society was not only the sector of relatively autonomous economic competition, but also the site of new forms of *cultural* production. The theory of taste (or the aesthetic) could thus be nurtured by the emergence of relatively new cultural producers, whose products were exchanged on the market, and who were thus "professionalized" rather than patronized. The theory of civil society remained incomplete so long as it did not give an account of the coterminous domain of the cultural (it was this defect, for example, which Gramsci's concept of "hegemony" finally attempted to address at the level of theory, just by way of reviving the problem of "civil society"). Moral philosophy was hardly prepared in its time to articulate a theory of the relation between the realm of culture and the realm of the economic, especially as it had no concept of class upon which to base such an articulation. It could, however, regard the cultivation of taste in the cultural domain as a means of checking the greed and social irresponsibility which were historically associated with "luxury," with uncontrolled consumption. The discipline of taste was to take the place of the long since abrogated sumptuary laws of feudal society, but without inhibiting the expansion of the commerce and industry upon which the nation depended. Here Caygill cites an exemplary statement of this position by Lord Kames:

> To promote the Fine Arts in Britain, has become of greater importance than is generally imagined. A flourishing commerce begets opulence; and opulence, inflaming our appetite for pleasure, is commonly vented on luxury, and on every sensual gratification: selfishness rears its head; becomes fashionable; and infecting all ranks, extinguishes the *amor patriae,* and every spark of public spirit. To prevent or retard such fatal corruption, the genius of an Alfred cannot devise any means more efficacious, than the venting opulence upon the Fine Arts; riches employ'd, instead of encouraging vice, will excite virtue. Of this happy effect Ancient Greece furnishes one shining instance; and why should we despair of another in Britain? (65)

The concept of "Fine Arts" already signals a vertical division of the field of cultural production, but what principle disposed the objects of art within this hierarchy? The uneasiness of the first consumer society with the lack of any systematic regulation of consumption produced as its end result a very curious new object: what we call the "work of art." Acknowledging the novelty of this object does not require us to deny the existence of poems or paintings before the eighteenth century, but rather to measure the effect of generalized commodity exchange on the discursive classification of objects, as well as on the practice of producing them. The "work of art" at the beginning of the eighteenth century is as yet any made thing, but as Adam Smith's tale of the manufacture of the pin in *The Wealth of Nations* reveals, there emerged in the course of the century, as a result of an increasingly complex "division of labor," marvelous new ways to make things. If the faculty of taste was to be exercised in the domain of consumption, it might proceed first to exclude from the objects presented to judgment the large category of objects which did not fall within the category of the "Fine Arts." Nevertheless such a sharp distinction was troubled by the production at its border of objects which shared some features of both categories:

On the one side, for example, novels and prints, which could mimic aspects of manufacture for the general population; and on the other, commodities of manifest utility which yet incorporated elements of design borrowed from the Fine Arts (Wedgwood china, or Chippendale furniture).[22] It was the apparent continuum of production, then, which required the exercise of taste, or a faculty of "discrimination" in the realm of consumption. Production and consumption proved to be the recto and verso of civil society, and a claim for civil society's autonomy in the sphere of the economic required a similar claim on behalf of cultural production. This claim took the form characteristically of a defense of a faculty of taste that was not "legislated," but which nevertheless obeyed an inexplicit law, a "je ne sais quoi."

The problem of the relation between production and consumption gives rise in this specific historical context to what Barbara Herrnstein Smith calls the "double discourse of value," a phrase which we may now give its proper due by emphasizing the word *discourse*. We need not deny that casual contrasts between the ethos of the market and the ethos proper to other social realms were always capable of being asserted; it is rather that such contrasts could now be worked up into distinct discourses. Moral philosophy could thus generate as the by-product of a double discourse of value an ontology of objects, a distinction between objects on the basis of whether they were directed to the end of utility (the commodity, the object of craft) or to the end of contemplation (the work of art). As obvious as this distinction may seem to us, it was by no means easy to formulate. For example, it was possible for Hume to propose a theoretical explanation of the sensation of "beauty" in his *Treatise of Human Nature* without making any ontological distinction at all between the kinds of objects produced by human "art." Thus he could derive the sensation of beauty directly from the perception of utility, which he saw as the source of "approbation" or pleasure common to all made objects. If this seems, after Kant, to be perverse, or after Barbara Herrnstein Smith, to be prescient, we can orient ourselves historically by recognizing that Hume not unreasonably assumed a continuum of production/consumption in which all made objects were alike in counting as "wealth." Hume looked at all objects from the point of view of those who possessed (or consumed) them, as a means to the end of gratification (of whatever kind), and in that sense all objects of production, even "works of art," were obviously commodities:

> What remains, therefore, but to conclude, that as riches are desired for ourselves only as the means of gratifying our appetites, either at present or in some imaginary future period, they beget esteem in others merely from their having that influence. This

indeed is their very nature or essence: they have a direct reference to the commodities, conveniences, and pleasures of life.[23]

This quotation from the *Enquiries* already points to what will become for
Hume the major complication in his conception of beauty: The pleasure of
the object is dependent upon its possession. Hume's theory of sympathy,
which Adam Smith picks up and revises, springs directly from this problem, and it attempts to answer the question of why objects of beauty (or
utility) are admired by those who do not own them, and who have no way
of using them for gratifying the "pleasures of life." In the *Treatise* Hume
incorporates what might otherwise be regarded as "disinterested" consumption into his utilitarian theory:

> The observation of convenience gives pleasure, since conve-
> nience is a beauty. But after what manner does it give pleasure?
> Tis certain our own interest is not in the least concern'd; and as
> this is a beauty of interest, not of form, so to speak, it must de-
> light us by communication, and by our sympathizing with the
> proprietor of the lodging. We enter into his interest by the force
> of imagination, and feel the same satisfaction, that the objects
> naturally occasion to him.
>
> This observation extends to tables, chairs, scritoires, chim-
> neys, coaches, sadles, ploughs, and indeed to every work of art,
> it being an universal rule, that their beauty is chiefly deriv'd
> from their utility, and from their fitness for that purpose, to
> which they are destined. But this is an advantage, that concerns
> only the owner, nor is there any thing but sympathy, which can
> interest the spectator.[24]

Caygill points out that the logic of Hume's theory "falters when it specifies
the beauty and utility of those peculiar objects which form the fine arts"
(72). In "The Standard of Taste," the very text so definitively refuted by
Herrnstein Smith, we find Hume arguing what looks like a version of
Smith's own very contemporary utilitarianism: "Every work of art [Hume
means here the *fine* arts] has also a certain end or purpose, for which it is
calculated, and is to be deemed more or less perfect, as it is fitted to attain
that end."[25] The specification of the end, however, is not as easy as in the
case of "tables, chairs, scritoires." In order to maintain the reduction of
beauty to utility, and thus the continuum of production, Hume has to imply, without actually elaborating, a concept of what Caygill calls "reflected
utility," a pleasure in consumption which more resembles the pleasure of
contemplating the beautiful objects of the rich man than it does the plea-

sure of possessing those objects. Because "The Standard of Taste" does not elaborate its concept of utility with specific reference to the work of art, it rather seems to contradict than to confirm the arguments of the *Treatise* and the *Enquiries*.

Even assuming a continuum of production, where no distinction is made between the commodity and the work of art, the concept of utility implies for Hume not a corresponding continuum of consumption, but two discontinuous modes of consumption: an immediate and a deferred or "reflected" utility. At some point it will be possible to correlate that distinction with the difference between the parcelized production of the industrial division of labor and the solitary production of the artist. But since the products of both kinds of labor were exchanged in the market as "wealth," it was in fact not easy to grasp the distinction which seems so obvious to us. Indeed, too obvious a distinction between the work of art and the commodity would have undermined the basis for an *aesthetic* of the social order: it was *production in general* which needed to be analogized to the harmony of a painting or a poem. Moral philosophy undertook to account for, and to justify, an undifferentiated realm of production, whose increasing division of labor was believed to be responsible for the nation's wealth, its "immense accumulation of commodities." When Adam Smith took up Hume's tenuous distinction between an immediate and a deferred utility, he did not go on to analogize the social order to the work of *fine* art, with its principle of deferred utility. On the contrary, he moved in another direction, deriving the beauty of the social order, the harmony of its unlegislated production, from a beauty he attributed directly to the *commodity*. Hence it was important for him to concede in *The Theory of Moral Sentiments* the Humean reduction of beauty to utility: "That utility is one of the principal sources of beauty has been observed by every body, who has considered with any attention what constitutes the nature of beauty."[26] The distinction of his theory—which Smith thought was his "original" idea but which we can see as more or less determined by the tendency of moral philosophy—emerges with his fuller analysis of what it is in the object that induces a desire for it. For Smith it is not simply or even primarily the end of consumption per se, but the degree and manner of the object's *fitness* for its end, a quality which elicits both admiration and discrimination:

> But that this fitness, this happy contrivance of any production of art, should often be more valued, than the very end for which it was intended: and that the exact adjustment of the means for attaining any conveniency or pleasure, should frequently be more regarded, than that very conveniency or plea-

sure, in the attainment of which their whole merit would seem
to consist, has not, so far as I know, been yet taken notice of by
any body. (179–180)

Smith does not concern himself with the distinction between works of art
and commodities, but rather points to a distinction internal to the commodity itself, a distinction between its being as means (its "beauty") and its
being as end (its use). In the following paragraphs of this chapter he defends
the theoretical need for what may seem a rather strained distinction by offering the distinction as the reason why, in the real world, the desire for the
object exceeds the gratification supplied by its use. If this were not the case,
no economy would develop beyond the level of production requisite for satisfying the minimal needs of human existence. Commodities are attractive,
then, not simply because they can be used to satisfy needs, but because they
possess an aesthetic dimension, because their "fitness" to use can be admired. In this way Smith finds in the *aesthetic disposition itself* the motor of
the economy:

> If we consider the real satisfaction which all these things are ca-
> pable of affording, by itself and separated from the beauty of
> that arrangement which is fitted to promote it, it will always
> appear in the highest degree contemptible and trifling. But we
> rarely view it in this abstract and philosophical light. We natu-
> rally confound it in our imagination with the order, the regular
> and harmonious movement of the system, the machine or
> oeconomy by means of which it is produced. The pleasures of
> wealth and greatness, when considered in this complex view,
> strike the imagination as something grand and beautiful and
> noble, of which the attainment is well worth all the toil and
> anxiety which we are so apt to bestow upon it.
>   And it is well that nature imposes upon us in this manner. It
> is this deception which rouses and keeps in continual motion
> the industry of mankind. It is this which first prompted them to
> cultivate the ground, to build houses, to found cities and com-
> monwealths, and to invent and improve all the sciences and
> arts. . . . (183)

If the aesthetic disposition is the motor of economic production, we should
not be surprised that an economy so organized should come to resemble
the very "beauty" of the *commodity,* in that everything in it aspires to the
condition of being "fit" to the end of satisfying desire: "We take pleasure in
beholding the perfection of so beautiful and grand a system. . . . " Smith

thus finds in the surplus "beauty" of the commodity over its actual use the source of the *social surplus,* the explanation of "wealth." And it is in this context that he can introduce what will later become the crucial trope of economic liberalism, the "invisible hand":

> The rich only select from the heap what is most precious and agreeable. They consume little more than the poor, and in spite of their natural selfishness and rapacity, though they mean only their own conveniency, though the sole end which they propose from the labours of all the thousands they employ, be the gratification of their own vain and insatiable desires, they divide with the poor the produce of all their improvements. They are led by an invisible hand to make nearly the same distribution of the necessaries of life, which would have been made, had the earth been divided into equal portions among all its inhabitants. . . . (184–85)

We will not have much difficulty in exposing the trick performed by the "invisible hand," since it is the oldest trick of "bourgeois ideology," and its secret has long since been published. Caygill observes in his closest approach to a Marxian ideology-critique that what Smith's account of the harmony of the social order hides from view is the "violence of production," the fact that the producers of commodities are not the entrepreneurs whose aestheticized cupidity motivates production but wage-laborers: "Yet the goods on which the virtuous circulation of civil society depends cost effort to produce, and were the source of conflict, but this conflict is relegated from civil society" (101). The "invisible hand" is really the multitude of invisible hands, the wage-laborers of manufacture, who were excluded as a group or class from the domain of aesthetic consumption or "taste." Caygill's persuasive hypothesis is that moral philosophy's problem of reconciling public good and private interest was "resolved" with Smith's invention of political economy as the discourse describing the "proportion of production and consumption," a harmony between the realm of production and the realm of need or desire. The internal division of the commodity into its aspect of beauty and its aspect of use was essential to this project, because it preemptively assimilated the distinction between the work of art and the commodity into the definition of the latter. It also firmly located the stimulus to production in the realm of consumption, thus attributing to all productive labor the motive of a consumption modeled on the reception of the fine arts rather than on the real motive of wage-labor, the motive of survival.

Yet the emergence of the "fine arts" as categorically distinct from other sorts of commodities complicated from the beginning the marriage of aesthetics to a defense of the socioeconomic order, because it exposed the discontinuum of production as the basis for the exercise of taste. The division of labor, the employment of wage-labor, vastly increased the accumulation of commodities, but it did not necessarily increase their fineness; it rather exposed the apparent aesthetic inferiority of commodities to works of art. Hence the qualitative distinction between the work of art and the commodity could be coordinated with class distinction as the distinction between taste and the lack of it. This, despite the fact that the new capitalist class emerged with the institution of a system of generalized commodity production. The theory which justified the social order by asserting the proportion of production to consumption proved inadequate for the purposes of class distinction. This contradiction ultimately assured the divorce of aesthetics from political economy or, rather, their precipitation as distinct discourses. Aesthetics could be developed in Adam Smith's writing, then, as a theory of consumption, but a consumption whose object was the commodity conceived as a "work of art." Political economy would soon enough have no need to theorize any object of consumption other than the commodity conceived under the aspect of utility, and therefore no need for an alliance with aesthetics.

The defense of the *harmony* of the social order was conducted by Adam Smith (as ever since) on the terrain of consumption, by arguing that production is driven by the desire to consume, and "fits" itself to that desire. In that sense, "neoclassical" economics, the economics of utility theory, or supply and demand, simply returns to this more explicit ideological agenda of classical political economy (newly armed, of course, with a "scientific" methodology).[27] Eighteenth-century discourse, however, was as yet incapable of such thorough self-deception, and hence it had to confront the fact that the theory of the proportion of production and consumption was inadequate to account for the most fundamental phenomenon of economic life, fluctuations in exchange value or price. As Caygill points out, proportion had to manifest itself in the marketplace, in the exchange relation. That relation was supposed to be structured according to a "logic of equivalence" (Baudrillard's term): the labor expended in the production of an object was supposed to be exchanged for an equal quantum of objectified labor, through the medium of the universal equivalent, money. The proportion of production to consumption had to be expressed in the exchange value of the commodity, which was supposed to express *both* the labor entailed in the commodity's production *and* the desire provoked in the consumer for the "use" of that commodity. But are these really commensurable phenomena? Can labor and desire really be expressed in the market by a *single* quantum, the money-price or "exchange value"? It was precisely in the context of exchange that the aesthetic theory of Smith's *Theory of Moral Sentiments* was brought up short, by failing to produce a *theory of value* that explained the phenomenon of market price. The desire for commodities might indeed explain the entrepreneurial drive to produce (in order to sell, in order to buy), but when the commodities produced arrived in the market, their surplus of beauty over use failed to yield a formula for the determination of their price, their exchange value. In order to arrive at a quantum for the latter value, Smith and his contemporaries were forced to shift their analysis to the terrain of production, and thus to account for the exchange value of a commodity by reference to the quantum of labor it embodied (or in Smith's variant of the "labor theory of value," the "cost of production"). Whatever happened in the realm of consumption was thus bracketed as irrelevant to the determination of price.

Caygill suggests that the quantity of labor, as Smith's "real measure of the exchangeable value of all commodities," functions in Smith as "an analogue of the standard of taste" (95). The choice of the term "analogue" is very precise here. Caygill does not speak of an "identity," and neither does Smith. To recur to Smith's own example of diamonds and water, we can say that in the case of the diamond the surplus of beauty over use approaches the infinite, in the sense that the diamond can suggest fairly explicitly the "beauty" of the commodity without also being a "work of art." Since the diamond stops short of being an object of "fine" art, its exchange value in the market will not be determined solely by its beauty but more obviously by the cost of its production (this is sometimes confused with "rarity," but the latter in fact indexes the difficulty of production). It is as though, in the determination of exchange value, the "standard of taste" were ideally an irrelevant consideration, even though it continues to function in the context of consumption to explain the desire that stimulates production itself. The circuit of production-exchange-consumption is never closed, then, and what emerges in the market is a disproportion between production and consumption rather than a proportion, the failure of the money equivalent to express both the labor embodied in a commodity and the desire of the consumer for that commodity. This disproportion is spectacularly evident in the case of the actual work of art, before which the labor theory of value disqualifies itself. Thus Ricardo:

> There are some commodities, the value of which is determined by their scarcity alone. No labor can increase the quantity of such goods, and therefore their value cannot be lowered by an increased supply. Some rare statues and pictures, scarce books

and coins, wines of a peculiar quality, which can be made only from grapes grown on particular soil, of which there is a very limited quantity, are of this description. Their value is wholly independent of the quantity of labour originally necessary to produce them, and varies with the varying wealth and inclinations of those who are desirous to possess them. (*Principles*, 6)

Political economy thenceforth will concern itself *only* with explaining the mechanism determining the price of objects produced within the system of generalized commodity production, or the division of labor.

If we were to ask then, how the work of art comes to be excluded from the discourse for which it initially provided a conceptual paradigm, a continuous analogy, the answer lies in the dialectical development of eighteenth-century moral philosophical discourse. Aesthetics and political economy were never closer than in Adam Smith's work, since they were *conjoined in the concept of the commodity;* but their convergence is immediately the occasion of their definitive separation. For Smith cannot after all explain the exchange value of a commodity solely by reference to the aestheticized concept of utility proposed in the *Theory of Moral Sentiments;* thus in *The Wealth of Nations* he must put forward a theory of value grounded in the pole of production. That theory can never find its way back to, or include within its formula for price, the "beauty" of the commodity. In order to reestablish the proportion of production and consumption, political economy must invent the concept of "use value," on the *analogy* of "exchange value." Casting its lot with an anthropology of needs, it has to forget the aesthetic theory which posited the surplus of beauty over use as the motor of production, as the engine of social life. The theory of taste becomes irrelevant to political economy, and the "invisible hand" can be reconceived, as it already is in *The Wealth of Nations,* in terms that sound more like Mandeville than like the Smith of the *Theory of Moral Sentiments:*

> By preferring the support of domestick to that of foreign industry, he intends only his own security; and by directing that industry in such a manner as its produce may be of the greatest value, he intends only his own gain, and he is in this, as in many other cases, led by an invisible hand to promote an end which was no part of his intention. Nor is it always the worse for the society that it was no part of it. By pursuing his own interest he frequently promotes that of the society more effectually than when he really intends to promote it. (456)

The conspicuous absence of the aesthetic analogy from this later invocation of the invisible hand argues for the following conclusion: The disproportion of production and consumption, which Caygill so brilliantly unearths in the texts of moral philosophy, is without question the origin of Herrnstein Smith's "double discourse of value." But the archaeology of that double discourse also unearths the largest aporia of social analysis: the problem of the relation between the economic and the cultural (a problem we know in many forms). For just as bourgeois political economists found it necessary to discard aesthetics, in order to make sense of the system of production and exchange, so did the bourgeoisie find it necessary to take up a "pure" aesthetics supposedly uncontaminated by economic considerations, in order to distinguish itself *culturally* from the class which produced what it consumed.

The failure to construct a theory of the harmonious relation between a continuum of production and a continuum of consumption marks the point of the irrevocable disengagement of political economy from aesthetic questions, and thus its emergence as a separate discourse. Aesthetics, on the other hand, continues to name a set of questions or a subdiscourse within the larger discourse of philosophy, from which it had no reason to detach itself, and never did. Nevertheless it still betrays its·consanguinity with political economy in several important respects: Once aesthetics has ceded to political economy the defense of the rationality of the social order (in the form usually of "equilibrium" theory, the theoretical grail of the neoclassical economist), it need no longer assume that all man-made objects are by definition "works of art," and it can define the "work of art" as distinct from both "craft" objects and the commodity. It then proceeds to analyze this object as though it had always existed, but it can only make such an assumption by *forgetting* political economy, by forgetting the fact that the "fine arts" emerged as such in contradistinction to commodities of immediate utility, or commodities as such. This distinction must be continuously reimposed upon the domain of production, in response to the fact that works of art continue to be exchanged in the marketplace as commodities which are commensurable with other commodities. The eventual transformation of the problem of taste or aesthetic judgment into the problem of aesthetic *value* sediments this sequence of historical determinations. A concept of specifically aesthetic value can be formulated only in the wake of political economy's discourse of exchange value. The immense pressure of that adjacent discourse eventually renders archaic the defining concepts of eighteenth-century aesthetics—concepts such as the "standard of taste"—and imposes upon later aesthetic theory the necessity of rephrasing the problem of aesthetic judgment as the problem of a peculiar kind of "value." This is why we were justified in raising the issue of anachronism in connection with arguments such as Tony Bennett's or Barbara Herrnstein Smith's: It is too easy to refute Hume or Kant as though their problem of *taste* were simply identical to our problem of aesthetic *value*. By ignoring the specificity of these terms, we lose sight of the historical moment when the "standard of taste" moved into analogical relation to the "measure of value." The moment of analogical correspondence effected, so to speak, a reversal of the charges between the discourses of aesthetics and political economy. Where, before the advent of Adam Smith's political economy, the harmony of the economic order could be analogized to the beauty of the work of art, subsequently it becomes possible and even necessary to reconceive aesthetic judgment by *analogy to exchange value*. The very concept of aesthetic *value* betrays the continued pressure of economic discourse on the language of aesthetics. Of course aesthetics immediately reasserted, against the universality of economic commensurability, a theory of the incommensurability of aesthetic and economic values, on the basis of the inutility of the aesthetic object. In that sense aesthetics learns to forget political economy just as political economy forgot aesthetics. This mutual forgetting constitutes aesthetics and political economy as antithetical discourses, which between them divide the world of cultural production into works of art and commodities.

The Absolute Commensurability of Everything

Kant's relation to the economic in *The Critique of Judgment* is worth remarking here, since the very complexity of his text is in part the result of a rigorous attempt to move aesthetic theory beyond the problematic which had allied it to political economy. *The Critique of Judgment*, as is well known, incorporated the topos of the inutility of the aesthetic—the famous "purposiveness without purpose"—into a systematic meditation on the faculty of judgment. The latter is conceived by Kant as the site of a possible solution to the long-standing problem in moral philosophy of the relation between the sensible and the intelligible; but the level of philosophical abstraction to which the Kantian critique raised the discourse of moral philosophy also had the effect of somewhat distancing the problems of the social order that moral philosophy had addressed directly. These problems now become the unexpressed referents of the philosophical system. Kant takes up the relation between the sensible and the intelligible by claiming that the judgment of taste is without recourse to the "concept," and hence to the intelligible, but also without "interest," not based on the gratification of the senses. Yet it has a relation to both, as it operates on the one hand "according to rule," and on the other hand as "a feeling of pleasure." Its peculiarly intermediate status is also confirmed by Kant's placement of judgment in the architecture of the critiques between understanding and reason, as the faculty conjoining both in its "free conformity to law." Caygill argues that the unifying project of the third critique could be carried through only as far as demonstrating that judgment appears as a contradictory faculty, or an "aporia." This is a consequence of its claim to a "subjective universality" which can be deduced neither a priori nor empirically, but only from a "feeling of pleasure" (27). Caygill rightly aligns the aporia of judgment with the disproportion of production and consumption, but it is not immediately apparent how the categories of production and consumption are translated into the language of the *Critique*. I would argue that the alignment to which Caygill points is evinced most convincingly by Kant's consistent preference for natural beauty over the beauty of the work of art, a preference which seems to have been determined in part by an attempt to displace the aesthetic as far as possible from the domain of manufacture.

In his brief discussion of the work of art in the "Analytic of the Sublime," Kant finds it very difficult to reconcile such an object with the principle of "purposiveness without purpose," primarily because the work of art is "directed designedly to our satisfaction" (144). Its purposiveness is still too possessed of a manifest purpose, unlike the natural object, whose purposiveness never discloses its purpose. Kant nevertheless goes on to distinguish the work of art from other objects of "handicraft" [*Handwerk*] precisely on the basis of the peculiar kind of purposiveness without purpose the work of fine art does possess: Art is purposive "in play," but the purpose of handicraft is "imposed upon one as work, i.e. as occupation which is unpleasant (a trouble) in itself and which is only attractive on account of its effect (e.g. the wage)" (146). What removes the commodity (and what other object is at issue here?) from the realm of the aesthetic is the fact which political economy was never disposed to consider, the real unfreedom of wage-labor, its coercion in the domain of production. This moment of rigor is not without consequence in Kant's theory, since the work of art, too, never quite loses the stigma of the "compulsory," and can only efface that stigma and distinguish itself from the commodity if its production is "removed from all constraint, and . . . change[d] from . . . work into mere play" (147). In short, the production of art must be removed from the arena of production altogether, on the face of it an impossibility. Such an impossible "work" will resemble a work of nature: "Nature is beautiful because it looks like art, and art can only be called beautiful if we are conscious of it as art while yet it looks like nature" (149). The Kantian aesthetic is very pure indeed, since it reinstates a proportion of production and consumption in the sphere of the aesthetic alone, and by the radical means of displacing the locus of that proportion to the subject's encounter with natural beauty, where the subject *produces* the very beauty it also simultaneously consumes. This beauty never passes through the market, and can never be assigned a value in exchange, because it is a form of production which is not "work." Kant cannot entirely forget, when he turns to works of art, that—as with commodities—some produce and others consume. If later aesthetic theory *can* forget this fact, and appropriate Kantian aesthetics as an aesthetics of the disinterested contemplation of the work of art, it can do this by taking the only way out of this impasse offered by Kant, by assimilating the work of art to a mystified and quasi-natural realm of production which always projects as its antithesis the production of commodities. The realm of work as "play" is thus strictly analogous to *natural* production (this gives Kant the basis for a theory of "genius"). If works of art still exchange in the market as a peculiar kind of commodity, this traffic can henceforth be deplored as the "commodification" of the work of art.

Since we have glanced briefly at the consequences for aesthetics of the sequence of events leading up to the separation at birth of aesthetics and political economy, it will be appropriate to consider, also briefly, the consequences for political economy. The purging of the aesthetic analogy from political economy entails likewise a conception of the commodity as the antithesis of the work of art. Hence, while political economy continues to seek in its own terms the proportion of production and consumption on the basis of the supposed tendency of the economy toward "equilibrium," it also continues to depend upon the concept of utility or "use value" to supplement a purely economic account of the relation of consumption to production. Even Marx's critique of political economy discovers no alternative to the anthropology of need, and it thus remains vulnerable to the more radical Baudrillardian critique.

Marx's comments on consumption are infrequent, but quite relevant in this context. The most interesting occur in the introduction to the *Grundrisse*, which takes up the systemic relations between "production, distribution, exchange, and consumption."[28] If Kant succeeds in establishing the proportion of production to consumption only by removing the work of art from the realm of economic production, Marx tacks in the opposite direction (but entirely in accord with the presuppositions of political economy) when he concedes that consumption "actually belongs outside economics except in so far as it reacts in turn upon the point of departure [production] and initiates the whole process anew" (89). In other words, consumption has to be a very simple activity in order to be represented within the system of political economy, which remains silent about what happens there, except to call it "use." Thus defined, the relations of production and consumption appear entirely circular, a *hyperproportionality:* Production is "immediately consumption" in that it consumes in order to produce, and consumption is "immediately production" in that "without consumption, no production." However, when Marx amplifies the latter formula—"consumption ideally posits the object of production as an internal image, as a need, as a drive and as a purpose"—he is clearly thinking of *new* commodities which must somehow be introduced into the steady-state of production-consumption. The very amplification of terms—image, need, drive, purpose—evokes the economy as an expanding spiral rather than a closed cycle. In order not to locate the mechanism of that expansion outside the realm of the *economic,* Marx is forced to refind within the system relating production to consumption an aesthetic aspect of the commodity. This will turn out to be the capacity of the commodity-object to create a need for itself in the absence of the consumer's prior experience of that need:

> Hunger is hunger, but the hunger gratified by cooked meat eaten with a knife and fork is different hunger from that which bolts down raw meat with the aid of hand, nail and tooth. Production thus produces not only the object but also the manner of consumption, not only objectively but subjectively. Production thus creates the consumer. . . . Production not only supplies a material for the need, but also supplies a need for the material. . . . The need which consumption feels for the object is created by the perception of it. The object of art—like every other product—creates a public which is sensitive to art and enjoys beauty. Production thus not only creates an object for the subject, but also a subject for the object. (92)

What reappears in this passage is of course the aesthetic analogy; but its reappearance is perhaps only the sign of the largest unresolved problem in social theory, the problem of the relation between the economic and the cultural. It is difficult to see what follows in Marx from his comments in the Introduction, although we can easily recognize in them an anticipation of Baudrillard's "ideological genesis of needs." The passage has also been claimed as an exemplary instance of self-deconstruction: Gregory Jay, for example, argues that Marx's analysis here "threatens to render the concepts and systems of political economy undecidable" as a consequence of failing to distinguish production from consumption, or subject from object.[29] In preemptive response to such a conclusion Marx appears to reassert the thesis that "production, distribution, exchange, and consumption . . . all form the members of a totality, distinctions within a unity." If that unity is so unconvincing—and it is—what does the disunity of economic discourse mean? It would be amusing indeed if political economy were really "deconstructed" in these few sentences—no need for *Capital!*—but the passage hardly bears such a reading. Marx is quite explicit in arguing that within the "unity" of the economic, the relation between production and consumption is quite decidable: production "produces consumption" (92). It is this asymmetry or *disproportion* which calls up from the prehistory of political economy the analogy of the work of art, as an example of the object's capacity to produce a need in the consumer that did not exist before. In that sense, Marx only acknowledges what the producers themselves had already realized, that consumption must be brought under the control of the productive apparatus (the project of the nascent advertising industry).

The "object of art" stands for what is momentarily in excess of present need—namely, desire—even if that desire can immediately be experienced as need (and what desire is not?). Marx resorts to the aesthetic analogy in order to maintain the priority of production: "production is the real point of departure, and hence also the predominant moment" (94). This account of the economic still excludes from consideration everything in the realm of consumption that will interest Simmel, Veblen, Baudrillard, or Bourdieu, everything that occurs at the level of symbolic struggles for distinction. The disproportion of production and consumption thus confirms the fact that political economy cannot give a systemic account of the system of production-exchange-consumption even in its own terms, without reluctantly attributing to the commodity what it *actually* possesses, an "aesthetic" aspect. In that sense the antithetical distinction between the work of art and the commodity names a real condition of social life which cannot be theorized away by conflating the two concepts. Commodities are works of art and works of art are commodities, but that is to say that both concepts are necessary to define both objects: The work of art is a certain *kind* of commodity. The commodity is a certain *kind* of work of art.

A few pages after the passage just quoted, the argument derails and comes to an abrupt halt in attempting to elaborate some very sketchy notes on the problem of art. This accident is worth replaying in slow motion, beginning with the moment of derailment:

> *The uneven development of material production relative to e.g. artistic development.* In general, the concept of progress not to be conceived in the usual abstractness. Modern art etc. This disproportion not as important or so difficult to grasp as within practical-social relations themselves. (109)

The work of art names a certain "disproportion" between the economy and the realm of cultural production, a disproportion entirely incompatible with the economism sometimes attributed to Marx and Marxism. If this rather dangerous note can then be expanded in another longer postscript into a meditation on the question of why the "flowering" of the arts in certain periods (the Greek, for example) is "out of all proportion to the general development of society," we can read this question as the theoretical problem of "disproportion" writ large, across the whole text of history. The question of "uneven development" (I pass over Marx's famous paragraphs elaborating this point) raises at this point what looks like our very contemporary dilemma of canon formation: "But the difficulty lies not in understanding that the Greek arts and epic are bound up with certain forms of social development. The difficulty is that they still afford us artistic pleasure and that in a certain respect they count as a norm and as an unattainable model" (111). Discounting Marx's own explanation in the following paragraph for the canonicity of Greek art—Marx produces a kind of Hegelian elegy for the childlike "charm" of an art devoid of "contradiction"—we can appreciate how the juxtaposition of the work of art with the world of commodity production could bring to the surface the problem of disproportion or incommensurability as the social condition of modernity. What would it add to the statement that Greek art "continues to please" to say, as we like to say, that it continues to have *aesthetic value?* Perhaps nothing at all, so far as particular judgments are concerned, but a good deal in the sense that the language of economic commensuration is so internalized in our discourse of judgment that we can continually be surprised by the simultaneous incommensurability and commensurability of aesthetic and economic values. It would be difficult if not impossible now to think of works of art as more or less "beautiful" without abstracting from the appearance of beauty a quantum of value—"aesthetic" value; but if it were possible to think of the aesthetic without also thinking of value, we would in effect have discarded the concept of the "work of art" as we know it. For that object is by definition the embodiment of a quantum of aesthetic value. According to aesthetic theory, it will ideally consist of nothing but the aesthetic essence, refined to the highest degree of purity by its extraction from the commodity-ore. When Marx finds in Greek art the essence of this essence, he is forced to describe Greek art as without "contradiction," and thus to name by negation the social condition—contradiction, disproportion—which gives rise to the category of object called the "work of art."

Because the commensurability or "commodification" of all objects is for us the inescapable horizon of social life, every discourse of judgment must now represent its object as the expression of a "value." The premise of our social life is the absolute commensurability of everything. The language of judgment has been transformed into the discourse of "value-judgments," a discourse which then raises as a perennial problem the relation between "economic" values and every other kind: religious values, moral values, family values, traditional values, patriarchal values, feminist values, liberal values, progressive values, socialist values, aesthetic values etc. Every social relation of any kind can be reified in discourse as a value, where it immediately becomes commensurable with all other values by virtue of its reified form. To return for one moment to Barbara Herrnstein Smith's critique, we can recognize the historical irony of cultural relativism's celebration of the plurality of values; for what is really being celebrated is precisely the condition of the absolute commensurability of everything:

> It appears from the present analysis, however, that just as the classic "value-form," money, operates within a market economy to commoditize (that is, to "put a price on" or assign a cash equivalence to) *everything,* so also, within the economy of the discourse of economy, *anything* that is indicated, predicated, or otherwise constituted either as a positivity within some economy or as the object of a need, desire, or interest (individual or collective) is measured, in the very moment that it is put forward as such, as so much "good". . . . (147)

By proposing the "good" as the universal equivalent, Smith collapses the "double discourse of value" into a single discourse of universal commensuration, the good as quantum. This is not so much a critique of the discourse of commensuration, as its apotheosis: the argument fails to recognize that the universalization of the "universal equivalent" of exchange value is the historical condition not of judgment in general but of the modern *discourse of value,* the discourse of universal commensuration, the commensurability of every object with every other.[30] In fact it is *only* the money-form which permits such commensuration, as it is entirely possible to conceive of different kinds of "good," of objects which need never be placed on the same scale of value, which need never be compared at all.

If it is virtually impossible now to imagine that particular objects and practices may be incommensurable, this fact goes a long way toward explaining why the pluralist or relativist discourse of value can so easily substitute for the analysis of objective social relations, and so easily confirm a very limited liberal-pluralist social agenda designed to revalue the values of dominated social groups by reasserting the cultural separation of those values. Let us sharpen this point on the hard surface of social reality: It will be easy enough to acknowledge that "races," for example, are incommensurable, because the discourse of their commensuration is called "racism." But it has been rather more difficult to counter the effects of the discourse and practice of racial commensuration with an analysis of the objective relations between races. The very extent to which the category of "race" remains a positivity in discourse (as we say, an "essence") measures the extent to which the discourse of commensuration can substitute for the analysis of social relations.[31] We may very well be incapable of overcoming the discourse of value at present, but the continued attractiveness of various forms of cultural separatism as a way of playing the social game of commensuration suggests how useful it would be to have some sense of how and why the practice of judgment could give way in a specific historical epoch to a discourse of "value judgments."

The conclusion to be drawn from this argument is not auspicious: Liberal pluralism confronts the absolutist posturing of particular discourses of value with the philosophical bad news that no metaphysical grounds exist for such posturing. The alternative to the tendential absolutism of value judgments seems obviously to be that all values are "contingent," a condition for which the variability of price in the market provides the most readily available analogy. But the fact remains that the market is the historical *condition* and not merely the proper analogy for the extension of the value-concept to all acts of judgment. The failure to recognize this fact has had the effect of making the economic analogy in recent critiques of aesthetics merely empty, an analogy that fails to represent the real complexity of economic relations, an analogy that erases the history of economic discourse. In the absence of any sense of what has been at stake historically in the emergence of political economy, the critique of value has been conducted as the most arid exercise in philosophical debate, as the choice between the two positions of relativism and absolutism. Hence the relativist critique of the absolutist position congratulates itself for having exposed the groundlessness of "absolute" values, without raising its own discourse of commensuration to the level of historical self-reflection. It is as though the critique of political economy had congratulated itself for having exposed the intrinsic worthlessness of paper money. The irrelevance of the philosophical critique to the actual circulation of values suggests that it is only in the graduate seminars that one can have the thrill of experiencing the "contingency" of value, a thrill which is produced by the very connotations of the word "contingency," its broad hint that values are merely arbitrary, that they have no ultimate determination beyond chance and circumstance. Any analysis of objective social relations will on the contrary reveal that both "values" and the discourse of value are historically *determined* as objective social facts. It is time now to replace the philosophical notion of the contingency of value with a historical account of the determination of value. From this perspective, the "objectivity" of values refers not to their supposed absolute or transcendent status, but to the objectivity of social relations. No particular social values can be transformed or superseded, then, by the declaration that *all* values are "relative," but only by transforming the social relations which are objectified in discourse as "values."

Enter Sociology: Bourdieu's Critique of the Aesthetic Disposition

> There is no way out of the game of culture.
> —BOURDIEU, *Distinction*

The "double discourse of value" is historically determined by the fact that while it is not possible for any object *not* to have a relation to the market, to the objective condition of universal commensuration, this relation cannot be defined by the simple reduction of the object (not even the commodity) to the quantum of exchange value. This point has been crucial for a sociological analysis such as Bourdieu's, since it is the basis for the distinction between material and cultural capital: "Symbolic goods are a two-faced reality, a commodity and a symbolic object: their specifically cultural value and their commercial value remain relatively independent although the economic sanction may come to reinforce their cultural consecration."[32] From this principle we may deduce the obverse proposition, that every commodity is also a "symbolic object." The latter principle follows also from the inadequacy of political economy to explain the exchange relation in its own terms. If it had been able to do so, it would not have had to inscribe the "double discourse of value" within its own terminology, in the form of the distinction between an unquantifiable "use value" and a quantified "exchange value." That political economy came to depend after Adam Smith on an implicit anthropology of needs in order to supplement its theory of exchange value suggests what price it paid when it discarded the aesthetic analogy. Despite the fact that the analogy never amounted to *more* than an analogy, it always implied that the relation between production and consumption had to be conceived as a fully social relation, involving potentially every aspect of social life, including the aesthetic. In retrospect, it seems evident that the aesthetic analogy provided a better entry into the complexity of social relations than an anthropology of human needs, especially as the truth of these relations was the *disproportion* of production and consumption. That truth could thereafter be misrecognized as the quasi-ontological distinction between the commodity and the work of art. The "two faces" of reality were turned away from one another, even though both commodities and works of art continued to exchange in the market by translation into the same universal equivalent, money.

The double discourse of value emerged as a way of assimilating the fact that exchange in the market really does function as an epitome of social relations, as everyone thought it did, but as the site of the objective disharmony of these relations, as the site of the commensuration of the incommensurable values objectified in every object. The "logic of equivalence," according to which every exchange is supposed to be an *equal* exchange, denies the crucial fact revealed in the market, that social relations do not *make sense*. The relation between the cultural and the economic cannot therefore be represented by reducing "noneconomic" values to economic values. Such a reduction would simply reinstate the proportion of production and consumption by crediting the "universal equivalent" with having accomplished its mission of adequating all objects in the market. The market is rather the place in which the struggles that take place in the domains of production (exploitation) and consumption (domination) are temporarily reified, objectified in always unequal exchanges. If the market is the omnipresent and inescapable horizon of social life, where the mirage of absolute commensurability always glitters, what this means most importantly is that the value-constitutive nature of struggle can be expressed not only at the site of exchange but in the inescapable relation of all aspects of social life to the economy.[33]

With that principle in mind we can turn finally to Bourdieu's sociology of art, with the intention of renegotiating the relation between aesthetic experience and the work of art as a form of cultural capital. To begin, we can note briefly the objection with which Bourdieu's sociology is usually confronted, that it reduces the cultural field to a reflection of the economic. Bourdieu has always emphasized, to the contrary, that the concept of cultural capital "was conceived in opposition to economism." In *Distinction,* the difference of a sociological from an economistic analysis is announced on the first page: "There is an economy of cultural goods, but it has a specific logic."[34] Even the fact of the mutual convertibility of cultural and material capital does not amount to the reduction of the former to the latter. There is no formula for such conversions, nor can there be; there is no "universal equivalent" for the adequation of cultural and material capital when the latter is *already* the order of the universal equivalent. The conversion of cultural into material capital (or vice versa) is precisely the condition of the commensuration of the incommensurable, an irresolvable social contradiction. Within this set of conditions, the relative autonomy of social fields, such as that of artistic production, generates specific logics (socio-logics) which are always in a specifically determinate relation to the economic logic of the market, the "restricted economy." For this reason, Bourdieu argues, practices within the cultural field can be said to "obey an economic logic without obeying narrowly economic interests."[35] This point is elaborated in more theoretical terms in Bourdieu's essay on "The Field of Cultural Production," where he represents that field as "the economic world reversed" at the same time that he insists on the inability of "all forms of economism, which seek to grasp the anti-economy in economic terms, to understand this upside-down world. The literary and artistic world is so ordered that those who enter it have an interest in disinterestedness."[36] To say that those who enter it have a "use" for such disinterestedness would also be true, but only in the trivial sense in which a use can be predicated of any subject's relation to any object or practice. The use of disinterestedness does not reduce disinterestedness to interest, or make disinterestedness vanish as a mere chimera. The "double discourse of value" cannot be collapsed into a single discourse, because the "specific logics" of the practices described by these discourses are different *in reality*.

Nevertheless the persistence of the charges of economism or reductionism point to what is genuinely problematic in Bourdieu's theory. The question before us now is, in the largest sense, the adequacy of a socio-logic to express the illogic of social existence. But we shall only have to address a specific version of this question: Is it possible to translate the (false) philosophical problem of "aesthetic value" into the sociological problem of "cultural capital"? I would like to propose an affirmative answer to this question, but with the qualification that the translation always has a remainder, which is nothing other than aesthetic experience. This experience is in a certain sense hypothetical, since it need never exist in a "pure" form. It is in practice always combined with other practices, and in such a way that its specificity may not be recognized discursively at all (as in the case, for example, of ritual objects or performances), or in such a way that its combination with other practices is denied (for example, in the "pure" work of art). For reasons that are entirely historical, the specificity of aesthetic experience was fully recognized only at the moment when that experience combined with another—the economic—and only in a discourse—the aesthetic—that denied this combination.

The work of art is defined from the point of view of consumption by the concept of "disinterested" or merely contemplative pleasure, and from the point of view of production by the concept of "autonomous" production. These are the elementary predicates of aesthetic discourse. The advantage of a sociological analysis of this discourse is its capacity to map the social field, and so to map the necessary conditions for such a discourse. This mapping is very efficiently accomplished by Bourdieu in perhaps his most crucial essay on cultural production, "The Market of Symbolic Goods." There he reprises a version of the narrative of cultural autonomization as follows: During the period when cultural production "progressively freed itself from aristocratic and ecclesiastical tutelage," it began to be represented as an autonomous field of production ("Market," 15). The nature of that autonomy was obviously "relative," in the sense that cultural production was from that point on increasingly subject to the impersonal forces of the market. Nevertheless the negotiation between producers and consumers proved to be much more complexly mediated by the market than by church, state, or noble patron—a mediation which was capable of being experienced as a relative measure of freedom from the direct determination of artistic forms or contents:

> By an apparent paradox, as the art market began to develop, writers and artists found themselves able to affirm the irreducibility of the work of art to the status of a simple article of merchandise and, at the same time, the singularity of the intellectual and artistic condition. . . . The emergence of the work of art as a commodity, and the appearance of a distinct category of producers of symbolic goods specifically destined for the market, to some extent prepared the ground for a pure theory of art, that is, of art as art. ("Market," 16)

Here we revisit the discontinuum of production—the distinction between the labor of artists and of wage-laborers—which is precisely echoed on the side of consumption by the emergence of a concept of "disinterested" pleasure, a mode of consumption which retroactively nominates any object so consumed as at least potentially a "work of art."

The difference of autonomous production entails a difference in the mode of consumption, then, but the latter difference is also dependent upon "objective structures that sociology apprehends in the form of probabilities of access to goods, services, and powers" (LP, 60). Initially, and to a certain extent always thereafter, the limitation of access to certain kinds of artwork (primarily work in the plastic arts) can be marked by a difference in price between such works and mass-produced commodities. This difference permits the discontinuum of consumption to be expressed in a relatively simple way through the class structure, since in ordinary circumstances only the wealthy will be capable of buying certified works of art. Nothing up to this point, of course, is either new or much in dispute. The difficulty arises with the fact that the distinction between works of art and commodities is an inherently unstable template upon which to articulate a cultural hierarchy, for all the reasons suggested in the preceding section, but also because it was difficult to fix the price of work in the *verbal* arts according to the principle of rarity that determined the price of plastic art. In addition to the fact that the cultural status of many verbal works (such as novels) was disputed, it was also the case that works in the verbal arts began to be produced and reproduced in more obviously commodified form as soon as the world of production was generally commodified. This was the burden of the eighteenth-century complaint, for example, against widely available and cheaply printed editions of the vernacular classics.[37] The status of canonical literary works as cultural capital was negotiated as though cultural capital were directly convertible into material capital, in which case works of high literary art ought to have been expensive, difficult of access. But the relation between the commodity and the work of art was not so symmetrical as that. The very autonomization of cultural production resulted in the possibility and indeed the actuality of much greater access to certain kinds of High Cultural products as a direct consequence of commodification. These cultural products included nearly all works of verbal art, but also "mechanical" reproductions of otherwise inaccessible work in the plastic arts. These products were included in what Bourdieu calls the "field of large-scale cultural production, specifically organized with a view to the production of cultural goods destined for non-producers of cultural goods, 'the public at large'" ("Market," 17). The dynamic established by this development could easily provoke among artists an adverse reaction to the demand of the market, which they could now perceive as a threat to the very autonomy the market itself had first made possible. These cultural producers seem to have acknowledged very early what Bourdieu calls their "structural domination" by the market, the fact that they had exchanged one master for another. In response to this development there emerged a "field of restricted production" in which producers saw themselves as producing for *other producers* in an imaginary space apart from market relations. It was in the interest of these producers to promote a distinct mode of consumption appropriate to the object (the work of art) whose determination by economic forces could now be denied. We live with this dynamic still because it is the dynamic *of* the work of art, of the tension between restricted and general cultural production.

What attracts Bourdieu's scrupulous attention is that the mode of consumption demanded by the products of restricted production offered to the dominant classes a more reliable means of restricting access to the work of art than the mechanism of price itself. This was a consequence of the fact that the mode of consumption appropriate to the objects of restricted production asssumed the possession of the cultural capital provided by a particular kind of *education:*

> So while consumption in the field of large-scale cultural production is more or less independent of the educational level of consumers (which is quite understandable since this system tends to adjust to the level of demand), works of restricted art owe their specifically cultural rarity to the rarity of the instruments with which they may be deciphered. This rarity is a function of the unequal distribution of the conditions underlying acquisition of the specifically aesthetic disposition and of the codes indispensable to the deciphering of works belonging to the field of restricted production. ("Market," 23)

To this concise formulation we can add the perhaps obvious corollary, that as cultural works recede into the past, they simultaneously gravitate into the realm of "restricted production" (whatever the context in which they were produced), by virtue of the fact that the knowledge required to decipher them is the cultural capital of the school. Hence the Renaissance plays and nineteenth-century novels which belonged to the field of popular culture or general production can no longer be consumed in that context, but only as High Art. The autonomy of the cultural producers is in no case absolute, since the consumption of their products is dependent upon the institutions of cultural capital which are themselves heteronomously organized by the class structure. For this reason, Bourdieu maps the field of cultural production within the larger social field as a *dominated* sector within the *dominant* class ("Field," 319).

We may now leave the artists and writers to fend for themselves and take account of how Bourdieu understands aesthetic discourse. Clearly it is in the interest of the dominant classes to cultivate an "aesthetic disposition" which endorses the conditions of restricted production. For Bourdieu this situation ensures the "incommensurability of the specifically cultural value and economic value in a work." ("Market," 22) "Disinterestedness" confirmed the autonomy of cultural production for the producers by distinguishing cultural value from economic exchange value, and in this way it could become the basis for a mode of consumption specific to the dominant classes. Bourdieu argues that acquisition of the aesthetic disposition depended upon access to the kind of knowledge possessed by the producers and was therefore relatively exclusive; and also that it permitted the dominant classes' perception of their real freedom from economic necessity to be conflated with the cultural producers' claim to have *freed themselves* from determination by the market. In *Distinction* Bourdieu does not take up the question of how the experience of aesthetic "disinterestedness" might be different for artists and for consumers of the dominant classes. The interest of these two groups in cultivating the aesthetic disposition is on the face of it rather different. But this difference is taken up elsewhere in Bourdieu's work in the context of his attempt to map the field of cultural production: There we discover that while there are *two* fields of production—the restricted (High Art) and general (cultural commodities)—there are *three* principles of legitimacy specific to these fields:

> First there is the specific principle of legitimacy, i.e. the recognition granted by the set of producers who produce for other producers, their competitors, i.e. by the autonomous, self-sufficient world of "art for art's sake," meaning art for artists. Secondly, there is the principle of legitimacy corresponding to "bourgeois" taste and to the consecration bestowed by the dominant fractions of the dominant class and by private tribunals, such as *salons*, or public, state-guaranteed ones, such as Academies, which sanction the inseparably ethical and aesthetic (and therefore political) taste of the dominant. Finally, there is the principle of legitimacy which its advocates call "popular," i.e. the consecration bestowed by the choice of ordinary consumers, the "mass audience." ("Field," 331)

Bourdieu does acknowledge here that there is a different principle of legitimacy at work for artistic producers and for the dominant consumers. This is the circumstance which will generate (eventually) the dynamic of the "avant-garde," the struggle of the cultural producers against the institutional forms of their domination: the galleries, museums, concert halls, schools, etc.[38] It has made quite a difference to the reception of Bourdieu's work, based as it is in the U.S. almost entirely on the reputation of *Distinction*, that the theme of autonomy, defining the position of the producers, is virtually absent from that text. *Distinction* takes up the question of aesthetics exclusively as a question of consumption, of the disinterested "aesthetic disposition," and thus it makes no distinction between that disposition as it is instantiated in the producers and in the dominant classes.

In this narrower context of class-based consumption, Bourdieu reads Kant's aesthetic as "the universalization of the dispositions associated with a particular social and economic condition" (493), specifically the universalization of the particular condition of freedom from economic necessity (55). While Kant (and aesthetic theory generally) is more than vulnerable to such a reading, it has the unintended effect of eliding the problem of production (noted above) in the third *Critique*. The absence of the question of production in Bourdieu's *Distinction* has the further effect, as we may now demonstrate, of making the specificity of the aesthetic experience, which Kant struggled to conceive as a mode of production, disappear altogether into the "aesthetic disposition," the mode of consumption. Let us pose, first, the question of the relation of aesthetic experience to the aesthetic disposition, before returning finally to the question of production in Bourdieu's theory.

For Bourdieu, aesthetic judgment comes in two forms: an elite aesthetic of the dominant classes, the "aesthetic disposition" proper, and a "popular" aesthetic of the dominated. These two aesthetics organize the world of cultural products into a hierarchy of cultural capitals specific to the domains of restricted and general production. In accord with the principle that "belief in the value of a work . . . is part of the reality of the work" ("Field," 317), we can say that in fact "aesthetic value" is nothing more or other than cultural capital. Even in the anomalous circumstance in which certain works or genres of lesser cultural capital—science-fiction, cartoons, popular music—are revalued (usually in an academic context) for consumption in the High mode, the effectiveness of this move in the game of evaluation depends upon the fact that these works simultaneously and transparently "appear as what they are, simple substitutes for legitimate assets" (88). The hierarchy of cultural capital is reconfirmed most especially when popular or mass art is consumed according to the High mode of consumption. The persuasiveness of this point is a particular achievement of Bourdieu's sociology. As a consequence, it may very well seem that the specific logic of the cultural field requires no other theory of the aesthetic than the theory of the "aesthetic disposition."

To say that the aesthetic disposition determines the relative cultural capital granted to any particular work is to say that the act of judgment is the assignment, or even the *recognition,* of cultural capital. Judgment is the act by which the aesthetic disposition expresses or externalizes itself, according to criteria which are relatively internalized, that is, neither capable of being fully rationalized, nor materially caused in the manner of a biological predisposition. The aesthetic disposition works just like what Bourdieu calls the "habitus," and in fact it can be said to function as an important, even crucial component of the habitus for the members of the dominant classes.[39] This is confirmed by the fact that the aesthetic disposition disposes the judgment not only of certified works of art but of all cultural productions, including simple commodities, as well as aspects of life-style. When the aesthetic disposition is forced to articulate its criteria of judgment, as it is in the interviews conducted with Bourdieu's respondents in *Distinction,* these criteria appear to be derived in a surprisingly direct way from the themes of aesthetic discourse, as though the members of the dominant classes had at least a passing familiarity with Kant. The most indispensable of these criteria is of course "disinterestedness," which is expressed initially as the quality of "deferred pleasure" (486) specific to High or legitimate art, but which is inevitably accompanied by expressions of *distaste* for lower-class or mass cultural productions which offer more immediate pleasures. Bourdieu quite rightly points to the fact that the pleasure of aesthetic judgment manifests itself curiously as a kind of unpleasure. If the pleasures of culture can then be distinguished in Kantian fashion from simpler, more immediate, pleasures—"pleasure without sensuousness" (493)—the nature of aesthetic pleasure itself is rendered entirely problematic: it seems incapable of articulating itself as anything but a pleasure either extremely attenuated in comparison to "sensuous" pleasures, or actually negative, the sense of disgust or distaste. The negative moment allows the aesthetic disposition to project as its "negative reference point" a working-class aesthetic which refers immediately to sensuous pleasure as its major criterion of judgment. But the latter pleasure is finally not *aesthetic* pleasure. It is produced rather by the agreeable contents of the work, a criterion that disallows, for example, the representation of ugly objects from being considered in any way "beautiful." It would seem, then, that at the level of the dominant aesthetic, the "pleasure" in aesthetic pleasure is ideally reduced to a zero-degree, to the experience of "distaste," while at the level of the popular aesthetic, the pleasure produced by cultural products fails to be aesthetic at all. At neither level is "aesthetic pleasure" actually experienced by anyone.

What appears in the place of aesthetic pleasure in the dominant classes is the pleasure *of distinction,* pleasure in the possession of cultural capital. Here Bourdieu cites as a convincing precedent a sentence from Marcel Proust, who describes the experience of High Culture as a peculiarly mixed or impure pleasure: "A sort of egoistic self-regard is inevitable in these mingled joys of art and erudition in which aesthetic pleasure may become more acute but not remain so pure" (499). Having cited no less a cultural authority than Proust, Bourdieu can conflate the "principle of pleasure" with the "denied experience of a social relationship of exclusion" (what Proust means by "erudition"). From the sociological point of view, the experience of any "pure" aesthetic pleasure is of no interest at all, since it can safely be assumed that no work of art can be experienced without also experiencing at the same time its status as cultural capital. But this is to say that aesthetic pleasure simply falls outside the sociological field as a merely hypothetical experience, incapable of articulation in the game of distinction, except as the pretext of the game. It is not necessary to experience aesthetic pleasure at all in order to enter this game, since judgment itself can be relegated to experts (as it is in the case of the corporate buyers of art), thus dividing the labor of consumption into the certification of cultural capital (by the critics) and its appropriation (by the collectors).

In the same way a certain muteness of aesthetic pleasure afflicts the popular aesthetic, in that the pleasure of popular cultural productions cannot, as Bourdieu demonstrates, easily be articulated as aesthetic, but is immediately conflated with pleasures associated with the objects represented. If the dominant aesthetic disposition knows only the "mingled joys of art and erudition," does this mean that within the dominated classes there is no experience that might be described as "mingled joys of art and *sensuousness*"? What Proust means by "impure" does not necessarily imply that in the mingled joys of art and erudition, or art and sensuousness, the pleasures of erudition and the pleasures of sensuousness always cancel out the pleasures of art.

This problem appears again in the second major criterion of judgment internalized in the aesthetic disposition of the dominant classes: the valorization of form over content. Here too it is a conventional topos of aesthetic discourse which is elicited by the interviews, a response to what the respondents *suppose* to be the legitimate criteria of aesthetic judgment. And again the respondents produce a kind of parody of their own discourse by insisting upon a reductio ad absurdum of aesthetic topoi—in the case of the dominant classes, the evacuation of content; in the case of the dominated, the rejection of form:

> The result [of the popular aesthetic] is a systematic "reduction" of the things of art to the things of life, a bracketing of form in favor of "human" content, which is barbarism par excellence from the standpoint of the pure aesthetic. Everything takes place as if the emphasis on form could only be achieved by means of a neutralization of any kind of affective or ethical interest in the object of representation which accompanies (without any necessary cause-effect relation) mastery of the means of grasping the distinctive properties which this particular form takes on in its relations with other forms (i.e., through reference to the universe of works of art and its history). (44)

The aesthetic disposition tends inevitably toward "aestheticism," as the ideal absence of content. There is indeed no question that aesthetic *discourse* makes available the conceptual antinomies which become internalized in the habitus of either class, where these dispositions have real social consequences. The moment of polarization, the mutual exclusion of form and content, betrays a certain inarticulateness of the aesthetic. However, it might be possible (indeed, necessary) to construct the relation of form and content as something other than a binary opposition. Adorno reminds us in *Aesthetic Theory* that it is merely a banal truth that there is no form without content, which is to say that form must refer to the relation between particular contents. It is difficult, then, to know what could logically be meant by the primacy of form over content (Adorno calls this a "pernicious equivocation"), since pure form, in the absence of the contents related, would be relations between nothing at all.[40] This formulation does not of course clear up the problem of form and content; it only correctly states the problem.

In practice, forms themselves can be objectified as contents, and brought into relation to other objectified relations. This is the sense in which certain conspicuously formalist or aestheticist works of art can take preexistent formal strategies as contents, something which all cultural products do to a certain extent anyway (consider the evolution of automobile design), and which produces the illusion of an immanent history of aesthetic objects. More importantly for Bourdieu, the same objectifications of the formal relations of contents can be fetishized by the aesthetic disposition as *pure* form. This is the sense in which one learns in school to distinguish Baroque from Classical styles of music, or Impressionist from post-Impressionist painting, without inquiring into how these forms bring their contents into relation. The fetishizing of such objectified formal relations (Bourdieu speaks consistently of aesthetic judgment as a "fetishization") effectively suppresses their specificity as relations of contents, which specificity we may designate as the specificity of the aesthetic. In that sense, the aesthetic disposition tends to recognize objectified (that is, culturally certified) forms, but not aesthetic experience itself, which falls silent before the monuments of culture. Conversely, the popular aesthetic's fetishizing of contents accomplishes the same silencing of aesthetic experience by the more direct route of rejecting the fetishized forms of the dominant aesthetic just because they are the recognizable signs of working-class cultural dispossession. In neither case, however, need we take the silence of the aesthetic at face value, as though the aesthetic disposition had actually neutralized for every member of the dominant classes the experience of aesthetic pleasure; or as though, for the members of the dominated classes, the fetishizing of content had actually disenabled the pleasures of form. It is only by taking the *articulation* of aesthetic discourse as identical to aesthetic experience that Bourdieu can present working-class culture as inimical to such aesthetic strategies as formal experimentation (the obverse of which is the dupe-like embrace of any formal experiment, however vapid, by the art-loving *haut bourgeois*). As Michael Denning has recently reminded us, there are innumerable examples in working-class cultural forms of formal experiment and variation;[41] it is precisely the experience of formal innovation which engages interest and admiration in these consumers, even though such manifestly aesthetic experience (by the very criteria of aesthetic theory) may fail to be recognized *as* aesthetic. There is no cultural product, then, which does not possess form, and therefore no way to experience cultural objects without having aesthetic experience.

Nevertheless we shall still have to say that so far as the object of sociology is concerned, nothing exists besides the cultural capital embodied on the one hand in the aesthetic disposition, and on the other in the cultural products judged according to the criteria internalized as the aesthetic disposition. It is easy enough to recognize here the largest effect of the discourse of canonicity: the illusion that aesthetic experience is really *restricted* to the experience of High Cultural works. Bourdieu is certainly right that it is impossible to experience any cultural product apart from its status as cultural capital (high or low); and even more, that it is impossible to experience cultural capital as disarticulated from the system of class formation or commodity production. There is no realm of pure aesthetic experience, or object which elicits nothing but that experience. But I shall nevertheless argue that the *specificity* of aesthetic experience is not contingent upon its "purity." Is this "mixed" condition not, after all, the condition of every social practice and experience? It may well be impossible, for example, to experience "just sex," exclusive of the social meanings of sexual acts. But it would be incorrect on that account to deny the specificity of the sexual. If the revelation of the impurity of the aesthetic tempts one to deny its *reality*, that logical misstep is the consequence of the historical determinations which have produced aesthetic discourse as a *discourse of purity*. Internalized as the aesthetic disposition, this discourse seems to determine whatever can be recognized as aesthetic; but the experience of *any* cutural work is an experience of an always composite pleasure, Proust's "mingled joys."

The overdetermination of the cultural capital of cultural products by the system of class formation and the market means that cultural capital is a "measure" as variable and inherently contradictory as the measure of exchange value. The recognition of cultural capital, otherwise known as aesthetic judgment, must deny, as a condition of its exercise, the ubiquity of aesthetic experience, the fact that such experience utterly pervades the field of cultural production. The worst that can be said of traditional aesthetics is that its conflation of the aesthetic with the work of art *is* its ideology. Such an aesthetics would be comparable to a theory of linguistics which only recognized as "language" the speech of the dominant classes. But this was the historical project, after all, of "grammar," which defined a legitimate speech, a linguistic capital, in precisely the same way that Bourdieu's "legitimate culture" restricts the aesthetic disposition to a restricted domain of consumption.

Bourdieu's sociology radically historicizes the "aesthetic disposition" by insisting upon its determination within a class-structured society, the same society in which many social practices—but chief among them, the economic—become relatively autonomous. Hence it is only in the context in which artistic producers can see themselves as relatively autonomous that the objects they produce can be seen to embody a specific form of cultural capital, the "aesthetic," which can then be conceived on the analogy of exchange value as a relative quantum of aesthetic value. One might conjecture that in societies structured differently, the aesthetic might not be experienced *as such;* and indeed there is a certain futility in attempting to differentiate the aesthetic in the cultural productions of the potters, the weavers, the dancers, the storytellers of premodern societies. At the same time it would be equally pointless to deny the exercise of judgment to these cultural producers, as though they did not distinguish between more or less beautiful, or more or less pleasing objects. We should rather have to speak of cultural capital in other social formations as differently constituted, even sometimes as constituted by the indistinction of its constituents. But of course this formulation would also be too simple, because implicitly "primitivist." This reflection is intended in any case only as a preface to a thought experiment, an analytic conjecture that will return us to the problem of "production" otherwise bracketed in Bourdieu's *Distinction.* If the status of cultural products as cultural capital is in certain historical circumstances overdetermined by limited access to certain works, or by limited access to the means of consumption, then one might hypothesize that a total democratization of access to cultural products would disarticulate the formation of cultural capital from the class structure and from the markets. In that event, what would constitute cultural capital?

We are fortunate in that this very thought experiment has already been performed by Marx in *The German Ideology,* with quite interesting results. Marx imagines that "with a communist organization of society" the division of labor that produces the "exclusive concentration of artistic talent in particular individuals" would disappear, along with the "very name of [the] activity" of painter, sculptor, etc. It would seem then, that the discourse of the aesthetic, in its traditional form, would have to disappear as a consequence of the disappearance of autonomous artistic production: "In a communist society there are no painters but at most people who engage

337

in painting among other activities."[42] These comments have often enough been dismissed as merely utopian, extravagantly so; but this is to miss their pertinence as a thought experiment, since what Marx represents as the disappearance of autonomous production can also be construed, after Bourdieu, as its *universalization*. No one is a painter because everyone is (or can be). The utopia of production Marx imagines reproduces Bourdieu's domain of "restricted production"—production for other producers—*as a condition of the entire society.* Or we might say that Bourdieu's sociology finds its way back to Marx's utopia of production by means of a certain idealization of the realm of "restricted production."[43] For what we discover in comparing *Distinction's* critique of consumption with Bourdieu's description elsewhere of restricted production is that the severity of his critique of consumption is inversely related to his idealization of autonomous production. Autonomy is both the condition of the cultural producer's implication in the socioeconomic order, and the condition for the construction of an imaginary social space in which cultural capital can be reconstituted as though *without relation* to that order:

> The *autonomous* principle of hierarchization, which would reign unchallenged if the field of production were to achieve total autonomy with respect to the laws of the market, is the *degree of specific consecration* (literary or artistic prestige), i.e. the degree of recognition accorded by those who recognize no other criterion of legitimacy than recognition by those whom they recognize. ("Field," 320)

Putting this point explicitly in "The Market for Symbolic Goods," Bourdieu can speak of the intellectual field as representing "the almost complete model of a social universe knowing no principles of differentiation or hierarchization other than specifically symbolic distinctions" ("Market," 19). The "utopian" tendency of this thought—for what else is an alternative "model of the social universe"?—is elsewhere still more explicit, for example, in the essay entitled "The Corporatism of the Universal: The Role of Intellectuals in the Modern World." There Bourdieu advocates the defense of autonomy as a necessary *political* strategy for all intellectuals: "Thus the first objective for a movement of intellectuals (broadly defined as artists, scholars, scientists, etc.) is to work collectively towards the defense of their own interests and towards the means necessary for the protection of their autonomy."[44] Bourdieu knows that *some* autonomy (relative autonomy) is the condition for the appropriation of the products of the cultural producers by the moneyed class; otherwise such products would have no "value," no status as cultural capital for the dominant classes who appropriate them. Nevertheless the struggle for autonomy is worth waging, on behalf of a "republic of artists and intellectuals," a domain in which the principle of restricted production is universalized.

The point of juxtaposing these perhaps surprisingly "utopian" statements to the analyses of *Distinction* is not to question them (in fact, I would endorse them), but to draw out an implication of Bourdieu's thought which may not be apparent to readers of *Distinction*. The idea of production for the producers (which by definition entails *consumption* by the producers) projects onto a utopian screen the disarticulation of cultural capital from the system of class formation, and thus from "distinction" based on inequality of access to cultural goods. Bourdieu calls this condition "total autonomy from the laws of the market." Such a condition does not, however, prophesy the disappearance of cultural capital. The universalization of restricted production would rather transform cultural capital into pure "symbolic distinction." The cultural capital embodied in cultural products would then be judged (and also contested) on aesthetic grounds, as the products already are, but not on the basis of their inaccessibility, the restriction of access guaranteed by the educational system: "The educational system, claiming a monopoly over the consecration of the past and over the production and consecration of cultural consumers, only posthumously accords that infallible mark of consecration, the elevation of works into 'classics' by their inclusion in curricula" ("Market," 26). Even were such an educational system no longer to regulate access to cultural capital in the grotesquely unequal way it presently does, cultural producers would still compete to have their products read, studied, looked at, heard, lived in, sung, worn, and would still accumulate cultural capital in the form of "prestige" or fame. But social distinctions reinstated on such an aesthetic basis would have to be expressed in social relations as distinctions in "lifestyle," in other words as a vast enlargement of the field of aesthetic judgment.

What we call canon formation would then become a much larger part of social life, because not restricted to the institutions of the materially advantaged. Bourdieu has recently made this implication of his argument more explicit, in response to readings of his work which impute to it an evaluative relativism he has never endorsed:

> [T]o deny evaluative dichotomies is to pass a morality off for a politics. The dominated in the artistic and the intellectual fields have always practiced that form of radical chic which consists in rehabilitating socially inferior cultures or the minor genres of legitimate culture. . . . To denounce hierarchy does not get us

anywhere. What must be changed are the conditions that make this hierarchy exist, both in reality and in minds. We must—I have never stopped repeating it—work to *universalize in reality the conditions of access* to what the present offers us that is most universal.[45]

In a culture of such universal access, canonical works could not be experienced as they so often are, as lifeless monuments, or as proofs of class distinction. Insofar as the debate on the canon has tended to discredit aesthetic judgment, or to express a certain embarrassment with its metaphysical pretensions and its political biases, it has quite missed the point. The point is not to make judgment disappear but to reform the conditions of its practice. If there is no way out of the game of culture, then, even when cultural capital is the only kind of capital, there may be another kind of game, with less dire consequences for the losers, an *aesthetic* game. Socializing the means of production and consumption would be the condition of an aestheticism unbound, not its overcoming. But of course, this is only a thought experiment.

NOTES

Preface

[1] The concept of class is as controverted as any other notion in social theory, and the class analysis I propose in this book will not wait for any definitive resolution of that controversy. Here I can only point to the larger features on the map in order to situate my own analysis (and Bourdieu's) in something like a region of this domain. For Marx and Marxism, class is defined by position in the relations of production, and there are only two of these: capital and labor; alternatively, the bourgeoisie and the proletariat (the existence of a "petty bourgeoisie" does not alter the dualism of this structure). The rigor of this model, which apprehends class distinction in economic terms, leaves largely unresolved the question of how cultural distinctions are articulated on the template of the capital-labor structure. The solution to this problem is ultimately what is at stake in every class analysis, including Bourdieu's. For the tradition of "bourgeois" sociology (Durkheim and Weber are as important in Bourdieu's theory as the work of Marx), class is primarily a cultural concept, although the expression of many cultural class traits will in practice depend on material resources. With the concept of "cultural capital" Bourdieu undertakes a certain negotiation between the domains of the economy and culture. Without pronouncing on the success of this negotiation, I would insist here that the aporia between the cultural and the economic is the most fundamental problem confronted by bourgeois sociology, as well as by that hypothetical "Marxist" sociology which Marx himself never produced. For Bourdieu's own account of the concept of capital, see "The Forms of Capital," in *The Handbook of Theory and Research for the Sociology of Education*, ed. John G. Richardson (New York: Greenweed Press, 1983), 241–58. Rather than offer here a precise definition of cultural capital, I have followed Bourdieu's own practice in constructing the concept through the contexts of its deployment.

[2] The concept of the "New Class" invokes Alvin Gouldner, *The Future of Intellectuals and the Rise of the New Class* (New York: Oxford University Press, 1979). The "professional-managerial class" invokes the groundbreaking essay of Barbara and John Ehrenreich, "The Professional-Managerial Class," in *Between Labor and*

Capital, ed. Pat Walker (Montreal: Black Rose Press, 1979). The controversy in the Walker volume over the question of whether the group of professional-managerial workers constitutes a class is scarcely settled in that volume. The Ehrenreichs proceed on the assumption that a class has both an economic and a cultural component, neither of which can be simply derived from, or reduced to, the other. This working assumption makes for a less than tidy theory of class, but the Ehrenreichs are not especially disturbed by this untidiness. Gouldner's conception of cultural capital casts the New Class in the role of a new bourgeoisie, the historical successors to the old. I have kept Gouldner's theory in mind, somewhat warily, preferring Bourdieu's less narrativizing mode of class analysis. For the more limited purposes of the argument I wish to make in this book, it perhaps does not matter whether the professional-managerial classes are conceived to be a distinct class, or, as Erik Olin Wright argues in his response to the Ehrenreichs in the Walker volume, a "contradictory location within class relations" (203). What matters to the present argument is that the emergence of the professional-managerial class has enormously altered the constitution and distribution of cultural capital in the school system, and that these new conditions remain the unremarked horizon of the canon debate.

Chapter One

¹See, for example, Allan Bloom, *The Closing of the American Mind* (New York: Simon and Schuster, 1987); Roger Kimball, *Tenured Radicals: How Politics Has Corrupted Our Higher Education* (New York: Harper and Row, 1990); Dinesh D'Souza, *Illiberal Education: The Politics of Race and Sex on Campus* (New York: The Free Press, 1991); and Alvin Kernan, *The Death of Literature* (New Haven: Yale University Press, 1990). These texts have provided the popular media with the handful of arguments and anecdotes with which it has prosecuted the case against the liberal academy, in articles now too numerous to list. E. D. Hirsch, Jr.'s *Cultural Literacy: What Every American Needs to Know* (New York: Houghton Mifflin, 1987) is often cited in association with this backlash, although its agenda is rather more complicated than that of the texts mentioned above. See pages 35–36 below.

²Gregor McLennan, *Marxism, Pluralism, and Beyond* (Cambridge, Mass.: Polity Press in association with Basil Blackwell, 1989), 18.

³As McLennan remarks, in ibid., "[W]hen the state is brought into this picture of competing, exchanging groups, the polity is represented as driven by a tendency to equilibrium, one in which the 'preferences' of interest groups can be expressed and to a large extent satisfied" (22).

⁴The phenomenon of "political correctness," recently the object of so much complaint in the right-wing media, can be seen in this context as the paradoxical triumph in the university of an otherwise defeated liberalism. It is not surprising that a progressive discourse, more or less routed in American culture, should find itself driven to police the borders of its diminished territory. As everyone on the left knows, the concept of political correctness was formulated within left discourse itself to critique the tendency to moralistic posturing provoked by the dire situation

of an increasingly reactionary social order. The usefulness of that concept is certainly at an end, but one may continue to speak of "identity politics" or what I would call "radical liberalism," a specific style of political discourse and practice distinct from the historical forms of socialism and Marxism. The argument of this chapter with liberalism, both traditional and radical, is not with any of its progressive objectives, but with those assumptions of its theory and practice which, because they are uncritically shared with American political culture in general, have disabled an effective response to the resurgence of reactionary politics. Taking the long view historically, there is considerable evidence for arguing that "identity politics" *is* now American politics, and that what we call identity politics exists on the same continuum of "interest-group" politics with positions that are manifestly conservative or reactionary. Identity politics makes no conceptual break as a *politics* with its precursors, even in its radical forms. I do not doubt that to those who are traumatized by the demise of liberalism, the alternative of a class-critique will seem even more quixotic; but it seems to me that it is in just this circumstance that a mode of systemic analysis recommends itself, and that certain foreclosed truths may become visible once again.

⁵The emergence of this topos into institutional prominence is marked by the publication of *English Literature: Opening Up the Canon,* selected papers from the English Institute, ed. Leslie Fiedler and Houston Baker (Baltimore: Johns Hopkins University Press, 1981). See also Paul Lauter, "History and the Canon," *Social Text* 12 (Fall 1985), 94–101, and William Cain, *Crisis in Criticism: Theory, Literature and Reform in English Studies* (Baltimore: Johns Hopkins University Press, 1984). Among feminist critiques of the canon are the following (others will be cited at later points in the chapter): Lillian Robinson, "Treason Our Text: Feminist Challenges to the Literary Canon," in *Critical Theory since 1965,* ed. Hazard Adams and Leroy Searle (Tallahassee: Florida State University Press), 572–85; Deborah Rosenfelt, "The Politics of Bibliography: Women's Studies and the Literary Canon," in *Women in Print,* ed. Joan Hartman and Ellen Messer-Davidow (New York: Modern Language Association, 1982), 11–31; Florence Howe, "Those We Still Don't Read," *College English* 43 (January 1981), 12–16. Howe writes: "What do we want? Nothing less than the transformation of the literary curriculum and the revision of critical theory and literary history that such a transformation would require" (16). See also Christine Froula, "When Eve Reads Milton: Undoing the Canonical Economy," *Critical Inquiry* 10 (December 1983), 321–48, and Adrienne Munich, "Notorious Signs, Feminist Criticism, and Literary Tradition," in *Making a Difference: Feminist Literary Criticism,* ed. Gayle Greene and Coppelia Kahn (London: Methuen 1985), 238–59.

⁶*Marxism, Pluralism, and Beyond,* 33.

⁷See Ernesto Laclau and Chantal Mouffe, *Hegemony and Socialist Strategy: Towards a Radical Democratic Politics* (London: Verso, 1985). Also interesting in this context, and perhaps neglected by literary postmodernists, is the work of Samuel Bowles and Herbert Gintis, particularly their *Democracy and Capitalism: Property, Community, and the Contradictions of Modern Social Thought* (New York: Basic Books, 1986). Because Bowles and Gintis, unlike Laclau and Mouffe, are

writing in response to an indigenous liberal tradition, they tend to emphasize the necessity for socializing the economy at the same time that it is democratized. Laclau and Mouffe do not disagree, but the very intimacy of their struggle with the Continental Marxist tradition, and the consequent vehemence of their post-Marxism, has had the unfortunate effect of underemphasizing for American readers the socialist commitments they also claim as their own.

[8]Basic statements of Bourdieu's theory of cultural capital may be found in his *Reproduction in Education, Society and Culture,* trans. Richard Nice (London: Sage Publications, 1977); "The Market of Symbolic Goods," *Poetics 14* (1985), 13–44; *Outline of a Theory of Practice,* trans. Richard Nice (Cambridge: Cambridge University Press, 1977); "The Production of Belief: Contribution to an Economy of Symbolic Goods," trans. Richard Nice, *Media, Culture and Society 2,* no 3. (1980), 261–93; *Distinction: A Social Critique of the Judgment of Taste,* trans. Richard Nice (Cambridge: Harvard University Press, 1984); "The Field of Cultural Production or: the Economic World Reversed," trans. Richard Nice, *Poetics 12* (1983), 331–56; *The Logic of Practice,* trans. Richard Nice (Stanford: Stanford University Press, 1990); *In Other Words: Essays towards a Reflexive Sociology,* trans. Matthew Adamson (Stanford: Stanford University Press, 1990).

[9]Rudolph Pfeiffer notes in his *History of Classical Scholarship from the Beginning to the End of the Hellenistic Age* (Oxford: Oxford University Press, 1968), that the analogy between the classics and the scriptural canon makes its first appearance in the work of the German philologist David Rühnken, in 1768. As late as Frank Kermode's *The Classic: Literary Images of Permanence and Change* (London: Viking Press, 1975), it was still possible to discuss what we call canon formation exclusively by reference to the word "classic."

[10]Henry Louis Gates, Jr., "The Master's Pieces: On Canon Formation and the African-American Tradition," *South Atlantic Quarterly* 89 (1990), 105. Elsewhere, it should be noted, Gates has produced very effective critiques of certain aspects of the "representation" view of canon formation, among them the fetishizing of authenticity and individual experience. For a more complete view of the complex evolution of Gates's thinking on the subject of the canon, see his *Loose Canons: Notes on the Culture Wars* (New York: Oxford University Press, 1992).

[11]In this context, see David Harvey, "Flexibility: Threat or Opportunity?" in *Socialist Review* 21 (1991), 74: "The postmodern embrace of ephemeral images, spectacle-type events, 'invented' traditions and heritages of all sorts, and perpetual novelty in the realm of cultural production deserves to be understood. . . . In recent years the cultural mass has pursued a whole host of political and ideological struggles that have general significance: anti-racism, feminism, and struggles concerning ethnic identiy, religious tolerance, cultural decolonization, and the like. Because postmodernism is associated with a democratization of voice within the cultural mass, many of the struggles against a central source of authority and power (white, male, elitist, and Protestant, for example) have enlisted under the postmodern banner. I think it is fair to say that efforts to counter various forms of gender, racial, ethnic, or religious oppression have been more successful within the cultural mass than in many other segments of society. The problem is that these fights are being

waged within a relatively homogeneous class context, where issues of class oppression, though always on the agenda for political reasons, are by no means as strongly and personally felt as they would be among, say, women factory workers in the Philippines or Mexico." Harvey's understanding of the socioeconomic forces driving postmodern culture leads him to a thoroughgoing skepticism about the "ideological struggles" of the newly constituted cultural minorities. While I do not share the degree of Harvey's skepticism about the political significance of these struggles, there is a sense in which we might see the critique of the canon in the context of the new social movements as the latest version of a kind of left Hegelianism. The idealism of this critique consists in the belief that in order to change the world it is only necessary to change our image of the world. This is a question not of the reality of images but of the virtual absence of economic or class analysis in liberal pluralist theory. The absence of such analysis permits First World pluralists to construe the question of postcolonialism, for example, primarily as one of rehabilitating our images of the native cultures and identities of postcolonial populations, a program that does not begin to address the steadily worsening effects of what Immanuel Wallerstein has called the "capitalist world-system." See also Harvey's *The Condition of Postmodernity: An Enquiry into the Origins of Cultural Change* (London: Basil Blackwell, 1980); also Immanuel Wallerstein, *Geopolitics and Geoculture: Essays on the Changing World-System* (Cambridge: Cambridge University Press, 1991).

[12]We are very far from being able to give a good account of the effects of images even within mass culture; this is one meaning, I take it, of the controversy over Spike Lee's film, *Do the Right Thing*. The provoking circumstance in that film's narrative of the absence of images of black Americans (the "brothers") from the wall of Sal's pizzaria (adorned with pictures of the heroes of Italian-American culture) suggests a rather obvious allegory of canon formation; but the subtler point, recently made by W. J. T. Mitchell, is that the provocation is beside the point when the narrative arrives at its complexly overdetermined moment of social violence. To see the images as the *cause* of the violence is to miss everything that overdetermines the social relations Lee is at such pains to evoke in their real complexity. Among its other accomplishments, the film suggests, then, not an allegory for the process of canon formation but for the liberal critique of the canon, that is, for our postmodern tendency to reduce the social to images of the social. See W. J. T. Mitchell, "The Violence of Public Art: *Do the Right Thing*," *Critical Inquiry* 16 (1990), 880–99.

[13]Hence the temptation to understand the process of canonical revision according to such political models as "affirmative action," a very dubious analogy which trivializes a necessary, fragile, and altogether too limited political practice whose site is very different—the site of employment. See, for example, Lillian Robinson, "Treason Our Text," on the necessity of including more female writers in the canon: "It is up to feminist scholars, when we determine that this is indeed the right course to pursue, to demonstrate that such an inclusion would constitute a genuinely affirmative action for all of us" (572). The fact that the "affirmative action" analogy is usually tacit in the rhetoric of canon revision indicates some uneasiness with it, an uneasiness that needs to be honestly acknowledged.

[14]Laclau and Mouffe, *Hegemony and Socialist Strategy*, 111. See also Joan W.

Scott's judicious reconsideration of this question in "The Evidence of Experience," *Critical Inquiry* 17 (1991), 773–97. Scott argues that "A refusal of essentialism seems particularly important once again these days within the field of history, as disciplinary pressure builds to defend the unitary subject in the name of his or her 'experience'" (791).

[15]In his more recent *New Reflections on the Revolution of Our Time* (London: Verso, 1990), 231, Laclau relates social identity to the context of representation as follows: "The notion of representation as the transparency of the identity between representer and represented identity was always incorrect, of course: but it is even more so when applied to contemporary societies in which the instability of social identities makes the constitution of the latter around solid and permanent interests much more ill-defined." For the latest of many attempts to "reanimate the author" on behalf of a "politics of author recognition," see Cheryl Walker, "Feminist Literary Criticism and the Author," *Critical Inquiry* 16 (1990), 551–71. Walker wants to reassert the "antifeminist implications" of theory's notion of the death of the author (560).

[16]For a good summary statement of the issues involved in this articulation, with extensive bibliography, see Ann Ferguson, "The Intersection of Race, Gender, and Class in the United States Today," *Rethinking Marxism* 3 (1990), 45–64.

[17]The concept of a "minority author" should itself be submitted to critique. The unresolved contradiction between the assertion of equivalence vis-à-vis the experience of marginalization or oppression and the assertion of difference at the level of specific gender, racial, or ethnic identity is one consequence of identity politics, and accounts for at least some of the tensions expressed between different minority groups over the actually quite limited resources available for compensating disadvantaged groups. These tensions follow from the fact that the name of "minority" is superimposed upon specific gender, racial, or ethnic identities as *another* identity, a general identity which paradoxically effaces the very specificity which is the basis for the claim to that general identity. This contradiction can only be superseded in the recognition that the concept of "minority" names a historically determinate relation between dominant and subordinate social groups in a specific social context. The tensions between such groups in the practice of identity politics suggests that in identity politics' practice of traditional interest-group politics, the interest of the group is defined on the basis of a hypothetically *preexistent* identity (essential, if not natural), and not on the basis of an analysis of the objective conditions giving rise to that identity. Hence the apparent absence of analogy between, say, one's racial identity, and one's identity as a "consumer"—but the obvious contingency of such "identities" as the latter is also the reason why it is so difficult to translate class position into the identity of "minority author."

[18]See for example Judith Butler's dismantling of some of the metaphysical presuppositions of identity politics in her *Gender Trouble: Feminism and the Subversion of Identity* (New York: Routledge, 1990): "Indeed, the fragmentation within feminism and the paradoxical opposition to feminism from 'women' whom feminism claims to represent suggest the necessary limits of identity politics. The suggestion that feminism can seek wider representation for a subject that it itself

constructs has the ironic consequence that feminist goals risk failure by refusing to take account of the constitutive powers of their own representational claims. This problem is not ameliorated through an appeal to the category of women for merely 'strategic' purposes, for strategies always have meanings that exceed the purposes for which they are intended" (4). Still powerful too is Alice Echols's early warning against the essentialist politics of cultural separatism, "The New Feminism of Yin and Yang," in *Powers of Desire: The Politics of Sexuality,* ed. Ann Snitow et al. (New York: Monthly Review Press, 1983), 439–59.

[19]Peter Osborne, "Radicalism without Limit? Discourse, Democracy, and the Politics of Identity," in *Socialism and the Limits of Liberalism,* ed. Peter Osborne (New York: Verso, 1991), 216–17.

[20]The social-institutional sites at which the articulation of different identities— or the coalition of minorities—can occur is actually very limited. For this reason we need to be cautious about generalizing the possibilities for such coalition from the experience of solidarities in the university. The latter version of solidarity is con- structed on the basis of a common *institutional* affiliation, the very strong tendency of teachers or students to affiliate strongly on the basis of their "identities" as teachers or students. The question is what social basis of affiliation might create the possibility for such political coalitions outside the university. The conditions that really determine relations *between* minorities in our culture are more accurately invoked by the names of Bensonhurst and Crown Heights than by the university's version of identity politics, with its Puritan wing of the politically correct. If the formulation and expression of a cultural identity are undeniably political acts, with political consequences, these consequences are at present very ambiguous. We do not know yet what kind of politics a real articulation of different identities would produce, what kind of "hegemony." Nor do we know of what mechanisms such a politics would consist. We only know that the bad conscience of identity politics about the identities always being "left out" of any community of common identities betrays the inability of radical liberalism to transcend the strategies of traditional liberal interest-group politics.

[21]The fact that liberal pluralism, in its current radical incarnation, has often been accused falsely of reducing the cultural to the political prevents one from seeing the fact that liberal pluralism's more serious problem is the reduction of the political to the cultural.

[22]Here we may note the precedent of Michel Pêcheux's work on identification, as yet largely unassimilated in American cultural theory. See his *Language, Semantics, Ideology,* trans. Harbans Nagpal (New York: St. Martin's Press, 1982). In his *New Reflections* Laclau also has some interesting comments on this question, which in my view go beyond the conclusions of *Hegemony and Socialist Strategy:* "the incorporation of the individual into the symbolic order occurs through *identifications.* The individual is not simply an identity within the structure but is trans- formed by it into a subject, and this requires acts of identification." Such a state- ment clearly implies a necessary distinction between identity and subject. In context (Lauclau's remarks are in reference to Lacan), that distinction points to the concept of the subject as defining what the individual does not know about the for-

mation of his or her identity. Is it not one of the peculiarities of identity politics that it has everything to say about identity and little to say about identification as a moment in a *process,* a process which gives birth to the *subject* (always, of course, the subject-in-process)? It was of course never the project of theory to make the subject simply disappear but to make its claim to rational self-determination (its free affirmation of its identity) suspect. Even Foucault's most radical statement on the subject, "What Is an Author?" which has been read incorrectly as arguing that authors do not exist (just when women authors and black authors were being discovered or rediscovered) clearly says just the opposite: "But the subject should not be entirely abandoned. It should be reconsidered, not to restore the theme of an originating subject, but to seize its functions, its intervention in discourse, and its system of dependencies." It will prove to be a rich irony of our post-theoretical era if our new prize of "identity" should prove in the end to be nothing other than the old Cartesian subject, the subject as it was conceived before theory called its self-determination into question and exposed its social and psychological determinations.

²³See McLennan, *Marxism, Pluralism, and Beyond,* 21. Giving class its due does not, it should be emphasized, reduce the phenomena of race and gender to aspects of class; the point of insisting upon the incommensurability of these categories is only that nothing explains class but class.

²⁴The difference between a research program and canonical revaluation is symptomatically confused in such statements as that by Marilyn L. Williamson, *Raising Their Voices: British Women Writers, 1650–1750* (Detroit: Wayne State University Press, 1990), which I quote for its representative puzzlement: "I do not therefore make aesthetic judgments the goal of my reading, and some readers will doubtless find much of the writing covered in this study deficient in quality and therefore not worth much attention. My work and that of other feminist critics offers the possibility of breaking out of the cycle of assuming that what is unknown or obscure deserves to be so. I do not claim to have discovered inglorious Miltons among the score of writers in this study, but I believe their work deserves atttention nonetheless. The neglect is historical: most were well-known, some quite famous, in their own time. Just as historians are beginning to read popular pamphlets along with Hobbes and Locke, so literary historians are reading far beyond the canon and the taste and values it informs" (9). Historians will be surprised to learn that they are just beginning to read archival material in connection with the study of major authors. But historical scholarship has sometimes been practiced by literary critics too, and in the university it has, historically speaking, been the norm. The dovetailing of new forms of historical scholarship with a critique of the canon has produced the quite interesting misapprehension that writing about a given author is equivalent to canonization of that author.

²⁵This fact remains an unspoken in such arguments as Lillian Robinson's "Treason Our Text," which grapples with the meaning of the feminist research program in the following terms: "The emergence of feminist literary study has been characterized, at the base, by scholarship devoted to the discovery, republication, and reappraisal of 'lost' or undervalued writers and their work. From Rebecca Harding Davis and Kate Chopin through Zora Neale Hurston and Mina Loy to Meridel

LeSueur and Rebecca West, reputations have been reborn or remade and a female counter-canon has come into being, out of components that were largely unavailable even a dozen years ago." A footnote supplies a bibliography for the authors cited, but appends the qualification: "The examples are all from the nineteenth and twentieth centuries" (575). There follows a statement to the effect that "Valuable work has also been done on women writers before the Industrial Revolution," along with a somewhat briefer bibliography of this work. From such an argument one can glean no understanding of why so many women writers have been recovered from the period following the Industrial Revolution, and indeed whether this fact has anything to do with the Industrial Revolution. It is simply taken for granted that any woman writer not currently canonical is ipso facto "lost or undervalued," as though it really did not matter how such texts came to be, or what social conditions enabled or constrained the practice of writing for different social groups.

While I have not undertaken to give a full account in the text of the relation between the distribution of cultural capital (access to the means of literary production) and the position of women in the system of distributions, the lineaments of such an account can be briefly indicated. We might begin by reconsidering two leading questions guiding the current account of women writers in the history of canon formation: First, is the fact of the transhistorical oppression of women sufficient to explain the exclusion of women from the means of literary production, if not from the canon itself? And second, does this fact imply that such oppression operates autonomously from class structure? Fortunately history does not enjoin upon us any choice between a transhistorical sexism and a historical class analysis. A properly historical question would be: What determines women's access or lack of access to the means of literary production at any given historical moment? While transhistorical sexism always makes women available to occupy disadvantaged locations in the social order, it is only the historical class system which determines how they will be so disadvantaged. In the premodern sexual division of labor, women occupy a different site in the system of production than they do after the emergence of generalized commodity production. The same system which "commodifies" women in new ways also permits them to produce new commodities (such as novels), to become new kinds of cultural producers. The historical class system of capitalism produces a new sexual division of labor, or a rearticulation of transhistorical sexism on the system by which material and cultural capital is distributed.

²⁶See for example the argument of Denise Riley, *Am I That Name? Feminism and the Category of "Women" in History* (Minneapolis: University of Minnesota Press, 1988).

²⁷F. R. Leavis, *The Great Tradition* (New York: New York University Press, 1964), 1.

²⁸Linda Nochlin, *Women, Art, and Power, and other Essays* (New York: Harper and Row, 1988), 150.

²⁹I have generally followed the lead of Brian Street's *Literacy in Theory and Practice* (Cambridge: Cambridge University Press, 1984) in his critique of Jack Goody's "autonomous" model of literacy. Street emphasizes the ambiguous effects of liter-

acy in any given set of social conditions, effects I have attempted to invoke continually by defining literacy as the systematic regulation of reading and writing. Literacy is now the subject of new and rather intense debate, centering on the very concrete and practical matter of how children are taught to read (or not to read) in our schools. See for example, Michael Stubbes, *Language and Literacy: The Sociolinguistics of Reading and Writing* (London: Routledge and Kegan Paul, 1980); W. Ross Winterowd, *The Culture and Politics of Literacy* (New York: Oxford University Press, 1989); John Willinsky, *The New Literacy: Redefining Reading and Writing in the Schools* (New York: Routledge, 1990); James W. Tollefson, *Planning Language, Planning Inequality: Language Policy in the Community* (London: Longman, 1991); and Tony Crowley, *Standard English and the Politics of Language* (Urbana: University of Illinois Press, 1989).

[30]I shall pose the question of distribution throughout this book as one of *access* to literacy; but the concept of "access" should not be confused with the ideological notion of "opportunity." We are not speaking here of providing individuals with the cultural capital necessary for "success." That notion is of course the cornerstone of American ideology, which employs a fiction of "equal opportunity" as the ideological means of justifying a system in which some individuals fail and others succeed—through their own fault. Access to literacy should be considered on the contrary an absolute right, not a means to success in any other cultural or economic sense.

[31]Barbara Herrnstein Smith, *Contingencies of Value: Alternative Perspectives for Literary Theory* (Cambridge: Harvard University Press, 1988), 51.

[32]*New York Times,* February 17, 1985.

[33]See, for example, Charles Altieri in "An Idea and an Ideal of a Literary Canon," *Critical Inquiry* 10 (September 1983), 55: "On this model, works do not address social life directly but elicit fundamental forms of desire and admiration that can motivate efforts to produce social change."

[34]Jeffrey Sammons, *Literary Sociology and Practical Criticism* (Bloomington: Indiana University Press, 1977), 134.

[35]See William Bennett, "To Reclaim a Legacy: Text of Report on Humanities in Education," *The Chronicle of Higher Education,* November 28, 1984, 18, where Bennett proposes his list of candidates for the canon of Western writers. The list contains a now obligatory nod to several minority texts, such as Martin Luther King's "Letter from a Birmingham Jail," and his "I Have a Dream" speech.

[36]Michael Ryan, "Loaded Canons: Politics and Literature at the MLA," *Boston Review* (July 1985).

[37]This mistake is pervasive, even among the most theoretically enlightened advocates of left pedagogy in the United States. Here I would cite, as an example, the otherwise judicious study of Patrick Brantlinger, *Crusoe's Footprints: Cultural Studies in Britain and America* (New York: Routledge, 1990). In his discussion of American literature in the context of "gender, class, race," Brantlinger remarks that "Great literature, my own education taught me, is not about public life or politics; it is instead about the experiences, lives, values of private, usually 'refined' individuals (lyric romantic poetry, portraits of the artist, remembrances of things past,

etc.). How then does one begin to understand and value literature which ignores refinement, etiquette, and 'taste' to tell the truth about a nation's past and to represent the struggles of majorities [sic] against slavery, sexism, poverty?" (155). But is it really the case that Melville's *Benito Cerino,* Twain's *Huckleberry Finn,* or Faulkner's novels "tell no truth" about the centrality of race and racism in the American experience, even if in the mode of sometimes expressing that racism? Or that they advertise hegemonic principles of taste and etiquette by habitually choosing to represent the lives of "refined" individuals? When Brantlinger cites Frederick Douglass's *The Narrative of the Life of Frederick Douglass* as a noncanonical text, he betrays the fact that the canon critique really does construe every literary work preferentially as *autobiography.* Yet even the canonicity of Douglass cannot finally be established on these grounds alone, because any text, even an autobiographical text which witnesses to the fact of racial repression, has to be *read.*

[38]Lillian Robinson, "Treason Our Text," 574.

[39]Nina Baym, *Women's Fiction: A Guide to Novels by and about Women* (Ithaca: Cornell University Press, 1978), 15.

[40]Myra Jehlen, "Archimedes and the Paradox of Feminist Criticism," *Signs* 6 (1981), 575–601.

[41]Jane Tompkins, *Sensational Designs: The Cultural Work of American Fiction, 1790–1860* (New York: Oxford University Press, 1985), xiv. On the subject of the distinction between serious and popular, see the argument of Peter Bürger in *Theory of the Avant-Garde,* trans. Michael Shaw (Minneapolis: University of Minnesota Press, 1984), liii: "For once the institution of art/literature has been thematized, the question about the mechanisms that make it possible to exclude certain works as pulp literature necessarily arises." One might add that "pulp literature" *as such* necessarily emerges simultaneously with the institution of the High Culture canon.

[42]Hans Robert Jauss, "Literary History as Challenge to Literary Theory," in *Toward an Aesthetic of Reception,* trans. Timothy Bahti (Minneapolis: University of Minnesota Press, 1982), 25.

[43]Stanley Fish, *Is There a Text in This Class?: The Authority of Interpretive Communities* (Cambridge: Harvard University Press), 11.

[44]Elizabeth Meese, "Sexual Politics and Critical Judgment," in *After Strange Texts: The Role of Theory in the Study of Literature,* ed. Gregory S. Jay and David L. Miller (Birmingham: University of Alabama Press, 1985), 90.

[45]The argument for a less anxious response to this state of affairs is exemplified in the several essays and books of Frank Kermode on issues relating to canon formation, most typically in "The Institutional Control of Interpretation," in his *The Art of Telling: Essays on Fiction* (Cambridge: Harvard Universtiy Press, 1983), *Forms of Attention* (Chicago: University of Chicago Press, 1985), and *History and Value* (Oxford: The Clarendon Press, 1989).

[46]On the issue of consensus and community I shall have more to say in Chapter 5. In the meanwhile we can concur with Gregor McLennan's observation that liberal pluralist theory tends to posit consensus as the ideal resolution to the competitive politics of interest groups (*Marxism, Pluralism, and Beyond,* 26). The canon cri-

tique follows faithfully in the logic of this politics by positing countercanons which are supposed to be consensual for given social subcommunities. For a very effective critique of the separatist tendencies in the institutionalized forms of canon revision, and the pluralist bases of those tendencies, see Cornell West, "Minority Discourse and the Pitfalls of Canon Formation," *Yale Journal of Criticism* 1 (1987), 193–202.

⁴⁷We might also note here that the very American style of liberal pluralist critique has made the entire debate about the canon seem rather mystifying to European critics. See, for example, Alice Jardine's and Anne Menke's interviews with fourteen French feminists in a recent issue of *Yale French Studies* 75 (1988). Jardine and Menke discovered to their surprise that French feminist writers found it difficult to become exercised over the problem of the canon, and that they were even incredulous that it had become a feminist issue in America: "It was hard for us to understand how so many could profess indifference to inclusion of their own work in the canon. And inclusion was not the only problem: for many of these women the word 'canon' does not refer to the literary tradition, and few of them see it as an area of feminist concern" (230). Here, to cite one response, are Monique Wittig's remarks, which are not untypical: "To say that writers have been excluded from the canon because they are women seems to me not only inexact, but the very idea proceeds from a trend toward theories of victimization. There are few great writers in any century. Each time there was one, not only was she welcome within the canon, but she was acclaimed, applauded, and praised in her time—sometimes *especially* because she was a woman. I'm thinking of Sand and Colette. I do not think that real innovators have been passed by. In the university, we ruin the purpose of what we do if we make a special category for women—especially when teaching. When we do that as feminists, we ourselves turn the canon into a male edifice" (257).

⁴⁸Commenting in an interview about the experience of editing the *Norton Anthology of Afro-American Literature,* Henry Louis Gates, Jr., points to the difference between a research program and the exercise of judgment in an institutional context: "When I was in grad school in the 1960s everything black that could be found was reproduced. But some of it was terrible. We've got to make discriminations within the corpus of black literature, and to keep that which is worth keeping." These remarks are reproduced in Dinesh D'Souza's *Illiberal Education,* p. 172.

⁴⁹Cited in Mary Louise Pratt, "Humanities for the Future: Reflections on the Western Culture Debate at Stanford," *South Atlantic Quarterly* 89 (1990), 14.

⁵⁰This sense of the noncanonical is well exemplified in the argument of Paul Lauter, "Race and Gender in the Shaping of the American Literary Canon: A Case Study from the Twenties," in *Feminist Criticism and Social Change: Sex, Class and Race in Literature and Culture,* ed. Judith Newton and Deborah Rosenfelt (New York: Methuen, 1985), 19–44, which provides an interesting and informative narrative about the construction of anthologies of American writing. Interpreting this information is not easy, however, since how one understands the narrative depends upon how adequate the paradigm of inclusion/exclusion is to describe the survival or disappearance of literary works. While Lauter states that "Obviously, no conclave of cultural cardinals establishes a literary canon," he is concerned to show

that "in the 1920s processes were set in motion that virtually eliminated black, white, female and all working-class writers from the canon." These processes were "the professionalization of the teaching of literature, the development of an aesthetic theory that privileged certain texts, and the historiographic organization of the body of literature into conventional 'periods' and 'themes'" (23). It is difficult to see how these criteria are intrinsically unfavorable to minority writers, but the ease with which they can be made to coincide with and explain the disappearance of any given minority writer from one anthology to the next is a measure of how difficult it is for us to imagine that the social identity of the author is not the *real criterion* for every judgment, no matter where or when. The processes Lauter discovers are on his own account considerably more complex than judgments based on the social identity of authors. It is perhaps time to recognize that it is only the emergence in our own time of social identity as a *positive* criterion of judgment (as the basis, in Lauter's phrase, of establishing a "more representative and accurate literary canon") that requires a revisionist history in which social identity is the major *negative* criterion of judgment.

⁵¹The agreement of Western thinkers about certain fundamental questions would have been surprising news to many of them, had they been privileged to receive this information in their own time. From an abundance of possible counterexamples, I choose the following passage from Thomas Hobbes (a canonical writer according to William Bennett): "To conclude, there is nothing so absurd, that the old Philosophers (as *Cicero* saith, who was one of them) have not some of them maintained. And I beleeve that scarce any thing can be more absurdly said in natural Philosophy, than that which now is called *Aristotles Metaphysiques;* nor more repugnant to Government, than much of that hee hath said in his *Politiques;* nor more ignorantly, than a great part of his *Ethiques.*"

⁵²The question of culture, and Western culture in particular, will be considered at length in the following section.

⁵³On this subject, see *The Invention of Tradition,* ed. Eric Hobsbawm and Terence Ranger (Cambridge: Cambridge University Press, 1983).

⁵⁴See Claude Lefort, *The Political Forms of Modern Society: Bureaucracy, Democracy, Totalitarianism,* ed. John B. Thompson (Cambridge: MIT Press, 1986), 195ff; and Cornelius Castoriadis, *The Imaginary Institution of Society,* trans. Kathleen Blamey (Cambridge: MIT Press, 1987), 115 ff. I have invoked a sense of the social imaginary somewhere between that of Castoriadis (for whom the imaginary converges upon the realm of the symbolic) and of Lefort (for whom it is closely associated with the theory of ideology).

⁵⁵See, for example, the Modern Language Association publication, *Professsion 88* (New York: Modern Language Association, 1988), with articles by Andrew Sledd and James Sledd, Helene Moglen, Robert Scholes, and Paul B. Armstrong.

⁵⁶Jean-François Lyotard, *The Postmodern Condition: A Report on Knowledge,* trans. Geoff Bennington and Brian Massumi (Minneapolis: University of Minnesota Press, 1984).

⁵⁷Hirsch, *Cultural Literacy.* Hirsch comments on the form of the list on p. 143: "Not least among the virtues of a list of cultural literacy is the fact of its finiteness.

As soon as one thinks about it, it is obvious that shared information in a large nation like ours must be limited. . . . Just to illustrate the finiteness of literate culture is useful. It should energize people to learn that only a few hundred pages of information stand between the literate and the illiterate, between dependence and autonomy." Hirsch does not go on to draw the appropriate conclusion, which is that the virtual infinitude of information in our culture corresponds to, is the "postmodern condition" of, the irreducible heterogeneity of the culture. The handy "finiteness" of the list is the ideological denial of that heterogeneity.

58In fact there exists a large body of critique on the subject of the curriculum and its function within the educational system, critique of which the canon debate has remained largely oblivious. See, for example, Michael Apple, *Teachers and Texts: A Political Economy of Class and Gender Relations in Education* (New York: Routledge, 1988), and Michael Apple, ed., *Cultural and Economic Reproduction in Education: Essays on Class, Ideology and the State* (London: Routledge, 1982); or Stanley Aronowitz and Henry Giroux, *Education Under Siege: The Conservative, Liberal, and Radical Debate over Schooling* (South Hadley: Bergin and Garvey, 1985). These works include extensive bibliographies as well. The absence of reference to such work in the debate about the canon, and indeed the absence of comment about the relation between the university curriculum and the curriculum at lower levels of the system, testifies to how entirely the debate has been conducted in the pedagogic imaginary of university teachers. On the actual state of the public school system in the U.S., see Jonathan Kozol's vivid account, *Savage Inequalities: Children in America's Schools* (New York: Harper, 1991).

59See for example the important article of Michael Apple, "Curricular Form and the Logic of Technical Control: Building the Possessive Individual," in *Cultural and Economic Reproduction in Education*, 247–74.

60Bourdieu makes this point in his essay "Systems of Education and Systems of Thought," *International Social Science Journal* 19 (1967), 349: "An individual's contact with his culture depends basically on the circumstances in which he has acquired it, among other things because the act whereby culture is communicated is, as such, the exemplary expression of a certain type of relation to the culture."

61William Bennett, "To Reclaim a Legacy," 21.

62See the entry for "culture" in Raymond Williams's *Keywords: A Vocabulary of Culture and Society*, revised edition (New York: Oxford University Press, 1976.1983), 87–93, for a lucid account of what is at stake in the different meanings of "culture" historically. We might sum up the difference between our national culture and our school culture by acknowledging that for national culture "Nike" is the name of an athletic shoe, for school culture a Greek goddess.

63Bourdieu, "Systems of Education and Systems of Thought," *International Social Science Journal* 19 (1967), 351, points to an analogous confusion when the concept of culture is made to refer indifferently both to popular culture and to school culture: "Just as Basil Bernstein contrasts the 'public language' of the working classes, employing descriptive rather than analytical concepts, with a more complex 'formal language,' more conducive to verbal elaboration and abstract thought, we might contrast an academic culture, confined to those who have been long subjected to the disciplines of the school, with a 'popular' culture, peculiar to those who have been excluded from it, were it not that, by using the same concept of culture in both cases, we should be in danger of concealing that these two systems of patterns of perception, language, thought, action and appreciation are separated by an essential difference. This is that only the system of patterns cultivated by the school, i.e. academic culture (in the subjective sense of personal cultivation or *Bildung* in German), is organized primarily by reference to a system of works embodying that culture, by which it is both supported and expressed."

[64]This argument should not be taken to deny the fact that the "West" is a real politico-economic entity, even though its cultural homogeneity lags far behind the unity of its politico-economic system. The *image* of that cultural unity remains the ideological support for the real unity of the West in its imperial relations with the Third World, or in its militarist competition with what was formerly the Eastern Bloc. The collapse of the Soviet Union as a result of that competition, and the consolidation of a Western alliance in the Persian Gulf War are sufficient evidence of what was and is at stake in maintaining the fiction of the cultural unity of the West. Finally, do we need to be reminded that it is Coca-Cola and not Plato which signifies Western culture in the realm of what Immanuel Wallerstein calls "geo-culture"? On this subject, see John Tomlinson, *Cultural Imperialism: A Critical Introduction* (Baltimore: Johns Hopkins University Press, 1991).

[65]This is the argument of Joan Shelley Rubin, *The Making of Middlebrow Culture* (Chapel Hill: University of North Carolina Press, 1992). Discussing John Erskine's original idea for a "great books" program at Columbia University, Rubin notes: "[B]y contending that 'great books' portrayed timeless, universal human situations [Erskine] permitted the conclusion that the classics of Western literature *were* the American heritage" (173).

[66]The example of Heidegger almost goes without saying, but not quite. Heidegger's belief in the deep affinity between the Greek and German languages, supposedly the only truly philosophical languages, forces us to recall that the text tradition which is the support of the notion of the West is itself supported in modern European thought both by philological and racial concepts of continuity.

[67]Bourdieu, "Systems of Education and Systems of Thought": "Because of its own inertia, the school carries along categories and patterns of thought belonging to different ages. In the observance of the rules of the dissertation in three points, for example, French schoolchildren are still contemporaries of Saint Thomas. The feeling of the 'unity of European culture' is probably due to the fact that the school brings together and reconciles—as it must for the purposes of teaching—types of thought belonging to very different periods" (352). What I have been calling a "text tradition" is obviously the site of critical judgment, in the sense that the entire domain of intertextuality, or response to earlier by later writers, is a powerful agency for the preservation of these writers. Nevertheless I have consistently argued for locating the site of canon formation in the school, for the reason implied by Bourdieu in the passage just quoted. The point of the sociological argument, for both Bourdieu and myself, is that authors learn whom to read and how to judge in the schools, and that even the judgment of recent but uncanonized work must even-

tually be validated in the passage of writers into school curricula in order for one to speak of canonicity. One should not forget that literary history is filled with the names of writers whose high standing with other, more famous authors was still insufficient to insure their canonicity.

[68]Schools do not always have to acknowledge the fact of deracination, nor do they necessarily have to employ historicizing strategies of recontextualization in classroom practice. Precisely to the extent that they deny the former and decline the latter, they can realize the objective of merely reproducing culture as dogma, as in the case of religious schools. The operation of culture as dogma will be taken up in Chapter 3.

[69]This point has been eloquently argued by Kwame Anthony Appiah in the context of the production and consumption of African cultural works: "If there is a lesson in the broad shape of this circulation of cultures, it is surely that we are all already contaminated by each other, that there is no longer a fully autochthonous *echt*-African culture awaiting salvage by our artists (just as there is, of course, no American culture without African roots). And there is a clear sense in some postcolonial writing that the postulation of a unitary Africa over against a monolithic West—the binarism of Self and Other—is the last of the shibboleths of the modernizers that we must learn to live without." "Is the Post- in Postmodernism the Post- in Postcolonial?" *Critical Inquiry* 17 (1991), 354.

[70]See Allan Bloom, *The Closing of the American Mind,* 352.

[71]Patrick Brantlinger, *Crusoe's Footprints,* 7.

[72]Alvin W. Gouldner, *The Future of Intellectuals and the Rise of the New Class,* 21. Gouldner argues persuasively that "An investment in education is not simply a consumable. Something is left over, which produces a subsequent flow of income. It is *cultural capital,* the economic basis of the New Class" (27). On the other hand, I am not convinced that the problem-solving orientation of the New Class constitutes what Gouldner calls a "culture of critical discourse." This is not to say that the professional-managerial class has not produced some forms of social criticism—it has—but that this criticism is seldom systemic (it is usually anti-state but not anti-capital). I am also aware that arguments *against* systemic critique have been made on certain "post-Marxist" grounds. Foucault's concept of the "specific intellectual" might in this context be compared to Gouldner's concept of the New Class intellectual. My own argument follows Bourdieu, however, in his version of systemic critique.

[73]Pratt, "Humanities for the Future," 9.

[74]Antonio Gramsci, *The Modern Prince and Other Writings* (New York: International Publishers, 1957), 126.

[75]Antonio Gramsci, *The Antonio Gramsci Reader: Selected Writings 1916–1935,* ed. David Forgacs (New York: Schocken Books, 1988), 317.

[76]Gramsci, *The Modern Prince,* 127.

[77]Gramsci, *The Antonio Gramsci Reader,* 318.

[78]There is reason to believe that the inevitable brevity and shallowness of the great-books tour are not so undesirable to the New Right. For they are less interested finally in inquiring closely into historical complexities or discursive ambi-

guities than in making sure that students come away from their experience of reading great works with the *right ideas*. This objective is quite openly acknowledged by the classicist Donald Kagan, who has been celebrated in the right-wing media for using his position as the dean of Yale College as a bully pulpit for what he calls "common studies." Mindful of the liberal persuasion of many of his faculty, however, the dean has expressed some doubt about their suitability to teach these works in the *right way:* "Consider what a core constructed by the current faculty would look like, and the consequences that would ensue if they also had the responsibility of teaching it." See Donald Kagan, "Yale University: Testing the Limits," *Academic Questions* 4 (1991), 33. On the historical origins of the idea of "great books" in American society, and the tendency toward the "superficial" assimilation of the books, see Rubin, *The Making of Middlebrow Culture,* 192ff. Rubin demonstrates persuasively that Mortimer Adler's transformation of John Erskine's notion of a great-books program into the Encyclopaedia Britannica's *Great Books of the Western World* produced nothing less than a monument of middle-brow culture. The almost exclusive emphasis on philosophical rather than literary works in the Britannica project called forth the famous "Syntopicon" of "Great Ideas," which virtually assured that no one would ever have to read the books themselves.

[79]Christopher L. Miller, "Literary Studies and African Literature: The Challenge of Intercultural Literacy," forthcoming in *Africa and the Disciplines: Contributions of the Study of Africa to the Humanities and Social Sciences,* ed. Robert H. Bates et al. (Chicago: University of Chicago Press).

[80]Walter Benjamin, *Illuminations,* trans. Henry Zohn (New York: Schocken Books, 1969), 256.

[81]On this thesis, see Bourdieu and Passeron, *Reproduction,* 32.

[82]Pierre Bourdieu, *Distinction,* 387.

[83]Bourdieu and Passeron, *Reproduction,* 98.

[84]Perhaps only "seems": For Bourdieu's response to the question about long-term historical transformation, see his *In Other Words,* 41–46.

[85]An example: If the sheer formal atavism of an institution such as the church suits the function of social reproduction, the prestige deriving from its atavistic features can as well become the ground of resistance in a complex agonistic game requiring the expenditure of that prestige as cultural capital. Consider the fate of the Sanctuary movement in the mid-1980s: This movement staged the literalization of the church's institutional autonomy as the autonomy of its physical space, the imaginary "sanctuary" within which political refugees from the right-wing Latin American dictatorships could take sanctuary. Before such an elegant atavism, even our authoritarian state paused, though not for long.

[86]John B. Thompson, *Studies in the Theory of Ideology* (Berkeley: University of California Press, 1984), 24.

[87]R. R. Bolgar, *The Classical Heritage and Its Beneficiaries* (Cambridge: Cambridge University Press, 1954), 24.

[88]Bourdieu and Passeron, *Reproduction,* 30.

[89]Ernst Robert Curtius, *European Literature and the Latin Middle Ages,* trans. Willard R. Trask (New York: Harper and Row, 1953), 250.

⁹⁰Quintilian, *Institutio Oratoria,* 4 vols., trans H. E. Butler (Cambridge: Harvard University Press, 1969), 1:63.

⁹¹Boris Eichenbaum, "Literary Environment," *Readings in Russian Poetics: Formalist and Structuralist Views,* ed. Ladislav Matejka and Kristyna Pomorska (Cambridge: MIT Press, 1971), 62.

⁹²P. N. Medvedev/M. M. Bakhtin, *The Formal Method in Literary Scholarship,* trans. Albert J. Wehrle (Baltimore: Johns Hopkins University Press, 1978), 81.

⁹³Medvedev/Bakhtin, 166.

⁹⁴For an elaborated version of this argument, see Roy Harris, *The Language Makers* (Ithaca: Cornell University Press, 1980), 1–32. The main lines of the argument were foreshadowed by V. N. Voloshinov in *Marxism and the Philosophy of Language,* trans. Ladislav Matejka and I. R. Titunik (Cambridge: Harvard University Press, 1986), 71: "At the basis of the modes of linguistic thought that lead to the postulation of language as a system of normatively identical forms lies a *practical and theoretical focus of attention on the study of defunct, alien languages, preserved in written monuments.*"

⁹⁵Mikhail Bakhtin, *The Dialogic Imagination,* ed. Michael Holquist, trans. Caryl Emerson and Michael Holquist (Austin: University of Texas Press, 1981), 381.

⁹⁶On this subject see Tony Bennett's helpful discussion in *Formalism and Marxism* (London: Methuen, 1979), 58 ff.; as well as Medvedev's comments, 160ff. Relevant passages of Shklovskii's *Rozanov* (1921) were translated for me by Christopher Caryll.

⁹⁷Tzvetan Todorov, *Mikhail Bakhtin: The Dialogical Principle,* trans. Wlad Godzich (Minneapolis: University of Minnesota Press, 1984), 58.

⁹⁸This position has been persuasively argued by Franco Moretti in *Signs Taken for Wonders: Essays in the Sociology of Literary Forms,* trans. Susan Fischer et al. (London: Verso, 1983), 13ff. See also Alastair Fowler's genre-oriented discussion of canon formation in *Kinds of Literature: The Theory of Genres and Modes* (Cambridge: Harvard University Press, 1982).

⁹⁹Raymond Williams, *Marxism and Literature* (Oxford: Oxford University Press, 1977), 45ff.

¹⁰⁰Charles Ferguson, "Diglossia," in *Language in Culture and Society,* ed. Dell Hymes (New York: Harper and Row, 1964), 435.

¹⁰¹Joshua Fishman, *The Sociology of Language: An Interdisciplinary Social Science Approach to Language in Society* (Rowley, Massachusetts: Newbury House, 1972), 102.

¹⁰²Erich Auerbach, *Literary Language and Its Public in Late Latin Antiquity and in the Middle Ages,* trans. Ralph Manheim (Princeton: Princeton University Press, 1965), 249.

¹⁰³On the instability of the fiction category, see William Nelson, *Fact or Fiction: The Dilemma of the Renaissance Storyteller* (Cambridge: Harvard University Press, 1973), 11–37. This instability obviously characterizes the conditions giving rise to the novel.

[104]Natalie Zemon Davis, *Society and Culture in Early Modern France* (Stanford: Stanford University Press, 1975), 232ff.

[105]Brian Stock, in his *The Implications of Literacy: Written Language and Models of Interpretation in the Eleventh and Twelfth Centuries* (Princeton: Princeton University Press, 1983), exhaustively surveys the effects of a reallocated literacy on religious controversy in the Middle Ages. The vernacular, of course, tends to be the language of heresy. According to Dick Leith in his *A Social History of English* (London: Routledge and Kegan Paul, 1983), 49, the English language begins to be used, though not exclusively, in government and law by the fourteeenth century.

[106]See Peter Burke, *Popular Culture in Early Modern Europe* (New York: Harper and Row, 1978), 58ff.

[107]Norbert Elias, *The Civilizing Process,* vol. 1, *The History of Manners,* trans. Edmund Jephcott (New York: Pantheon Books, 1982).

[108]*Literary Criticism of Dante Alighieri,* trans. Robert S. Haller (Lincoln: University of Nebraska Press, 1973), 3.

[109]Antonio Gramsci, *Selections from Cultural Writings,* trans. Geoffrey Nowell-Smith (Cambridge: Harvard University Press, 1985), 233. James Bown, in *A History of Western Education* (New York: St. Martin's Press, 1981), 2: 218, points out that court tutors were to be found in almost all Italian aristocratic homes by the early fifteenth century. These tutors resurrected classical pedagogy (Quintilian, for example), and with that pedagogy classical literature. The progress of vernacular literacy thus came to depend upon the revival of classical literacy among a group no longer exclusively clerical.

[110]Perry Anderson, *Lineages of the Absolutist State* (London: Verso, 1974), 18.

[111]Antonio Gramsci, *Selections from the Prison Notebooks,* 7.

[112]Graham Pechey, "Formalism and Marxism," *Oxford Literary Review* 4 (1980), 80.

[113]An interesting light is thrown upon the ambivalence of the Humanists in relation to the vernacular by a letter of Gabriel Harvey's regarding the state of learning at Cambridge (the letter is dated April 17, 1580): "Tully and Demosthenes nothing so much studyed, as they were wont: Liuis and Salust possiblye rather more, than lesse: Lucian never so much: Aristotle much named, but little read . . . Machiavell a great man: Castilio of no small reputation: Petrarch and Boccace in every mans mouth. . . . The French and Italian when so highly regarded of Schollars: The Latine and Greeke, when so lightly?" *Works,* ed. Alexander Grosart, 3 vols. (1984–85), 1:69.

[114]In *A Discourse Concerning the Original and Progress of Satire,* Dryden sees no way to alleviate his linguistic anxiety except by the establishment of an "Academy": "We have yet no English *prosodia,* not so much as a tolerable dictionary, or a grammar; so that our language is in a manner barbarous; and what government will encourage any one, or more, who are capable of refining it, I know not: but nothing under a public expense can go through with it." *Of Dramatic Poesy and Other Essays,* 2 vols., ed. George Watson (New York: Dutton, 1962), 1: 152.

[115]Erich Auerbach, "La Cour et la ville," in *Scenes from the Drama of European Literature* (Minneapolis: University of Minnesota Press, 1984), 157.

116Auerbach, *Literary Language and Its Public,* 333.

117One may recall here Joseph Addison's well-known statement in *Spectator,* No. 10: "I shall be ambitious to have it said of me that I have brought Philosophy out of Closets and Libraries, Schools and Colleges, to dwell in Clubs and Assemblies, at Tea-Tables and in Coffee-Houses."

118Thomas Sheridan, *British Education: Or the Source of the Disorders of Great Britain* (New York: Garland Publishing, 1970). For an interesting and provocative argument about the relation between canon formation and British imperialism, see Gauri Viswanathan, *Masks of Conquest: Literary Study and British Rule in India* (New York: Columbia University Press, 1989). Viswanathan tends to date the formation of the English vernacular canon somewhat later than I do, but we share some assumptions about the nationalist motives which are in part the support of the school system and of the imperialist project.

119The implications of this fact within the developing discourses of Romanticism have been summarized most astutely by Michel Beaujour in an essay entitled "Genus Universum," *Glyph 7* (Baltimore: Johns Hopkins University Press, 1980): "If this segregation [of scripture from other forms of writing] corresponds but imperfectly to the distinction between the uses of Latin and the Vulgar tongues in medieval culture, it seems clear that the coexistence of a priestly tongue and various lay languages resulted in the institutionalization of a dichotomy: it is no accident therefore that the post-Romantic period attempted to re-instate this duality within various vulgar literatures in order to counteract the tendency to homogenization and equality that accompanies the removal of a sacred hierarchical principle, and the fading away of a hieratic language used at the top (and beyond the top) of the scale" (18). The "re-instatement" took the now familiar but little understood form of a supposed transcendence of genre by truly "literary" works; these works form the super-genre or *genus universum* of literature itself.

120William Wordsworth, Preface to *Lyrical Ballads, Poetical Works,* ed. Thomas Hutchison and Ernest de Selincourt (Oxford: Oxford University Press, 1969), 736.

121Renée Balibar and Dominique Laporte, *Le Français national: politique et pratique de la langue nationale sous la revolution* (Paris: Hachette, 1974); and Renée Balibar, *Les Français fictifs: le rapport des styles littéraires au français national* (Paris: Hachette, 1974). More recently there have appeared somewhat similar studies of English, *Re-Reading English,* ed. Peter Widdowson (London: Methuen, 1982), and *Re-Writing English,* ed. Janet Batsleer et al. (London: Methuen, 1985).

122Pierre Macherey and Etienne Balibar, "Literature as an Ideological Form: Some Marxist Propositions," trans. James Kavanaugh, *Praxis 5* (1981), 47.

123William Strunk, Jr., *The Elements of Style,* with Revisions, and Introduction, and a Chapter on Writing by E. B. White. 3d ed. (New York: Macmillan, 1979), 77.

124Anyone who has forgotten what these texts are may remember the charming occasion of the press conference in which President Reagan and Secretary of Education Bennett recited together Robert Service's "The Cremation of Sam McGee." At least one of these two individuals seems to have been more familiar with Service and company than with the "great works" of Western literature. The literary syllabus in the grammar schools and the high schools was always, as we know, very canonically organized; but this is a subject which has as yet provoked no comment in the canon debate.

125With reference to Strunk and White, we might add that E. B. White himself now occupies the strange canonical limbo of a writer who survives to delight while instructing in the *elements* of style. More sophisticated writers and readers know that "literature" often violates precisely these elements.

126On this subject, see the informative essay by Myron Tuman, "From Astor Place to Kenyon Road: The NCTE and the Origins of English Studies," *College English* 48 (1986), 339–49.

127E. D. Hirsch, Jr., *The Philosophy of Composition* (Chicago: University of Chicago Press, 1977), 44; and James Kinneavy, "Writing Across the Curriculum," *Profession 83* (New York: Modern Language Association, 1983), 18.

128Edward Corbett, "Literature and Composition: Allies or Rivals in the Classroom?" in *Composition and Literature,* ed. Winifred Bryan Horner (Chicago: University of Chicago Press, 1983), 180. Corbett may represent what was the mainstream of composition practice, which apparently policed prose as a means of regulating reading. The policing metaphor is Corbett's, not my own: "It was fairly easy for me to monitor the teaching of that small band of instructors; but every year I would discover some them . . . bootlegging literary texts into the course" (181). It would seem that this practice of writing is founded on a peculiar animus against the reading of literary works. The new school of composition theory represented by Richard Lanham and others provides an interesting retrospect on the disciplinary distinction between composition and literature. See, for example, Lanham's "Composition, Literature, and the Lower-Division Gyroscope," *Profession 84* (New York: Modern Language Association, 1984), 13: "Up to now we have, in composition courses, taught a neutral, denotative, transparent theory of language . . . and then in the first literature course changed the rules completely and taught an opposite theory of poetic meaning, one that a bewildered student once described to me as the OWH, or obscurity-wordiness-hypocrisy, theory of language." Lanham rightly recommends the use of both literary and nonliterary texts in composition courses, but this measure reveals how mutually constitutive these syllabi have always been. This fact is confirmed too by the recurrence of certain "canonical" prose works in composition textbooks. One might add finally that there is no reason why composition classes cannot also be the site of a politically astute and critical pedagogy, as no doubt many are.

129Macherey and Balibar, "Literature as an Ideological Form," 57.

130Lyotard, *The Postmodern Condition,* 48.

131The assumption that critical thinking is only possible in "Standard English" is an error exploded by the many works of William Labov with reference to Black English. See especially "The Logic of Non-Standard English," in *Language in the Inner City: Studies in the Black English Vernacular* (Philadelphia: University of Pennsylvania Press, 1972). With regard to the relation between writing and the sociolects of minority groups, one may cite the political use to which the King James Bible has been put in the cause of civil rights. It would not be inaccurate to say that this alliance of Jacobean writing and spoken Black English has produced the only public oratory (or "rhetoric") we know today, in comparison with which our public speakers of Standard English barely evince any rhetorical skills at all. In this context see Ishmael Reed's apposite comment on the misuse of Standard English by white politicians (and why it does not matter to the distribution of political power), in "How Not to Get the Infidel to Talk the King's Talk," in *The State of the Language,* ed. Leonard Michaels and Christopher Ricks (Berkeley: University of California Press, 1980), 180–81.

Chapter Two

[1]Leslie Stephen, *Hours in a Library* (London: Smith, Elder, 1909), 97. Stephen raises the issue to be considered presently, of the effect of banality: "'The Bard' and the lines upon Eton have become so hackneyed as perhaps to acquire a certain tinge of banality."

[2]Edmund Gosse, *Gray,* The English Men of Letters Series (New York: Harper, 1882).

[3]I note that "The Elegy Written in a Country Churchyard" is an item in the list which defines E. D. Hirsch's concept of cultural literacy. See his *Cultural Literacy: What Every American Needs to Know* (Boston: Houghton Mifflin, 1987), 169. Thomas Gray's name, however, does not appear on the list.

[4]A discussion of the form and contents of Gray's commonplace books may be found in Roger Martin, *Essai sur Thomas Gray* (London: Oxford University Press, 1934), 187–200.

[5]R. P. Gillies, *Memories,* 1851, II, 165, quoted in the annotation to Johnson's *Life of Gray, Lives of the English Poets,* ed. George Hill, 3 vols. (Oxford: Clarendon Press, 1905), 2:441.

[6]The importance of the "notebook" in early modern education is stressed by R. R. Bolgar, in his *The Classical Heritage and Its Beneficiaries,* 272ff. Bolgar quotes the detailed instructions of Vivès: "make a book of blank leaves of a proper size. Divide it into certain topics, so to say, nests. In one, jot down the names of subjects of daily converse . . . in another, sententiae" (237). In this context see also the invaluable discussion of Terence Cave, *The Cornucopian Text: Problems of Writing in the French Renaissance* (Oxford: Clarendon Press, 1979), which elaborates more than I am able here upon the difference writing makes to the mnemotechniques of the "commonplace." For a useful discussion of commonplace books in the early modern period, see Ruth Mohl, *Milton and His Commonplace Book* (New York: Frederick Ungar, 1969), 11–30.

[7]Johnson, *Lives of the English Poets,* 1:77.

[8]The connection between property and landscape painting was suggested by John Berger, *Ways of Seeing* (Harmondsworth: Penguin Books, 1972), 106. The relation between enclosure and landscape in literature is briefly discussed by James Turner, *The Politics of Landscape: Rural Scenery and Society in English Poetry, 1630–1660* (Oxford: Basil Blackwell, 1979), 124ff., and extensively in John Barrell's *The Idea of Landscape and the Sense of Place, 1730–1840* (Cambridge: Cambridge University Press, 1972), from which I would extract the following key

statements: "because of their dependence on the sort of techniques of organizing and composing landscape that I have been discussing, the cultivated classes in England felt much more at ease, in the eighteenth and early nineteenth centuries, in landscape which had been enclosed" (32). And: "The effect, far from suggesting any sense of locality, instead serves to show that one locality . . . can be treated in much the same way as another, in that it can be persuaded to illustrate the same rhetorical commonplaces." I propose that the effect of generality in locodescriptive poetry is precisely the reinhabiting of the emptied "common" by the rhetorical commonplace. The process of enclosure is discussed at length by Barrell, 64ff.

[9]*The Complete Poetical Works of James Thomson,* ed. J. Logie Robertson (London: Oxford University Press, 1908).

[10]John Barrell, *An Equal, Wide Survey: English Literature in History, 1730–1780* (London: Hutchinson, 1983).

[11]See, for example, "Summer," 1438ff. for Thomson's survey of English literature.

[12]William Empson, *Some Versions of Pastoral* (New York: New Directions, 1950), 4.

[13]For the concept of interpellation, the "hailing" of the subject in ideology, see Louis Althusser, *Lenin and Philosophy and Other Essays,* trans. Ben Brewster (New York: Monthly Review Press, 1971), 170ff.

[14]I.A. Richards, *Practical Criticism: A Study of Literary Judgment* (New York: Harcourt, Brace and World, 1929), 197.

[15]Frank Brady, "Gray's Elegy: Structure and Meaning," in *Twentieth Century Interpretations of Gray's Elegy* ed. Herbert W. Starr (Englewood Cliffs, N.J.: Prentice-Hall, 1968).

[16]Roy Porter, *English Society in the Eighteenth Century* (Harmondsworth: Penguin Books, 1982), 65, cites a typical statement of Defoe's: "Men are every day starting up from obscurity to wealth." The question of social mobility is no longer a simple one, if it ever was, and I must therefore add the following qualifications. Historians are now inclined to emphasize a disparity between the perception of upward mobility and the actual rate at which this mobility occurred. Doubtless if one confines the definition of mobility to actual examples of the bourgeoisie passing into the ranks of the nobility, the numbers of those passing, as Lawrence Stone has demonstrated in *The Open Elite? England 1540–1880* (Oxford: Clarendon Press, 1984), are relatively small. Stone biases his study by constricting his definition of the ruling elite to the landed country "squirearchy," and he is thus able to conclude that the "perennial openness of England's landed elite to penetration by members of newly enriched bourgeoisie is clearly no more than a hoary myth." Now this statistical revisionism is based upon what can only be an arbitrary judgment about precisely what minimum number of aristocratized bourgeois would qualify the elite as "open." Setting aside the question of whether this use of statistics is not intended to confound the very possibility of a class analysis, one may at least argue that the perception of upward mobility, which was ubiquitous and even hysterical in the eighteenth century, is a real event with real historical consequences. For a somewhat different analysis than Stone's, see Peter Laslett's *The World We Have*

Lost (New York: Charles Scribner's Sons, 1965). The perception of upward mobility is related to the demonstrable imitation of aristocratic manners by the professional middle classes and the haute bourgeoisie. The concept of upward mobility therefore cannot be confined to the actual expansion of the landed elite: its site is rather the cultural homogenization of the aristocracy and the bourgeoisie, which Auerbach describes in the literary/linguistic sphere. Here the evidence Stone himself collects suggests the cardinal importance of education in this process of homogenization (27, 408), particularly the significance of the professional middle classes, the "middling sort," who were more easily capable of acquiring the knowledge and manners of the aristocracy than of acquiring vast landed capital. It is this version of social mobility which is crucial to the present argument.

[17]In this context, consider the "commonplace" statement of Edward Young, *Conjectures on Original Composition* (1759), ed. Edith J. Morley (London: Longmans, Green, 1918): "Many a genius, probably, there has been, which could neither write, nor read" (17).

[18]John Barrell, *An Equal Wide Survey,* 119.

[19]See James Bowen, *A History of Western Education,* 3 vols. (New York: St. Martin's Press, 1972), 1:138ff. For a general discussion of this subject, see also John Lawson and Harold Silver, *A Social History of Education in England* (New York: Methuen, 1973) 193ff. They note that the lending libraries were initially opposed by the Anglican clergy (236).

[20]John Barrell, *An Equal Wide Survey* (140), points out that eighteenth-century English grammars were designed as much to limit as to disseminate knowledge of language. On the matter of education for the working class, see R. K. Webb's discussion of Hannah More and the SPCK, in his *The British Working Class Reader* (New York: Augustus M. Kelley, 1971), 25ff. On the monitorial system, see Karen Jones and Kevin Williamson, "The Birth of the Schoolroom," *Ideology and Consciousness* 6 (1979), 59–110. On the relation of the middle class to newer developments in education, see Brian Simon, *Studies in the History of Education, 1780–1870* (London: Lawrence and Wishart, 1960), 107ff.

[21]Bowen, *A History of Western Education,* 3:138ff.

[22]John Locke, *Some Thoughts Concerning Education* (1693), in *The Educational Writings of John Locke,* ed. James L. Axtell (Cambridge: Cambridge University Press, 1968), 268.

[23]Bowen, *A History of Western Education,* 3:139.

[24]Nicholas Hans, *New Trends in Education in the Eighteenth Century* (London: Routledge and Kegan Paul, 1951): "By the end of the eighteenth century, classical education had become simply a sign of social prestige." Hans discusses the revival of the grammar schools and the classical curriculum in the nineteenth century— that is, the revival of aristocratic caste traits—when the objectives of social emulation were no longer satisfied by vernacular literacy.

[25]I am following here the excellent discussion of Richard D. Altick, *The English Common Reader: A Social History of the Mass Reading Public, 1800–1900* (Chicago: University of Chicago Press, 1957), 42ff.

[26]One recalls in this context the characteristic rhetoric of Dryden's evaluative

criticism, for example, this passage from the "Defense of the Epilogue," in *Of Dramatic Poesy and Other Critical Essays,* 2 vols, ed. George Watson (London: Dutton, 1962): "But malice and partiality set apart, let any man who understands English read diligently the works of Shakespeare and Fletcher; and I undertake that he will find in every page either some solecism of speech, or some notorious flaw in sense" (1:171). This problem is accurately characterized by Richard Foster Jones, *The Triumph of the English Language: A Survey of Opinions Concerning the Vernacular from the Introduction of Printing to the Restoration* (Stanford: Stanford University Press, 1953): "The Elizabethans had sought to make their language eloquent rather than grammatical" (283).

[27]John Barrell, *An Equal Wide Survey,* 34.

[28]Ibid., 36. Barrell quotes Steele's generalizing statement, to the effect that a gentleman is "a Man compleatly qualify'd as well for the Service and Good, as for the Ornament and Delight, of Society." See also Barrell's discussion beginning 133ff., as well as Stone's comment on the effects of education, in his *The Open Elite,* 411. For a nuanced discussion of the "class of the polite," see Susan Staves, "Pope's Refinement," *The Eighteenth Century: Theory and Interpretation* 29 (1988): 145–63.

[29]Benedict Anderson, *Imagined Communities: Reflections on the Origin and Spread of Nationalism* (London: New Left Books, 1983), 74.

[30]Quoted in Johnson's *Life of Gray,* 3:430.

[31]Thomas Sheridan, *British Education: Or the Source of the Disorders of Great Britain* (New York: Garland Publishing, 1970), 180, 192.

[32]This agenda is quite specific in Sheridan's work, which seeks to institute the "study of oratory" as a politically oriented practice on the model of "Athens and Rome."

[33]Herbert McLachlan, *English Education Under the Test Acts* (Manchester: Manchester University Press, 1931), 216. In a recent study, *The Pristine Culture of Capitalism: A Historical Essay on Old Regimes and Modern States* (London: Verso, 1991), p. 82, Ellen Meiksins Wood remarks how narrow this linguistic practice could be: "Britain is certainly not alone among European nations to identify social classes by means of differential sound patterns in their habits of speech. But it *is* perhaps distinctive in the extent to which sound patterns, the conventions of pronunciation, predominate over other linguistic criteria of social difference."

[34]Wood, *The Pristine Culture of Capitalism,* 216.

[35]William Enfield, ed. *The Speaker: or Miscellaneous Pieces, Selected from the Best English Writers, and disposed under proper heads, with a view to facilitate the improvement of youth in reading and speaking* (London: Joseph Johnson, 1774).

[36]The significance of middle-class women in this movement has been recently stressed by Nancy Armstrong, "Literature as Women's History," *Genre* 19 (Winter 1986), 367: "Today few of us realize that many features of our standard humanities curriculum came from a curriculum designed specifically for educating polite young women who were not of the ruling class, or that the teaching of native British literature developed as a means of socializing children, the poor, and foreigners before we became a masculine profession." Barbauld was uniquely privileged in her

educational opportunities (she even persuaded her father, Dr. Aiken, to teach her Latin and Greek), although she was not an advocate of schools for women. She seems to have promoted instead the more unofficial instruments of literary culture as a means of disseminating knowledge to women.

³⁷See Terence Cave's comment on Ciceronian topics in *The Cornucopian Text*, 13.

³⁸*The Poems of Thomas Gray, William Collins, Oliver Goldsmith,* ed. Roger Lonsdale (London: Longmans, 1969), 126.

³⁹George T. Wright, "Stillness and the Argument of Gray's 'Elegy,'" *Modern Philology* 74 (1977), 382.

⁴⁰For a brief account of Old Corruption, see Philip Corrigan and Derek Sayer, *The Great Arch: English State Formation as Cultural Revolution* (Oxford: Basil Blackwell, 1987). We might contextualize Gray's ignoble/noble strife here by pointing also to the *libelles* of the French underground press, which actively delegitimized the French nobility in the decades before the revolution. Robert Darnton writes in *The Literary Underground of the Old Regime* (Cambridge: Harvard University Press, 1982), 29: "The *grand monde* was the real target of the *libelles*. They slandered the court, the church, the aristocracy, the academies, the salons, everything elevated and respectable, including the monarchy itself, with a scurrility that is difficult to imagine today, although it has a long career in underground literature." Similarly, the ethico-satiric productions of English High Culture sublimate Grub Street productions by the same techniques of "normalization" to which Gray's classical sources are subjected. Darnton's study is quite pertinent to the general argument of this essay, though it would lead us to an account of how differently the nationalizing of French literature proceeds. Darnton notes in passing that the Academie Française restricted literary immortality to "forty privileged individuals" (21). For a recent consideration of "Grub Street," as this notion is mystified by the distinction between High and Low Culture, see Kathy Macdermott, "Literature and the Grub Street Myth," in *Popular Fictions: Essays in Literature and History,* ed. Peter Humm et al. (London: Methuen, 1986), 16–28.

⁴¹Pierre Bourdieu, *Outline of a Theory of Practice,* trans. Richard Nice (Cambridge: Cambridge University Press, 1977), 72, 77.

⁴²For a discussion of this and other Theocritean topoi, see Thomas G. Rosenmeyer, *The Green Cabinet: Theocritus and the European Pastoral Lyric* (Berkeley: University of California Press, 1969), 105.

⁴³See Arnold's Romantic reading of Gray's career, "Thomas Gray," in *The Complete Prose Works of Matthew Arnold,* 11 vols. (Ann Arbor: University of Michigan Press, 1973), 9:189–204.

⁴⁴This question has been unfortunately confused in some critical accounts by the invention of another character, the "stonecutter," who is presumably the youth who dies at the end of the poem. The present argument declines this hypothesis without resorting to a simplistic biographical reading. For the "stonecutter controversy," see the essays by Herbert W. Starr, Frank H. Ellis, and John H. Sutherland collected in Starr, *Twentieth Century Interpretations of Gray's Elegy.*

⁴⁵John Sitter, *Literary Loneliness in Mid-Eighteenth Century England* (Ithaca: Cornell University Press, 1982), chap. 3.

⁴⁶See Jürgen Habermas, *The Structural Transformation of the Public Sphere,* trans. Thomas Burger (Cambridge: MIT Press, 1989).

⁴⁷Norbert Elias, *The Civilizing Process,* volume 2: *Power and Civility,* trans. Edmund Jephcott (New York: Pantheon Books, 1978), 8 and passim.

⁴⁸On this subject see the recent article by Linda Zionkowski, "Bridging the Gulf Between: The Poet and the Audience in the Work of Gray," *ELH* 58 (1991), 331–50, which argues for Gray's reaction to the commodification of literature. I have provided below a slightly different (though not contradictory) context for Gray's characteristic posturing in the complex overlapping of poetry and literature, as categories of cultural production.

⁴⁹Waller, "Of English Verse," in *The Poems of Edmund Waller,* ed. G. Thorn Drury (London: George Routledge and Sons, 1893).

⁵⁰*The Works of Thomas Gray,* ed. Edmund Gosse, 4 vols. (London: Macmillan, 1903), 2:108.

⁵¹See Lonsdale, *The Poems of Gray, Collins, Goldsmith,* 113.

⁵²See Habermas's comment on this moment in the development of the English public sphere, in his *The Structural Transformation of the Public Sphere:* "Two years after *Pamela* appeared on the literary scene the first public library was founded; book clubs, reading circles, and subscription libraries shot up. In an age in which the sale of the monthly and weekly journals doubled within a quarter century, as happened in England after 1750, they made it possible for the reading of novels to become customary in the bourgeois strata. These constituted the public that had long since grown out of early institutions like the coffee houses, *salons,* and *Tischgesellschaften* and was now held together through the medium of the press and its professional criticism" (51).

⁵³Raymond Williams, *Marxism and Literature* (Oxford: Oxford University Press, 1977), 47.

⁵⁴John Hill Burton, *The Life and Correspondence of David Hume,* 3 vols. (New York: Garland Publishing), 3:28.

⁵⁵On peasant poets, see Morag Shiach, *Discourse on Popular Culture* (Stanford: Stanford University Press, 1989), 35–70.

⁵⁶Jerome Christensen, *Practicing Enlightenment: Hume and the Formation of a Literary Career* (Madison: University of Wisconsin Press, 1987), 49.

⁵⁷See Geoffrey Tillotson, "Eighteenth Century Poetic Diction I," in his *Essays in Cricitism and Research* (Cambridge: Cambridge University Press, 1942), 69. In the following paragraphs I take up some reflections of Donald Davie, *Purity of Diction in English Verse* (New York: Oxford University Press, 1969), 202.

⁵⁸Johnson, in *Rambler,* No. 37. In *The Rambler,* ed. Walter Jackson Bate, 3 vols. (New Haven, Yale University Press, 1969), 1:202.

⁵⁹Davie, *Purity of Diction,* 13. For an interesting longer view of the significance of prose, see Jeffrey Kittay and Wlad Godzich, *The Emergence of Prose: An Essay in Prosaics* (Minneapolis: University of Minnesota Press, 1987).

⁶⁰John Aiken, "Essay on Ballads and Pastoral Songs" (1793), quoted in *A Book of English Verse,* ed. John Barrell and John Bull (New York: Oxford University Press, 1975), 435. One might remark here on a certain tension between the nationalist agenda carried by the forging of a vernacular standard and the invention of "traditions," the latter manifested by the movement to collect specimens of the earliest English poetry (Percy's *Reliques,* for example). This tension might be described as the difference between the cultural value of the bourgeois sociolect and the ideological value of "authentic" English dialect; perhaps the hypothetical grounding of the bourgeois sociolect in peasant speech was one way of resolving this tension.

⁶¹In *Wordsworth's Literary Criticism,* ed. W. J. B. Owen (London: Routledge and Kegan Paul, 1974).

⁶²A. D. Harvey, *English Poetry in a Changing Society, 1780–1825* (London: Alison and Busby, 1980), 66.

⁶³Coleridge, *Biographia Literaria,* ed. George Watson (New York: Dutton, 1971).

⁶⁴Johnson, in *Rambler,* No. 4, in Bate, *The Rambler,* 3:19.

⁶⁵Coleridge's mention of the "Gradus" betrays the impact of vernacular literacy upon the Latin grammar school itself, since students there are no longer so immersed in classical literature as to be able to practice composition without the aid of already compiled commonplace texts.

⁶⁶Since the High Culture canon is for us a given of higher education, its relation to "juvenile" literature—which no less than "great" works has a history of canon formation in the schools—has been unfortunately obscured. I would like to open up the question of this other canon, if it cannot be thoroughly explored here, by invoking some of the names in its pantheon (randomly selected): O. Henry, Ambrose Bierce, Washington Irving, Richard Connell (author of "The Most Dangerous Game"), Edgar Allan Poe, James Thurber, Robert Louis Stevenson, John Masefield, Carl Sandburg, Edwin Arlington Robinson, A. E. Housman, Amy Lowell, Robert Frost. The fact that some of these names appear in the High Culture canon is an interesting, not an invalidating, complication of the present thesis. Gray's "Elegy" is itself an example of this dual citizenship, since it has so frequently been taught at the primary and secondary levels.

Chapter Three

¹Francis Mulhern, *The Moment of Scrutiny* (London: New Left Books, 1979); Chris Baldick, *The Social Mission of English Criticism, 1848–1942* (Oxford: Oxford University Press, 1983).

²T. S. Eliot, *Selected Essays* (New York: Harcourt, Brace, Javonovich, 1932), 392; hereafter cited as SE in the text.

³Pierre Bourdieu, *Outline of a Theory of Practice,* 164.

⁴Mulhern, *The Moment of Scrutiny,* 35 ff.

⁵T. S. Eliot, "Tradition and the Individual Talent," in *The Sacred Wood* (London: Methuen, 1920; 1960), 50; hereafter cited as SW in the text.

⁶See also Eliot's "Poetry and Drama," in his *On Poetry and Poets* (New York:

Farrar, Strauss, and Cudahy, 1957): "Reviewing my critical output for the last thirty-odd years, I am surprised to find how constantly I have returned to the drama" (75). Further references cited as OPP in text.

[7]A particular passage of Eliot's is worth noting in "What Is a Classic?" OPP: "The predecessors should be themselves great and honoured: but their accomplishment must be such as to suggest still undeveloped resources of the language, and not such as to oppress the younger writers with the fear that everything that can be done has been done, in their language" (58).

[8]There is an additional motive to be mentioned in this connection—Eliot's unhappy feeling that religious poetry will aways be regarded as minor: "For the great majority of people who love poetry, *religious* poetry is a variety of *minor* poetry" ("Religion and Literature," SE, 345).

[9]T. S. Eliot, *John Dryden: The Poet, the Dramatist, the Critic* (New York: T. and E. Holiday, 1932), 24.

[10]Ibid., 5.

[11]See also Eliot's remark in "Virgil and the Christian World," OPP: "A poet may believe that he is expressing only his private experience; his lines may be for him only a means of talking about himself without giving himself away; yet for his readers what he has written may come to be the expression both of their own secret feelings and of the exultation or despair of a generation" (137).

[12]T. S. Eliot, "The Classics and the Man of Letters," in *To Criticize the Critic* (New York: Farrar, Strauss, and Giroux, 1965), 147.

[13]T. S. Eliot, *After Strange Gods: A Primer of Modern Heresy* (New York: Harcourt, Brace, 1933), 22.

[14]T. S. Eliot, *The Idea of a Christian Society* (New York: Harcourt, Brace, 1940), 26.

[15]On the decline of the "bourgeois public sphere," see Jürgen Habermas, *The Structural Transformation of the Public Sphere,* 141ff.

[16]Ibid., 42.

[17]T. S. Eliot, *Christianity and Culture* (New York: Harcourt, Brace, 1968), 99.

[18]T. S. Eliot, *The Idea of a Christian Society,* 34. Eliot goes on to associate, as well as to distinguish, his notion from the Coleridgean idea of the "clerisy," but the very fact that Eliot takes such care with his relation to Coleridge on this issue suggests that there is much more continuity than Eliot would like to acknowledge between Romantic notions about the function of literary culture and his fantasy of a Christian culture.

[19]See Edward W. Said, *The World, the Text, and the Critic* (Cambridge: Harvard University Press, 1983), 290–92.

[20]Gerald Graff, *Professing Literature: An Institutional History* (Chicago: University of Chicago Press, 1987), 145ff.

[21]Robert Penn Warren, "A Conversation with Cleanth Brooks," in *The Possibilities of Order: Cleanth Brooks and His Work,* ed. Lewis P. Simpson (Baton Rouge: Louisiana University Press, 1976), 19.

[22]Cleanth Brooks, *Modern Poetry and the Tradition* (Chapel Hill: University of

North Carolina Press, 1939), 203. For an even less restrained polemic against science, see John Crowe Ransom, *God Without Thunder: An Unorthodox Defense of Orthodoxy* (Hamden: Archon Books, 1965), 117–38.

²³Cleanth Brooks, *The Well Wrought Urn: Studies in the Structure of Poetry* (New York: Harcourt, Brace, and World, 1947), 252; hereafter cited as WWU in the text.

²⁴Arthur Marotti, *John Donne, Coterie Poet* (Madison: University of Wisconsin Press, 1986).

²⁵See also WWU: "I should certainly dislike to be thought to maintain that English poetry ceased with the death of Donne, to be resumed only in our own time" (224). Elsewhere Brooks returns to the project of revaluation in another mood: "The truth of the matter is that an increased interest in criticism will not render literary history superfluous. It will rather beget more literary history—a new literary history, for any revised concept of poetry implies a revised history of poetry. I think that it is possible to foresee what some of the revisions will be, and in *Modern Poetry and the Tradition* I was rash enough to make some predictions about them. If the discussions of eighteenth- and nineteenth-century poems in the present book correct some misapprehensions, that is all to the good. What is relevant to say here is that the same discussions confirm my view that a new history is desirable and necessary . . . that certain poets deserve a higher place than they have been accorded in the past, and some a lower" (237).

²⁶The consistency of this strategy is impressive in *The Well Wrought Urn*. Keats's "Ode on a Grecian Urn," for example, presents a challenge for the theory because its concluding lines seem to present a blatant statement. Tennyson likewise "is perhaps the last English poet one would think of associating with the subtleties of paradox and ambiguity." One by one these challenges are met by virtuosic displays of close reading.

²⁷Craig S. Abbott, "Modern American Poetry: Anthologies, Classrooms, and Canons," in *College Literature* 17 (1990), 209–21.

²⁸Cleanth Brooks and Robert Penn Warren, *Understanding Poetry,* fourth edition (New York: Holt, Rinehart, and Winston, 1976), 137.

²⁹Another consequence, which may have been equally serious, was that literary education relieved one of the necessity of "reading" mass cultural artifacts. If the refusal of reading (that is, of interpretation) in the domain of mass culture no longer has the excuse it once had, it has not been without considerable resistance that interpretation has been wrested from its privilege as the High Cultural mode of consumption. Witness the struggle of Film Studies to establish its legitimacy in the university.

Chapter Four

¹The following abbreviations for works by or about Paul de Man are used throughout this chapter:

AR=*Allegories of Reading: Figural Language in Rousseau, Nietzsche, Rilke, and Proust* (New Haven: Yale University Press, 1979).

BI=*Blindness and Insight: Essays in the Rhetoric of Contemporary Criticism,* second edition (Minneapolis: University of Minnesota Press, 1983).

CW=*Critical Writings, 1953–1978* (Minneapolis: University of Minnesota Press, 1989).

EM= "The Epistemology of Metaphor," in *On Metaphor,* edited by Sheldon Sacks (Chicago: University of Chicago Press, 1978).

RDR=*Reading de Man Reading,* edited by Lindsay Waters and Wlad Godzich (Minneapolis: University of Minnesota Press, 1989).

RR=*The Rhetoric of Romanticism* (New York: Columbia University Press, 1984).

RT=*The Resistance to Theory* (Minneapolis: University of Minnesota Press, 1986).

YFS=*The Lesson of Paul de Man,* Yale French Studies 69 (New Haven: Yale University Press, 1985).

²Barbara Johnson, *A World of Difference* (Baltimore: Johns Hopkins University Press, 1987), 4.

³In the argument to follow, I will be using the term "symptomatic" in the specific sense developed by Althusser in *Reading Capital,* trans. Ben Brewster (London: Verso, 1970), 28. For a somewhat different use of Althusser's technique of symptomatic reading to interpret de Man's oeuvre, see Ellen Rooney's *Seductive Reasoning: Pluralism as the Problematic of Contemporary Literary Theory* (Ithaca: Cornell University Press, 1989). Rooney very persuasively demonstrates the fact that pluralism is a problematic which underlies much critical theory, even theories which appear to contradict each other. She finds in de Man another version of the problematic of "general persuasion" which posits "a homogeneous community of readers" (161). While I would agree that de Man shares certain pluralist assumptions with much other contemporary criticism, I have attempted to discern in this chapter a problematic which is more specific to the project of deconstructive theory in its symptomatic relation to the institutionalized theory syllabus.

⁴I use the terms "deconstruction" and "rhetorical reading" interchangeably, despite the fact that the former term is attached equally to the work of Jacques Derrida. In making this terminological choice I mean to draw explicit attention to the problematic conflation of rhetorical reading with the concept of deconstruction in general usage. While the term "deconstruction" encloses the work of de Man and Derrida within a set of generalized theoretical motifs and procedures, it does so *only* in the practice of literary criticism. This fact has ensured the consequence that Derridean philosophy is largely transmitted to literary critics through the lens of his reception in the immediate context of de Man's critical writing. It is through de Man's work that the *term* deconstruction is disseminated, as the name of a school of criticism; in the preface to *Allegories of Reading,* he remarks that he "first came across" the term in Derrida's writing. On the question of the differences between de Manian and Derridean deconstruction, it is customary to defer to Rodolph Gasché's scrupulous appraisal, "Deconstruction as Criticism," in *Glyph* 6 (Baltimore: Johns Hopkins University Press, 1979). I would of course agree with Gas-

ché that there are crucial differences between the respective projects of de Man and Derrida which need to be, so to speak, "reiterated." But where does that leave the term "deconstruction"? It is my supposition that there is very little "deconstructive" criticism which is not capable of being regarded as a version of "rhetorical reading." To this point we may add a reiteration of the differences, first by de Man, then by Derrida. From *The Resistance to Theory:* "In some cases, a direct link may exist between philosophy and literary theory. More frequently, however, contemporary literary theory is a relatively autonomous version of questions that also surface, in a different context, in philosophy, though not necessarily in a clearer and more rigorous form" (RT, 8). And from the Afterword to *Limited Inc:* "But it may be permissible to underscore that I have never assimilated or reduced, as is often said, concept to metaphor. . . . Instead, I have sought to deconstruct the concept of metaphor itself and proposed an entirely different 'logic,' 'a new articulation' of the relations between concept and metaphor, which is to say, also, between philosophy, science, logic on the one hand, and rhetoric on the other. Deconstruction, as I have practiced it, has always been foreign to rhetoricism—which, as its name indicates, can become another form of logocentrism—and this despite or rather because of the interest I have felt obliged to direct at questions of language and at figures of rhetoric. What is all too quickly forgotten is often what is most massively evident, to wit, that deconstruction, that at least to which I refer, *begins* by deconstructing logocentrism, and hence also that which rhetoricism might owe to it" (*Limited Inc* [Evanston: Northwestern University Press, 1988], 156).

5 "Portrait: de Man," in *Rhetoric and Form: Deconstruction at Yale,* ed. Robert Con Davis and Ronald Schleifer (Norman: University of Oklahoma Press, 1985), 70.

6 See Freud, "The Dynamics of the Transference" (1912), in *Therapy and Technique* (New York: Collier Books, 1963): "It is undeniable that the subjugation of the transference-manifestations provides the greatest difficulties for the psychoanalyst; but it must not be forgotten that they, and they only, render the invaluable service of making the patient's buried and forgotten love-emotions actual and manifest; for in the last resort no one can be slain *in absentia* or *in effigie*" (114–15).

7 *The Four Fundamental Concepts of Psycho-analysis,* trans. Alan Sheridan (New York: W. W. Norton, 1981), 231.

8 Monique David-Menard, "Lacanians Against Lacan," *Social Text* 6 (1982), 86–111.

9 Roustang, *Dire Mastery: Discipleship from Freud to Lacan,* trans. Ned Lukacher (Baltimore: Johns Hopkins University Press, 1976), 58.

10 Lacan, *Television,* trans. Denis Hollier et al. (New York: W. W. Norton, 1990), 130.

11 See, for example, the argument of Peggy Kamuf, "Pieces of Resistance," RDR, 136–54, about the relation between psychoanalytic terms and de Man's essay.

12 Frank Lentricchia argued some time ago for the special relation between de Man and Sartre, in his *After the New Criticism* (Chicago: Chicago University of Chicago Press, 1980), 283ff.

13 Lacan, *Four Fundamental Concepts,* 126.

¹⁴Freud, *Introductory Lectures on Psychoanalysis,* trans. James Strachey (New York: W. W. Norton, 1920; 1966), 452.

¹⁵See David Macey, *Lacan in Contexts* (London: Verso, 1988), 170ff.

¹⁶See Lindsay Waters, "Paul de Man: Life and Works," CW: "The ease with which the insights he had earned were mimicked made him wince. He told me so" (lxi).

¹⁷De Man, "Sign and Symbol in Hegel's *Aesthetics," Critical Inquiry* 8 (1982), 762.

¹⁸Jonathan Culler, *The Pursuit of Signs: Semiotics, Literature, Deconstruction* (Ithaca: Cornell University Press, 1981), 16.

¹⁹Miller, "The Function of Literary Theory at the Present Time," in *The Future of Literary Theory,* ed. Ralph Cohen (New York: Routledge, 1989), 110.

²⁰Consider, for example, Wordsworth's insistence in the Preface to *Lyrical Ballads* that the proper antithesis of "poetry" is not prose but "Matter of Fact, or Science."

²¹*Friedrich Nietzsche on Rhetoric and Language,* ed. and trans. Sander L. Gilman et al. (New York: Oxford University Press, 1989), 23.

²²Gerard Genette, "Rhetoric Restrained," in *Figures of Literary Discourse,* trans. Alan Sheridan (New York: Columbia University Press, 1982). The argument of Genette's essay is in my view as yet unassimilated in the "rhetoricist" episteme of literary theory. See also Roland Barthes' discussion of this subject in his *The Semiotic Challenge,* trans. Richard Howard (New York: Hill and Wang, 1988): "this third part of the *techne rhetorike* [is] known as lexis or *elocutio,* to which we are accustomed to pejoratively reducing rhetoric because of the interest the Moderns have taken in the figures of rhetoric, a part (but only a part) of *elocutio*" (83).

²³De Man's deconstruction of Locke in "The Epistemology of Metaphor" should not obscure the fact that his epistemology is much closer to Locke's than it is to Bachelard's or Wittgenstein's, a historical irony which is entirely lost by taking de Man's distinction between the epistemological and the historical as an axiomatic antithesis. It is just such a distinction that the work of both Bachelard and Wittgenstein calls into question.

²⁴See Suzanne Gearhart's "Philosophy *Before* Literature: Deconstruction, Historicity, and the Work of Paul de Man," *Diacritics* 13 (1983), 63–81. I am greatly indebted to Gearhart's still unsurpassed analysis of the dominant tendency in de Man's work, and I hope to have extended that analysis in the direction of a full-scale ideology critique.

²⁵The recurrence of the Jakobsonian binarism at the heart of de Man's "rhetoricist" overthrow of linguistic (grammatical) terminology is rather impressive evidence of the episteme at work. The history of the binarism long predates Jakobson, however. It has been traced by Genette (*Figures,* 107) to the attempt by French rhetoricians of the nineteenth century to simplify or systematize the taxonomy of tropes, a systematization which ultimately produced the "bookends of our modern rhetoric," metaphor and metonymy. The point of depriviveging (not deconstructing) this binarism is to question precisely the slippage from a taxonomy of tropes to a "system" of tropes. The drive toward such systematicity forms no part of classical

rhetoric, which might have extended the list of tropes indefinitely, but it is very much the means by which rhetoric can be fitted over the template of a modern discourse such as linguistics.

[26]This point has been recognized in Neil Hertz's perceptive reading of de Man, "Lurid Figures" (RDR). Hertz speaks of a "pathos of uncertain agency" a concept to which I shall return below.

[27]De Man, "Phenomenality and Materiality in Kant," in *The Textual Sublime: Deconstruction and Its Differences,* ed. Hugh J. Silverman and Gary E. Aylesworth (New York: State University of New York Press, 1990), 108.

[28]Fredric Jameson seems to me entirely correct in remarking that "De Man was an eighteenth-century mechanical materialist, and much that strikes the postcontemporary reader as peculiar and idiosyncratic about his work will be clarified by juxtaposition with the cultural politics of the great Enlightenment philosophes." *Postmodernism or, The Cultural Logic of Late Capitalism* (Durham: Duke University Press, 1991), 246. I would qualify this statement only by deemphasizing the idiosyncracy of this materialism, and arguing for the symptomatic generality of theoretical notions such as the "materiality of the letter."

[29]Perhaps it is worth recalling Marx's words on this question: "The chief defect of all materialism (including Feuerbach's) is, that the object, reality, what we apprehend through our senses, is understood only in the form of the object of contemplation; but not as sensuous human activity, as practice; not subjectively. Hence in opposition to materialism the active side was developed abstractly by idealism, which does not know real sensuous activity as such. Feurbach wants sensuous objects, really distinct from the thought objects, but he does not conceive human activity itself as *objective* activity." From "Theses on Feurbach," in *The German Ideology,* ed. C. J. Arthur (New York: International Publishers, 1947, 1970), 121.

[30]See also in this context Rodolph Gasché's analysis of de Man's "formal materialism" in his "In-difference to Philosophy: De Man on Kant, Hegel, and Nietzsche" (RDR, 259–94). Gasché regards de Man's argument as at once a fully articulated philosophical position, almost a "positive philosophy," and at the same time curiously indifferent to the philosophical question of difference itself. Gasché's formulation of de Man's thesis is worth quoting in part here: "Considering the sheer arbitrariness and intrinsic senselessness of the material and signifying agencies of language, the randomness of their individual occurrences, the relative independence of their play, and the opacity of their literal materiality, all experienceable meaning appears *superimposed* upon [the text's figural and conceptual constructs]" (278). Gasché concludes that de Man's "materiality of language in its unwrought or native state . . . is a cause devoid of all meaning, of all semantic depth, which stands in a relation of eccentricity to what it appears to effect." And therefore: "between the linguistic act constitutive of signification and meaning itself there is no relation of any sort" (280). I would accept the terms of this analysis, only emphasizing that the question of causality has driven the argument all along; for what Gasché calls de Man's "formal materialism" produces an indeterminate or "random" relation between the materiality and the meaning of the signifier, a relation which is itself inexorably "caused." Hence de Man's assertion that "the

positing power of language" is "both entirely arbitrary in having a strength that cannot be reduced to necessity, and entirely inexorable in that there is no alternative to it. It stands beyond the polarities of chance and determination" (RR, 116). The latter statement is what de Man's "miniature philosophy" (Gasché's phrase) strives to assert, what I would call determinate indeterminacy. But the vacuum that lies beyond the polarities of chance and determination borrows its power to evacuate meaning from the very ambiguity of the terms "necessity" and "determination" in the above quotation. Causality in de Man is really material, but when it is conceived within the terms of a "metaphysics," where a transcendental subject is the "cause" of some action, it is called "necessity." Clearly what de Man wants is a theory of signification which is not teleological (meaning determined by what one *wants to say*), and what he gets is a causality that is at once like chance and like *fate*. I differ from Gasché in reading this argument as "ideological," as invested in a determinism which is sentimental and which only signifies as a "philosophy" in a very specific institutional context of discipleship.

[31]Johnson, *A World of Difference,* 15

[32]Gasché, "Edges of Understanding," in *Responses: On Paul de Man's Wartime Journalism,* ed. Werner Hamacher et al. (Lincoln: University of Nebraska Press, 1989), 218.

[33]Andrzej Warminski, "Terrible Reading (preceded by 'Epigraphs')," in *Responses,* 389.

[34]J. Hillis Miller, "The Function of Theory at the Present Time," 105–6.

[35]Andrew Parker, in *Displacement: Derrida and After,* ed. Mark Krupnick (Bloomington: Indiana University Press, 1987), 136.

[36]*Memoires for Paul de Man,* trans. Cecile Lindsay et al. (New York: Columbia University Press, 1986), 142–43.

[37]For an interesting reading of the de Man affair which seeks to displace the context of his criticism from his alleged pro- or anti-Nazi sentiments to the political context of the decades during which he did his major work, see David Simpson, "Going on about the War without Mentioning the War: Other Histories of the Paul de Man Affair," *Yale Journal of Criticism* 3 (1989), 163–73.

[38]Christopher Norris, *Paul de Man: Deconstruction and the Critique of Aesthetic Ideology* (New York: Routledge, 1988), xiii.

[39]Johnson, *A World of Difference,* 11.

[40]"The Anxiety of American Deconstruction," in Silverman and Aylesworth, *The Textual Sublime,* 157.

[41]This, and Weber's other discussions of charisma, have been collected in *Max Weber: On Charisma and Institution Building,* ed S. N. Eisenstadt (Chicago: University of Chicago Press, 1968), 21.

[42]For a rather different analysis of the kind of "work" that goes on in English departments, see Evan Watkins, *Work Time: English Departments and the Circulation of Cultural Value* (Stanford: Stanford University Press, 1989). Watkins emphasizes the function of the "evaluation" of students in his analysis rather than, as I have, the process of credentialization in linguistic or other knowledges.

[43]See especially, Stanley Fish, "Profession Despise Thyself: Fear and Self-Loath-

ing in Literary Studies," *Critical Inquiry* 10 (1983), 349–64, for a response to Bate's complaint interestingly and prophetically different from de Man's.

44Max Weber, *Economy and Society: An Outline of Interpretive Sociology,* 2 vols., ed. Guenther Roth and Claus Wittich (Berkeley: University of California Press, 1968), 2:1002.

45Cornelius Castoriadis, *Political and Social Writings,* vol. 2, trans. and ed. David Ames Curtis (Minneapolis: University of Minnesota Press, 1988), 272.

46Weber, *On Charisma,* 20.

47Claude Lefort, *The Political Forms of Modern Society: Bureaucracy, Democracy, Totalitarianism,* ed. John B. Thompson (Cambridge: MIT Press, 1986).

48*Karl Marx: Early Writings,* trans. Rodney Livingstone (New York: Vintage Books, 1975), 107.

49In a remarkable passage, which owes much to Hegel, Weber goes a long way toward identifying *Geist* with that bureaucracy whose Prussian form was the immediate context of Hegel's own celebrations of the state: "An inanimate machine is mind objectified. Only this provides it with the power to force men into its service and to dominate their everyday working life as completely as is actually the case in the factory. Objectified intelligence is also the animated machine, the bureaucratic organization, with its specialization of trained skills, its division of jurisdiction, its rules and hierarchical relations. Together with the inanimate machine it is busy fabricating the shell of bondage which men will perhaps be forced to inhabit some day, as powerless as the fellahs of ancient Egypt" (*Economy and Society,* 2:1402).

50See André Gorz's discussion of the relation between autonomy and heteronomy in his *Critique of Economic Reason,* trans. Gillian Handyside and Chris Turner (London: Verso, 1989): "The economic and administrative apparatuses become differentiated, more complex and bureaucratized in synergy. The result of this, for individuals in their work, is that their *field* of responsibility and scope for initiative (but not necessarily their responsibility and initiative as such) are narrowed and what is more, the coherence and goals of the organization—within which they are more or less consenting cogs—become less intelligible. . . . I term the *sphere of heteronomy* the totality of specialized activities which individuals have to accomplish as functions co-ordinated from outside by a pre-established organization" (32).

51David Harvey makes this point in his essay "Flexibility: Threat or Opportunity?" *Socialist Review* 12 (1991): "University-based intellectuals, for example, now find themselves faced with far shorter turnover times in the realm of ideas and far stronger pressures to increase output than was the case in the 1960s" (77).

52Magali Scarfatti Larson, *The Rise of Professionalism: A Sociological Analysis* (Berkeley: University of California Press, 1977).

53A similar point has been argued by Alvin Gouldner in *The Future of Intellectuals and the Rise of the New Class:* "Unlike the older bureaucrats, the new intelligentsia have extensive cultural capital which increases their mobility. . . . They need not, moreover, seek status solely within their own organization and from its staff or clients. Rather, they also seek status in professional associations; they wish the good regard of the knowledgeable" (51).

⁵⁴In addition to *The Future of Literary Theory* and *The Textual Sublime*, from which I have already cited, see also Joseph Natoli, ed., *Literary Theory's Future(s)* (Urbana: University of Illinois Press, 1989), and Thomas M. Kavanagh, ed., *The Limits of Theory* (Stanford: Stanford University Press, 1989). See also Steven Knapp and Walter Benn Michaels's "Against Theory," *Critical Inquiry* 8 (1982), 723–42, and the subsequent controversy over this argument.

⁵⁵I emphasize once again that "theory" and "deconstruction" were virtually synonymous in both the "journalistic" accounts of deconstruction and the various specifically academic media of dissemination. Journalism can hardly be held responsible for this confusion, since the journalists only confirmed the considerable homogenization of theory in the graduate schools, the solidification of an epistemic rhetoricism which colored the practice of many different and on the surface conflicting theories. The villainizing of journalism in the wake of the de Man scandal is only a belated consequence of this homogenization effect, the inverse mirror image of deconstruction's self-image as the premier theory of its day. The level of anathema heaped upon the journalistic accounts of the de Man scandal is convincing testimony to how crucial the celebrity system always was to the dissemination of theory, how thoroughly theory's dissemination conformed to the cultural paradigms of the mass media.

⁵⁶Pierre Bourdieu, "The Market of Symbolic Goods," *Poetics* 14 (1985), 33.

⁵⁷The only critic I have encountered who has remarked on the "cathexis" of boredom in the practice of rhetorical reading is D. A. Miller, who detects and exposes such a cathexis in J. Hillis Miller's citation of precisely this passage from de Man's work. See "The Profession of English: An Exchange," J. Hillis Miller and D. A. Miller, *ADE Bulletin* 88 (1987), 42–58.

⁵⁸It seems evident in retrospect that deconstruction's solution to the problem of autonomy has been displaced in recent years by a more openly professionalist discourse that vehemently reasserts professional autonomy by celebrating precisely the "blending of personal and organizational prestige." Such an ideology of professionalism once again represses the bureaucratic determination of professional activity, though it is no less troubled by the omnipresence of such heteronomy; it wishes rather to play the game well, "pragmatically." Most importantly it no longer needs to project its solution to the problem of work autonomy onto a theory of *reading*. Indeed, the versions of pragmatism and relativism now circulating in the wake of theory can display a relaxed disdain for theory's "rigor," as that term signifies a kind of prior restraint upon professional activity. In that sense pragmatism is the theory of which professionalism is the practice.

⁵⁹Gerald Graff, *Professing Literature: An Institutional History* (Chicago: University of Chicago Press, 1987), 1987.

⁶⁰Williams, *Marxism and Literature*, 54.

⁶¹On the relation between technical knowledges and the practice of composition, see the interesting remarks of Stanley Aronowitz and Henry A. Giroux, *Education Under Siege: The Conservative, Liberal, and Radical Debate over Schooling* (Hadley, Mass.: Bergin and Garvey, 1985), 52ff.

62John Frow, *Marxism and Literary History* (Oxford: Basil Blackwell, 1986), 234.

63Raymond Williams has always argued forcefully for maintaining a sense of the historical interrelation between High and Low Cultural works. See his comment in "The Future of Cultural Studies," in *The Politics of Modernism: Against the New Conformists* (London: Verso, 1989): "It is necessary and wholly intellectually defensible to analyse serials and soap operas. Yet I do wonder about the courses where at least the teachers—and I would say also the students—have not themselves encountered the problems of the whole development of naturalist and realist drama, of social-problem drama, or of certain kinds of serial form in the nineteenth century, which are elements in the constitution of these precise contemporary forms, so that the tension between that social history of forms and these forms in a contemporary situation, with their partly new and partly old content, partly new and partly old techniques, can be explored with weight on both sides" (159).

Chapter Five

1Hume remarks that "The want of humanity and of decency, so conspicuous in the characters drawn by several of the ancient poets, even sometimes by HOMER and the GREEK tragedians, diminishes considerably the merit of their noble performances," although that judgment does not prevent Hume from saying in the same essay that "The same HOMER, who pleased at ATHENS and ROME two thousand years ago, is still admired at PARIS and LONDON." See David Hume, *Essays Moral, Political, and Literary* (Indianapolis: Liberty Classics, 1985), 246, 243.

2Gayatri Chakravorty Spivak, "Scattered Speculations on the Question of Value," *Diacritics* (Winter 1985), 74.

3Immanuel Kant, *Critique of Judgement,* trans. J. H. Bernard (New York: Hafner Press, 1951), 46.

4Barbara Herrnstein Smith, *Contingencies of Value: Alternative Perspectives for Critical Theory,* (Cambridge: Harvard University Press, 1988), 34.

5We have recently been reminded of this fact by Patrick Brantlinger in his *Crusoe's Footprints: Cultural Studies in Britain and America* (New York: Routledge, 1990), 73.

6See Althusser's "Letter on Art in Reply to André Aspre," in *Lenin and Philosophy,* trans. Ben Brewster (New York: Monthly Review Press, 1971).

7T. W. Adorno, *Aesthetic Theory,* trans. C. Lenhardt (London: Routledge, 1970), 9.

8Eagleton's views of the work of art in this context are fairly represented by his chapter on "Marxism and Aesthetic Value," in *Criticism and Ideology* (London: Verso, 1976). Lentricchia has recently repudiated those literary materialists who "speak as if the real enemy were the aesthetic" in an inteview with Imre Salusinszky, *Criticism in Society* (New York: Methuen, 1987), 200. More recently Perry Anderson has observed in his *English Questions* (London: Verso, 1992): "For aesthetic value is not to be dispatched so easily—the wish to finish with it recalling Dobrolyubov, or Bazarov, more than Marx or Morris. Railing at canons is not the same as replacing them, which they have resisted. Evacuation of the terrain of literary evaluation in the traditional sense necessarily leaves its conventional practitioners in place" (243).

[9]Tony Bennett, "Really Useless 'Knowledge': A Political Critique of Aesthetics," in *Thesis Eleven* 12 (1985), 33.

[10]Mary Louise Pratt, "Linguistic Utopias," in *The Linguistics of Writing: Arguments between Language and Literature,* ed. Nigel Fabb et al. (New York: Methuen, 1987), 56.

[11]Suzanne Kappeler, *The Pornography of Representation* (Minnesota: University of Minnesota Press, 1986), 221. The dismissal of the aesthetic on behalf of political objectives is hardly defensible on "strategic" grounds, a point which can be illustrated again with the example of the antipornography movement. The coincidence of fundamentalist and feminist opposition to pornographic images of women in no way implies the unambiguous advantage for women of censorship legislation. The political objective of the fundamentalist antipornography movement is certainly to *reconfirm* the subjection of women by resacralizing the female body; such a gesture is the precise obverse of pornography's supposed objectification of female bodies. It remains to be seen which group, fundamentalist or feminist, has the more accurate understanding of the long-term effects of censorship on the status of women.

[12]*New York Times,* September 25, 1990, A16.

[13]Joanna Russ, *How to Suppress Women's Writing* (Austin: University of Texas Press, 1983), 120.

[14]See, among other texts, Peter Fuller, *Seeing Berger: A Revaluation* (London: Writers and Readers Publishing Co-operative, 1980).

[15]Jan Mukarovsky, *Aesthetic Function, Norm and Value as Social Facts,* trans. Mark E. Suino (Ann Arbor: University of Michigan Press, 1979), 88.

[16]This point, one would hope, clarifies a confusion that derives from the apparent discrepancy between Smith's willingness to speak on the one hand of some works as "information-rich," and on that basis more likely to become canonical in the first place (51), and on the other hand to insist that any evaluative distinction between, for example, "Shakespeare's poetry" and "doggerel" is simply contingent in the sense that one may "prefer" doggerel in those contexts where it is the function of doggerel that one is interested in. True enough! But does it matter that these latter functions are *never* going to be those in which the canonical status of the work is at issue? It is simply not likely that Shakespeare's poetry and some example of doggerel verse are ever going to be seriously compared in the first place. The interesting question is why we might think that we need to give some account of why it is Shakespeare's poetry and not some example of doggerel verse which comes to be canonical. In the actual circumstances of commensuration, doggerel verse will be compared to other doggerel verse, or Shakespeare's work to other work in similar genres.

[17]Georg Simmel, *The Philosophy of Money,* trans. Tom Bottomore and David Frisby (Boston: Routledge, 1978), 56.

[18]Adam Smith, *An Inquiry into the Nature and Causes of the Wealth of Nations,* 2 vols, ed. W. B. Todd (Indianapolis: Liberty Classics, 1976), 1:44.

[19]See the crucial essay "Beyond Use-Value," in *For a Critique of the Political Economy of the Sign*, trans. Charles Levin (St. Louis: Telos Press, 1981), 130ff.

[20]David Ricardo, *The Principles of Political Economy and Taxation* (New York: Dutton, 1973), 5.

[21]Howard Caygill, *Art of Judgement* (London: Basil Blackwell, 1989).

[22]On this and related issues in the eighteenth century, see Neil McKendrick et al., *The Birth of a Consumer Society: The Commercialization of Eighteenth-Century England* (Bloomington: Indiana University Press, 1982).

[23]David Hume, *Enquiries Concerning Human Understanding and Concerning the Principles of Morals*, third edition (Oxford: Clarendon Press, 1975), 247.

[24]David Hume, *A Treatise of Human Nature* (London: Penguin Books, 1969), 412–13.

[25]David Hume, *Essays, Moral, Political, and Literary*, 240.

[26]Adam Smith, *The Theory of Moral Sentiments* (Indianapolis: Liberty Classics, 1982), 179.

[27]Readers familiar with the history of economic theory will note that I have not granted any credibility to the "marginal utility" theory of the later nineteenth century, from which our "supply and demand" notions descend, as an alternative to the classical problematic of value. In fact I have assumed throughout what others have argued more skillfully than I, that this economic theory is manifestly inadequate to account for the phenomenon of exchange value. See, for example, Robert Heilbroner, *Behind the Veil of Economics: Essays in the Worldly Philosophy* (New York: W. W. Norton, 1988): "[O]ne might ask why such a clearly inadequate approach to value commands such near-unanimous support among contemporary economists. I think the answers are two. First, very few economists actually use utility analysis as a serious means of resolving the value problematic. . . . It is striking in this regard that economists regularly resort to a cost-of-production approach when compiling data for gross national product or when comparing the products of two or more years. From a view that sees utilities as the fundamental and irreducible building blocks of price, gross national product is a meaningless concept, the 'summation' of individual experiences of pleasure and pain. This has no more validity than the summation of enjoyments of an audience at a concert. . . . Second, I suspect that the utility approach . . . recommends itself because it avoids troublesome considerations of class conflict and cooperation as the fundamental problem of social order, and puts in their place a view of social order as the outcome of individuals contending for pleasure or avoiding pain in an environment of scarcity" (129–30). I quote these remarks at length in order to emphasize the point argued in the text that neo-pragmatism's rediscovery of utilitarian notions only rediscovers the longstanding ideology of capitalist political economy.

[28]Karl Marx, *Grundrisse: Foundations of the Critique of Political Economy*, trans. Martin Nicolaus (Harmondsworth: Penguin Books, 1973). It is clear from Marx's exposition that "distribution" really means in context what is otherwise referred to as the "mode of production": in the case of capitalist production, the fact that the producers own neither the means of production nor the commmodities produced, but sell their labor-power.

29Gregory S. Jay, "Values and Deconstructions: Derrida, Saussure, Marx," *Cultural Critique* (Winter 1987), 184.

30One might return in this context to Herrnstein Smith's polemic against Bataille and Baudrillard for their supposed denial of the principle of economic utility. A response to that polemic would obviously point out that both Bataille and Baudrillard are concerned with the *historical* conditions of capitalist social relations, specifically with the universalization of *exchange*. Whether or not their accounts of these relations reproduce a mythologizing narrative of a "fall" into economism (Smith makes this charge, and it is true enough in a narrow sense), that narrative still retains greater analytical accuracy than an analysis based on the simple opposition between utilitarianism and anti-utilitarianism. These terms are entirely inadequate in any case to grasp the real historical differences between so-called primitive and modern economies. On the former, see for example, Marshall Sahlins, *Stone Age Economics* (New York: Aldine, 1972): "Intergroup exchange does not simply answer to the 'moral purpose' of making friends. But whatever the intent and however utilitarian, it will not do to make enemies. Every transaction, as we already know, is necessarily a social strategy. . . . As it happens, the safe and sane procedure is not just measure-for-measure, a reciprocity precisely balanced. The most tactful strategy is economic *good measure,* a generous return relative to what has been received, of which there can be no complaints. One remarks in these intergroup encounters a tendency to *overreciprocate.* . . . " (303). The practice of *equal exchange* produces a very different social world than the practice of *overreciprocation,* whether or not one chooses to idealize the latter. Whatever deficiencies characterize the theories of Bataille and Baudrillard (and let us grant deficiencies), surely the interest of their work does not lie in whether they have adopted a position which is, in Smith's terms, the *correct* philosophical position. Bataille and Baudrillard are less interested in the philosophical issue which exercises Smith than they are in producing a critique of the culture of capitalism. For the same reason I would suggest that there is somewhat less in common between Smith's work and Pierre Bourdieu's than may at first appear. It would be a serious misrepresentation of Bourdieu's argument to claim that he is a "relativist," since he is never averse to representing objective social relations. The method of his "reflexive sociology" is to "objectify more completely one's objective and subjective relation to the object" (*The Logic of Practice,* 1). But this formulation already takes us into quite a different universe of discourse than the "objective/subjective" opposition Bourdieu calls "ruinous" and which seems to dominate thinking about the social in American discourse. For Bourdieu's critique of utilitarianism, see his *In Other Words: Essays Towards a Reflexive Sociology,* trans. Matthew Adamson (Stanford: Stanford University Press, 1990), p. 108.

31On this subject see the important argument of Anthony Appiah, "The Uncompleted Argument: Du Bois and the Illusion of Race," *Critical Inquiry* 12 (1985).

32Pierre Bourdieu, "The Market of Symbolic Goods," *Poetics* 14 (1985), 16 (henceforth cited within the text as "Market").

33The problem addressed in this paragraph takes us by an only apparently circuitous route back to Marx's theory of exploitation as the extraction of "surplus value," a concept which functions to critique political economy by striking at the central ideological thesis of the discourse: the "equal exchange" of the market. "Surplus value" defines the disproportion between production and consumption in the realm in which the laborer sells his or her labor-power. In the simplest of the formulations of this disproportion, Marx says that the "use value" of labor exceeds its "exchange value." We may acknowledge the difficult and perhaps intractable conceptual problems raised by Marx's theory of exploitation, without losing the sense of the theory as a way of pointing to the non-sense of the economic relation. The nature of the non-sense is clear enough: it is the problem of translating labor into a quantum of exchange value, a problem which has engaged Marxist and non-Marxist economists for a very long time. See for example, Diane Elson, ed., *Value: The Representation of Labour in Capitalism* (London: Humanities Press, 1979); Ian Steedman et al., *The Value Controversy* (London: Verso, 1981); Ian Steedman, *Marx after Sraffa* (London: Verso, 1977). The same problem appears in another version, somewhat closer to home for literary critics, in Gayatri Chakravorty Spivak's "Scattered Speculations on the Question of Value," in the form of the distinction between "idealist" and "materialist" constructions of the "subject," which determine two different trajectories for the question of value. The idealist determination leads to the question of canon formation and "cultural" value; the materialist determination to the question of economic exchange value. Spivak argues quite interestingly for reintroducing certain "idealist" concepts such as "representation" into the analysis of exchange value. Whether or not she succeeds in the project of rereading Marx's theory of value, it is telling that she never returns to the issue of canon formation.

³⁴Pierre Bourdieu, *Distinction: A Social Critique of the Judgment of Taste,* trans. Richard Nice (Cambridge: Harvard University Press, 1984), 1.

³⁵Pierre Bourdieu, *The Logic of Practice,* trans. Richard Nice (Stanford: Stanford University Press, 1990), 50. Bourdieu generally distinguishes in his work between a "field" and a "market," emphasizing always that a field has a necessary relation to the market.

³⁶Pierre Bourdieu, "The Field of Cultural Production, or: The Economic World Reversed," *Poetics* 12 (1983), 321. Hereafter cited within the text as "Field."

³⁷See Roy Porter, *English Society in the Eighteenth Century* (New York: Penguin Books, 1982): "De Saussure, for example, was amazed that artisans—even, he claimed, shoe-blacks—lounged about browsing the papers in London coffee houses. Pastor Moritz found his London landlady read Milton and other classics of English literature: 'The English national authors are in all hands, and read by all people, of which the innumerable editions they have gone through are a sufficient proof'" (239).

³⁸Bourdieu, interestingly, has little to say about the historical avant-garde in *Distinction,* where he makes no distinction between the consumption of avant-gardist and High Cultural productions. His work has not surprisingly provoked critical response from those who, like Peter Bürger, see the avant-garde as expressing a critique of the *institutions* of art, and of the very concept of the artwork. In this context see Peter Bürger's critique of Bourdieu in his essay, "The Problem of Aesthetic

Value," in *Literary Theory Today,* ed. Peter Collier and Helga Geyer-Ryan (Ithaca: Cornell University Press, 1990).

[39]For a discussion of the "habitus," see Chapter 2 above and Bourdieu, *The Logic of Practice,* 52ff.

[40]Adorno, *Aesthetic Theory,* 203ff.

[41]See Michael Denning, "Mass Culture and Working Class, 1914 to 1970," *International Labor and Working Class History* 37 (1990), 16.

[42]Karl Marx and Frederick Engels, *The German Ideology,* Part One, ed. C. J. Arthur (New York: International Publishers, 1947, 1970), 109.

[43]A more complex reconsideration of consumption as a *productive* activity is currently being worked out in a forthcoming book by Jennifer Wicke, *Consuming Subjects: Gender, Modernity, and the Work of Consumption.* I am indebted to Ms. Wicke for allowing me to examine this work.

[44]Pierre Bourdieu, "The Corporatism of the Universal: The Role of Intellectuals in the Modern World," *Telos* 81 (1989), 103.

[45]Pierre Bourdieu and Loïc J. D. Wacquant, *An Invitation to Reflexive Sociology* (Chicago: University of Chicago Press, 1992), 84–85.

INDEX

Abbott, Craig S., 170–71
Addison, Joseph, 97
Adorno, Theodor, 36, 156, 171, 273, 335
Aesthetics, xv, 20, 270–340; aesthetic
    pleasure, 327, 333–40; and commodity,
    308–17, 326, 328; and disinterested-
    ness, 275, 319, 327, 330–34; and
    Marxism, 273–82, 287, 297–98, 301–
    2, 319–22; and moral philosophy, 303–
    17; and political economy, 272, 274,
    296–325; and pornography, 279–81,
    379 n. 11; and taste, 305–17; and work
    of art, 292–94, 307–22, 326, 328–29,
    336. *See also* Community; Ideology;
    Marxism; Mass culture; Value
Agamemnon, 36
Agnew, Spiro, 36
Aiken, John, 101, 103
Alcibiades, 187
Althusser, Louis, 91, 179, 180, 181, 273
Altieri, Charles, 350 n. 35
Ancients and the moderns, quarrel be-
    tween, 118
Anderson, Benedict, 98–99, 118, 278
Anderson, Perry, 74, 378 n. 8
Anthologies, 28–29, 30, 62, 64, 101–3,
    170–71
Appiah, Kwame Anthony, 356 n. 69,
    381 n. 31
Aquinas, Thomas, 42
Aristotle, 42, 43, 88, 89; on topics, 218–
    19

Armstrong, Nancy, 365 n. 36
Arnold, Matthew, 114, 135–36, 137, 138
Auerbach, Erich, 71–73, 75
Augustine, 32
Aulus Gellius, 62
Austen, Jane, 17
Austin, J. L., 217

Bachelard, Gaston, 220
Bacon, Francis, 32
Bakhtin, M. M., 64–68, 70, 72, 74, 77,
    129, 206–7
Baldick, Chris, 135
Balibar, Etienne, 79
Balibar, Renée, 77, 78
Barbauld, Anna Laetitia, 103–6, 118,
    119, 124
Barrell, John, 89, 90, 97, 98, 99, 362 n. 8
Barthes, Roland, 373 n. 232
Bate, Walter Jackson, 247
Bates, Katherine Lee, 171
Baudrillard, Jean, 301, 302, 313, 319,
    320, 321
Baumgarten, Alexander, 304, 306
Baym, Nina, 23
Beardsley, Monroe, 272
Beaujour, Michel, 360 n. 119
Benjamin, Walter, 55–57, 62
Bennett, Tony, 274–79, 281, 282, 317,
    358 n. 96
Bennett, William, 20–21, 39, 41–42, 44,
    46, 47, 50, 56

Berger, John, 362 n. 8
Bloom, Allan, 46
Bolgar, R. R., 60, 61
Boswell, James, 99
Bourdieu, Pierre, ix, x, xvi, 6, 40, 46, 48, 57, 58, 59, 61, 96, 112, 121, 136–37, 151, 153, 207, 208, 231, 251, 252, 256, 259, 287, 298, 325–40, 341 n. 1; on aesthetic disposition, 330–40; on disinterestedness, 327, 330, 331, 333, 334; on doxa, orthodoxy, and heterodoxy, 136–37; and economism, 326–27; sociology of art, 326–40; on school culture, 354 n. 63, 355 n. 67. Works: "The Corporatism of the Universal," 338; *Distinction,* 326, 330, 332–37, 338, 339; "The Field of Cultural Production," 327, 330, 331, 332, 338; *Logic of Practice,* 328; "The Market of Symbolic Goods," 328–30, 338, 339. *See also* Cultural capital
Bourgeois public sphere, 117–18, 121–24, 133, 153, 155, 367 n. 52
Bowles, Samuel, 343 n. 7
Brady, Frank, 93
Brantlinger, Patrick, 44, 350 n. 37
Brennan, J. Keirn, 167
Brooks, Cleanth, 138–40, 141, 156–75; and motif of secularization, 162–66; and philologists, 165–66; and reading of Donne's "The Canonization," 160–66. Works: *Modern Poetry and the Tradition,* 157–58; *Understanding Poetry,* 168, 173; *The Well Wrought Urn,* 156–58, 160–75. *See also* New Criticism
Brower, Reuben, 156
Brown, Capability, 89
Burger, Peter, 351 n. 41, 382 n. 38
Burke, Edmund, 305
Burns, Robert, 126
Butler, Judith, 346 n. 18
Byron, George Gordon (Lord), 129

Caesar, Julius, 111, 118
Calvin, John, 32
Canon debate: and affirmative action analogy, 345 n. 13; and category of experience, 10; and class, x, xi, 6, 13, 14, 341 n. 1; and concept of "classics,"

6; and concept of the noncanonical, 9–11, 15–17, 20; and conservative backlash, 3–4; and cultural relativism, 20; and feminist critique of canon, 14–19, 23–27, 37–38, 58, 280–82, 348 n. 24, 352 n. 47; and identity politics, 11–14, 279, 346 n. 18; as imaginary politics, 7–14; and integrationist and separatist strategies, 3, 9, 19–28, 44, 47, 279–80, 323–24; and modernization of curriculum, 32, 38; and representation of minorities, x, xi, 4–12, 15, 18, 19, 21, 29, 37, 47, 53, 59–60, 80–81; and reproduction of social relations, xi, 52, 55–63, 80; and research programs, 15–19, 52; and syllabus, ix, 29–38; and value judgments, xv, xvi, 19–28, 29, 269–71, 336, 339–40. *See also* Classical canon; Literary reputation; Literature; Relativism; Schools; Value; Vernacular canon
Castoriadis, Cornelius, 35, 248
Cato, 111, 118
Cave, Terence, 362 n. 6
Caygill, Howard, 303–7, 309, 312, 313, 314, 316, 318
Christensen, Jerome, 123
Cicero (Tully), 111, 118, 123, 218
Class. *See* Canon debate
Classical canon (curriculum), xi–xiii, 6, 31–33, 43, 51, 60, 62, 70–72, 96–101, 119, 123, 136, 213, 343 n. 9, 364 n. 24
Coleridge, Samuel Taylor, 85, 124, 127–32
Community: as basis of value judgment, 34–36, 274–82, imagined community, 278–79, interpretive community, 26–28, 59
Composition: ideology of, 80, and New Class sociolect, 79–80, and relation to theory, 263–65, syllabus of, 79–81, 263, 361 n. 128
Conrad, Joseph, 17
Corbett, Edward, 80, 361 n. 128
Core curriculum, 42, 45–55
Cowper, William, 126, 129
Crabbe, George, 107
Crisis of the humanities, 44–45, 48, 54

Index

Cromwell, Oliver, 111, 112, 114, 118

Crozier, Michel, 251–52

Culler, Jonathan, 207

Cultural capital, ix–xvi, 6, 36–41, 45–56, 59–71, 73, 81, 86, 96, 100–102, 118, 121, 124, 133, 165, 168, 171, 172, 174, 263, 269, 281, 295, 325–40; and linguistic capital, xi, xii, 61–71, 81, 121, 171

Cultural literacy, 35, 36, 87

Cultural studies curriculum, 265

Curriculum. *See* Canon debate; Core curriculum; Literature; Philosophical canon; Schools; Vernacular canon

Curtius, Ernst Robert, 62, 71

Dante, 43, 74, 151, 177, 182, 258

Darnton, Robert, 366 n. 40

David-Menard, Monique, 188

Davie, Donald, 124, 125, 132

Davis, Natalie Zemon, 73

Deconstruction. *See* Theory

de Man, Paul, xiv, 176–265, 271, 273; and "aesthetic ideology," 271, 273; and Austin, 217; on Bakhtin, 206–7; and canon of theory, 176–81, 203–5, 212, 230, 258–65; and countertransference, 186–98; and fetishization of rigor, 231–36, 248, 257–58; and foreclosure of psychoanalysis, 192–207, 234–36, 246; and pathos, 97, 199, 204, 229, 233–66, 257–58; and question of agency, 227–30, 258–59; and relation to phenomenology, 208–9; and routinization of charismatic authority, 244–59; and wartime journalism, 178–79, 240, 255–56, 375 n. 37, 377 n. 55. Works: "Aesthetic Formalization in Kleist," 205; *Allegories of Reading,* 192–94, 200, 203–4, 208, 216, 220, 221–30, 235, 236, 258, 260; *Blindness and Insight,* 193, 205, 207, 208, 211, 214, 215; *Critical Writings, 1953–78,* 231–32, 236; "Dialogue and Dialogism," 206–7; "Epistemology of Metaphor," 212, 220; "Hegel on the Sublime," 239; "Hypogram and Inscription," 205; *The Resistance to Theory,* 178, 190–91, 193, 195–201, 205–6, 208–11, 216, 237, 239, 241–42, 246–47, 257, 271, 273; *The Rhetoric of Romanticism,* 228–29, 234; "Sign and Symbol in Hegel's *Aesthetics,"* 205; *Yale French Studies: The Lesson of Paul de Man,*184–87, 192, 195, 200. *See also* Theory

Denham, John, xiii, 100, 104, 105

Denning, Michael, 336

Derrida, Jacques, 180, 203, 237, 239–40, 241, 246, 371 n. 4

Dickens, Charles, 17

Dodsley, Robert, 119

Donne, John, 135, 139, 160. Works: "The Canonization," 161–75

Dryden, John, 75, 141–43, 146, 148, 149, 154

Dyer, John, 103

Eagleton, Terry, 273

Echols, Alice, 346 n. 18

Ehrenreich, Barbara, 341 n. 2

Ehrenreich, John, 341 n. 2

Eichenbaum, Boris, 65

Elegy Written in a Country Church Yard, 85–124; class structure in, 93, 99, 116, 119; and canon formation, 109–11; and educational system, 95–107, 119; and ideology, 85–86; and literacy, 116; and literary culture, 112–14, 118; and pastoral, 99, 102–28; and public sphere, 117; and repression of literary ambition, 106–16, 119

Elias, Norbert, 73, 119

Eliot, George, 17, 21

Eliot, Thomas Stearns, 134–55, 157, 158, 160, 166, 167, 173; and canonical revaluation, 141–55; and dissociation of sensibility, 139, 148, 150, 151, 153, 158, 160, 174; on literary tradition, 142–54, 155, 158; on minor poets, 140, 141–55. Works: *After Strange Gods,* 152; "Milton I," 147; *Murder in the Cathedral,* 153; *"In Memoriam,"* 149–51; "John Dryden," 141–42; "The Possibility of a Poetic Drama," 144–46, 149; "Tradition and the Individual Talent," 142–45, 146, 152; "What Is a Classic," 151; "What Is Minor Poetry," 146–47; *The Waste Land,* 149–50; *The Use of Poetry and the Use of Criticism,* 146

Elliot, Gilbert, 122
Empson, William, 86, 91–95, 106, 108, 109, 124, 126
Enfield, William, 101, 103
Ennius, 71
Erasmus, Desiderius, 88

Ferenczi, Sandor, 235
Ferguson, Charles, 69
Feuerbach, Ludwig, 287
Feyerabend, Paul, 220
Fielding, Henry, 212
Fish, Stanley, 26, 247, 277
Fishman, Joshua, 69, 71
Flaubert, Gustave, 25
Fontanier, 217–18
Foucault, Michel, 203, 219, 237, 287, 348 n. 22
Fowler, Alastair, 358 n. 98
Freud, Sigmund, 177, 183, 190, 191, 193, 194, 200, 201, 203, 235
Frow, John, 264–65
Fuller, Peter, 285, 290

Gasché, Rodolph, 238, 374 n. 30
Gates, Henry Louis, Jr., 7, 352 n. 48
Gearhart, Suzanne, 221
Genette, Gerard, 217
Gintis, Herbert, 343 n. 7
Goldsmith, Oliver, 103
Gorz, André, 376 n. 50
Gosse, Edmund, 87
Gouldner, Alvin, 46, 48, 356 n. 72, 376 n. 53
Graff, Gerald, xiii, 155–57, 160, 161, 167, 260
Gramsci, Antonio, 38, 48–53, 74, 153, 306
Gray, Thomas, xii, 85–124, 127, 128, 168; and commonplace book, 87–89; and common reader, 91–92, 118, 121; and emulation, 96–107, 113, 114, 119, 365 n. 24; as "gentleman," 99, 102, 118, 119; and literary ambition, 110–14; and "man of letters," 122–24. See also *Elegy Written in a Country Church Yard*
Green, Matthew, 103
Greimas, A. J., 210

Habermas, Jürgen, 117, 367 n. 52
Hamacher, Werner, 198, 212, 220
Hammett, Dashiell, 173
Hampden, John, 111, 112, 118
Hans, Nicholas, 364 n. 24
Hartman, Geoffrey, 242
Harvey, A. D., 126, 129
Harvey, David, 344 n. 11
Harvey, Gabriel, 359 n. 113
Hawthorne, Nathaniel, 24
Hazlitt, William, 85
Hegel, G. W. F., 32, 184, 205, 229, 249, 306, 322
Heidegger, Martin, 177, 203, 355 n. 66
Heilbroner, Robert, 380 n. 27
Herodotus, 32
Hertz, Neil, 233–35, 257, 374 n. 26
Hirsch, E. D., 35–36, 42, 50, 80, 353 n. 57
Hölderlin, Friedrich, 177, 182, 258
Homer, 21, 40, 41, 51
Horkheimer, Max, 171
Humanism, 74–76, 119, 359 n. 109
Hume, David, 122–23, 213, 270, 272, 284, 304, 308–10, 317
Hurston, Zora Neale, 32
Hutcheson, Frances, 304, 305

Ideology, xi, xiii, 61–63, 77–78, 80, 85–86, 94–95, 134–41, 142; and aesthetics, 275–76, 282, 296, 302, 312, 320, 336; and New Criticism, 134–41, 157, 161; and theory, 180, 238–40, 262–65, 271, 273. See also Canon debate

Jakobson, Roman, 211, 213, 214, 223
James, Henry, 17, 183, 184
Jameson, Fredric, 273, 374 n. 28
Jauss, Hans Robert, 25–26, 205, 206
Jay, Gregory, 320
Jehlen, Myra, 23
Jenyns, Soam, 95
Johnson, Barbara, 176, 207, 231, 243
Johnson, Samuel, 75, 89–92, 97, 120, 125, 129, 130
Jones, Richard Foster, 325 n. 26
Jonson, Ben, 75
Joyce, James, 32

Kagan, Donald, 357 n. 78
Kames, Lord (Henry Home), 305, 307
Kamuf, Peggy, 242
Kant, Immanuel, xv, 25, 26, 32, 228, 229,
284, 290, 291, 293, 308, 317, 331–33.
Works: *Critique of Judgment,* 271, 274–
76, 302–4, 317–19
Kappeler, Suzanne, 280–81
Kermode, Frank, 351 n. 45
Kilmer, Joyce, 171
Kinneavy, James, 80
Kleist, Heinrich, 205
Knapp, Steven, 377 n. 54
Kristeva, Julia, 203

Labov, William, 361 n. 131
Lacan, Jacques, 187, 188, 202, 203, 224.
Works: *Seminar XI: The Four Fundamen-
tal Concepts of Psycho-Analysis,* 187–
89, 194–99
Laclau, Ernesto, 5, 10, 12, 13, 346 n. 15
Lanham, Richard, 361 n. 128
Laporte, Dominique, 77–78
Larson, Magali Scarfatti, 253–54
Laslett, Peter, 363 n. 16
Lauter, Paul, 352 n. 50
Lawrence, D. H., 14
Leavis, F. R., 17, 134, 139–41, 154, 166
Lefort, Claude, 35, 249, 250
Leibniz, Gottfried Wilhelm, 304
Lentricchia, Frank, 273, 378 n. 8
Liberal pluralism, 3–14, 17, 18, 21, 28, 34,
52–55, 287, 296, 323–24, 342 n. 4,
345 n. 12, 347 n. 21, 351 n. 46, 371 n. 3
Lindsay, Vachel, 170
Literacy, xii, 15–16, 18–19, 23, 35, 36, 38,
53–54, 61–62, 71, 73–74, 77–82, 91,
349 n. 29, 350 n. 30; and classical liter-
acy, 96–100, 118–23, 131, 259 n. 109;
and vernacular literacy, 73–74, 77–82,
86, 98–102, 116, 118–21, 123, 131,
359 n. 113, 368 n. 60. *See also* Cultural
capital; *Elegy Written in a Country
Church Yard;* Schools
Literary culture, 139, 152–54, 165–66,
173–75, 180, 264–65
Literary reputation, 17, 64, 70, 135, 146
Literature: category of, xi–xv, 27, 60, 64–
69, 72, 77–82, 121–24, 130–33, 135,

208–30, 262–65; and composition, 79–
81; and diglossia, 69–71, 74, 78; and
grammar, 61–62, 66–68, 70–78, 97,
208–30; and *Hochsprache,* 71–75, 97,
119, 131; and ideology, xi, xiii, 61–63,
77, 78, 80, 85–86, 94–95, 134–35; and
literary language, 63–71, 78–80, 132–
33; and literariness, 65–67, 77; and mass
culture, 171–75; and oral literature, 43;
and poetics, 213–14; and rhetoric, 71,
79, 88, 207–31; and religion, 136–41;
and science, 158–60, 213–14, 219–20;
and sociolects, 79–82; and theory, 212–
16, 237, 260–65; transhistorical definition of, 69–70. *See also* Bourgeois public
sphere; Serious vs. popular literature;
Standard English; Tradition; Vernacular
canon
Locke, John, 32, 88, 95, 96, 304
Lonsdale, Roger, 106
Lowell, Amy, 170
Lukács, Georg, 36, 297
Luther, Martin, 139
Lyotard, Jean-François, 36, 81, 82, 203

MacCannel, Juliet Flower, 183
Macey, David, 202
Macherey, Pierre, 79
McLennan, Gregor, 4, 5, 14, 351 n. 46
Mallarmé, Stéphane, 303
Mandeville, Bernard, 304, 306, 315
Mann, Thomas, 32
Mapplethorpe, Robert, 279–81, 295
Marotti, Arthur, 163
Marx, Karl, 3, 155, 274, 283, 297, 301,
302, 319, 322; and survival of Greek art,
320–22, 321. Works: *German Ideology,*
337–38; *Grundrisse,* 273, 319–22
Marxism, ix–xi, 4–6, 11, 18, 65; and aes-
thetics, 273–82, 287, 297–98, 301, 302,
319–22, 378 n. 8; and class, 341 n. 1;
and sociology, 297–98, 300. *See also*
Canon debate; Class; Value
Mass culture, 8, 36, 37, 53, 80, 139–41,
167, 263, 265, 370 n. 29
Masters, Edgar Lee, 170
Mauss, Marcel, 112
Medvedev, P. N., 65–66
Meese, Elizabeth, 26

Melville, Herman, 24

Michaels, Walter Benn, 377 n. 54

Miller, Christopher, 53

Miller, D. A., 377 n. 57

Miller, Jacques-Alain, 202

Miller, J. Hillis, 212, 377 n. 57

Milton, John, 85, 99, 105, 111, 112, 114, 115, 118, 125, 128, 130, 131, 133, 134, 141–43, 148, 149, 154, 177, 182, 258

Mitchell, W. J. T., 345 n. 12

Montaigne, Michel de, 32

Moretti, Franco, 358 n. 98

Mouffe, Chantal, 5, 10, 12, 13

Mukarovsky, Jan, 272, 290–91

Mulhern, Francis, 135, 136, 139

Multiculturalism, 38–55

Nelson, William, 358 n. 103

New Class. *See* Professional-managerial class

New Criticism, 134–41, 155–75; and close reading, 141, 168; and critique of modernity, 155–60, 167; and difficulty of poetry, 168–72; and modernist canon, 155, 167, 168–71; and university, 140, 158, 165–75. *See also* Ideology; Literature

Nietzsche, Friedrich, 25, 177, 182, 203, 216, 218

Nochlin, Linda, 18

Norris, Christopher, 243

Novels (and canon formation), 67–68, 77, 122, 124, 129–33, 213, 308, 329. *See also* Literature; Vernacular canon

Osborne, Peter, 12–13

Ovid, 32

Parker, Andrew, 239

Passeron, Jean-Claude, 207–8, 231, 251, 252, 259

Pecheux, Michel, 219

Pechey, Graham, 75

Philips, Katherine, 16

Philosophical canon, 42, 177, 181, 215, 220–21, 230, 258, 262, 264, 356 n. 78. *See also* Core curriculum; Theory

Plato, 32, 40, 41, 43, 51, 182, 187, 214, 219

Poe, Edgar Allan, 156

Poetic diction, 120–29, 132–33. See also *Elegy Written in a Country Church Yard*

Political correctness, 342 n. 4. *See also* Canon debate

Political economy, 303–25; and civil society, 304–6, 308, 312; and labor theory of value, 314–17; and Marxist theory of value, 381 n. 33; and neoclassical economics, 313, 316, 380 n. 27. *See also* Aesthetics; Value

Porter, Roy, 363 n. 16

Pottle, Frederick, 172

Pound, Ezra, 148

Pratt, Mary Louise, 46, 277

Profession (professionalism), 59, 247–55

Professional-managerial class (New Class), xii, xiv, 45–47, 58, 79–81, 261–65, 341 nn. 1,2, 356 n. 72, 376 n. 53. *See also* Cultural capital

Proust, Marcel, 32, 177, 204, 221–27, 230, 258, 333–34, 336

Puttenham, George, 213

Quintilian, 62

Rabelais, François, 32

Radcliffe, Anne, 133

Raphael, Max, 269

Reed, Ishmael, 362 n. 131

Relative autonomy, xvi, 250–51, 304–6, 326, 328, 330, 337, 338, 357 n. 85. *See also* Aesthetics; Bourdieu, Pierre; Marxism

Relativism (neopragmatism), 177, 256, 273, 277–303, 323–25. *See also* Aesthetics; Smith, Barbara Herrnstein

Rhetoric, 207–31, 264–65; and metaphor and metonymy, 221–31, 258; and persuasion, 217–20; and relation to grammar, 223–30; "rhetoricism," 180, 230; and topics, 218–20. *See also* de Man, Paul; Literature; Theory

Rhetorical reading. *See* Theory

Ricardo, David, 274, 301, 314–15

Richards, I. A., 91–92, 158, 159

Rifaterre, Michael, 206

Rilke, Rainer Maria, 204

Rinehart, Mary Roberts, 173

Robinson, Lillian, 23, 348 n. 25

Rooney, Ellen, 371 n. 3

Rorty, Richard, 277, 283
Rosso, Stephano, 240, 246
Rousseau, Jean-Jacques, 32, 184, 215, 227, 233
Roustang, François, 189, 198
Russ, Joanna, 281
Russel, Jemmy, 123
Russian Formalism, 64–68. *See also* Literature
Ryan, Michael, 22

Sahlins, Marshall, 381 n. 30
Said, Edward, 154
Sandburg, Carl, 170
Sartre, Jean-Paul, 193, 240, 247
Saussure, Fernand de, 177, 180, 203, 209, 211, 214, 220, 225
Schools, ix–xiv, 15–19, 22, 28–55, 75–82, 95–107, 131–33, 139–40, 165, 270, 330, 339, 354 n. 58; and Dissenting Academies, xiii, 100–107; and graduate seminars, 255–65; and pedagogic imaginary, 28–38; scene of transference, 182–207; school culture vs. national culture, 38–55, 354 nn. 60,62,63; unitary school, 48–50; and the university, 38–55, 172–75, 241, 245–48, 250–65. *See also* Canon debate; Literacy; Theory; Vernacular canon
Scott, Joan W., 345 n. 14
Scott, Sir Walter, 129, 133
Serious vs. Popular literature, 23–25, 131–33, 351 n. 41, 378 n. 63. *See also* Literature; Mass culture; New Criticism
Shaftesbury, Third Earl of, 304, 305, 306
Shakespeare, William, 21, 75, 112, 116, 121, 133, 145, 146, 166, 287, 295
Shelley, Percy Bysshe, 229, 235
Sheridan, Thomas, 76, 100–102
Shklovskii, Victor, 68
Sidney, Sir Philip, 74, 75
Simmel, Georg, 297–98, 300, 321
Simpson, David, 375 n. 37
Sitter, John, 117
Smith, Adam, 274, 301, 302, 305–7, 309, 313, 317, 325. Works: *Theory of Moral Sentiments,* 310–12, 314; *Wealth of Nations,* 315–16
Smith, Barbara Herrnstein, xv, 19–20, 271–72, 274, 275, 277, 278, 283–303,

308–9, 316; and aesthetic axiology, 272; and aesthetic function, 288–95; and Bourdieu, 381 n. 30; and canon formation, 293–95; and concept of contingency, 283–88; and concept of personal economy, 288–95, 298–302; and "double discourse of value," 296, 302, 308, 316, 323, 325, 327; and Simmel, 297–98, 300
Socrates, 187
Spectator, 96
Spenser, Edmund, 125, 146
Spivak, Gayatri Chakravorty, 271, 382 n. 33
Standard English, 76–82, 92, 97–98, 121, 126, 131–32, 136, 171, 263, 361 n. 131. *See also* Classical canon; Literature; Vernacular canon
Stephen, Leslie, 87
Stock, Brian, 359 n. 105
Stone, Lawrence, 363 n. 16
Stowe, Harriet Beecher, 17, 24
Strunk, William, 78
Swift, Jonathan, 97
Swinburne, Algernon, 150
Syllabus, 29–38, 56, 59; as fetishized list, 30–38

Temple, William, 99
Tennyson, Alfred Lord, 149–51
Thayer, Tiffany, 173
Theory: and bureaucratization of intellectual work, 248–55, 256–62, 376 nn. 49,50; canon of theory, 176–181, 203–5, 212, 230, 258–65; and composition syllabus, 263–65; and concept of literariness, 209, 212–16, 260; and discipleship, 179, 182–207, 235, 243–45; and fetishization of rigor, 231–36, 238, 248; and gender, 233–35; identification of theory with deconstruction, 178–79, 371 n. 4; institutionalization of, 244–57; and literary canon, 179, 203–5, 208, 237, 258, 261–65; and Marxism, 240; and materiality of the letter, 228–29, 232, 236, 374 nn. 28,29,30; politics of, 181, 231–45, 263–64; and professionalism, 247–55, 377 n. 58; relation to canon critique, 176–77, 237, 262–65; resistance to, 190–207, 241–45, 255–56; routinization of, 244–57; and sci-

Theory (*continued*)
 ence, 197, 198, 201–2, 219–20, 232, 373 n. 23; thematization of rhetoric, 221–30, 231, 262; transference onto theory, 183–207, 216, 243–45, 255, 259; transmission of, 189–207; and tropes, 209, 216–30, 236. *See also* Literature; de Man, Paul; Rhetoric; Schools
Thompson, John B., 59
Thomson, James, 89–90
Tompkins, Jane, 24–26
Tönnies, Ferdinand, 34, 35
Tradition, 23, 33–34, 42–43, 56, 57, 59, 62, 63, 87; and concept of "text tradition," 43–44, 59, 62, 63, 355 n. 67
Tully. *See* Cicero
Tynjanov, Jurij, 65

Value: and aesthetics, 269–340; contingency of, 284–88, 324–25; and cultural relativism, 277–303, 323, 324–35; double discourse of, 296, 302, 308, 316, 323, 325, 327; use value distinguished from exchange value, 296–302; and valuing communities, 274–82, 283–87. *See also* Canon debate; Marxism; Relativism; Smith, Barbara Herrnstein
Veblen, Thorstein, 321
Vernacular canon (curriculum), xi–xiii, 43, 51, 74–82, 85–133, 329, 360 n. 118, 365 n. 36, 368 n. 66, 379 n. 16, 382 n. 37; and canonization of the novel, 129–33; emergence of vernacular curriculum, 85–133; and New Criticism, 134–75. *See also* Cultural capital; Literacy; Literature; Schools
Virgil, 32, 43, 51, 72, 150, 151

Viswanathan, Gauri, 360 n. 118
Voloshinov, V. N., 358 n. 94

Waller, Edmund, xiii, 100, 119
Warminski, Andrej, 201
Warner, Susan, 24
Warren, Robert Penn, 168
Warrington Academy, 101, 103–7, 119
Waters, Lindsay, 244
Watkins, Evan, 375 n. 42
Weber, Max, 244–46, 248–50, 252–54, 297, 298, 376 n. 49
Weil, Simone, 32
West, Cornell, 352 n. 46
West, Richard, 120, 128
Western culture (Western civilization), 21, 31, 39–55, 355 nn. 64,66; and Stanford Western Culture course, 31–33
White, E. B., 78
Wicke, Jennifer, 383 n. 43
Wilkie, William, 122
Williams, Raymond, 68, 81, 119, 122, 262, 378 n. 63
Williamson, Marilyn L., 348 n. 24
Wittgenstein, Ludwig, 220
Wittig, Monique, 352 n. 47
Wolff, Christian, 304
Wood, Ellen Meiksins, 365 n. 33
Woolf, Virginia, 32
Wordsworth, William, 77, 85, 88, 124–33; on poetic diction, 126–29, 132; on the vernacular canon, 129–33
Wright, Erik Olin, 341 n. 2
Wright, Richard, 32
Wroth, Lady Mary, 16

Xenephon, 32

Zionkowski, Linda, 367 n. 48